Y0-BYV-930

A Modern Legal Ethics

A Modern Legal Ethics

ADVERSARY ADVOCACY IN
A DEMOCRATIC AGE

Daniel Markovits

PRINCETON UNIVERSITY PRESS   PRINCETON AND OXFORD

Copyright © 2008 by Princeton University Press

Published by Princeton University Press, 41 William Street, Princeton, New Jersey 08540
In the United Kingdom: Princeton University Press, 6 Oxford Street, Woodstock,
Oxfordshire OX20 1TW

All Rights Reserved

Library of Congress Cataloging-in-Publication Data

Markovits, Daniel, 1969–
A modern legal ethics : adversary advocacy in a democratic age / Daniel Markovits.
        p. cm.
    Includes index.
    ISBN 978-0-691-12162-8
 1. Legal ethics—United States.   2. Attorney and client—United States.   I. Title.
            KF306.M36 2009
      174′.30973—dc22   2008018368

British Library Cataloging-in-Publication Data is available

This book has been composed in Sabon

Printed on acid-free paper. ∞

press.princeton.edu

Printed in the United States of America

1   3   5   7   9   10   8   6   4   2

For my parents

Lawyers, I suppose, were children once.
   —*Charles Lamb*

———————————

CONTENTS

ACKNOWLEDGMENTS

MANY, MANY PEOPLE, both individually and in groups, have helped me to write this book. All of them deserve thanks.

Anthony Kronman sympathetically supervised a student paper that developed an early version of the book's central ideas, which eventually became an article, entitled "Legal Ethics from the Lawyer's Point of View," published in the *Yale Journal of Law & the Humanities*. The faculties of the Law Schools at Florida State University, Harvard University, New York University, Stanford University, The University of Alabama, The University of Michigan, The University of Pennsylvania, The University of Toronto, and Yale University heard and commented on this article in workshops. And Geoffrey Hazard, Ted Schneyer, and Alec Walen contributed sustained and careful responses to the article to a mini-symposium published in a later issue of the *Yale Journal of Law & the Humanities*. Finally, Bruce Ackerman, Arthur Applbaum, Sarah Bilston, Guido Calabresi, David Cross, Owen Fiss, Risa Goluboff, Dan Kahan, Rick Lempert, Meira Levinson, Richard Schragger, Gil Seinfeld, Kenji Yoshino, and Noah Zatz provided informal but invaluable assessments of early versions of the argument. Without the observations and criticisms of these attentive readers, I could not have corrected and elaborated the initial formulation of the argument as the book has demanded.

As the book came into being, many of its parts benefited from receiving additional individual attention from still other readers. Dan Callcut and David Owens offered incisive assessments of some of the arguments concerning integrity in Part II. And audiences at Fordham University Law School's conference titled "The Internal Point of View in Law and Ethics," Washington & Lee University's 28th Annual Legal Ethics Institute, and the 2006 Meeting of the Law & Society Association in Berlin, Germany, made important contributions to the argument of chapter 8. Greg Cooper, Ali Denham, David Luban, James Mahon, Bill Simon, and Brad Wendel made especially significant individual contributions to the chapter's argument on these occasions. A version of this chapter was also published, under the title "Adversary Advocacy and the Authority of Adjudication," in a symposium issue that the *Fordham Law Review* devoted to the Fordham Conference, and a much shorter and more informal account of the chapter's argument appeared in the *Yale Law Journal's Pocket Part*, under the title "In Praise of the Supporting Cast."

The completed book received equally generous attention from many more readers, who worked their way through the entire manuscript.

These included two anonymous readers for Princeton University Press, as well as Bruce Ackerman, Sarah Bilston, Bo Burt, Owen Fiss, Bob Gordon, Michael Graetz, Paul Kahn, Ian Malcolm, Richard Markovits, Jerry Mashaw, Jed Rubenfeld, Vicki Schultz, Alan Schwartz, and Brad Wendel. Once again, the observations and criticisms made by these readers uniformly improved the book.

I could not have written without still further help from many more people. Alicia Bannon, Craig Estes, Dan Korobkin, and Jonathan Manes provided outstanding research assistance, and, independently, commentary and criticism; the editors of the *Yale Journal of Law & the Humanities*, the *Fordham Law Review*, and the *Yale Law Journal*, improved both the mechanics and the substance of every text that they touched, and Karen Williams and Brad Hayes provided excellent administrative support.

Finally, Ian Malcolm, who acquired the book for Princeton University Press and managed its production was a fabulous editor. He made the mechanics of publication as simple and clear as possible and, much more importantly, provided enormously helpful substantive criticism and advice concerning every facet of the argument.

INTRODUCTION

IF THE BASIC TASK of ethics is to say how one should live,[1] then the basic task for a professional ethics is to explain how the actions, commitments, and traits of character typical of the profession in question may be integrated into a life well-lived.

For some professions—perhaps for medicine—answering this question is an essentially happy affair. The medical profession's core ethical appeal is never seriously in doubt, and so its professional ethics is primarily concerned with elaborating the values that account for this appeal and analyzing marginal cases (such as end-of-life care), where it is unclear just what conduct these values recommend. For other professions—for example, for torturers—professional ethics is an essentially unhappy affair. The torturer's professional commitments cannot, finally, be seen as anything other than a retreat from ethical life, and so his professional ethics become inevitably a masquerade, which can at most disguise the ethical failings of a basically degenerate occupation.[2]

There exists also a third class of professions, for which the nature of professional ethics is essentially uncertain. These professions have obvious ethical appeal but also display obvious ethical shortcomings; and although virtuous professional administration may enhance the professions' appeal and diminish the shortcomings, these will never be more than incremental changes to substantial entries on both sides of the ethical ledger. Accordingly, it is an open question, for such professions, whether a life lived within them may be a life well-lived, overall.

Law is just such a profession. On the one hand, lawyering is intimately connected to the deep and enduring ethical ideals of respect for persons that justice involves. On the other hand, the legal profession also has an ethically troubling aspect. Lawyers—at least when they function as adversary advocates—do not pursue justice itself, directly and impartially. Instead, they are charged loyally to represent particular clients, whose interests and aims may diverge from what justice requires.[3] This entails that adversary advocates commonly do, and indeed are often required to do, things in their professional capacities, which, if done by ordinary people in ordinary circumstances, would be straightforwardly immoral.[4] These practices make it uncertain whether the life of the lawyer is, finally, worthy of commitment.*

I shall seek, in these pages, to confront the uncertainty about lawyers' ethical lives by developing a professional ethics that comes down essentially in favor of lawyers, articulating a powerful and distinctively lawyerly virtue and explaining how this virtue renders lawyers' professional commitments ethically worthwhile. At the same time, the argument raises questions about whether this lawyerly virtue is practically available to modern lawyers, so that the vindication it offers is only bittersweet, at least when assessed from lawyers' own points of view.

AN OVERVIEW OF THE ARGUMENT

The basic argument of the book may be simply stated, in three parts. First, lawyers' professional obligations to behave in ways that would ordinarily be immoral are not simply the results of excessive or perverse partisanship. Instead, they are deeply ingrained in the genetic structure of adversary advocacy. Uncertainty about the ethical appeal of the legal profession therefore cannot be resolved simply through incremental changes in the positive law governing lawyers. Second, while it may be that lawyers' professional obligations to act in ordinarily immoral ways are necessary parts of a moral division of labor that best serves justice overall, this is not enough to redeem their professional ethics. Division of labor arguments cannot cast lawyers' professional lives as in themselves worthy of affirmation and commitment, which is what a successful legal ethics requires. And third, an alternative approach to legal ethics, which develops an account of distinctively lawyerly virtue to complement division of labor arguments, can render lawyers' lives ethically appealing and so bring their professional ethics to a successful conclusion. But although this vindication is possible in principle, recent developments in the structure of the legal profession

---

*Lawyers may, of course, behave unethically in other ways also. Most notably, lawyers who select clients based simply on the clients' ability to pay fees contribute to creating an unfair distribution of legal services. This raises a host of questions concerning ethical obligations to provide legal services pro bono and, more broadly, the economic structure of the legal profession. I will not address these questions here, however, save for some brief reflections in chapter 8. Lawyers' roles cannot plausibly be said to obligate them to distribute their services on the basis of the ability to pay fees (in civil cases, at least, no one has a right to whatever lawyer he can afford). And insofar as it is immoral for lawyers to sell their services to the highest bidders, this wrong is incidental rather than essential to the lawyer's professional role (doctors behave in similar ways). An argument about the basic nature of adversary advocacy should therefore avoid relying on such contingent features of any particular adversary legal practice.

threaten to deny contemporary lawyers practical access to the ideals on which it depends.

Part I: Adversary Advocacy

The book's argument begins by describing the complexities that underwrite the uncertain prospects for lawyers' professional ethics. To this end, the first part of the book embarks on a systematic interpretive engagement with the professional obligations of adversary advocates. This engagement generates a detailed and robust account of the ordinarily immoral conduct to which lawyers are professionally committed even as, in the very same breath, it sows the seeds of a parallel conception of distinctively lawyerly virtue. In both respects, Part I sets the stage for the rest of the book.

The legal process writ large may be designed to promote accurate assessments of factual and legal claims in the service of just adjudication. But the individual lawyers who shepherd clients through the legal process do not pursue truth or justice directly. Instead, the lawyer-client relationship is governed by principles of *lawyer loyalty* and *client control* that require lawyers to repress personal impressions of what is true or fair in deference to their clients' interests and instructions. This places lawyers in an unusually complex ethical position.

Most familiarly, the ideals of lawyer loyalty and client control subject adversary advocates to professional obligations to violate otherwise applicable principles of impartiality. As Geoffrey Hazard and William Hodes declare in the leading treatise on legal ethics, "the law of lawyering imposes a clear and mandatory favoritism when a lawyer must choose between the interests of clients and non-clients."[5]

Moreover, this thin, generic idea of partisan preference operates (although now in less-acknowledged ways) through thicker and more structured professional duties to embrace forms of conduct that would ordinarily be classed as vices, with familiar names.

Unlike juries and judges, adversary lawyers should not pursue a true account of the facts of a case and promote a dispassionate application of the law to these facts. Instead, they should try aggressively to manipulate both the facts and the law to suit their clients' purposes. This requires lawyers to promote beliefs in others that they themselves (properly) reject as false. Lawyers might, for example, bluff in settlement negotiations, undermine truthful testimony, or make legal arguments that they would reject as judges. In short, lawyers must lie.

And unlike legislators, adversary lawyers should not seek to balance competing interests and claims so that all persons get what they deserve. Instead, they should strive disproportionately and at times almost exclusively to promote their clients' interests. This requires lawyers to exploit strategic advantages on their clients' behalves even when they themselves (correctly) believe that the clients are not entitled to these advantages. Lawyers might, for example, employ delaying tactics, file strategically motivated claims, or exploit a law's form to thwart its substantive purposes. In short, lawyers must cheat.

These charges have of course been leveled at lawyers before,[6] but they nevertheless prove surprisingly controversial. Suggestions that lawyers display professional "vices" and, more specifically, that they "lie" and "cheat" are startling, unwelcome, and even off-putting to many lawyers, who resist (and resent) them (even as they accept, as a matter of course, that lawyers must display generic partiality in favor of their clients).[7] The principal burden of Part I is to render plausible the claims that lawyers are professionally obligated to lie and to cheat, both under the positive law of lawyering as it stands and under any alternative regime of professional regulation that remains consistent with adversary adjudication's basic commitment to a structural separation between advocate and tribunal.

I therefore devote substantial attention to elaborating lawyers' professional duties in considerable detail. In order to do so, I take up the specific doctrinal regime that makes up the law of lawyering in most U.S. jurisdictions today, including in particular the American Bar Association's (ABA's) Model Rules of Professional Conduct, as supplemented and amended from time to time. But although I turn to the American case to provide the doctrinal detail necessary for persuading skeptics, and indeed for informing the open-minded, I use the positive law for illustrative purposes only. The center of gravity of my argument remains the genetic structure of adversary lawyering, and in particular the separation between advocates and tribunals that constitutes adversary adjudication's core, rather than what someone once called "the ethical codes' discrete body of subrules."[8] I turn to the ethics codes out of a belief that the best path to understanding what is essential to adversary advocacy in general is through careful attention to one particular variety of adversary advocacy.

Moreover, in order to avoid the mistake of attributing the idiosyncrasies of one particular species to the basic morphology of the genus, I arrange my interpretive engagement with the positive law around the distinction between the necessary and contingent features of this body of doctrine. In particular, I demonstrate that the pressures to lie and to cheat that the positive law exerts on lawyers arise out of broad and organic rules that establish the necessary foundations of adversary lawyering, whereas the constraints that the positive law imposes on lawyers' professional vices arise out of rules that are narrow, technical, and contingent. I argue that these technical limits, even when they substantially restrict lawyers' conduct, cannot possibly cancel out the adversary advocate's partisanship or eliminate the professional vices that the adversary system's foundational commitment to a structural separation between advocates and judges entails.

However, even as professional ethics requires lawyers to betray their own senses of truth and justice in ways that contravene the ethic of self-assertion that dominates ordinary morality, this ethics also promises to establish distinctively lawyerly virtues. Most notably, lawyers who specialize in suppressing their own judgments of truth and justice, as lawyer loyalty and client control require, develop a distinctive facility (which others do not share) for assisting persons who cannot themselves speak in a way that engages the authoritative institutions of government to state their claims in an undistorted and yet effective fashion. Part I concludes by foreshadowing the distinctively lawyerly virtue associated with this capacity to give voice to the voiceless in high *fidelity*. Lawyerly fidelity involves more than merely partisan partiality in favor of clients over others; it also includes the capacity accurately to identify and to articulate clients' points of view, including even in clients who are themselves inarticulate (and to do so without distortion from the lawyers' own views of what their clients deserve or ought to prefer). Fidelity, understood as a distinctively lawyerly virtue, offers lawyers their best hope for ethical vindication of their professional lives.

That the argument concludes by vindicating lawyers' professional commitments (at least in principle) should be remembered while considering the account of the lawyerly vices from which it begins. For one thing, this will serve as a useful reminder that even in its most critical moments, the argument's ultimate sympathies lie with lawyers rather than with their detractors. Moreover, and more importantly, remembering these sympathies even in the midst of criticism will serve to emphasize the argument's deep commitment to ethical complexity, both for the special case of lawyers' professional ethics and for the modern moral condition more generally. A successful defense of lawyers' professional ethics must be more than just a whitewashing. The tensions between lawyers' professional commitments and the ethical ambitions of ordinary good people are too deep and too pervasive to ignore; and criticisms that lawyers' professional activities are vicious are too prominent, and too resonant with ordinary moral experience, to dismiss as ignorance or hostility. Instead, friends of partisan lawyers will be most effective if they treat ethical doubts about the legal profession seriously and respectfully and, in spite of the discomfort involved, hard-headedly acknowledge that the charges that lawyers display characteristic professional vices are, on their own terms, accurate. The mark of the complexity of lawyers' professional ethics is that the legal profession remains worthy of commitment even in spite of its attendant vices. Finally, lawyering is not unique in respect of this complexity, which instead pervades modern moral life quite generally. A sympathetic but honest appraisal of the legal profession therefore promises to yield insights beyond legal ethics, concerning the generally fractured state of modern moral life.

Part II: Integrity

These reflections suggest that the invocation of vice and virtue in Part I is not idle talk, and the second part of the book takes the philosophical measure of the professional vices that Part I identifies. It treats the language of vice and its effects—including the resistance of good lawyers to claims that they lie and cheat—as themselves important features of lawyers' professional ethics. Part II thus asks what it is like—what it is like not emotionally or psychologically but *ethically**[9]—to practice law with an adversary advocate's professional commitments. This question opens up a new front in legal ethics. The forms of argument that dominate traditional debates in legal ethics are by nature inadequate to sustaining the appeal of any life that involves the lawyer's professional vices, so that even if these traditional defenses succeed on their own terms, they cannot render the life of the lawyer worthy of commitment and therefore cannot bring lawyers' professional ethics to a satisfactory conclusion, all things considered.

This is not to say that traditional approaches to legal ethics have been hostile to lawyers. To the contrary, the leading argument in traditional legal ethics—the adversary system excuse—seeks to defend lawyers' professional conduct. According to this argument, the perception that adversary advocates behave immorally is an illusion only, brought on when lawyers' professional activities are viewed through too narrow a lens. In fact, a broader view reveals that aggressively partisan lawyers play an essential part in an impartially justified division of moral labor. Although lawyers may appear impermissibly to favor their clients over others, a

---

* The emphasis on ethics is important here, particularly in respect of the distinction between the ethical and emotional life of lawyers.

Lawyers, especially young lawyers, work increasingly long hours, and, especially in large city firms, increasingly work on tasks far removed—by two or three layers of seniority—from the clients and causes of action that they supposedly serve. These features of law-firm life, which can make practicing law at once stressful and uninteresting, figure prominently in what it is like emotionally to be a lawyer. But they are much less important to what it is like ethically. I point this out in order to emphasize that my argument in this book does not depend on the organizational structure of (especially large) law firms or on the economic pressures that principally determine this structure.

broader view reveals that competition among partisan advocates concerned primarily, and indeed almost exclusively, for their clients produces, on balance, the best justice for all.

This defense of aggressive partisanship has not gone unchallenged, of
course. Indeed, a lively debate about the outer limits of the partisanship
that the adversary system excuse can justify has come to dominate legal
ethics.

At one extreme is the view that the adversary system excuse justifies a
nearly absolute moral division of labor, so that the lawyer's partisan duties to her client know virtually no limits. This view appears vividly in
Lord Brougham's remark (perhaps the most famous in legal ethics) that
a lawyer "by the sacred duty which he owes his client, knows, in the
discharge of that office but one person in the world—THAT CLIENT AND
NONE OTHER" so that a lawyer must continue pressing his client's interests "by all expedient means" and "reckless of the consequences," and
even though (as in the case of Lord Brougham's own defense of Queen
Caroline's divorce case) he should "involve his country in confusion for
his client's protection."[10] This was surely an extravagant way of speaking, as it was meant to be,[11] but the basic sentiment that Lord Brougham
immodestly expressed—that a lawyer's partisan duties to her client
should control her professional life—remains the standard conception
of legal ethics today.

On the other side of the debate, critics of the standard conception
argue that in spite of its familiarity and intuitive appeal, the adversary
system excuse justifies only a much more limited moral division of labor
than is commonly supposed, under which lawyers' partisan obligations
to clients are much more narrowly cabined and their direct obligations
to truth and justice sweep more broadly. To begin with, these critics
question how much partisanship the adversary system excuse can justify
in actual, as opposed idealized, legal systems. They observe that when
the underlying law is unjust or the underlying distribution of legal services is unequal, it becomes simply implausible that the extravagant partisanship associated with the standard view will best serve justice for all,
even only on balance.[12] Moreover, critics observe that even in an ideal
legal system, adversary advocates commonly promote their clients' interests through actions that violate the rights of others. In such cases, the
aggregative conception of impartiality on which the traditional statement
of the adversary system excuse relies faces challenges from rival conceptions, associated with deontological moral theories, that apply impartiality separately to every relation between persons. These conceptions insist
that when a lawyer's preference for her client violates a third party's
rights, this cannot be simply offset by benefits that arise elsewhere in the
adversary administration of justice. And so the adversary system excuse

must be adjusted to reflect the constraints imposed by rights, most likely in ways that narrow the partisanship that it ultimately justifies.[13]

These complications together fix the principal focus of contemporary legal ethics. Reformers propose that they require a retreat from the orthodox view—associated with Lord Brougham's professed intentions to remain loyal to his client "reckless of the consequences"—that the adversary advocate must use every arguably legal means to promote any legal ends her client sets. Traditionalists, for their parts, resist (in whole or in part) such efforts to temper adversary advocacy.[14] And so the issue is joined and the debate that, as I have said, dominates legal ethics gets underway.

The lawyerly vices, however, will endure regardless of how these disagreements concerning the metes and bounds of lawyers' impartially justified partisanship are resolved. As Part I argues, lawyers' professional obligations to mislead and to exploit are incidents not of any specific, extreme elaboration of the adversary ideal but rather of that ideal itself. They arise ineliminably out of the structural separation between advocate and tribunal, and the associated principles of lawyer loyalty and client control, that belong to every conception of adversary advocacy, no matter what its limits.

This renders the dominant debate in legal ethics (in spite of its obvious importance in other respects) on its face inadequate to resolving the basic question whether or not the professional life of the lawyer is worthy of commitment. The adversary system excuse never denies that lawyers must adopt professional vices but merely justifies these vices on the grounds that it is best overall for lawyers to display them. And the insistent focus, among legal ethicists, on the outer limits of the partisanship that the adversary system excuse justifies draws attention away from the important question of whether this argument, within the scope of its competence, can sustain lawyers' commitment to a professional life that requires them to embrace the lawyerly vices within the scope of their partisanship, wherever its limits are set.

Moreover, there are strong reasons to suspect that the success of the adversary system excuse cannot sustain an appealing professional ethics—one that renders the lawyers' professional lives worthy of commitment—in the face of lawyers' enduring professional vices. At best, the success of the adversary system excuse casts lawyers, who remain required to lie and to cheat in the service of justice, as, so to speak, usefully vicious. But even as it does so, lawyers themselves, as evidenced by their resentful responses to accusations that they lie and cheat, badly wish not to be vicious at all.

This wish may seem to rest on a moral confusion. Surely if the adversary system excuse is correct—so that lawyers' partisanship does in fact serve justice and therefore is impartially justified—then this is all that lawyers need to say in defense of their profession. Indeed, it is tempting to *define* lying and cheating as involving *unjustified* deception and advantage-taking, so that a successful impartialist defense of lawyers' professional conduct undermines the suggestion that they lie and cheat immediately and at a stroke.

But this view proceeds too quickly. Certainly it is inadequate to the experience of lawyers, and others, who are asked to do acts that would ordinarily be immoral because, in the circumstances at issue, they serve impartial justice. The tension in lawyers' professional ethics is not resolved so easily, and the everyday morality of viciousness does not melt away at the first (successful) mention of extenuating circumstances. Ordinary notions of truthfulness and fair play have more staying power than this, so that they continue to exert their pull even the face of the adversary system excuse. That is why the charges of lying and cheating rankle so.

Part II of the book attempts a philosophical reconstruction of lawyers' dissatisfaction with being cast even as usefully vicious. This effort begins by developing a distinction between two fundamentally different forms of moral argument: impartial argument, which concerns a person's duties to others in light of their equal importance as sources of free-standing moral claims; and first-personal argument, which concerns a person's interest in achieving her own (suitable) ambitions and emphasizes the special relation of authorship that a person has to her own actions and life plans. I develop the idea of integrity in connection with this distinction and argue that lawyers betray their integrity when, abandoning their ordinary ambitions to honesty and fair play, they lie and cheat, including even when, as under the adversary system defense, they are impartially justified in doing so. I argue that this problem of integrity endures regardless of the conception of impartiality that the adversary system defense employs, including in particular when the adversary system defense is adjusted to reflect the deontological conception of impartiality that prominent critics of traditional conceptions of aggressive partisanship have employed. Moreover, I argue that integrity is a substantial (and indeed essential) moral ideal, so that lawyers' resentment at betraying their integrity in the service of their impartially justified professional obligations is no mere self-indulgence.

Part II therefore raises doubts whether lawyers might retain their integrity even as they satisfy their professional obligations. It reveals that this inquiry is every bit as important to lawyers' professional ethics as the inquiries involved in more familiar discussions about the adversary system excuse and the metes and bounds of justified partisanship.

A profession that destroys the integrity of its practitioners cannot be worthy of their commitment.

Part III: Comedy or Tragedy?

Legal ethics must therefore ask whether it is possible for lawyers to conceive of their professional activities, including those associated with lawyerly vices, in a way that permits lawyers to sustain their integrity. To do so, lawyers must develop a professional ethics that speaks not only impartially but also in the first-personal register, casting lawyers' professional commitments as part of a life that a person might honorably pursue. This requires answering the charges that lawyers lie and cheat head-on, arguing not only (as under the adversary system excuse) that these vices are impartially justified, but also that the conduct in question is not in fact vicious at all. The third part of the book assesses lawyers' prospects for pursuing the ethical ideas that their integrity requires.

Part III begins by suggesting that certain familiar ideas in the ethics of role—reinterpreted, along unfamiliar lines, not as a substitute but rather as a complement for impartial morality—are formally suited to preserving lawyers' integrity against the threats posed by their professional obligations. Specifically, role morality allows lawyers directly to reject (as the adversary system defense and cognate impartialist moral arguments did not) the accusations that they lie and cheat by replacing descriptions of their professional conduct that emphasize these ordinary vices with descriptions that emphasize distinctively lawyerly virtues. Such role-based redescription allows lawyers to achieve their wish not to conceive of themselves as vicious at all and in this way to preserve their integrity against the threats that their professional obligations would otherwise pose.

Next, Part III develops a substantively appealing conception of the lawyer's role, which elaborates in detail on the distinctively lawyerly virtue introduced briefly at the end of Part I and recasts the professional activities that ordinary first-personal ethics calls vicious as expressions of this virtue. In this emphasis, my argument resembles an earlier attempt by Anthony Kronman to deploy a distinctively lawyerly conception of virtue—which is embodied in what he calls the "lawyer-statesman," who displays an uncommon prudence or practical wisdom, a "special talent for discovering where the public good lies and for fashioning those arrangements needed to secure it"[15]—in the service of rendering the lawyer's life worthy of commitment, or as he puts it, explaining "the capacity of a lawyer's life to offer fulfillment to the person who takes it up."[16] Nevertheless, the substantive account of the lawyer's characteristic virtues that I offer in this book is very different from the ideal that Kronman proposes. In particular, whereas the states-manship that Kronman champions involves self-assertion by lawyers who are cast as leaders—for being especially skilled at forming and identifying their own views of the good—the account of the lawyerly virtues that I develop requires a kind of self-effacement in lawyers who are cast as servants. This is implicit in the initial statement of the lawyerly virtue of fidelity that appears at the end of Part I, and in particular in the ideals of accuracy and deference that fidelity includes—in the fact, as I have said, that fidelity involves not just lawyer loyalty but also client control (not just partisan preference for clients over other persons but also deference to clients in determining what this preference requires).

Part III elaborates this ideal of fidelity. The argument begins by describing in detail the content of lawyerly fidelity, with a particular emphasis on the ways in which fidelity requires more than the partisan preference in favor of clients that loyalty *simpliciter* involves. The description develops a surprising analogy between lawyers and poets, which provides the raw materials out of which lawyers might construct lawyerly virtues that make it possible to square their professional obligations with their personal integrity. According to this account, lawyers, like poets, are specialists in what I call (following Keats) *negative capability*: that is, in the capacity to speak not in one's own voice but rather, effacing one's private judgments, faithfully and authentically to render the subjectivity of another—in the case of lawyers by giving voice to clients who would otherwise remain inarticulate.*[17] The argument continues by

---

* Note that opportunities to display fidelity, as I understand it, arise in every dispute, no matter how inconsequential. Accordingly, these opportunities are open to all lawyers, no matter how banal or mundane their practices. Kronman's statesmanship, by contrast, is a much grander virtue, and the opportunities for statesmanship are concentrated in lawyers who play important roles in governing the societies to which they belong.

In past eras relatively many lawyers may have played such roles. Certainly local politics was more likely to involve basic questions of collective self-rule, and therefore to call for lawyers to exhibit statesmanship, before political power became as concentrated in the national government as it is today. Kronman is therefore perhaps right to invoke the country lawyer as one of the pillars of statesmanship, at least insofar as he is discussing historical lawyers, and to insist that in its nineteenth-century heyday statesmanship was always sufficiently near to hand that it might serve as an "ennobling thought, even for those who . . . found that they had only limited opportunities in their own work to exercise [this] virtue."

But over the course of the twentieth century, and in particular as principled decisions concerning collective self-government became concentrated at the national level, relatively fewer and fewer lawyers faced professional engagements that called for statesmanship. And, today, opportunities for statesmanship are intensely concentrated in the very highest echelons of the bar.

This does not, of course, mean that statesmanship is not a real virtue. But it does limit the service that statesmanship can render lawyers' integrity, because it limits the class of

explaining the importance of lawyerly fidelity, so understood. Specifically, the argument, employing an analogy to the democratic political process, connects the fidelity that adversary advocates display to the legitimacy of adjudication. These reflections, which embed legal ethics in political theory, make it possible to supplement the formal support for lawyers' integrity identified by the purely moral argument concerning the ethics of role with a rich, substantive account of the characteristically lawyerly virtues through which integrity-preserving role-based redescription might proceed. Lawyerly fidelity is a high calling, I argue, both in its intrinsic merit and in its central role in sustaining social life more broadly in the face of the disputes that threaten, at every moment, to tear society apart. And the opportunity to cultivate and exercise lawyerly fidelity therefore renders the lawyer's professional life worthy of commitment, even in the face of the fact that, in the eyes of nonlawyers, this life requires lawyers to lie and to cheat.

These considerations incline toward bringing lawyers' professional ethics to a positive conclusion, suggesting that whatever nonlawyers might think, the professional life of the lawyer is in principle worth pursuing for those who are prepared to immerse themselves in it. But the third part of the book (and therefore also the book's overall argument) concludes by returning the argument to a less happy register. I ask what a role must be like in order to be capable in practice of sustaining the forms of integrity-preserving role-based redescription that I propose, and I answer that the role must be authoritatively insular—that is, capable of sustaining idiosyncratic first-personal moral ambitions in its occupants, even as those who do not occupy the role systematically reject these role-based ambitions in favor of more ordinary alternatives. I then trace the history of the American legal profession from the years immediately following the Civil War to the present day and conclude that this history involves the systematic removal of all the key incidents of insularity from the lawyer's role. Lawyering has therefore become increasingly incapable of sustaining any distinctive forms of moral life and increasingly deferential to outside judgments, or, as I say, increasingly and anxiously cosmopolitan. The practice of law, as Kronman has warned, has "los[t] its status as a calling and degenerat[ed] into a tool with no more inherent moral dignity than a hammer or a gun."[18]

Regardless of what is possible in *principle*, the recent history of the legal profession has left contemporary U.S. lawyers without *practical* access to integrity-preserving role-based redescription. Accordingly, the ethical circumstances of adversary advocates today are, overall, anything

lawyers who can appeal persuasively to statesmanship in the role-based redescriptions on which their integrity depends.

but happy. Certainly the biblical charge—"Woe unto you also, ye lawyers! for ye lade men with burdens grievous to be borne, and ye your-
selves touch not the burdens with one of your fingers"[19]—does not apply
today. If anything, its opposite is true: even as lawyers are called on to
integrate clients into a process of adjudication that would otherwise be
alien, they are denied the cultural resources needed to shoulder the ethical burdens that arise on answering this call. These burdens threaten to
dis-integrate the lawyers themselves.

Finally, the same egalitarian and democratic ideals that render negatively capable lawyers essential to the legitimacy of adjudication also
account for the cosmopolitanism of the modern bar. The very forces that
make adversary advocacy essential to sustaining social order and therefore in principle worthy of commitment also conspire to shut lawyers
out from the ideals that would allow them to sustain this commitment,
preserving their integrity against the threats that their partisanship poses.
This connection introduces a note of irony, and indeed of tragedy, into
the life of the modern lawyer.

• • •

This brief statement of the main ideas of the book is schematic and
incomplete, of course, and the body of the book will elaborate systematically what I have only hinted at here. But before embarking on that
substantive effort, a few brief reflections about the nature of the argument are in order, specifically with respect to its scope and method.

SCOPE

I have so far been speaking of lawyers as an undifferentiated mass, but
of course they are not. Rather, lawyers inhabit many roles and perform
many tasks, which bear at most a family resemblance to one another.
This makes it necessary to ask: To which lawyers, or classes of lawyers,
does my ethical analysis of the legal profession apply?

Certainly this analysis does not apply equally to all lawyers in all legal
systems. As the language in which I have introduced them reveals, the
professional obligations to behave immorally that lawyers face arise out
of lawyers' adversary advocacy: that is, out of lawyers' narrowly partisan
loyalties to particular clients and, more specifically, out of their efforts to
promote these clients' interests, even at the expense of the interests of
more deserving others. But not all lawyering is equally adversarial. First,
legal systems differ (across both space and time) in the degree of partisanship that they require or indeed permit lawyers to display. It may

seem that lawyers in legal systems that de-emphasize partisanship face much less ethical uncertainty about professional obligations that they may simply embrace. And second, even in legal systems (such as the American one) that generally affirm lawyerly partisanship, not everything that lawyers do involves advocating for clients and against others with whom they stand in direct competition. Some lawyers—most obviously, judges, but also arbitrators and other "third party neutrals"[20]—staff tribunals rather than advocating before them. And even lawyers who loyally serve particular clients often work in contexts that involve little or no advocacy. Rather, they focus on counseling clients concerning the legal, economic, and even moral consequences of some project, for example, or on preparing opinions that characterize a client's legal situation for others.[21] Finally, the justification of lawyers' partisanship that I propose will not apply equally to all lawyers even on its home turf, adjudication: in particular, as a later argument will explain, litigators for the government may justifiably display only much more modest partisanship than I describe, if they may display any partisanship at all. For all these reasons, some portion of the professional conduct of people called lawyers may entirely avoid the ethical difficulties that I make my subject here.

This is not a weakness of the approach to legal ethics developed here but rather a strength. For one thing, the class of lawyers who are subject to the moral difficulties from which my argument departs is larger and more inclusive than might perhaps be thought. Certainly, the question whether the professional life of the lawyer is worthy of commitment applies broadly enough so that asking it is no mere curiosity and answering it no idle parlor game. Instead, these activities belong to the natural preoccupations of self-reflective morality, arising directly out of the lived experience of a large group of persons who, moreover, exert a disproportionately prominent hold over humanity's collective moral imagination.

Thus, although they of course do so to differing degrees, most legal systems require lawyers to display some measure of adversariness in the sense required for the problems of legal ethics, as I identify them, to appear. To begin with, the partisan element of adversary lawyering arises, and calls the ethical standing of the profession into question, whenever lawyers, practicing in the shadow of a structural separation between advocate and tribunal, serve rather than judge their clients' causes. As Part I emphasizes, the ethical arguments that I develop do not depend on any particular, and certainly not on any extreme, account of the extent of lawyers' partisanship, but instead apply even when lawyers' loyalties to their clients are constrained by rules that prevent partisan excess. Although I elaborate my argument through an intensive engagement specifically with contemporary U.S. legal practice, this is only to fix ideas. Many of the reflections that I develop would survive reforms to the American legal profession and indeed might be applied, mutatis mutandis, to lawyers in other legal systems also.

After all, the structural separation between advocate and tribunal that serves as my starting point is not uniquely American. Indeed, in spite of my invocation of adversary advocacy, my ethical analysis is not even confined to one side of the distinction between adversary and inquisitorial processes of dispute resolution. That contrast principally refers to whether, as a matter of procedure, the legal and factual record in a dispute is developed primarily by the disputants or by the tribunal. And, although this choice has important consequences, including for the professional dispositions of lawyers,[22] the structural separation between advocate and tribunal may endure however it is made. Even lawyers who practice under inquisitorial procedures generally retain some measure of the partisan loyalties that cast them as adversaries in the sense at issue here. As a prominent comparativist has observed, "the familiar contrast between our adversarial procedure and the supposedly nonadversarial tradition has been grossly overdrawn."[23] German legal practice, which may be taken as representative of the broader inquisitorial tradition (at least on the European continent), illustrates this point nicely. Although German lawyers play only a very limited role in developing the facts, they "advance partisan positions from first pleadings to final arguments."[24] They "suggest legal theories and lines of factual inquiry, they superintend and supplement judicial examination of witnesses, they urge inferences from fact, they discuss and distinguish precedent, they interpret statutes, and they formulate visions of the law that further the interests of their clients."[25] All in all, then, "outside the realm of fact-gathering, German civil procedure is about as adversarial as our own."[26] And German lawyers, as indeed are lawyers in inquisitorial systems generally, are therefore subject to the ethical complexities and uncertainties that adversary advocacy involves.

Furthermore, although not every activity in which lawyers engage constitutes adversary advocacy, most lawyers do act as adversary advocates at least some of the time. The basic division of labor between advocates on the one hand and tribunals (judges or judge-surrogates) on the other ensures that partisanship penetrates deep into the legal profession. Judges and others who staff tribunals account for only a small fraction of lawyers. And although many more lawyers act principally as counselors and negotiators rather than directly as advocates, these lawyers advise and bargain in the shadow of the law,[27] that is, against the backdrop of what they can achieve for their clients through more direct advocacy. Indeed, the regulatory regimes that govern lawyers' conduct in these roles, for example, the ethical regime governing lawyers who give tax advice,[28] are often designed in express contemplation of end-games that involve such direct advocacy. Additionally, some of the professional duties that lie at the foundation of lawyers' partisanship unquestionably arise even outside the orbit of open advocacy. Thus, the duty to preserve client confidences applies quite generally to all forms of lawyering,[29] and may even apply more strictly outside of litigation, when it is less likely to run up against competing duties requiring candor before tribunals.[30] Accordingly, many more lawyers than the small minority who regularly engage in litigation count as adversary advocates, so that the ethical uncertainty about lawyering applies well beyond this narrow group.

Indeed, the ethical argument that I develop may also apply, although in an attenuated form, beyond the confines of the legal profession. The central themes of this argument—a circumstance in which persons must abandon their ordinary ethical ambitions in order to satisfy the contingent demands associated with their places in a moral division of labor; the threat to integrity that is posed by acquiescing in this division of labor; and the fragile and perhaps unsustainable hope that this threat might be answered by embracing one facet of the division of labor in order to sustain an ethical identity that stands apart from ordinary ethical ambitions—all reappear throughout modern ethical life. They are simply a working out of one of the characteristic dilemmas of modernity, namely, the problem of being a situated individual, with idiosyncratic commitments and plans, in a pluralist society that can hope stably to sustain social cooperation only on impartial, deindividuated terms. Lawyers focus this problem into particularly sharp relief because they are directly charged with integrating the idiosyncratic perspectives of individual persons into the impartial system. And legal ethics serves, in this respect, as a miner's canary, giving advance warning of ethical problems that, sooner or later, trouble all modern persons. These broader implications of legal ethics will remain mostly in the background in these pages, although I shall again address them more directly in a brief postscript.

Finally, the argument's focus on the genuinely partisan aspects of legal practice is a strength rather than a weakness for another reason also. For various reasons that will become plain in Parts II and III, this focus picks out the segment of the bar whose professional life is morally and politically distinctive, that is, unreplicated elsewhere in the social division of labor, and that plays an important and utterly unique role in this division of labor. Philosophical analysis should organize its energies according to such basic structural distinctions rather than deferring to the often arbitrary, or at least shallowly contingent, categories adopted by a profession for purposes of self-description. Legal ethics is no exception, and insofar as it aspires to be a philosophically serious field, it should organize itself according to categories that reflect basic moral realities rather than mere conventions.

METHOD

The book's central ambition is to understand the lawyer's circumstances rather than to intervene in ongoing controversies over the positive law governing lawyers or indeed even to prescribe, more generally, a course of conduct for "ethical" lawyers to pursue. Each part of the book elaborates one facet, to repeat a phrase that I have used before, of what it is like to adopt the professional commitments of an adversary advocate: Part I sets out the basic principles of lawyer loyalty and client control that are inscribed in the genetic structure of adversary advocacy and identifies the vices, and gestures toward the virtue, that these principles engender; Part II explains the ethical burdens, specifically with respect to personal integrity, associated with embracing these vices as adversary advocates must; and Part III places the lawyer's legal and ethical practices into a broader social and political context. This focus—on diagnosis rather than cure—is necessary and natural, especially given the connection between legal ethics and the broader ethical dilemmas of modernity. How, after all, could a philosophical argument possibly cure the condition of modernity? But it is also somewhat unusual in legal ethics; and it certainly involves methodological commitments that are highly unusual and therefore worth discussing in some detail before commencing with the argument proper.

Most legal ethics, and indeed most applied ethics more generally, tends towards casuistry:* it begins by identifying general principles of

---

* Legal scholarship in general has the same tendency, even when it does not invoke immediately ethical ideas. Ever since the realist revolution exploded the formalist myth that legal rules are connected to one another by logic and are independent of the rest of the normative universe, the focus of legal scholarship—and especially of interdisciplinary legal scholarship—has been on asking what values outside of the law a legal regime should serve and what system of legal rules might serve these values best. I have no desire to revive the formalist conception of law as hermetically sealed off from morals or politics. There is anyway no less plausible site for such an ambition than the law governing lawyers, which is obviously rent through with extralegal moral and political ideals. But I do believe that even though the law is ultimately beholden to extralegal values, legal regimes can construct edifices of doctrinal, and indeed human, relationships that cast long shadows in the light of these extralegal values. Life in these shadows is, then, neither purely legal nor purely independent of the law but instead consists of the patterns that extralegal values take on when they are, to change metaphors, refracted through the prism of the

value and right action (which it has usually borrowed wholesale from more abstract work in moral and political theory) and then applies these principles to a particular set of facts in order to generate prescriptions about what should be done. Certainly the many arguments about the adversary system defense have this character, as their express reliance on antecedent theories of justice and their insistent return to the question of the metes and bounds of lawyers' justified partisanship attest.

I am dubious of this approach. To begin with, the general principles from which casuistic arguments in applied ethics begin tend to be too simplistic, and the facts to which the arguments apply these principles tend to be too stylized, for the casuistry to be persuasive. Moreover, it is probably not realistic to expect philosophy to have such mechanical and immediate regulative implications for ethical life as casuistry supposes. After all, moral and political philosophers are notoriously not better or more just than other people, and not only because they are no better at resisting the temptations to do wrong. Instead, ethical life requires forms of sensitivity and judgment that philosophical expertise makes no claims to providing. Ethics—at least in the sense of living well—simply is not a technical subject in the way casuistry presumes, and we mark this linguistically by distinguishing ethical excellence, which we call virtue, from mere technical excellence, or skill.* Ethical life involves complexities and offers possibilities for practical and indeed ethical creativity and judgment that casuistic approaches to applied ethics, which emphasize technical expertise, cannot encompass, so that these approaches tend to have an unappealing air of naïveté and even unreality. Indeed, a person who treats casuistry respectfully, deferring to a casuist's claims of expertise much as a patient defers to her doctor's expertise in a more naturally

---

law. The distinctive forms of life and action that arise in this context—the values and ideals that are immanent in the law—will be understudied by a scholarly method that stands outside the law and proceeds with the principal purpose of shaping the law to promote one or another set of extralegal ends. So it is, I believe, with much contemporary scholarship in legal ethics.

* We have inherited this distinction from the ancient Greeks (for example, Aristotle in the *Nicomachean Ethics*), who insisted (much more clearly than we do now) on the difference between virtue and what they called techne.

Our language is not uniformly helpful in resisting casuistry, however. Indeed, the suggestion that philosophers are appropriate sources of regulative principles for living may owe part of its prominence to nothing more than a quirk of language, namely that the English word "ethics" refers to both the art of living well and the philosophical study of the values that living well involves. If this were not the case—if there were different words for these distinct things—the casuistic impulse would probably seem less compelling. The situation would be more as it is in art, where the fact that "beauty" and "aesthetics" are different words makes it easy to resist the idea that the second offers a regulative guide to creating the first.

technical subject such as medicine, has already committed an ethical error. She has accepted a kind of ethical authority that is inconsistent with her own freedom and responsibility.

This is not to claim (which would be absurd) that philosophy is irrelevant to ethics. Philosophers, including by applying their professional expertise, are unusually able to explain the conceptual structure of an ethical practice, to identify the relationships in which various ethical practices stand to one another, and even to explain what is at stake in a particular ethical conflict. In all these ways, philosophers, and characteristically philosophical forms of thought, do indeed have distinctive contributions to make to ethical life. But their contributions are primarily *interpretive* and *reconstructive* rather than directly *regulative*.

The task of philosophical ethics is therefore primarily to elaborate what is rather than to command what should be. Of course, a philosophical advance in understanding of a form of ethical life may lead to changes in that form of life, as participants and indeed outsiders adjust their engagements with the form of life in light of how they have come to understand it. (In the case at hand, philosophical argument shows that a life of committed professionalism, both in law and more generally, can in principle be reconciled with the broader obligations that apply to persons generally, and that the prospects for a successful reconciliation depend on the social and political structures in which that life is embedded.) But the choices involved in actually making these adjustments have an *independent* ethical content of their own, involving ethical creativity and judgment.[31] They are not entailed by the mechanical application of philosophical understanding to ethical life.

The question that I have set myself here accepts this account of the limits and possibilities of philosophical ethics: it resists casuistry entirely and invites interpretive reconstruction. I do not attempt to say whether the adversary system is justified or wrongheaded and certainly make no effort to identify the optimal specification of lawyers' professional obligations. Instead of evaluating them with an eye to reform, I take the basic outlines of adversary advocacy for granted and ask, as I have said, what legal, ethical, and political values and forms of life are immanent in this professional regime. To be sure, I intend the philosophical understanding that I present here to influence the ethical life of the legal profession, and indeed of our wider society. But I insist that how this influence plays out depends on further ethical interventions, of a nonphilosophical nature, which my philosophical account of legal ethics therefore necessarily leaves somewhere off the page.

The methods of argument that I apply throughout the book follow from the question that I have set myself and the view of philosophical ethics that this question reflects. Thus I begin my argument not from an

abstract philosophical theory of goodness or justice to which I claim the
law governing lawyers should conform but rather from the detailed
body of rules that constitutes the law of lawyering as it stands, from
which I propose to excavate the ethical content of adversary advocacy.
And throughout my argument, I return repeatedly to interpretive engagements with other features of the legal profession, for example, its
historical development and institutional structure. Moreover, my commitment in favor of interpretive over regulative approaches to applied
ethics works itself inward in my argument, into the details of my engagement with the positive practice of adversary lawyering. Most immediately, I resist the temptation, which often overcomes even the most
reflective legal ethicists, to focus discussions of legal ethics on extraordinary cases—for example, cases in which lawyers present an alibi defense
that they know to be false,[32] keep a life-threatening secret,[33] intimidate
an adverse party by investigating her sexual history,[34] or even bring a
false murder prosecution.[35] Instead, I emphasize the ethical questions
that arise in adversary legal practice quite generally, in the banal conduct of lawyers' workaday professional lives.

Sensational cases may be suited to casuistry, because they usefully
support intuitive tests of the limits of justified partisanship. They may
even underwrite more theoretical investigations of the limits of the adversary system defense's power to recast lawyers' partisan attachment
to their clients as part of a more broadly impartial scheme of justice.*
But exceptional cases are much less useful for my purposes, which are
to elaborate a philosophical reconstruction of the constant core of adversary advocacy rather than to fix its variable boundaries, and to identify the moral and political complexities that every form of adversary
lawyering, no matter how mild, necessarily involves, because they arise
inevitably in the shadow of the structural division of labor between
advocate and tribunal. In order to know what a practice is really like,
it is better to ask what it is ordinarily like rather than to fixate on what
it becomes as it starts cracking under pressure. Sensational cases, which
are the mainstays of most discussions of legal ethics, are attention-
grabbing, to be sure. But it is a mistake to emphasize them: just as
great cases make bad law,[36] so they make bad legal ethics.

Finally, the interpretive approach to legal ethics that I adopt here requires the argument to be relentlessly interdisciplinary, stepping out, at

---

*An undue emphasis on sensational cases can cause troubles even within the casuistic
paradigm, insofar as fixating on extraordinary dilemmas overshadows lawyers' more common ethical concerns. It allows critics of the adversary system to paint the entire practice
in its harshest colors, and (probably more damagingly) it allows adversary advocacy's defenders to obscure the ethical difficulties that arise in everyday legal practice behind the
favorable contrast between ordinary and exceptional cases.

various places, not just into legal doctrine and moral philosophy, but also into political philosophy, history, sociology, and even literary theory. The central role that adversary advocates and adversary adjudication play in legal, moral, and political life brings legal ethics into contact with all these neighboring disciplines. And whereas casuistic approaches to legal ethics naturally narrow their focus according to the concerns of the purely philosophical theories from which they begin, the reconstructive ambition that I am pursuing here requires that my methods adapt themselves flexibly to address all the many aspects of adversary advocacy, each in its own native idiom. As James Agee said of another reconstructive effort, "[i]f complications arise," they come of trying to address a subject "not as journalists, sociologists, politicians, entertainers, humanitarians, priests, or artists, but seriously."[37]

PART I

Adversary Advocacy

Chapter 1

THE WELLSPRINGS OF LEGAL ETHICS

Adversary advocates practice as partisans in the shadow of the structural division of labor between lawyer and judge and represent particular clients rather than justice writ large. They therefore come under professional obligations to do acts that, if done by ordinary people and in ordinary circumstances, would be straightforwardly immoral. They unfairly prefer their clients over others and, moreover, serve their clients in ways that implicate common vices with familiar names: most notably, lawyers lie and cheat. These vices will play a prominent role in the moral and political discussions to come, and the three chapters that constitute the first part of the book's larger argument therefore devote themselves to establishing that adversary advocates are in fact necessarily professionally obligated to display them.

Thus I begin, in this chapter, by identifying broad principles of professional conduct that every adversary system must recognize and explaining the genetic pressures that these principles exert on lawyers who practice under them. In addition, I elaborate some on the nature of lying and cheating, in order to forestall the objection that, especially when applied to more modest adversary systems, my argument depends on an unduly rigorous moralism. Then, in chapter 2, I consider the rules through which a regime of professional responsibility might regulate these pressures and argue that, although such rules can cabin lawyers' professional vices, they cannot eliminate them. Finally, in chapter 3, I present an alternative doctrinal characterization of lawyers' professional obligations, which answers certain objections that my earlier doctrinal arguments invite. Even as they cement lawyers' professional obligations to lie and to cheat, the doctrines at issue in chapter 3 also sow the seeds of a distinctively lawyerly virtue, which I introduce at the end of the chapter under the name *fidelity*. In this way, the first part of the book sets the stage not just for the ethical troubles that will dominate Part II but also for the ethical hopes that will dominate Part III.

Critics of the legal profession often take the law governing lawyers to adopt extreme adversarialism.[1] The profession's defenders respond, sometimes angrily, that the critics wrongly emphasize contingent adversary excesses in the positive practice of lawyering—that they attribute the unprofessional intemperance of a minority of lawyers to the legal profession as a whole, and certainly that they ignore the many ways in which the positive law expressly limits lawyers' partisanship.[2] Although I accuse lawyers of displaying professional vices, I am sympathetic to the professions' defenders on this point. Philosophical legal ethics should treat legal practice respectfully, and it is a mistake to proceed as if lawyers must serve their clients single-mindedly or to take any other extreme view of the partisanship that lawyers must display. Accordingly, I accept that the partisanship at the core of lawyers' professional obligations is limited, and indeed encroached on, from all sides by more specific rules of legal ethics that bind lawyers to values besides their clients. I claim only that these constraints do not, and could not possibly, eliminate the lawyerly vices that the underlying commitment to partisanship entails.

It is therefore important to proceed cautiously in writing about the lawyerly vices, and in particular to follow my earlier admonition to avoid sensational cases and instead to focus on the banalities of everyday adversary legal practice. Moreover, it is important to demonstrate that the lawyerly vices are not artifacts of one or another contingent (and misguided) elaboration of the adversary ideal in the positive law but are instead inscribed in the genetic structure of adversary advocacy, in all its forms. My approach reflects these challenges. In addition to preferring the commonplace over the extraordinary, I attend constantly to the distinction between the essential and the merely contingent features of adversary advocacy. Although I will repeatedly take up the positive law of lawyering, often in considerable detail, I will never analyze positive law for its own sake but always, rather, to illustrate the possibilities and limits of adversary advocacy in all its forms. I can therefore accept that the legal profession's defenders are right about the constraints on partisanship that the positive law incorporates and claim that lawyers nevertheless come under professional duties to lie and to cheat. I argue, moreover, that the formal structure of adversary advocacy means that not just these constraints but any constraints that are consistent with the adversary ideal will necessarily be unable to purge the legal profession of the lawyerly vices.

Three Foundational Principles of Adversary Advocacy

The foundations of adversary advocacy remain constant across all forms of adversary legal practice and therefore do not depend on any particular formulation of positive law. But they are nevertheless inscribed in positive law, including in the ABA's Model Rules and their several predecessors. The basic structure of adversary advocacy may therefore be discerned from the study of the law governing lawyers. This structure involves three foundational principles, which I call *lawyer loyalty*, *client control*, and *legal assertiveness*.

Lawyer Loyalty

Two provisions of the Model Rules display the basic structure of adversary advocacy in a particularly clear light, and I use these provisions as a template to organize the discussion. Model Rule 1.3 (addressed in this section) establishes the lawyer's duty of loyalty to her client; and Model Rule 1.2 (addressed in the next) establishes the client's control over the ends that the lawyer pursues. Both provisions articulate open-ended standards that reflect the basic assumptions of adversary legal practice rather than narrow rules that call for technical application.

Perhaps the adversary advocate's most familiar duty is to represent her client loyally. This duty of loyalty, which is familiarly expressed in the language of zealous advocacy, has in one form or another maintained a constant presence in all major codes of legal ethics adopted over the past century. The 1908 ABA Canons of Professional Ethics stated that the lawyer should represent her clients with "warm zeal."[3] The ideal was carried forward in the 1969 ABA Model Code of Professional Responsibility: The Canons (announcing the broad norms underlying the Model Code) include the principle that "a lawyer should represent a client zealously within the bounds of the law";[4] and the more specific Disciplinary Rules state that "a lawyer shall not intentionally fail to seek the lawful objectives of his client through reasonably available means permitted by law and the Disciplinary Rules."[5] Much the same duty appears in the Model Rules: Model Rule 1.3 requires lawyers to display "diligence" in serving clients;[6] the Official Comments to this Rule, which "provide guidance for practicing in compliance with the Rule[],"[7] add that lawyers should "take whatever lawful and ethical measures are required to vindicate a client's cause or endeavor" and must therefore "act with commitment and dedication to the interest of the client and with zeal in advocacy upon the client's behalf";[8] and the Preamble to the Model Rules mentions zeal three times.[9] These commands are not controversial. The Restatement of the Law Governing Lawyers summarizes the substance of loyalty, saying that a lawyer must "proceed in a manner reasonably calculated to advance a client's lawful objectives."[10] And Hazard and Hodes, who place loyalty at the very center of adversary lawyers' professional ethics, observe that "the single most fundamental principle of the law of lawyering is that so long as lawyers stay within the bounds of law, they serve society best by zealously serving their clients, one at a time."[11]

The law governing lawyers, moreover, shores up the primary duty of loyalty though secondary rules that guard against certain particularly

worrisome or prominent forms of disloyalty.[12] The most important of
these are the conflict of interest rules, which regulate, or even forbid,
a wide range of activities through which lawyers might be tempted
to betray their clients. Most generally, these rules impose restrictions—
including procedural restrictions requiring written informed consent[13]
and substantive restrictions against waivers of the duty to be competent
and diligent[14]—on lawyers' freedom to represent clients when "the representation of one client will be directly adverse to another client"[15] or,
more broadly still, when "there is a significant risk that the representation of one or more clients will be materially limited by the lawyer's responsibilities to another client, a former client or a third person or by a
personal interest of the lawyer."[16] More narrowly, the rules take aim at
certain especially troublesome behaviors. For example, they forbid lawyers from "using information relating to representation of a client to the
disadvantage of the client unless the client gives informed consent."[17]
They impose an outright ban on representations that "involve the assertion of a claim by one client against another client represented by the
lawyer in the same litigation or other proceeding before a tribunal."[18]
They forbid lawyers from writing themselves into their clients' wills[19] or
appropriating literary or media rights in their clients' stories,[20] and they
quite generally insist on substantive fairness in business transactions between lawyers and their clients.[21] And they forbid lawyers from being
paid to represent clients by third parties who interfere with the lawyer-
client relationship.[22] In these and other ways, the Model Rules emphasize and enforce the lawyer's duty of loyalty.

Client Control

In spite of its central importance to legal ethics, lawyer loyalty cannot
stand alone. Loyalty carries no content apart from the end to which it
refers—loyalty, even zealous loyalty, requires an object. And the loyalty
and zeal provisions in the ethics codes, even when supplemented by the
conflicts rules, do not adequately fix their own objects, because identifying "the client" as the object of the lawyer's loyalty and the end of her
zeal is not enough to fix the lawyer's professional duties in a meaningful
way. Saying simply that the lawyer should be loyal to the client does not
determine to what about the client the lawyer's loyalty should attach,
and this choice will dramatically affect the nature of the lawyer's ethical
life. Indeed, in the extreme case, if the lawyer's loyalty were tied to the
client's interest in moral or legal rectitude—to the client's justice, as one
might say—then the lawyer would cease to be meaningfully an adversary advocate at all. In order to represent her client loyally, she would
be required first to judge her client's cause to determine what protecting

his rectitude required. (The ends of the representation, which would depend upon the right outcome of the case, simply could not be identified apart from this judgment.) Lawyer loyalty underwrites a distinctively adversary legal practice only if it is owed more narrowly and immediately to the client than the suggestion about moral or legal rectitude allows. Adversary advocacy—indeed, the structural separation between advocate and tribunal—requires not just loyalty but also a client- rather than justice-centered approach to loyalty.

The ethics codes must therefore supplement the lawyer's duty of loyalty by specifying loyalty's ends, and they must (if they are to retain their adversary character) set ends that look more or less narrowly to the client. The codes fulfill both requirements, specifically through provisions that allocate decision-making authority between lawyers and clients in ways that give clients control over the basic purposes of a legal representation—control to fix the objectives that lawyers must loyally pursue. Moreover, the ethics codes establish just how the lawyer's loyalty will be client-centered, specifically by directing lawyers to pursue clients' instructions and not just clients' interests—that is, to defer to clients' beliefs about what ends they should pursue. The ethics codes allocate authority between lawyer and client in a way that supplements lawyer loyalty with client control and requires lawyers (within limits, of course) to be the servants of their clients' points of view.

The Model Rules announce the basic principle of client control in Rule 1.2, which gives clients broad power to determine "the objectives of representation."[23] The Model Code similarly directs the lawyer to "seek the lawful objectives of his client."[24] And the Restatement elaborates on this basic structure of client control, stating that that "[a] client may instruct the lawyer during the representation" and that lawyers should act "to advance a client's objectives as defined by the client."[25] The convergence concerning client control is not absolute,[26] but the basic idea is the same in all three regimes. That is not surprising: "The attorney-client relationship," as one court has observed, "is one of agent to principal, and as an agent the attorney must act in conformity with his . . . instructions and is responsible to his principal if he violates this duty";[27] and the ethics codes borrow their ideas about lawyer loyalty and especially client control from the general law of agency.[28] The law governing lawyers proceeds, against this background, to elaborate the agency relation between lawyer and client in ways that emphasize client control.

Most importantly, the ethics codes protect client control over ends from encroachment by the lawyer's superior knowledge and technical expertise, which often pose the gravest threats to client autonomy. Thus, although the ethics codes recognize lawyers' technical expertise by giving them limited control over the means through which to pursue the ends that clients set,[29] the line between "means" and "ends" is given a flexible rather than rigid interpretation—one that emphasizes client control. In particular, choices that would ordinarily be classed as involving mere means and therefore allocated to the lawyer—for example, respecting the aggressiveness of a cross-examination—are treated as involving ends and allocated to the client as soon as they impinge on the client's broader values. As the comment to Model Rule 1.2 says, when disputes about what would ordinarily be classed as means arise, "lawyers usually defer to the client regarding such questions as the expense to be incurred and concern for third persons who might be adversely affected."[30] (The juxtaposition of harm to others and cost to the client is striking in this context, and fortifies the client's right to subject even means to the test of his broader values, because client control over cost is particularly clear and unchallenged.) In this way, the ethics codes restrict lawyers' control over means to areas in which lawyers have "special knowledge and skill"—in effect, to "technical, legal and tactical matters."[31] Indeed, the lawyer's control over means is best understood not as an independent value at all but rather as an instrument to serve the client's control over ends: the client's power to set and pursue ends is made more valuable by giving the client access to a lawyer with discretion to devote her expertise to pursuing the client's ends more skillfully than the client could do on her own.

Lawyers are, to be sure, permitted, and perhaps even encouraged, to offer clients independent counsel even within the sphere of client authority—that is, not just in matters of technical law but also, as the Model Rules say, concerning "other considerations such as moral, economic, social and political factors, that may be relevant to the client's situation."[32] But even the practice of counseling clients concerning the ends of a representation serves, finally, to reemphasize the clients' ultimate authority over these ends. Lawyers may advise but must never command, and they should take care, in offering advice, to avoid unduly influencing their clients.

This is prominently reflected in the professional ideology of client counseling. For example, an important handbook instructs that "though you may ultimately provide a client who asks for it with your opinion, you should do so only after you have counseled a client thoroughly enough that you can base your opinion on your client's subjective values, not your own."[33]

Courts are also attentive to the line between advice and control. In one case, a court criticized the ethics of capital defense lawyers who sought to impose their own objections to the death penalty on their client. The lawyers exerted psychological pressure on their client to "compel" the client to "to accept [their] point of view" and plead guilty in the hope that this would spare him the death sentence.[34] The court observed that the desire to avoid death came from the lawyers rather than from their client, so that the lawyers exerted pressure to change their client's ends rather than merely to influence tactics through which to pursue ends fixed by the client. The lawyers acted, as the court put it, in order to "accommodate themselves, not their client."[35] The court therefore concluded that the lawyers' conduct "may very well have exceeded the bounds of ethical norms" concerning client counseling. (Although the court was hearing the client's habeas petition challenging the voluntariness of his guilty plea, it went out of its way to observe that "counsel's conduct may require further consideration by the Illinois Attorney Registration and Disciplinary Commission."[36])

Even though lawyers should advise their clients broadly, they may not use their positions as advisers to subvert clients' autonomy. The strong principle of lawyer loyalty is supplemented, in the ethics codes, by an equally strong principle of client control.

Legal Assertiveness

Even taken together, lawyer loyalty and client control do not fix the nature of lawyers' professional obligations. The duties that lawyer loyalty and client control actually impose on lawyers depend on the range of objectives that clients and their lawyers may jointly pursue and the range of means that clients and their lawyers may use to pursue these objectives. And the questions therefore remain just what clients may command their lawyers to do and just what client commands lawyers may follow.

The creation of an agency relation binds the agent to her principal but does not generally alter the scheme of duties that the principal and the agent (as his stand-in) owe third parties: a principal generally may not pursue ends through an agent that he may not pursue directly himself; and, an agent generally cannot avoid obligations to others by hiding behind the agency relation. Thus the law makes both principals and agents liable when agents take actions on behalf of their principals that tortiously harm third parties.[37] Accordingly, if the assertion of legal claims were governed by a standard of strict liability or even negligence, so that clients who asserted and lawyers who promoted losing or unreasonable claims were liable for the harms that they caused, then this liability would impose external constraints on the loyalty that clients might demand and that lawyers might display. Tort law would require both clients and lawyers to pursue justice or its reasonable approximation and therefore would effectively erase lawyers' partisanship.

Lawyer loyalty and client control are accordingly not the exclusive possessions of the law governing lawyers but instead arise against a broader background framework that allows clients to press their claims and makes room for the lawyer-client relationship to arise. For lawyer loyalty and client control to be meaningful in lawyers' professional lives, this larger framework must give lawyers substantial latitude in assisting clients who themselves enjoy substantial latitude in pressing their legal claims.

The legal structures that arise in and around adversary advocacy do just this, through a set of legal rules that allow lawyers wide latitude in assisting disputants who may press colorable but losing claims. Most narrowly, these rules give lawyers a literal privilege—which is expressly inscribed in legal doctrine—with respect to certain specific forms of conduct. For example, lawyers are in most jurisdictions absolutely immune from tort liability for defamatory statements that they make in court.[38] Similarly, although a little more broadly, lawyers are expressly protected against certain forms of legal liability that might otherwise attach to persons who do what lawyers do for their clients: A lawyer who encourages a client to breach a contract is not liable to the client's promisee for tortious interference with contract;[39] a lawyer who gives legal advice to a corrupt business is not guilty of racketeering;[40] and, more broadly still, a lawyer who gives good faith legal advice cannot be held liable as an accessory to tortious actions that her client takes on the basis of this advice.[41] In these ways, lawyers enjoy express protection against liability for the burdens that the assistance they give their clients imposes on others.[42]

These express protections, moreover, stand atop a much larger zone of protection that both clients and lawyers enjoy against liability for asserting and assisting legal claims. This zone of protection receives expression not just directly, in doctrines that narrowly cabin liability for bringing or defending lawsuits, but also indirectly, in the law's decision not to extend generally applicable standards of liability to conduct that involves asserting legal claims or defenses. Indeed, the express immunities that lawyers enjoy are made explicit precisely because they help to define the outside edge of these broader immunities.

To begin with, both the law governing lawyers and the broader law of procedure protect lawyers and their clients from liability for the full harms that they cause by asserting mistaken or even unreasonable legal claims (for example, claims that are dismissed or that lose on summary judgment), unless these claims are in some way frivolous or malicious.*[43]

---

* Fee-shifting, which requires losing parties to pay winning parties' fees and costs, imposes some liability on those who assert losing but nonfrivolous legal positions. Fee-shifting has been widely adopted in Great Britain and selectively in the United States.

Model Rule 3.1, for example, requires only that lawyers have a "basis in law and fact" for the claims they make "that is not frivolous, which includes a good faith argument for an extension, modification or reversal of existing law."[44] And the Federal Rules of Civil Procedure similarly require only that filings are not made for an improper purpose, are non-frivolous, and have or are likely to have evidentiary support.[45] The precise limits on the adversary assertiveness that these rules allow is of course a subject of substantial dispute (and one to which I return in chapter 2). But it is unquestioned that these rules do not impose strict liability or even negligence standards on lawyers and disputants. Strict liability would hold disputants liable whenever they asserted claims or defenses that eventually lost. And even negligence would (following a prominent interpretation of reasonableness) hold disputants liable whenever their arguments failed to minimize the total costs—including both error costs of inaccurate dispute resolution and transactions costs of litigation—that they, their opponents, and third parties had jointly to bear. Regardless of how the interpretive controversies that surround the rules against frivolous litigation are resolved, the rules clearly give disputants and lawyers substantially greater leeway than these standards of liability would allow.

Moreover, this retreat from ordinary standards of liability for harming others is carried over in the often unnoticed but important fact that tort law also declines to apply the ordinary law of negligence to harms caused when one person asserts legal claims, including losing legal claims, against another. Thus, although there do exist torts of malicious prosecution and abuse of process, they are subject to narrow limits and certainly do not apply generally to impose liability in connection with unreasonable lawsuits or legal arguments that burden others, even when the lawsuits should have been predicted to fail.[46] Once again, the law clearly does not require clients or their lawyers to proceed only with claims that are reasonable (for example, in the sense of joint cost minimizing).

These rules (and indeed the narrower immunities discussed a moment ago) do not of course protect clients or even lawyers from liability for all actions taken in connection with asserting legal claims, and I take up the limits on adversary ethics in more detail in the next chapter. It is enough for now that the adversary system writ large unambiguously insulates parties and their lawyers from liability for the harms that they impose simply

---

Although fee-shifting arrangements bring the standard of liability for pressing legal claims more nearly into line with the standards applied elsewhere in the law, the liability that they impose is limited to the direct costs of adjudication and does not include the often much larger (and potentially enormous) indirect costs—for example involving lost opportunities or lost reputations—imposed by the mistaken claims.

by asserting losing (including predictably losing) claims. This is a subtle but enormously important point. The legal system entitles clients, with the help of their advocates, aggressively to pursue their legal claims by denying legal recognition to many of the harms that persons' assertions of their legal rights cause others. Indeed, the protection that lawyers enjoy against liability for pressing losing claims is a mark of the distinction between advocate and judge, and the protection that losing clients enjoy is similarly a mark of the parallel distinction between party and judge. Both give an unfamiliar but important gloss on the common idea that the rule of law forbids a person from being a judge in her own case. This idea is ordinarily understood to say that judges ought not be partisans. But the arguments just rehearsed reveal that it has a second meaning also, namely that disputants and their advocates may be partisan and should not be required to bear the responsibility of judging their own causes.

● ● ●

The discussion of legal assertiveness provides the background needed to complete a basic characterization of the lawyer's professional role. When set against a backdrop of legal assertiveness, the principles of lawyer loyalty and client control together give substance to the adversary system's core commitment to placing lawyers at their clients' disposal. The principle of legal assertiveness entitles clients to press even losing (and even unreasonable) legal claims and entitles lawyers to assist them. And with this license in place, the principle of client control allows clients to choose the legal claims that they assert and to set the ends that they and their lawyers pursue, while the principle of lawyer loyalty requires lawyers to advance legal and factual arguments designed effectively to promote the ends that their clients have set.

THE LAWYERLY VICES

The foundational principles of adversary advocacy require lawyers to promote the causes and assert the claims that their clients choose, even when they doubt (or indeed reject) the claims' merits. Lawyers must assert their clients' factual and legal positions even when they privately find the opposing positions more compelling; and lawyers must promote their clients' causes even when they privately conclude that their clients do not fairly deserve to have these causes succeed. Moreover, lawyers must act in these ways even when their private doubts about their clients' positions are correct and even when their clients' positions are (within limits) unreasonable.

These professional obligations are not morally neutral. Instead, the forms of conduct that they describe arise in moral life more generally and have familiar names: to deceive others by asserting a proposition that one privately (and correctly) disbelieves is to lie; and to exploit others by promoting claims or causes that one privately (and correctly) thinks undeserving is to cheat.

Lawyers, as I have observed, commonly object to such charges. This response—including in respect of its intensity—is in itself an important feature of lawyers' professional ethics. Indeed Part II of the book may be read as an extended effort to render lawyers' intuitive objections to being charged with the lawyerly vices philosophically articulate—to demonstrate that lawyers' resentment at being said to lie and to cheat is not merely defensive self-indulgence, or any other form of special pleading, but instead expresses philosophically respectable and indeed foundational moral ideals. Moreover, the book's third part proposes a principled argument through which lawyers might resist claims that they lie and cheat (although it also worries that this argument might be no longer practically accessible to lawyers today).

But although the charge that lawyers are professionally obligated to lie and to cheat may be *answered*—so that the lawyer's professional life remains, even in the face of this charge, at least in principle worthy of commitment—it remains a substantial claim, both philosophically and ethically. The arguments of Parts II and III therefore take as their points of departure that the accusations commonly leveled at lawyers are, in a way, accurate and appropriate. Although they may be answered, they must be addressed respectfully, which is to say by means of arguments whose foundations go sufficiently deep into the ethical structure of the lawyer's professional life.

Not everyone agrees that the lawyerly vices deserve to be taken so seriously, however. Defenders of the legal profession, and in particular lawyers who wish for a quick and easy vindication of their own conduct, sometimes propose simply to dismiss the charges that they must lie and cheat as involving simple-minded mistakes about the legal profession, ordinary morality, or both. The success of these ready rejoinders would render the subtler defense of the legal profession that I offer unnecessary and indeed mistaken, because it would flatten the moral complexity that my approach takes to be essential to lawyers' professional ethics. Accordingly, before I develop my own efforts to defend lawyers' professional conduct, I explain why the more straightforward defenses that have been offered by others fail.

On the one hand, lawyers argue that the description of their professional obligations from which charges that they are professionally vicious begin is inaccurate—in particular, that it ignores the web of rules through which the law governing lawyers, both in its actual and certainly in its ideal state, constrains lawyers' partisanship to prohibit the very conduct on which the charges of lawyerly viciousness are based. In the next chapters, I investigate the more detailed rules that regulate the conduct of adversary advocates, both as they are and as they might be, in considerable detail and argue that lawyers' professional obligations to lie and to cheat are robust in the face of these rules and arise in any legal order that adopts the basic commitments of adversary advocacy, no matter how narrowly or carefully it constrains lawyers who operate within them.

On the other hand, lawyers reject the moral characterizations of their professional conduct that charges of professional viciousness involve. Lawyers argue that although they are not quite candid and indeed encourage false beliefs, what they do falls short of *lying*, and that although they are not committed to any rich ideal of fair play and indeed exploit unfair advantages, what they do falls short of *cheating*, properly so called. These arguments propose that lawyers' professional commitments to clients over truth and justice do not quite amount to professional *vices* and therefore do not deserve the harsh censure associated with the terms I am using. I devote the remainder of this chapter to identifying the arguments that lawyers make in this connection and explaining why they fail. This exercise emphasizes that if adversary advocates must in fact behave as I have said they must behave, then it is appropriate to say that they must lie and cheat.

First, and perhaps most implausibly, lawyers sometimes argue that there are no antecedently established facts for them to lie about or entitlements for them unfairly to undermine. This response is as old as Johnson's answer to Boswell's wonder that he could in good conscience support a bad cause—"Sir, you do not know it to be good or bad til the judge determines it . . . . An argument which does not convince yourself may convince the judge to whom you urge it; and if it does convince him, why then, sir, you are wrong and he is right. It is his business to judge; and you are not to be confident in your opinion that the cause is bad, but to say all you can for your client, and then hear the judge's opinion."[47]

The argument is as bad as it is familiar, however. It cannot, by its own terms, apply to the many circumstances in which lawyers act other than before tribunals, for example during settlement negotiations; and even as it concerns conduct before tribunals, the argument is simply false.

Thus, there is nothing in adjudication that makes it mysterious to say that lawyers mislead others. There is a truth of the matter about facts apart from the factfinder's decision, and there is no mystery or paradox in the claim that a lawyer has persuaded a factfinder to reach a false conclusion. Indeed even questions of law may sensibly and indeed naturally be said to be wrongly decided, save perhaps in a narrow class of cases that fall within a judge's discretion to establish new precedents.

Moreover, it is similarly unmysterious to say that lawyers exploit others. Lawyers' stratagems can deny persons their legal entitlements, even though they do not violate the law governing lawyers, because legal entitlements have substantive grounds and arise independently of whether they can as it happens be effectively secured through the adversary process. The argument that lawyers cannot cheat would be persuasive only if adversary adjudication presented a case of pure procedural justice, in the Rawlsian sense of a process that is constitutive of the justice of its outcomes. But this is plainly absurd, and, moreover, inconsistent with the defense of adversary advocacy that lawyers themselves most commonly offer, which touts the *accuracy* of adversary adjudication as a technique for securing independently established rights, thereby treating the adversary legal process not as a case of pure procedural justice but simply as an ordinary procedure. Indeed, certain doctrines in the law of procedure would be *incomprehensible* if the adversary legal process were understood as a case of pure procedural justice. *Res judicata* is a prominent example: the outcomes of a system of pure procedural justice are necessarily correct, so that it is incoherent to worry about relitigating issues or to champion the virtues of repose in such a system, because there is literally nothing left to litigate about.

None of this is to deny that it is for courts (that is, judges and juries) rather than lawyers to assess evidence and weigh arguments and on this basis to find facts and decide law. But these are claims about decision-making *authority*, and it is simply confused to elevate them into claims about epistemology or even metaphysics. The ultimate authority of the court does not mean that the lawyer has no independent access to facts, law, and justice, or that there are no facts, laws, or rights, apart from what the court decides. Indeed even as lawyers *say* that there are no truths for them to disguise and no entitlements for them to deny, they *act* as if there are. Lawyers seek to persuade courts by arguments that address public, intersubjective standards, and not just by private appeals to the personalities of the judge or jury. And they seek to vindicate rights rather than to create them.

Second, lawyers sometimes argue that even lawyers who advance propositions they privately disbelieve do not lie because they are merely retelling their clients' stories as advocates rather than affirming anything in their own voices.* Lawyers, so the argument goes, are in two ways

---

* Some lawyers might try to draft this argument in the service of denying that they cheat, by claiming that they merely promote their clients' causes as champions rather than

like actors: lawyers' statements do not assert anything, and certainly do not assert what they literally say; and, lawyers themselves are dissociated from their statements, and certainly do not personally vouch for the statements' propositional content.[48] But neither element of the analogy to actors is ultimately persuasive—lawyers' statements are in both respects more like ordinary lies than actors' lines.

On the one hand, lawyers come much nearer to making ordinary assertions than actors ever do. In particular, whereas actors' statements promote only the suspension of disbelief, lawyers' statements promote false belief. Indeed, this is an essential part of the adversary legal process, whose claims to function as a truth-generating mechanism require that courts treat lawyers' statements as serious propositions, in the sense of being open to believing what they assert. Theatergoers, of course, are not (in any ordinary sense) open to believing what the actors say.*

On the other hand, lawyers are not nearly so dissociated from their statements as the analogy to actors supposes. Certainly lawyers have far less *role-distance* than actors, who may comfortably step out of their roles to speak in their own voices and denounce the characters that they play.[49] An effective advocate, by contrast, may not disparage her client's claims and moreover must, as is commonly said, "exude confidence and enthusiasm that contribute to the credibility of his client's cause."[50]

Thus, as Robert Post has observed, "a lawyer can perform his job only if he 'appears' to be and in fact convinces us that he is sincere."[51] This is, moreover, no mere figurative characterization but is instead a literal demand on the lawyer. Although we may know generally that lawyers often do not privately believe what they say, if we come to know this specifically, with respect to a particular argument made by a particular lawyer, the lawyer will have failed. To know in detail a lawyer's private doubts is to find him no longer persuasive on the point at issue. As Post observes, "unlike the actor, then, the lawyer's job requires that he totally conceal his performance."[52]

Indeed, courts worry that emphasizing even the narrow role-distance lawyers do have threatens fatally to undermine their effectiveness as adversary advocates. Specifically, courts have disapproved of the prosecutorial practice of telling juries that although prosecutors may not bring

---

claiming anything for themselves. But this application of the argument is too transparently foolish to tempt anyone for long. It is, after all, perfectly easy to cheat on someone else's behalf.

* This difference is vividly illustrated by an occasion at the National Theater in London, at which an audience member answered Richard's plea "my Kingdom for a horse," shouting "for God's sake, somebody give the man a horse." Courts, of course, answer the litigants' pleas all the time. In fact, this is precisely what they are charged to do.

charges that that they privately disbelieve, defense lawyers are ethically permitted to distort what they privately concede is the truth.[53] Courts have even held that this practice deprives defendants of effective assistance of counsel, because it puts the defense counsel in the position of "defend[ing] his own honor" rather than his client.[54] And although the constitutional dimension of this claim depends on the criminal context, the basic idea that an adversary advocate may not dissociate herself from her statements in court applies quite generally, so that lawyers simply may not warn that they do not necessarily believe what they say.[55] This is not merely an incidental feature of the positive law, moreover, but instead reflects the deeper nature of adversary advocacy. Unlike an academic discussion whose participants take all sides in a cooperative effort to determine the truth, the adversary system involves a real and not just provisional division of labor between advocate and tribunal. This requires lawyers to intend to succeed even when they should fail— that is, to intend to deceive—and lawyers may not hedge this intent with warnings that court failure, not even when the failure is, in the end, deserved.

To be sure, lawyers remain separate from their roles insofar as they do not, and indeed may not, personally *vouch* for the claims that they make on behalf of their clients—they may not, in the words of the Model Rules, "assert personal knowledge of facts in issue . . . or state a personal opinion as to the justness of a cause, the credibility of a witness, the culpability of a civil litigant or the guilt or innocence of an accused."[56] But it is quite possible to lie even without vouching, simply by employing other means in the service of an intent to deceive. As this suggests, most lies probably do not involve vouching. The ordinary morality of lying emphasizes that whereas truthfulness allows a person's listeners to share in her view of the world, and so creates a kind of community of understanding, lies place a speaker out of community with her listeners because the combination of knowledge and ignorance that lies create makes it impossible for liar and listener to share a point of view. Whereas truthfulness makes it possible for persons to interact on free and equal terms, lies engender manipulation and disrespect.[57] This account sweeps broadly, and it surely includes intentional deception quite generally and not just deception accomplished through personal vouching, because intentional deception generally renders shared understanding impossible, regardless of whether the deception is accomplished by vouching or by some other means. Nor will it do to call adversary lawyers truthful on the ground that that even where their narrowest intent is to deceive in the service of their clients' positions, they act more broadly to support the adversary system and that system's capacity impartially to resolve disputes. This confuses intent with motive, and as white lies make plain, even well-motivated deception counts as a lie.*

And third, and finally, lawyers cannot avoid the charges that they lie and cheat by construing these vices artificially narrowly: for example, by identifying lying with perjury and cheating with fraud; or, more modestly, by exploiting a distinction between actively making affirmatively false statements and creating unfair advantages one the one hand, and merely failing, passively, to correct false beliefs or to reverse unfair advantages on the other.[58]

Even if such a distinction could be sustained, it would offer lawyers only partial comfort: many of the lies that lawyers tell—for example, to persuade a tribunal of legal arguments that the lawyer privately rejects, to impeach a witness whose testimony the lawyer privately believes, or to deceive a third party about a client's bargaining position—are active rather than passive. And many of the ways in which lawyers cheat—for example, by creating undeserved adverse publicity—are active also.

Moreover, the distinction is itself highly dubious. The forms of manipulation and disrespect that make lying and cheating immoral can arise quite apart from any active misrepresentation or affirmative misuse. They arise whenever a person fails to correct a false belief in circumstances in which respectful relations require shared knowledge of the truth or fails to undo an undeserved advantage in circumstances in which respectful relations require equality. The morality of truthfulness and fair play imposes duties to correct as well as duties not to deceive or to exploit, which lawyers transgress whenever they allow others to remain mistaken or disadvantaged in the face of these duties. Certainly the duties of truthfulness and fair play extend well beyond purely formal obligations to make only true assertions and to play by the rules. Thus it is clear, for example, that Vice President Cheney lied in the lead up to the invasion of Iraq, even though his statements, parsed technically and narrowly, may never actually have asserted the false connection between Iraq and the World Trade Center bombing that they were clearly designed to convey. Similarly, there is no doubt that an athlete who takes a steroid cheats, even when the specific drug has not yet been formally banned.

Indeed, legal doctrine repeatedly recognizes that conduct that conforms to the formal rules of adversary adjudication may nevertheless constitute cheating. This recognition receives direct expression in the

---

* Both mistakes exaggerate the capacity of persons to detach themselves from the moral properties of their actions: in the first case, by avoiding certain highly personal means; and, in the second, by emphasizing collective outcomes over personal contributions to these outcomes. The limits of moral detachment will figure prominently in Parts II and III of my larger argument.

principle that, in contrast to ordinary advocates, the first duty of prosecutors is not to win but to see that justice is done.[59] It also receives indirect expression in any number of ways, including (in an ironic turn) in the rule that a bar applicant who employs the technical defenses that lawyers must employ for clients on her own behalf, for example by seeking a discharge in bankruptcy of her student loans, casts her character in a sufficiently adverse light to justify denying her admission to the bar on grounds of moral unfitness (that is, for cheating).[60]

A person's duties of truthfulness and fair play cannot be cabined by formalisms because they must answer, finally, to substantive ideals concerning what makes the activity in which she engages an honorable one. This is especially true when the broader subject is professional ethics, since that subject calls, as I have said from the start, for an account of why the profession in question is worthy of commitment. The legal profession simply cannot be rendered part of a life well-lived through formal and cramped ideas about truthfulness or fair play, which divorce these virtues from the broader project of living well.[61]

A More Careful Reassessment

The principles of lawyer loyalty and client control, and the background condition of adversary assertiveness, are ineliminable parts of every adversary system rather than contingent features of some adversary systems but not others. But even though these sources of the lawyerly vices cannot be removed from adversary legal practice, the vices themselves may be constrained. And even as the organic structure of adversary advocacy presses lawyers to lie and to cheat, the more technical provisions of the various ethics codes certainly do cabin such professional duties. The Model Rules, for example, observe that even though the client has "ultimate authority to determine the purposes to be served by legal representation"[62] nevertheless "[a] lawyer is not bound . . . to press for every advantage that might be realized for a client."[63] And the ethics codes, including the Model Rules, devote substantial energies to elaborating limits on lawyers' partisanship and identifying actions that lawyers need not, and indeed may not, employ to promote their clients' ends.

Critics of the legal profession, as I have said, often ignore these limits, and the profession's defenders consequently complain that the critics invent an extreme adversarialism that has never existed and so attack a straw man. It is therefore critically important to show that my claims about lawyers' professional duties do not depend on any extreme or straw-man characterization the adversary system but instead survive the substantial limits on adversary advocacy that the law governing lawyers imposes and indeed any limits that an adversary law of lawyering could impose.

In the next chapters I take up in greater detail the limits that the positive law imposes on adversary advocacy. I argue that even when lawyers respect these technical limits, they must nevertheless lie and cheat. The argument develops the contrast between the broad and organic ethics rules that command the lawyerly vices and the narrow technical rules through which the law governing lawyers limits these vices. (The structure of lawyers' professional morality is in this respect the exact opposite of the structure of ordinary morality, which contains a general, organic duty to truth and fair play and then allows certain technical exceptions to this duty, say for white lies and harmless fouls.) I hope, by engaging the law governing lawyers in greater detail, to demonstrate that the technical limits cannot eliminate the effects of the organic principles.

This approach depends on developing a detailed doctrinal account of what the law governing lawyers ultimately requires adversary advocates to do. I display the ways in which the organic morals of adversary advocacy—the principles of lawyer loyalty, client control, and legal assertiveness—inevitably bleed through the technical limits on partisanship that the law governing lawyers imposes. I argue that although the positive law's limits on adversary advocacy should not be underestimated—although there are indeed many things that even adversary lawyers may not do—these limits only moderate, and do not eliminate, lawyer loyalty and client control. Even in modest adversary systems, clients retain substantial authority to instruct lawyers to argue facts and law that the lawyers disbelieve and to pursue outcomes that the lawyers disapprove.

I try, in developing this argument, to follow my earlier maxim that great cases make bad legal ethics. Instead of elaborating lawyers' professional duties by reference to extraordinary cases, I emphasize the banalities of everyday adversary legal practice: I avoid the perjured alibis,[64] life-threatening secrets,[65] sexual intimidation,[66] and false murder prosecutions[67] that figure so prominently in academic legal ethics in favor of the misleading legal arguments, deceptive cross-examinations, technical defenses, and strategic counterclaims that dominate the actual practice of adversary advocacy. Maintaining this focus on the banal is particularly important in arguments about lawyers' duties to lie and to cheat. Those who doubt such charges associate these vices with extreme adversary excess—with the idea that "the lawyer must—or at least may—pursue any goal of the client through any arguably legal course of action and assert any nonfrivolous legal claim."[68] And they emphasize the limits on adversariness that the positive law governing lawyers imposes, which, they say, mean that "[i]n practice, . . . , professional morality rarely will conflict with common moral norms . . . ."[69] This is probably right with respect to sensational cases of immorality, which the positive law generally does forbid. But the overlap between professional and common morality runs out at the edges of the adversary system and certainly does not extend to the banalities of everyday adversary advocacy, where lawyers must regularly do acts that ordinary morality considers wrong, although in less arresting ways.

Chapter 2

THE LAWYERLY VICES

IN THE LAST CHAPTER, I introduced the principles of lawyer loyalty, client control, and legal assertiveness that together elaborate the genetic structure of adversary advocacy. I argued that these principles subject lawyers to professional obligations to advance legal arguments and factual characterizations that they privately (and correctly) disbelieve, and to exploit undeserved advantages in the services of causes that they privately (and correctly) disapprove. I claimed, moreover, that these obligations are organic features of adversary advocacy, which cannot be cured by technical restrictions that forbid extremes of adversary conduct, and in particular that they are not cured by the technical restraints adopted in the positive law governing lawyers.

These claims are essential to my larger argument, most notably to its ambitions to address the essence of adversary advocacy in all forms rather than making a fetish of extreme partisanship. I devote this chapter to defending them. I take up in detail the technical rules through which the positive law restricts the lies that lawyers must (or indeed may) tell and the ways in which they must (or may) cheat and explain how lawyers' underlying professional duties to lie and to cheat survive these restrictions. Although the argument proceeds through a close reading of the ethics rules that are most prominent in American legal practice today (including some prominent proposals for reform), I approach the positive law not for its own sake but rather in order to illustrate the possibilities and limits of adversary advocacy quite generally. I argue that the restrictive rules are necessarily technical and secondary, and that although they create specific (and even substantial) exceptions to the background principles of partisanship inscribed in the genetic structure of the lawyer-client relation, they do not alter the basic nature of adversary advocacy or eliminate the lawyerly vices. I argue, moreover, that the resilience that lawyers' professional duties to lie and to cheat display against rules that limit them in specific cases arises out of the formal contrast between the broad and organic character of the underlying duties and the technical and mechanical character of the limiting rules: by their natures, the technical rules can only moderate, and never eliminate, the obligations that the broad standards create. The engagement with the positive law therefore suggests more generally that no technical restrictions could completely eliminate the vices that are built into the organic structure of adversary advocacy.

LAWYERS LIE

Adversary advocates neither must nor indeed may advance every falsehood that promotes their clients' interests. The positive law of lawyering unquestionably imposes significant limits on a lawyer's duty, and indeed license, to lie.[1] Moreover, nothing in the nature of adversary advocacy disapproves of these limits, and certain lies may even undermine the adversary system.

First, lawyers owe duties of candor to the tribunals before which they appear. These are strongest concerning direct communications with tribunals and with respect to facts. Thus the Model Rules, for example, forbid lawyers from knowingly making false statements of material fact to tribunals or offering evidence that they know to be false,[2] and, moreover, require lawyers to correct false statements of material fact that they have previously made and to take reasonable remedial measures if they come to learn that evidence that they offered in good faith is false.[3] Similarly, the Model Rules require lawyers who represent a client before a tribunal to take reasonable remedial measures, including disclosure to the tribunal, when they know of criminal or fraudulent acts related to the adjudicative proceedings at issue.[4] Indeed, these basic principles apply, although perhaps in an attenuated form, even to criminal defense lawyers: the Supreme Court has held, in *Nix v. Whiteside*,[5] that it is not unconstitutionally ineffective assistance of counsel for a defense lawyer to refuse to assist her client in committing perjury and indeed to force her client to testify honestly (or not at all) by threatening to reveal his perjury. These duties of candor expressly trump the duty of confidentiality that ordinarily governs lawyer-client relations.[6] Finally, lawyers, at least in civil proceedings, may generally refuse to offer evidence to a tribunal when they reasonably believe (even if they do not know) that the evidence is false.[7]

Lawyers' duties of factual candor toward tribunals also extend, although less rigorously, to circumstances in which tribunals are only indirectly involved and to actions that are only indirectly communications. Even when not immediately before a tribunal, lawyers must preserve, and in some instances hand over, evidence.[8] They may not falsify evidence or counsel or assist witnesses to testify falsely,[9] or (more broadly) counsel or assist clients to commit fraud on tribunals.[10] And even when factual statements are not directly involved, lawyers may not assert claims or defenses that are factually frivolous or that neither have nor are expected to develop a reasonable basis in fact.[11]

Lawyers also owe tribunals duties of candor with respect to law, although these duties are perhaps weaker than their duties with respect to facts. Thus the Model Rules, following a long line of authority, forbid lawyers from knowingly making false statements of law to tribunals and, moreover, require lawyers to disclose controlling legal authorities that they know are directly adverse to their clients' causes.[12] And the Model Rules, in conjunction with the law of procedure, forbid lawyers from asserting arguments whose legal basis is frivolous.[13] Finally, the Model Rules probably allow lawyers to refuse to argue against their most fundamental legal and moral beliefs, in particular by withdrawing from representations,[14] or declining court appointments,[15] that would require them to do so.*

Second, lawyers owe duties of candor even to third parties, although these are in important ways weaker and narrower still. Most straightforwardly, the Models Rules forbid lawyers from affirmatively assisting clients in conduct that the lawyers know is criminal or fraudulent, and they also more broadly prohibit lawyers from knowingly making false statements of material fact or law to third persons.[16] Moreover, although more controversially, the Model Rules require lawyers to take corrective action when they discover certain frauds against third parties,† by disclosing material facts when this is necessary to avoid assisting their clients in criminal or fraudulent acts, but only insofar as they can do so without breaching the professional duty of confidentiality.[17] Under the current version of the Model Rules,[18] this regime requires lawyers to make disclosures necessary to avoid assisting clients in frauds that threaten reasonably certain death or substantial bodily harm or that use the lawyers' services and are likely to result in substantial harm to the property of third parties. In addition, lawyers *may* (but need not) make

---

* Lawyers may not, however, withdraw from a representation or decline an appointment simply because they find a client's claim unpersuasive. I elaborate this important point later in this chapter.

† It is sometimes suggested that lawyers should be further required to make reasonable investigative efforts to ensure that their clients are not committing fraud.

Such proposals face intense opposition from the bar, no doubt partly because it is worried that their adoption would reduce the demand for lawyers. But whatever their merits, all-things-considered, these proposals merely contemplate an additional technical restriction on partisan excess rather than a basic retreat from lawyers' foundational adversary commitments. Accordingly, the proposals are of a piece with the other restrictions on adversary excess discussed in this chapter and, for the reasons discussed below, would not eliminate lawyers' professional obligations to lie and to cheat.

To eliminate the lawyerly vices, the law of lawyering would have to change much more radically, to permit lawyers affirmatively to seek out and publicize not just deliberate fraud but rather all weaknesses that they (privately) perceive in the cases even of clients who act in good faith.

disclosures necessary to prevent reasonably certain risks of death or substantial bodily injury even apart from any crime or fraud and even when the lawyers' services have not been involved in creating the risks.[19] Finally, lawyers sometimes have duties under generally applicable law to disclose certain facts to third parties. Most prominently, the rules of procedure require lawyers to cooperate with discovery, sometimes including by identifying, even without a discovery request, persons and documents that they will use to assert their claims or defenses.[20] The law of fraud, insofar as it treats nondisclosure as participation in a fraud, also requires lawyers to make certain disclosures.[21] And other, narrower and more idiosyncratic legal regimes, for example, concerning threats to children, require disclosure as well.[22] The Model Rules support these externally created duties to disclose: they specifically forbid lawyers from refusing reasonable discovery requests;[23] and, more broadly, they now permit lawyers to break client confidences in order to comply with the law.[24]

Taken together, the provisions of the law governing lawyers place significant limits on lawyers' professional duty (and indeed license) to lie for their clients. But the restrictions remain technical and self-consciously narrow and certainly fall short of an organic injunction to promote truth or avoid dishonesty. Indeed, the one element of the Model Rules that might be thought to attack lawyers' lying in more general terms—Model Rule 8.4's command that lawyers shall not engage in conduct "involving dishonesty, fraud, deceit, or misrepresentation"[25]—has been reduced in application to the narrowest and most technical rule of all. Thus Model Rule 8.4 clearly does not trump the duties to preserve client confidences imposed by Model Rule 1.6, and it does not in practice add anything to the duties of candor imposed by Model Rules 3.3 and 4.1. Instead of presenting an organic standard in favor of truthfulness, Rule 8.4 functions, in practice, as a narrow corrective for technical gaps in other secondary rules, for example to extend Rule 4.1's prohibition on knowing misrepresentation directed against third parties by also forbidding knowing misrepresentations directed against a lawyer's own firm.[26] Moreover, this is no accidental or contingent interpretation but instead reflects a self-conscious understanding that any broader interpretation would be inconsistent with the deep structure of the adversary process. Thus the Restatement, for example, warns that Rule 8.4 could not possibly impose the broad duties of candor that its literal language suggests, because it is so vague that its application would trigger concerns about due process.[27]

The law governing lawyers thus counterbalances the organic pressures to lie established by lawyer loyalty and client control with a series of restrictions that, although surely important, remain self-consciously and insistently technical. Such technical limits undoubtedly constrain the lawyer's professional duty to lie. But constraints on certain specific forms of lying do not amount to a general, affirmative commitment to truthfulness. It is therefore not hard, even in the shadow of the restrictions that the law imposes on the lies that lawyers may tell, to identify specific ways in which lawyers may and indeed must mislead others into accepting propositions that they personally disbelieve. And although the deceit involved in these cases is less extravagant than the lies that are forbidden, it nevertheless would, if perpetuated by an ordinary person in ordinary circumstances, be straightforwardly immoral.

Deceiving Tribunals

First, in spite of the restrictions on the means that they may use, lawyers remain permitted—and, insofar as clients wish, are often required—to try to persuade tribunals to accept false (and even unreasonable) characterizations of fact and law.

CONCERNING FACTS

Even as regards facts, where the Model Rules and their cognates elsewhere in the law give lawyers their greatest professional obligation to the truth, lawyers continue to be committed to engendering false beliefs in many kinds of cases.[28]

To begin with, the prohibition (under Model Rule 3.1 and Rule 11 of the Federal Rules of Civil Procedure) against bringing claims that are factually frivolous or without reasonable factual basis has never been seriously thought to require lawyers to restrict themselves to claims whose factual bases they privately believe or indeed even just think sufficiently plausible so that the claims' social benefits outweigh their social costs. Certainly lawyers do not violate this prohibition simply by bringing claims that lose on summary judgment.

Nor are the rules that limit lying any more comprehensive where direct statements of fact are at issue. Although Rule 3.3 forbids a lawyer from suborning perjury, her *duty* not to present false evidence does not extend to cases in which she only believes but does not actually know that evidence is false.[29] And although an advocate may not willfully avoid knowledge or "ignore an obvious falsehood,"[30] and even though knowledge is imputed to a lawyer who tries,[31] a lawyer should, the Model Rules explain, "resolve doubts about the veracity of testimony or other evidence in favor of the client."[32] Certainly "a mere suspicion of perjury . . . does not carry with it the obligation to reveal that suspicion to the court under Rule 3.3."[33]

Indeed, even the *permission* that the Model Rules give lawyers to refuse to offer evidence that they reasonably believe (but do not know) is

false is narrowly construed.[34] The Official Comments observe, in the
only explanation they give of this permission, that "[o]ffering such proof
[that is, evidence that the lawyer reasonably believes false] may reflect
adversely on the lawyer's ability to discriminate in the quality of the evidence and thus impair the lawyer's effectiveness as an advocate."[35] In
other words, the focus of the permission is not on the lawyer's pursuit
of the truth as she sees it but rather on her effectiveness at promoting
her client's broader agenda. This emphasis on partisanship over truth is
reaffirmed elsewhere in the Official Comment, which states (in drawing
a contrast to *ex parte* proceedings) that "ordinarily an advocate has the
limited responsibility of presenting one side of the matters that a tribunal should consider."[36] As Hazard and Hodes observe, even under the
relatively modest version of the adversary system established by the current Model Rules, a lawyer should not place much weight on his own
view of the truth. "In practice, a lawyer must always be open to the
possibility that *he* is the one who is mistaken,"[37] and "it is only at a
point not far short of [the] extremes [of perjured or falsified evidence]
that an advocate even has discretion to refuse to present evidence, without risk of being charged with malpractice or lack of diligence."[38] All in
all then, lawyers may not make false claims when doubt evaporates and
truth becomes inescapable, but they need not seek truth and should take
advantage of doubts to make claims that are probably false (and that
they privately believe false) when doing so benefits their clients.*[39]

Moreover, in addition to presenting favorable evidence that they privately disbelieve, adversary advocates must attack and discredit unfavorable evidence that they privately do believe. Lawyers have professional

---

* The obligation to resolve all doubts in favor of the client, and to insist on the truth
only when it becomes unavoidable, is strongest in criminal defense lawyers, whose refusal
to present evidence that is merely doubtful threatens to deprive defendants of constitutionally guaranteed effective assistance of counsel. (Note that although this conclusion
nominally sounds in constitutional law, it depends on ideas in the law of lawyering—in
particular on the idea that an effective defense counsel must serve as an adversary to the
state and must advocate for rather than judge her client.)

The Model Rules expressly exclude "the testimony of a defendant in a criminal matter"
from the zone of the lawyer's discretion to refuse to offer evidence she reasonably believes
is false. And some courts have even gone so far as to suggest that only absolute, incontrovertible proof of its falsehood—typically a client's affirmative statement of his intent to
commit perjury—can justify a criminal defense lawyer's refusal to offer evidence.

Moreover, it is not clear that the constitutional argument runs out at the defendant's
own testimony—instead, criminal defense lawyers may be quite generally required to present evidence that they privately disbelieve but that benefits their clients. Thus a court has
held that an appellate counsel who reported that his client challenged the evidence that
convicted him but added that he was "not in agreement with this contention" rendered
ineffective assistance of counsel. The lawyer, the court held, failed in his duty of "setting
forth all arguable issues, and the further duty not to argue the case against his client."

duties to undermine the true statements of others, most dramatically, by cross-examining truthful but hostile witnesses. Such lying cross-examinations are basic parts of everyday legal practice. As Jerome Frank observed, "an experienced lawyer uses all sorts of stratagems to minimize the effect on the judge or jury of testimony disadvantageous to his client, even when the lawyer has no doubt of the accuracy and honesty of that testimony. The lawyer considers it his duty to create a false impression, if he can, of any witness who gives such testimony."[40]

And although the Model Rules—as part of their ban on tactics that "have no substantial purpose other than to embarrass, delay, or burden a third person"[41]—probably do forbid outrageously hurtful cross examination techniques, they do not forbid all efforts to make a truthful witness appear untruthful, and they implicitly countenance many such efforts. Impeachment generally does have a substantial and legitimate purpose, namely to test the evidence in the hope of shaking it—and this testing purpose does not disappear simply because the lawyer privately believes the evidence to be truthful.[42] Accordingly, even a lawyer who privately believes a witness should nevertheless seek to impeach the witness in order to test the witness's credibility for the jury. Indeed, the lawyer should proceed even if she privately concludes that her impeachment has exaggerated the witness's weaknesses. The lawyer who holds back abandons her advocate's role and usurps the factfinder by denying it an independent opportunity to weigh credibility.[43] Cross-examination therefore provides another instance of the adversary advocate's professional duty to promote false beliefs.*[44]

---

* This duty is once again particularly strong in criminal defense lawyers. As Justice White once observed, "[i]f [defense counsel] can confuse a witness, even a truthful one, or make him appear at a disadvantage, unsure, or indecisive, that will be his normal course." And even when courts forbid particularly aggressive or deceptive methods of cross-examination, they affirm the basic principle that "[v]igorous advocacy by defense counsel may properly entail impeaching or confusing a witness, even if counsel thinks the witness is truthful." Indeed, although courts do not require defense counsel to assist a defendant who wishes to commit perjury, and although courts are generally reluctant to second-guess lawyers' strategic situation sense and find ineffective assistance of counsel when lawyers fail to take advantage of strategic opportunities, courts have suggested that defense counsel in a criminal trial has a Sixth Amendment obligation to conduct meaningful cross-examinations, including even of truthful witnesses. Thus the Supreme Court, in commenting on a case in which a trial court disallowed defense cross-examination, has said that "if counsel entirely fails to subject the prosecution's case to meaningful adversarial testing, then there has been a denial of Sixth Amendment rights that makes the adversary process itself presumptively unreliable." Indeed, the Court held cross-examination to be so important a part of criminal procedure that although ineffective assistance of counsel claims generally require showings of both deficient performance and prejudicial effect, a failure of meaningful cross-examination is presumptively prejudicial and so deprives a defendant of effective assistance of counsel without more. And the same analysis

Furthermore, in addition to attacking unfavorable evidence that they privately do believe, lawyers have broad rights and duties to keep tribunals from ever learning of unfavorable but accurate evidence in the first place. To begin with, lawyers' duties to preserve and reveal evidence under Model Rule 3.4 have narrow limits. Although a lawyer may not destroy evidence or counsel others to do so,[45] a lawyer may counsel clients not to retain documents that might be damaging to them and may probably also counsel clients to destroy possibly damaging documents as long only as they are not yet relevant to any actual or immediately foreseeable proceeding.[46] And although a lawyer may, of course, counsel clients concerning the morality of concealing the truth,[47] she must be careful not to overstep her advisory role in this respect and must certainly also advise her clients of the instrumental benefits of failing to keep or destroying potentially damaging documents and support a client who takes advantage of these strategies to the fullest extent permitted by law.[48] Indeed lawyers are expressly permitted, under Model Rule 3.4, to assist clients who wish to repress the truth, for example, by asking relatives, employees, or agents of clients to remain silent unless faced with specific, authoritative requests for information (and to answer even these requests only in the presence of the lawyer herself) and probably even by suggesting that an employer threaten to fire employees who do not agree.[49]

Moreover, although the law of procedure and the legal ethics codes require lawyers to cooperate with discovery—so that they may not refuse reasonable discovery requests and must sometimes even identify

---

presumably applies when cross-examination of prosecution witnesses is abandoned because of defense counsel's beliefs instead of the court's. Although "the Sixth Amendment does not require that counsel do what is impossible or unethical . . . at the same time, even when no theory of defense is available, if the decision to stand trial has been made, counsel must hold the prosecution to its heavy burden of proof beyond a reasonable doubt."

Moreover, the ethics codes, which in general govern the cross-examination of truthful witnesses by implication only, expressly approve of impeaching truthful witnesses in the course of conducting a criminal defense. Thus the ABA's Standards for Criminal Justice state that "[d]efense counsel's belief or knowledge that the witness is telling the truth does not preclude cross-examination." And although the Commentary observes that "the mere fact that defense counsel can, by use of impeachment, impair or destroy the credibility of an adverse witness does not impose on counsel a duty to do so" and adds that "[i]f defense counsel can provide an effective defense for the accused and also avoid confusion or embarrassment of the witness, counsel should do so," this conditional statement carries the clear implication that if the only way to provide an effective defense is to discredit a truthful witness, defense counsel must impeach.

Finally, even critics who seek narrower constraints on defense counsel's cross-examinations, and who speak of giving defense lawyers a "monitoring" rather than an "advocacy" role, do not entirely reject the impeachment of truthful witnesses but instead suggest only that defense counsel should decline to cross-examine when she knows beyond a reasonable doubt that a witness is truthful.

sources of evidence that will help the other side in formulating its discovery plan[50]—it remains true, as the Comments to the Model Rules observe, that "[o]rdinarily an advocate has the limited responsibility of presenting one side of the matters that a tribunal should consider,"[51] so that a lawyer "generally has no affirmative duty to inform an opposing party of relevant facts."[52] In spite of the duty to cooperate with discovery, lawyers need not reveal even the sources of harmful evidence insofar as they use no evidence from these sources in their own cases, and lawyers need not reveal the content of evidence (no matter how critical) unless the evidence is made the subject of a specific discovery request.[53] And outside of the narrow exceptions discussed earlier,[54] the duty to preserve client confidences means that lawyers may not reveal what they need not reveal. As Hazard and Hodes say, the discovery regime gives lawyers "a duty . . . to use reasonable efforts to ensure that their clients have complied with the discovery rules, but [also] a duty to the client to resist illegitimate demands and . . . to ensure that nothing beyond what has been requested is in fact produced."[55]

And finally, lawyers' duties to promote false beliefs about facts also reappear piecemeal, in the myriad cases that, for one reason or another, do not quite trigger the technical requirements of the duty of candor that the Model Rules establish. For example, when a prosecution witness incorrectly fixes the time of a crime, a defense lawyer whose client has an alibi for the incorrect time may (and insofar as this will be effective, must) establish the alibi even though the client cannot account for his whereabouts at the time the crime in fact occurred and even though the lawyer privately believes the client guilty.[56] The lawyer need not remedy the mistake because she did not call the mistaken witness; and the testimony that she will offer to establish an alibi for the incorrect time is true.[57] (Similarly, if a sentencing court independently develops the false belief that a lawyer's client has no criminal record, the lawyer need not and indeed may not correct it.[58]) Alternatively, a suspicious lawyer's remedial duties may be cut off by her client. For example, if a lawyer who strongly suspects but does not know that her client has lied in a deposition is fired, then she must keep her suspicions to herself even if the lie could easily be uncovered. Because she does not yet know that the client lied—she has not yet taken the simple measures needed to check—she has no duty to correct the client's statement and therefore has an affirmative duty not to reveal anything. And, because she has been fired, she has no further duty to investigate.[59] Indeed, even when a lawyer develops certain knowledge that she has presented false evidence, her duties to take remedial action expire at the "conclusion of the proceeding" in question.[60]

These examples may seem artificial and contrived, but they may be endlessly multiplied, and they collectively illustrate that the adversary advocate's underlying duty to lie bleeds through the inevitable gaps in the technical rules though which the law governing lawyers expresses its commitment to candor. Thus it is familiar to observe that "[u]nless one of [the] special circumstances [requiring affirmative candor] exists, trumping the ordinary duty of confidentiality set forth in Rule 1.6, a lawyer is not only not required to make disclosure but is *prohibited* from doing so."[61]

CONCERNING LAW

Lawyers' obligations to mislead tribunals become even greater with respect to legal arguments. Certainly the various rules by which the law governing lawyers restricts the aggressiveness of lawyers' legal arguments do not absolve adversary advocates of the professional duty to make, and to try to persuade courts to accept, statements about the law that they privately think mistaken.

Although lawyers may not bring frivolous claims and must disclose directly adverse controlling precedent,[62] there is a large gap between these restrictions and any suggestion that lawyers may make only arguments that they themselves believe should win the day. Thus even as it forbids frivolous legal arguments, Model Rule 3.1 expressly says that a legal argument is not frivolous if it "includes a good faith argument for an extension, modification, or reversal of existing law."[63]

This gives adversary advocates enormous leeway to promote accounts of the law that they privately reject. Indeed, the Official Comment to the Rule explicitly observes that an argument ". . . is not frivolous even though the lawyer believes that the client's position ultimately will not prevail."[64] In practice, moreover, doubts about lawyers' legal arguments are resolved in favor of finding them nonfrivolous.[65] And although lawyers of course enjoy broad tactical discretion to refuse to make losing arguments when they believe that this will harm rather than advance their clients' causes, the underlying principles of lawyer loyalty and client control forbid them from refusing to make effective arguments simply because (even though a court might be persuaded) the lawyers privately think the arguments false.*[66] For example, even as a court reprimanded a lawyer for selectively citing and editing precedent to create a false impression of what earlier courts had *said* on a subject, the court observed that the lawyer might of course properly have sought

---

* Criminal defense lawyers' obligations to make legal arguments that they privately disbelieve are, unsurprisingly, stronger still, although they are not of course unbounded.

to *distinguish* precedents whose language she had accurately reported, including, presumably, even when she did not personally accept the distinctions that she made on her client's behalf.[67] Thus, although lawyers may not mislead courts by *doctoring the texts* of the law, they may and indeed must mislead courts by promoting false *characterizations* of these texts' meanings.

Moreover, (and in contrast to the regime governing factual claims[68]) lawyers' obligations to lie about the law extend even to circumstances in which their claims are unlikely ever to be subjected to adversary testing or indeed to any meaningful scrutiny at all. For example, tax lawyers are permitted, according to an ABA Formal Ethics Opinion, to submit tax returns to the Internal Revenue Service that take aggressive positions as long as the positions enjoy "some realistic possibility of success if the matter is litigated,"[69] a standard that allows a lawyer to "advise reporting a position even when the lawyer believes the position probably will not prevail, there is no 'substantial authority' in support of the position, and there will be no disclosure of the position in the return."[70] Lawyers, in other words, may assist clients who take advantage of the IRS's inability (because of administrative costs) to scrutinize every return that is filed and report positions that will likely lose if the Service challenges them. And lawyers may do this even though the Service's own standard for tax reporting imposes penalties if tax returns fail to disclose positions that are not supported by "substantial authority."[71] Indeed, the Ethics Opinion self-consciously states that a "realistic possibility of success" is less than "substantial authority" and that a lawyer who tells her client that there is no "substantial authority" but that there is a "realistic possibility of success" has discharged her ethical duty. Moreover, lawyers engaged in negotiations and settlements with the IRS after it has noticed and questioned an aggressive position are governed by a still laxer ethical standard, which requires only that the lawyers advance no positions that lack a "reasonable basis."[72] And finally, if the "realistic possibility of success" standard is not met, a lawyer may of course instruct her client to pay the tax in question and then advocate the client's position in seeking a refund, as long only as the position is not frivolous. As always, lawyers may counsel their clients that over-aggressive tax reporting is unethical, but they must not insist if clients decide to be over-aggressive nevertheless.

Deceiving Third Parties

In addition to deceiving tribunals, lawyers may—and, insofar as clients wish, often must—also deceive third parties. Indeed, lawyers' commitments to clients over truth grow stronger when only third parties, rather than tribunals, might be deceived.

Even the strictest part of the duty of truthfulness toward third parties—the rule that lawyers may not knowingly make affirmatively false statements of law or fact to others[73]—contains many exceptions. These exceptions arise most immediately in connection with negotiations: the Official Comment to the Model Rules, for example, expressly contemplates that lawyers may lie about what their clients will accept to settle a case;[74] and the case law generally declines to discipline lawyers for "puffing" in negotiations more broadly.[75] In addition, lawyers may lie affirmatively in subtler and more indirect ways also. For example, a lawyer who drafts a contract containing an intentionally ambiguous term in the hope that it will later sustain an interpretation in favor of her client and against the other contracting party need not, and in fact may not, reveal to the other party the possible interpretation that she has in mind.[76] Probably, a lawyer may even draft a contract that contains terms that have been held unenforceable because unconscionable in the hope that the other party does not discover this and complies nevertheless, and she certainly may include terms that she only believes will be held unenforceable.[77] In all these ways, lawyers may—and insofar as their clients command it must—affirmatively promote false beliefs.

Moreover, lawyers have only limited duties, and indeed limited rights, to correct falsehoods that they have innocently told—for example by repeating information given them by trusted but deceitful clients. Although lawyers must, under Model Rule 4.1, disclose material facts "when disclosure is necessary to avoid assisting a criminal or fraudulent act by a client," the Rule (in contrast to the Rule requiring lawyers to correct frauds on tribunals[78]) makes an express exception for cases in which "disclosure is prohibited by [the duty to keep client confidences established under] Rule 1.6."[79]

Until recently, this exception almost entirely swallowed the rule: an expansive duty of confidentiality permitted lawyers to break confidence only to "prevent the client from committing a criminal act that the lawyer believes is likely to result in imminent death or substantial bodily harm,"[80] and lawyers were therefore broadly forbidden from correcting false statements that implicated client confidences, including even statements that had contributed to client frauds.[81] In 2003, amendments to Model Rule 1.6 narrowed the duty of confidentiality and hence broadened the duty to correct fraud against third parties. Specifically, the 2003 amendments expanded the circumstances in which lawyers may (but need not) disclose client confidences additionally to allow disclosure to the extent reasonably believed necessary to prevent or rectify client crime or fraud that uses the lawyer's services and that is likely to result in substantial financial injury to third parties. And when the 2003 amendments expanded the scope of disclosure that Rule 1.6 *permits*, they also expanded the scope of disclosure that Rule 4.1 *requires*.[82]

But even under this expanded regime (whose adoption has been far from universal*[83]), lawyers' duties and rights to correct falsehoods remain limited. Lawyers whose false statements have contributed to merely moral wrongs (for example, by deflecting blame in a divorce) and to even legal wrongs that fall short of crime or fraud (for example, by deflecting responsibility for a tort) may and indeed must refuse to disclose client confidences that would correct the wrongs.

Finally, lawyers may not (with very narrow exceptions) disclose client confidences in order to prevent or correct false beliefs that they have played no role in creating, even when the false beliefs cause third parties to suffer substantial moral or legal wrongs. Certainly a lawyer may not correct a third party's exaggerated understanding of her client's legal entitlements. As an ABA Ethics Opinion observes, the Model Rules "do not require a lawyer to disclose weaknesses in her client's case to an opposing party" and "the lawyer who volunteers such information without her client's consent would likely be violating her ethical obligation to represent her client diligently, and possibly her obligation to keep client confidences."[84] Indeed, a lawyer is generally not permitted to correct any independently formed third-party belief that benefits her client, at least insofar as she must reveal client confidences to do so. And the permissions to reveal confidential information "to prevent reasonably certain death or substantial bodily harm"[85] and "to comply with other law [outside legal ethics] or a court order,"[86] again create only narrow and

---

* Some jurisdictions retain the pre-2003 version of Model Rule 1.6 and therefore impose only more limited duties under Rule 4.1 to correct fraud against third parties. Even under this regime, however, lawyers are forbidden, by Rule 1.2, from affirmatively participating in ongoing fraud once they learn of it and might be required to withdraw from representing a client whose fraud is completed, insofar as a jurisdiction's generally applicable law of fraud treats nonwithdrawal as giving ongoing support to the client's past fraud. Indeed, lawyers must withdraw *noisily*—that is, in a way that disaffirms the fraudulent documents or statements in which they were involved—insofar as a jurisdiction treats failure to withdraw noisily as giving ongoing support to past fraud. (In these jurisdictions the law of fraud treats failing to withdraw (noisily) as participating in ongoing fraud, and the law governing lawyers therefore requires withdrawing (noisily) under Rule 1.2, quite apart from Rules 1.6 and 4.1.)

The Model Rules, moreover, recognize this possibility of withdrawal, and indeed noisy withdrawal, when they observe that: "A lawyer may not continue assisting a client in conduct that the lawyer originally supposed was legally proper but then discovers is criminal or fraudulent. The lawyer must, therefore, withdraw from the representation of the client in the matter. In some cases, withdrawal alone might be insufficient. It may be necessary for the lawyer to give notice of the fact of withdrawal and to disaffirm any opinion, document, affirmation or the like."

isolated exceptions to a broad principle of confidentiality, which leaves lawyers, in the ordinary practice of their profession, inevitably implicated in their clients' lies.*[87]

For example, although a lawyer who learns of a client's fraudulent business plans may not, of course, support the fraud, she may also not reveal it if she discovers, after the conclusion of the representation, that the client is instigating the fraud without her.[88] Where the lawyer's own services have not been involved, a lawyer emphatically may not break confidences to prevent less than serious physical crimes, she may not break confidences to prevent any financial frauds or crimes, she may not break confidences to correct any past crimes, and she may not break confidences to prevent any purely moral wrongs. And although nondisclosure in sensational cases—for example, in a case in which lawyers refused to disclose where their client had hidden the body of a girl he had murdered[89]—generates hand-wringing and even urgent calls for changes to the legal ethics rules,[90] there is wide-ranging support among lawyers and legal ethicists for principles of confidentiality that forbid lawyers from correcting broad classes of their clients' more ordinary lies.[91]

LAWYERS CHEAT

Adversary advocates of course neither must nor indeed may wholeheartedly abandon fair play. As the Official Comment to the Model Rules says, a "lawyer is not bound to press for every advantage that might be realized for a client."[92] Moreover, the positive law of lawyering unquestionably forbids certain extreme forms of cheating. Once again, nothing in the nature of adversary advocacy disapproves of these limits, and certain forms of cheating may even undermine the adversary system.[93]

To begin with, lawyers may not *subvert* the adversary process entirely. Thus, a lawyer may not seek illegally to influence a judge or juror[94] or intentionally to disrupt a tribunal.[95] Moreover, lawyers are forbidden certain less direct means that undermine the legal process, so that, for

---

* Here it is worth noting, moreover, that the duty of confidentiality may arise based on the transmission of confidential information even without the creation of a formal lawyer-client relationship. This occurred, for example, in *Westinghouse Electric v. Kerr-McGee*, in which a law firm representing a trade association that received confidential information from its members was held to suffer a conflict of interest when one of its other clients became involved in a lawsuit against one of the association's members. Although the opinion formally addressed the conflict of interest rules, the argument turned on the idea that the firm had a duty to maintain the confidences of the trade association's members, even though it did not formally represent them. Lawyers are, in other words, unusually susceptible to taking on confidential secrets.

example, a lawyer who participates in litigating a matter may not seek through publicity to prejudice the adjudication of the matter.[96] Finally, a lawyer may not knowingly disobey the rules of a tribunal.[97]

Similarly, lawyers may not *transgress* the boundaries of the adversary process by extending their adversary practices to circumstances outside the adversary system's structural frame. Thus, a lawyer may not exploit circumstances in which her opponents are absent. She may not communicate *ex parte* with judges or jurors save where she is authorized to do so by law or court order;[98] and even when *ex parte* communications are permitted, she must dampen her adversariness and may not exploit an opponent's absence to present a one-sided view of a dispute.[99] In addition, a lawyer may not misuse persons who do not understand her adversary role. Thus, a lawyer who communicates, on behalf of a client, with unrepresented third persons may not deceive them into thinking she is disinterested and must, moreover, make reasonable efforts to correct even misunderstandings of her role that she did not cause.[100]

These restrictions are not surprising. Without the restrictions against subverting the adversary process, or their functional equivalents, adversary adjudication would become simply impossible, because the adversary frame in which it occurs would collapse. Without the restrictions against transgressing the adversary process, or their functional equivalents, adversary lawyering would become unbalanced, because it would be disconnected from the process that underwrites its justification. Practices relate actions to the structural circumstances in which the actions occur, and they cannot countenance conduct that escapes their internal logic.

Lawyers also come under duties not to *misuse* the adversary process in certain ways, although these duties are less insistent and far less comprehensive.*[101] To begin with, a series of related and interlocking rules forbid a range of outrageous litigation tactics. As is by now familiar, Rule 3.1 (together with its cognates in the rules of procedure, statutes

---

* Rule 8.4(d) of the Model Rules—which forbids lawyers from engaging in conduct "that is prejudicial to the administration of justice"—appears to impose a comprehensive prohibition on cheating. But once again, this Rule is not in practice interpreted to add anything to the more specific provisions through which the Model Rules restrict partisan excesses, and (in spite of its language) the Rule certainly does not generally commit lawyers to fair play. Thus Model Rule 8.4 adds little to the more specific duties to support the administration of justice established by Model Rules 3.1 to 3.6 and 4.4, and has even been said to "appear[] redundant" in this respect. (The Restatement's warning that giving greater effect to a rule as vague as Rule 8.4 violates due process of course also applies in this connection.) Moreover, applications of 8.4(d) again tend to focus on narrow cases of outrageous conduct that is somehow not quite covered by another rule—for example berating and verbally assaulting an opposing party in the courthouse hallway or charging, with a reckless disregard for truth, that a judge is "crooked."

establishing the federal courts, and even certain inherent powers of the courts) forbids asserting frivolous or unreasonable claims or defenses.[102] Moreover, this Rule is supplemented by others that further constrain advantage-taking in litigation. Perhaps most prominently, Model Rule 3.2 commands that a lawyer must "make reasonable efforts to expedite litigation consistent with the interests of the client,"[103] and the Official Comment to the rule makes plain that delay is not reasonable "if done for the purpose of frustrating an opposing party's attempt to obtain rightful redress or repose" and that "realizing financial or other benefit from otherwise improper delay in litigation is not a legitimate interest of the client."[104]

This forbids a range of unscrupulous litigation tactics, for example, bringing one suit merely to delay enforcement of a judgment in another in order to gain time to raise money for a supersedeas bond (only to dismiss the second suit once the money has been raised),[105] asserting a frivolous defense on appeal solely to delay an inevitable judgment for specific performance,[106] filing a frivolous cert petition solely to delay the finality of a judgment and allow a client to benefit from the spread between market interest rates and the interest rates applied to court judgments,[107] or employing scheduling shenanigans designed purely to waste an opposing party's resources or inconvenience its witnesses.[108] Similarly, Model Rule 3.4 forbids lawyers from making frivolous discovery requests or resisting legally proper discovery requested by the other side[109] and from alluding in trial to matters that they do not reasonably believe relevant and supported by admissible evidence.[110]

Moreover, Model Rule 4.4—which forbids a lawyer from promoting a client's interests through "means that have no substantial purpose other than to embarrass, delay, or burden a third person"[111]—extends the ban on unscrupulous tactics to include circumstances in which non-litigants are burdened, or even in which there is no litigation at all. This rule forbids morally outrageous or exploitative forms of advantage-taking that misuse process in ways that cannot plausibly be connected to any adversary values (and, therefore, in the language of the rule, serve "no substantial purpose" that commands respect).

Thus Model Rule 4.4 forbids lawyers from using morally outrageous cross-examination techniques, for example techniques (like abusive attacks on the sexual morality of rape victims) that make no effort rationally to test a witness's evidence but instead seek merely to intimidate the witness into retracting her testimony or to appeal to bigotry and thereby to prejudice a factfinder against the witness.[112] Model Rule 4.4 also condemns certain manipulative bargaining tactics, for example baseless threats to inform a prosecutor or regulator of an opposing party's conduct.[113] And finally, Model Rule 4.4 (in conjunction with other

legal regimes) permits and may in some circumstances even require a
lawyer to return and refuse to exploit confidential documents that they
have improperly received.[114]

These rules combine to constrain lawyers' advocacy and prevent the
most sensational excesses of adversary cheating. Moreover, the rules that
establish these constraints understandably dominate the secondary rules
through which the positive law fixes the metes and bounds of lawyers'
professional obligations: As Hazard and Hodes say, "[t]he emphasis on
limitations is not hard to explain. In the ethos of partisan representation, American lawyers rarely need any special exhortations to be zealous when acting as advocates."[115] But the primary principles of lawyer
loyalty and client control maintain a persistent presence beneath this fa-
cial emphasis on constraints, and these primary ideals inevitably bleed
through the gaps in the technical rules by which the positive law limits
lawyers' partisanship, so that adversary advocates remain obligated to
exploit others on behalf of their clients. Indeed, it is not difficult to identify specific ways in which adversary advocates must cheat, even within
the constraints established by the law governing lawyers. These are less
sensational than the forbidden forms of exploitation, to be sure, but
they remain squarely cheating nevertheless.

Exploiting the Adversary Process

First, although the rules that forbid lawyers from subverting or transgressing the adversary process are firm and inflexible, the rules against
misusing the adversary process are shifting and elastic. Indeed, these
rules are sufficiently limited so that lawyers may and even must in many
circumstances take strategic advantages that have nothing to do with
the merits of the disputes in which they become involved. Although
lawyers may not overwhelm the adversary process, they may, and indeed must, exploit it.

To begin with, the ban on frivolous claims announced by Model Rule
3.1—and by its several companions elsewhere in the law, including most
importantly the requirement of Rule 11 of the Federal Rules of Civil
Procedure that lawyers may press only claims that are not legally frivolous and that have or are expected to have a reasonable basis in fact—
falls far, far short of a general ban against lawyers' making legal claims
that they believe will (and should) lose. This is expressly recognized on
the face of the Rule, which classes as nonfrivolous any "good faith argument for an extension, modification or reversal of existing law."[116]
The Rule thus takes a narrow view of frivolous legal arguments, according to which, as Hazard and Hodes suggest, "frivolousness is sometimes
closely related to incompetence."[117] Moreover, Rule 3.1 also permits

lawyers to accept at face value their clients' (plausible) accounts of the facts and therefore to bring claims that foreseeably lack adequate factual support.[118] As long as courts remain permitted to expand on or modify existing law, and lawyers continue to represent clients who might benefit from changes in the law, the leeway that lawyers enjoy under Model Rule 3.1 is ineliminable.

This is of course familiar already from the earlier discussion of the lawyer's professional duty to lie.[119] But the point may be expanded in a way that is relevant to the lawyer's professional duty to cheat. In particular, Model Rule 3.1 and its cognates (including in particular Rule 11 of the Federal Rules of Civil Procedure[120]), in addition to allowing lawyers to bring claims that they do not believe will succeed, do not (in spite of sometimes using the word "reasonable") require lawyers to bring only claims that are reasonable in the tort-law-like sense that their expected social benefits exceed their expected social costs. Indeed, these rules do not require even that the exclusive motive for bringing a dubious claim is the (small) chance that the claim might succeed. Instead, a partially strategic motive for bringing a claim does not render the claim frivolous or unreasonable for purposes of Model Rule 3.1 and Rule 11, not even when the strategic advantages that the claim secures are inefficient and undeserved.

Courts have given this license to exploit procedure practical effect. In a typical case, a lawyer defending a lawsuit brought against his client by the bank of Israel threatened to countersue, pointing out that the countersuit would embarrass the bank politically and might slow foreign investment in Israel. Although the countersuit was clearly an effort to exploit a political vulnerability in order to extract a favorable settlement, the Second Circuit refused to sanction the lawyer, observing that "it is both common and proper for lawyers to send demand letters to potential defendants, hoping that the threat will bring a desirable settlement but preparing for litigation if settlement is not possible. The purpose of [the lawyer's] threats and the suit he eventually filed was to put pressure—including the pressure of negative publicity—on his clients' opponents in litigation. There is nothing 'improper' about that, so long as the suit threatened or actually filed is not frivolous."[121] Similarly, courts generally refuse to find that lawyers for unsuccessful tort plaintiffs have violated Model Rule 3.1 (or indeed to find lawyers liable for common law malicious prosecution), even when they bring lawsuits that aim principally at forcing a settlement rather than winning in court.[122] In other words, the rules against bringing frivolous or unreasonable claims do not forbid a lawyer from benefiting her client by exploiting an opponent's undeserved strategic vulnerability to nonfrivolous, but ordinarily pointless, claims.

Moreover, the other rules against misusing the adversary process leave analogous openings within which lawyers may and indeed must cheat on behalf of their clients. Thus Rule 3.2, on expediting litigation, allows many forms of strategically motivated delay.[123] The rule requires "reasonable efforts to expedite litigation" only insofar as these are "consistent with the interests of the client,"[124] and therefore appears, on its face, to countenance lawyers' employing widespread delay as long only as the delay serves their clients. And although the Official Comment expressly limits the "interests of the client" in whose service lawyers may delay litigation—by calling a failure to expedite unreasonable "if done for the purpose of frustrating an opposing party's attempt to obtain rightful redress or repose"[125] and adding that "[r]ealizing financial or other benefit from otherwise improper delay in litigation is not a legitimate interest of the client"[126]—this does not narrow the permissible grounds for delay nearly enough to forbid all forms of exploitation that obstruct the progress of litigation. Instead, the Comment expressly permits delay whenever "a competent lawyer acting in good faith would regard the course of action as having some substantial purpose other than delay."[127]

Once again, many purposes justify strategic delay under this test even though the delay exploits strategic advantages that are themselves unjustified and that may even be caused by the wrongful conduct of the party that exploits them. Thus a lawyer may intensively pursue probative evidence and nonfrivolous arguments, even when this approach to litigation is partly motivated by the prospect of exhausting the other side and triggering an advantageous settlement, and even (moreover) when the imbalance in the litigants' patience on which the strategy depends is caused by the very actions of the more patient party whose legality is under dispute.[128] To fix ideas, imagine that a cancer victim sues a polluter for causing his cancer and that the polluter conducts an exhaustive but nonfrivolous defense, involving many experts on many subjects who aggressively test the plaintiff's causal claim, partly in order to exploit the fact that the plaintiff cannot, because he is dying of cancer, afford to delay whatever recovery he receives.

The delay tactics associated with this intensive approach to litigation clearly do not fall foul of Rule 3.2—they serve the undoubtedly substantial purpose of establishing the factual and legal basis of the case (whether the defendant's pollution culpably caused the plaintiff's cancer). Indeed, these forms of advantage-taking through delay are too common and too widely accepted even to receive comment in connection with Rule 3.2, whose practical application is instead confined to cases in which (as in the earlier examples) delay is not just unfair but frivolous.[129] Nor, finally, could this be otherwise. As one commentator has observed, "litigation by its nature involves delay," because courts must "carefully consider conflicting evidence and arguments . . . before rendering a decision," so that "[a]sking a court to avoid a too-hasty decision is part of the lawyer's function."[130] Lawyers must look principally to their client's interests in deciding how much delay is appropriate and certainly may not defer to an opposing party's lower tolerance for delay, not even when the opposing party deserves to win the dispute at issue. Any other rule would require lawyers to judge their client's cases and would convert lawyers from adversary advocates into impartial referees.

And finally, Model Rule 4.4 also falls well short of imposing a general ban on cheating, and indeed for reasons much like those developed in connection with Rule 3.2. Instead of imposing a blanket ban on conduct prejudicial to third parties, Model Rule 4.4 forbids only conduct that has "*no substantial purpose other than* to embarrass, delay, or burden a third person."[131] Accordingly, lawyers are not required to *balance* the purpose of delay against its costs and to seek delay only when this balance favors it. Instead they need look only to one side of the ledger and may embarrass, delay, or burden third parties as long as there exists a sufficiently good other reason for their actions.

Once again, the caveat concerning substantial other purposes allows lawyers to exploit many strategic advantages to which their clients are not entitled. Most commonly, a lawyer may exploit a witness's shyness or embarrassment in order to obtain information that the witness has no legal obligation to provide.[132] Getting the information is a substantial other purpose, and as one commentator has observed, "[w]here the purpose is permitted, the Rule appears to tolerate a high level of negative effect," so that "the fact that [the] examination of [a witness] was humiliating and degrading would not likely, by itself, lead to violation of Rule 4.4."[133] Similarly, a lawyer may extract favorable testimony through threats to sue uncooperative witnesses (as long as the threatened suits are not frivolous or vexatious);[134] and a lawyer in a civil matter may, in certain circumstances, even secure a favorable settlement through threats to present criminal charges against an opposing party.[135] Other exploitative strategies permitted under Rule 4.4 are more idiosyncratic and include, for example, counseling a client to stop paying child support in order to compel an opposing party in a contested divorce to return from another state to attend a hearing.[136]

Thus courts accept, even in light of Rule 4.4, that "some pressure tactics are not necessarily inappropriate" as long as they do not go "beyond the bounds of vigorous representation . . . ."[137] Moreover, this once again cannot be otherwise. Litigation by its nature harms third parties, who are drawn into costly disputes even though they are merely innocent bystanders. And adversary assertiveness permits clients and their lawyers to weight such harms less than impartially. The law governing lawyers may take steps (as under Rule 4.4) to protect third parties against harms that are gratuitous, or perhaps even just sufficiently egregious. But it cannot protect third parties absolutely, or absolutely prevent litigants from exploiting third parties' vulnerabilities. Any such general ban would require lawyers to judge their clients' causes in order to determine which harms to others the causes can justify, and which they cannot. And that would once again require lawyers to abandon their roles as adversary advocates and become, instead, impartial referees.

Exploiting the Substantive Law

Second, the law governing lawyers does not forbid lawyers from taking advantage of the underlying substantive law in ways that produce unfair results. The Official Comment to Rule 3.1 elaborates the lawyer's duty to avoid frivolous arguments by observing that "the *law*, both procedural and substantive, establishes the limits within which the advocate may proceed."[138] The turn to the law (rather than to underlying principles of fairness) in establishing the boundaries of the duty to avoid frivolous claims further emphasizes the professional obligations to cheat that survive in the Model Rules. Even as they forbid extreme excesses of zeal, the secondary rules that cabin lawyers' adversariness emphasize their own narrow, technical character and, moreover, reaffirm the organic principles of lawyer loyalty and client control.

Lawyers' professional obligations to make a "zealous[] assert[ion]" of their clients' claims are constrained by the "rules of the adversary system,"[139] to be sure, but these rules expressly abjure broad-ranging commitments to fairness in favor of a narrow deference to positive law. Whereas ordinary morality often obligates people not to exploit the fullest extent of their legal rights, lawyers have a professional obligation to exploit the fullest extent of their clients' legal rights when the clients wish it (even if the clients are acting immorally). The law governing lawyers therefore expressly contemplates that, notwithstanding technical bans on specific forms of adversary excess, lawyers will in general help their clients secure benefits that the law allows even when the clients are not, finally, entitled to the benefits, including even when the benefits contravene the law's broader purposes. In addition to exploiting the adversary process, lawyers may, and indeed must, exploit substantive law.

Thus it is one of the banalities of legal ethics that a lawyer must assert technical defenses to defeat morally valid claims—claims that her client has a moral obligation to honor. For example, a lawyer must assert the statute of limitations to defeat a morally valid debt that her client wishes to avoid even though, as in a famous case, the debtor is "in a position of some affluence" and the poorer creditor is a former employee and an "old friend."[140] To fail to assert the statute of limitations when the client wanted to would violate Rule 1.2 (on client control), and to fail to inform the client that the statute of limitations allowed him to avoid the debt would violate Rule 1.3 (on diligence).* Nor is the statute of limitations the only technical argument that lawyers must exploit to secure undeserved benefits for their clients. Lawyers must, for example, also assert the statute of frauds and the right to a discharge in bankruptcy to help clients who wish it to avoid morally binding obligations to others.

Lawyers may secure undeserved advantages for their clients in more complex ways also. A lawyer may, for example, structure a taxicab service as many independent partnerships in order to minimize her client's exposure to tort liability. And if one of the taxis in a service that is structured this way causes an accident, the lawyer may argue that the formal structure of the service, rather than its economic underpinnings, governs its tort obligations.[141] Similarly, a lawyer may help delay regulation to allow a client to continue selling medical products, even if she privately believes that the products are defective and the regulation proper.[142] Moreover, as earlier discussions made familiar,[143] a lawyer may report an aggressive position on a tax return without highlighting the position, even if she believes that the position ought to lose on the merits and that it will succeed principally by exploiting the IRS's inability to audit every return. A lawyer may even draft contract terms that are likely unenforceable in the hope that her client's contracting partner remains ignorant of the legal doubts about them and simply complies. Nor is it hard to come up with still further examples.[144]

Indeed, although the reported cases are rare (probably because lawyers rarely insist that clients abandon legal rights in the name of moral principle), they plainly rebuke and even sanction lawyers who seek too strenuously to prevent their clients from unfair advantage-taking. In one case,[145] for example, a lawyer was publicly censured for threatening to seek contempt sanctions against a former client who refused to make

* That these duties arise out of the principles of zealous advocacy rather than out of any sense of the fairness of the statute of limitations may be seen from the further fact that a lawyer must attempt to *avoid* the statute of limitations whenever this benefits her client. Thus a lawyer for creditors may not abandon collection efforts simply because a debt is time-barred and certainly may not inform a debtor that the statute of limitations has run. Indeed, because the statue of limitations creates only an affirmative defense, which is waived if not asserted, it is not fraudulent or frivolous (under Rules 3.3 and 3.1) for a lawyer to file a time-barred lawsuit to recover a debt.

repayment of a debt as contemplated in a divorce settlement. The client sought to avoid the debt (which was her share of a joint debt she had owed together with her ex-husband) through a bankruptcy proceeding, and even though the repayment that the lawyer urged was not just morally but also legally required (because the bankruptcy did not absolve the client of her obligations under the divorce decree), the lawyer was found to have violated his duty, under DR 7–101 of the Model Code, not intentionally to "fail to seek the lawful objectives of his client through reasonably available means permitted by law and the Disciplinary Rules."[146]

In another, possibly still more striking, case,[147] a lawyer representing a corporation was censured for betraying and frustrating the immoral (and possibly illegal) efforts of the corporation's president to avoid paying monies owed to his ex-wife. The president's divorce settlement allocated the corporation to the president but gave the president's ex-wife a 45 percent share of any settlement that the corporation received in an unrelated action in which it appeared as plaintiff. The corporation was offered a settlement in that action that the lawyer regarded as fair, but the president refused to settle, presumably in order to avoid paying his ex-wife her share of the proceeds. The lawyer informed the judge supervising the president's divorce of the settlement offer and stated that he regarded it as reasonable, and the judge authorized and instructed the lawyer to accept the settlement on the corporation's behalf. Even though the settlement was fair, and the president's efforts to reject it were at least immoral and possibly fraudulent, the lawyer was found to have violated Model Rule 1.6 (on confidentiality) by informing the divorce court and to have violated Model Rule 1.2 (on client control) by accepting the settlement against the president's instructions. The lawyer was publicly censured by the state disciplinary commission, and a reviewing court affirmed, adding that "had this case been litigated, the sanction may well have been more severe."[148]

The clients in both cases clearly sought to cheat, and the lawyers were sanctioned for resisting their clients' efforts in the name of fairness.[149] These results are not in the end surprising. The principle of client-control means that a lawyer whose client wishes to exploit these or similar underserved legal advantages must pursue the advantages the client seeks.

APPOINTMENT AND WITHDRAWAL

In all these ways, lawyers must lie and cheat more or less whenever they represent clients whose causes they privately (and correctly) believe should be defeated. But although lawyers are open to these professional obligations while they represent a client, lawyers are not required to represent every client who desires their services, or even every client who is willing to pay them. And this might seem to open up a way out of the professional vices that the ethics codes (necessarily) impose within ongoing representations, giving lawyers the freedom that they need to avoid these vices by avoiding the representations that demand them—that is, by refusing to take on clients whose claims they reject and withdrawing from representations that they have accepted whenever sufficient doubts about their clients' claims arise. In fact, however, the deep structure of adversary advocacy reasserts itself here, to limit lawyers' freedom to avoid representations based on their private judgments and, in this way, to cement lawyers' professional obligations to lie and to cheat.

Now it may seem obvious that adversary advocates cannot avoid the lawyerly vices simply by choosing their clients carefully. After all, an adversary legal system could in practice function so that lawyers never represented clients whose claims they rejected only if persons with unreasonable or even just losing claims never secured legal representation, and persons whose legal claims were reasonable and indeed justified were unfailingly matched with lawyers who happened to find the claims persuasive. And even in a legal system that, like the American one, does not guarantee legal representation in civil cases, that is an impossibly tidy allocation of legal services. The economics of legal practice, and indeed human nature, entail that even clients whose claims are unreasonable will sometimes find lawyers and that some clients whose claims are justified will inevitably find lawyers who nevertheless privately reject them.

But this injection of realism is not enough to shore up my larger argument. I am claiming that lawyers are *professionally obligated* to lie and to cheat, and not just that they will in practice tend to do so. And no account of the realities of legal practice, no matter how ironclad its economic or psychological foundations, can produce the required obligation. Instead, the argument can make good its claims only by returning to the law governing lawyers and displaying, in this body of law and especially in its deeper structure, doctrines that *require* lawyers to represent clients whose claims they privately reject.

Such limits on lawyers' freedom to choose their clients exist in the law. To begin with a court may *appoint* a lawyer to represent a client (especially in criminal and even in some civil matters), and her private doubts about the client's claims are generally not good grounds for avoiding the appointment. Moreover, and in practice much more importantly, even a lawyer who might freely have declined to take on a client to begin with often cannot *withdraw* from an ongoing representation simply because she has developed private doubts about her client's claims.

Appointment

The law governing court-appointed legal representations straightforwardly requires lawyers to accept court-appointments even when doing
so would require the lawyers to lie and to cheat on behalf of their clients. Model Rule 6.2 states that "[a] lawyer shall not seek to avoid appointment by a tribunal to represent a person except for good cause."[150]
And although the Rule adds that "good cause" includes that "the client
or the cause is so repugnant to the lawyer as to be likely to impair the
client-lawyer relationship or the lawyer's ability to represent the client,"[151] this provision expressly picks out only the narrow class of cases
in which a lawyer's objections to a representation are so great that they
would incapacitate her, and render her professionally incompetent,
were the appointment imposed upon her. Other cases of good cause
for declining an appointment that the Rule lists—for example, that the
appointment will likely result in a violation of the Model Rules[152]—
reinforce this emphasis on threats to the lawyer's professional competence. And it is therefore hornbook law that "Rule 6.2(c) applies only
when the lawyer's feeling of repugnance is of such intensity that the
quality of the representation is threatened,"[153] so that a lawyer may not
avoid a court-appointed representation simply because she disapproves
of the client's cause.

Nor is this an innovation in the Model Rules, whose narrow construction of the right to decline a court-appointed representation simply
follows a long tradition, made even more explicit in the earlier Model
Code. Like the Model Rules, the Model Code insists that a lawyer may
decline a court-appointed representation only for "compelling reasons."[154] And although the Model Code (again like the Model Rules)
accepts that a lawyer "should decline appointment if the intensity of his
personal feelings . . . may impair his effective representation of a prospective client,"[155] it expressly adds that "compelling reasons do not include
such factors as the repugnance of the subject matter of the proceeding,
the identity or position of a person involved in the case, the belief of the
lawyer that the defendant in a criminal proceeding is guilty, or the belief
of the lawyer regarding the merits of a civil case."[156]

Moreover, courts have not wavered in implementing this principle, so
that it is easy to find cases that simply parrot the ethics codes as they
deny lawyers' requests for relief from court-appointed representations.[157]
Indeed, ethics panels have even construed the exception that the principle allows for cases in which a client's repugnance threatens the lawyer's
competence, which is on its face narrow, more narrowly still, so that
lawyers have been forced to accept court appointments that require
them to argue against their personal beliefs not only in the banal ways

that I have documented, but also in more sensational ways. One ethics panel, for example, has suggested that a lawyer's religious opposition to abortion is not good cause for avoiding a court appointment to represent a minor seeking an abortion without parental consent.[158] This ruling insists that a lawyer accept an appointment even when this will require him, as he sees things, to tell untruths not just about banal factual or technical legal matters, but also in ways that offend against his most basic religious and moral commitments.

The law of lawyering, both in the formal rules governing court appointed representations and in the rules' practical application, therefore constrains lawyers' freedom to choose their clients and in this way reinforces lawyers' professional obligations to lie and to cheat. But court appointments are rare, especially in civil cases, and they might, taken alone, be treated as the exception that proves the rule that a lawyer generally may select clients whose causes she believes in. In fact, however, unwanted court appointments are only a small fraction of the cases in which lawyers must represent clients whose causes they privately doubt. The much larger class of such cases arises in the shadow of limits on a lawyer's right to withdraw from a representation that she has freely begun.

Withdrawal

Even if a lawyer accepts clients selectively, so that she always commences a representation believing in her clients' causes, this belief will sometimes be shaken as a representation progresses. Facts will come to light, or legal developments will occur, that weaken a client's claims. The client's initial account of his case may turn out to have been confused or incomplete, or a client may have concealed an aspect of his case from the lawyer, or even misrepresented the case. And even if the developments are new to both the lawyer and her client, the two may disagree about their interpretation or importance, and hence about how they affect the accurate and just resolution of the client's claims. In any of these circumstances, the lawyer will develop doubts about her client's claims that the client does not share, doubts that will sometimes harden into certainties. Consequently, even lawyers who chose clients in order to avoid the lawyerly vices will in some cases come to believe that clients whom they enthusiastically accepted are in fact in the wrong and that advantages to which they initially thought clients were entitled are in fact exploitative. Such doubts will inevitably arise, and not just in exceptional cases, no matter how carefully a lawyer screens her clients before taking them on. And in these unavoidable cases, continuing the representation will require the lawyer to lie and to cheat just as surely as if her doubts about the clients had existed from the start.

Of course, a lawyer might carry client-screening forward, as an ongoing practice, throughout the life of every representation that she undertakes. She might withdraw from any representation as soon as she came to doubt its merits. But although the right of withdrawal is often proposed as a way of avoiding the lawyerly vices,[159] this is in the end a false hope.*[160] Although lawyers may in some circumstances withdraw from representing clients who ask outrageous things of them, their freedom to withdraw is much narrower than would be necessary for them to use withdrawal as a way of avoiding altogether the lawyerly vices.

Lawyers do enjoy a broad right to withdraw from a representation for more or less any reason, including on moral grounds, when withdrawing has no materially adverse effects on their clients' interests.[161] This is unsurprising, because a harmless withdrawal does not offend the principles of lawyer loyalty and client control that generate lawyers' professional morality. The difficult cases—the cases that establish the effects of the possibility of withdrawal on lawyers' professional obligations—arise when a lawyer's withdrawal will harm her client. When a lawyer whose client pursues unjustified claims cannot withdraw without prejudicing the client, she becomes caught between ordinary morality on the one hand and the professional ideology of adversary advocacy on the other: continuing in the representation requires her to

---

* Indeed, the law's primary engagement with the question when lawyers may withdraw from awkward representations does not concern cases in which continuing a representation is morally troublesome. Unsurprisingly, most cases in which lawyers seek to withdraw from representing their clients involve prosaic difficulties that do not implicate morality in any way. Instead, lawyers seek to withdraw because bad health interferes with their work. Or they seek to withdraw because of breakdowns in the lawyer-client relation in which clients refuse to pay the lawyers' fees or lose confidence in them. In these and related cases, withdrawal appears in the modality not of professional morality but rather of commercial reality: although lawyers are a profession, they are also a service industry in which questions of customer satisfaction arise.

The greatest practical effect of the withdrawal rules is to serve as an interface between these modalities, to give the commercial realities of legal practice a professional gloss. This interface receives its most direct doctrinal expression in the interaction between Rule 1.16(a)(1), which requires lawyers to withdraw when continuing in a representation is likely to result in the violation of the Model Rules and Rule 1.1, which requires lawyers to provide clients with competent representation and in this way makes the adequacy of legal services a matter of professional morality and not just customer satisfaction. Together these rules require a lawyer to withdraw from a representation when an ordinary commercial dispute with a client becomes so serious as to make competent representation going forward impossible, even when the client is in the wrong.

All of this emphasizes how little of the law's attention is focused on cases in which lawyers seek to withdraw from representing clients on moral grounds, and it therefore serves to suggest, even before the doctrinal argument commences, that withdrawal is not a promising starting place for a principled rebuttal of the claims that lawyers have professional obligations to lie and to cheat.

lie and to cheat, but withdrawing violates the principles of lawyer loyalty and client control.

The ethics rules concerning prejudicial withdrawal must therefore strike a balance between ordinary morality and the adversary ideal. Perhaps unsurprisingly, the withdrawal rules roughly reaffirm the balance struck by the several rules discussed above, creating a nontrivial right of exit that is nevertheless not sufficiently comprehensive to allow lawyers to avoid the lawyerly vices altogether. The possibility of withdrawal therefore does not fundamentally alter adversary advocates' professional obligations but instead reinforces, at the point of exit, the regulatory scheme that governs ongoing relations.

This is illustrated, in the positive law, by Model Rule 1.16, which incorporates into the withdrawal regime the balance between partisanship and restraint that governs ongoing representations by making express reference to the rules that strike this balance. Most straightforwardly, Rule 1.16(a)(1) insists that a lawyer *must* withdraw, including when withdrawing prejudices her client, if continuing in a representation "will result in violation of the rules of professional conduct or other law."[162] For example, a lawyer must withdraw, including prejudicially, if her client insists on committing what the lawyer knows to be perjury, because continuing in the representation would violate Model Rule 3.3(a)(3), which forbids lawyers from offering evidence that they know to be false.[163] Similarly, a lawyer must also withdraw, again even prejudicially, if her client insists on filing frivolous claims or making frivolous arguments, because a lawyer who continued to represent a client in these circumstances would violate Model Rule 3.1[164] and its cognates outside the law governing lawyers (including Rule 11 of the Federal Rules of Civil Procedure).*[165]

---

*This analysis unsurprisingly becomes more complicated in the case of lawyers who represent criminal defendants, because constitutional principles that guarantee those accused of crimes the right to a vigorous defense oppose withdrawal in some cases in which it would otherwise be allowed. This generates an interplay between constitutional law and legal ethics concerning withdrawal that parallels the interplay (discussed earlier in this chapter) between constitutional law and legal ethics within ongoing representations of criminal defendants.

Thus it is not difficult to find cases that raise the threshold of justification that a lawyer must have for her belief that a client will commit perjury before ethics rules requiring withdrawal in the face of client perjury may take effect, for example by insisting that criminal defense counsel must have a "firm factual basis for believing" that perjury is in the offing and that "it will be a rare case in which this factual requirement is met." Nevertheless, constitutional law recognizes that even a criminal defense lawyer *may* withdraw, and therefore accepts legal ethics rules that say that a lawyer *must* withdraw, when her client's perjury is *certain*.

Criminal defense counsel's freedom to use withdrawal as a way to avoid asserting frivolous claims is similarly reduced by constitutional concerns. For example, in *Anders v.*

Additionally, a lawyer *may* withdraw (although she is not generally required to) when a client "persists in a course of action involving the lawyer's services that the lawyer reasonably believes is criminal or fraudulent,"[166] or when a client "has used the lawyer's services to perpetrate a crime or fraud,"[167] even though continuing in the representation would not violate any ethics rule or other law.[168] Just as the previously discussed provisions import principles that require candor and respect toward tribunals during ongoing representations into the law of withdrawal, so these provisions import some of the principles that promote respect for third parties during ongoing representations into the law of withdrawal.

These rules identify several classes of cases in which lawyers may (and indeed sometimes must) withdraw from representations when continuing in the representations would involve them in adversarial excess. But because the relief that the rules offer closely tracks the relief offered by the constraints on adversary excess that the law governing lawyers anyway imposes within ongoing representations, these rules are best understood not as announcing new restrictions on adversary advocacy but rather as supporting the restrictions that are already familiar, by constructing an escape path for lawyers whose clients demand adversary excess. Were it not for the possibility of withdrawal, lawyers with such clients would be caught between the general commands of lawyer loyalty and client control and the more specific rules by which the law of lawyering limits these demands; withdrawal gives lawyers a way out of representations that exploit their loyalty in the specific ways that the Model Rules identify.

This is not, however, a general way out of all representations that impose professional obligations to lie and to cheat. Indeed, the withdrawal rules could not possibly provide such general relief, because they track rules governing ongoing representations that themselves fail to underwrite any general release. The withdrawal rules merely expand the ways in which lawyers may respond to clients who demand adversary conduct that is excessive according to already established principles. They do not alter the underlying balance that the law governing lawyers strikes

---

California the Constitution was interpreted to require that although a criminal defense lawyer may withdraw from a frivolous appeal, she must first file a brief that reports "anything in the record that might arguably support the appeal." Failure to file such an *Anders* brief requires reversal even without a showing of prejudice. Nevertheless, even criminal defense lawyers may distance themselves from frivolous arguments as they may not from arguments that they merely think mistaken: the required brief must only *identify* the arguments, it need not *assert* them, and it may even identify them as frivolous. The dissent in *Anders* was therefore mistaken when it argued that the majority would have lawyers violate professional ethics by asserting frivolous claims.

between ordinary morality and the adversary ideals of lawyer loyalty and client control, and they therefore do not expand the class of conduct that counts as adversary excess. Instead of domesticating adversary advocacy by asserting broad moral principles against adversary excess, the withdrawal rules discussed so far merely reprise the narrow and technical restrictions on adversary conduct that are already familiar.

The Model Rules, however, identify another, broader class of cases in which a lawyer may (even though she need not) prejudicially withdraw from representing a client even when continuing in the representation would not violate the law of lawyering or any other law, and even when the client has not implicated her in crime or fraud. Even when the technical requirements of the other withdrawal rules are not satisfied, a lawyer may prejudicially withdraw from a representation when the "the client insists upon taking action that the lawyer considers repugnant or with which the lawyer has a fundamental disagreement."[169]

This aspect of the withdrawal regime, which I shall call the *repugnant-client withdrawal* rule, has no counterpart in the rules governing ongoing representation. It is therefore important to ask how broadly the rule sweeps and, in particular, whether it sweeps broadly enough to allow lawyers systematically to avoid the professional duties to lie and to cheat that they would otherwise come under. Although the repugnant-client withdrawal rule seems promising in this respect—in particular because it seems to announce broad ethical standards rather than just adding technical rules—lawyers' professional vices survive the rule. They survive because the right to withdraw from representing repugnant clients that the rule creates is not (nor on reflection could it be) a general invitation to stop serving clients and instead begin judging them.*[170]

---

* Here it is worth noting, although I shall not rely on the point in my main argument, that even a much broader right to withdraw from representing distasteful clients would not entirely relieve lawyers of their professional duties to lie and to cheat. Especially where lawyers have already been implicated in their clients' wrongs, the ordinary morality of truthfulness and fair play often requires the lawyers to do more than simply dissociate themselves from their clients. Even the prejudice that a lawyer's withdrawal does to her client's wrongful plans going forward may not be enough to undo the wrong that has already been done, and truthfulness and fair play may require a lawyer who has aided in her client's wrongful conduct actively and not just passively to undermine the client's wrongful future plans and, moreover, to force the client to make restitution for his past wrongs.

But even where the law of lawyering permits lawyers prejudicially to withdraw, it does not, save perhaps in the narrow exceptions in which it permits noisy withdrawal, permit them to go this far. Thus Hazard and Hodes observe that "a lawyer may not *sabotage* a client's lawful cause . . . because the lawyer considers the cause repugnant." Moreover, the Model Rules themselves make this clear, reminding lawyers that they should comply with their obligations of confidentiality when explaining their withdrawal, and insisting that even a lawyer who may prejudicially withdraw "shall take steps to the extent reasonably practicable to protect a client's interests." This idea also appears in the Restatement,

The repugnant-client withdrawal rule does, to be sure, allow lawyers prejudicially to withdraw from representing repugnant clients in sensational cases, and even (in such cases) to withdraw in order to save themselves from becoming implicated in purely moral wrongs, and not just in violations of the law governing lawyers or other law. A defense lawyer who opposes the death penalty, for example, might be allowed to withdraw from representing a client who instructs her to argue that he should be executed.[171] Similarly, a lawyer who has been hired to secure a broadcast license might be allowed to withdraw if the client subsequently discloses that he wishes to use the license to broadcast racist propaganda.[172] In these cases, and in others like them, lawyers who continue to represent their clients must betray their most sacred and fundamental moral convictions. And in this narrow class of cases, the repugnant-client withdrawal rule relieves lawyers of the professional obligations to behave immorally that the core adversary principles of lawyer loyalty and client control would otherwise impose.

But in order to eliminate these professional obligations entirely, and thus to enable lawyers to avoid every professional duty to lie and to cheat, the rule would have to allow lawyers prejudicially to withdraw from representing clients in a much broader class of cases. Instead of allowing withdrawal only in sensational cases, in which continuing in a representation affronts a lawyer's most fundamental and sacred moral commitments, the repugnant-client withdrawal rule would have to allow lawyers to withdraw in banal cases, whenever they concluded that their clients' claims should, on balance, fail. Any less general right of withdrawal leaves lawyers sometimes obligated zealously to advance arguments whose factual or legal predicates they regard as untrue and to promote outcomes that they regard as unfair.

Some commentators have indeed proposed a broad view of the repugnant-client withdrawal rule, suggesting that the rule allows even prejudicial withdrawal whenever a client takes a position that violates public policy or opposes the common interest.[173] But this broad view must be rejected in favor of a much narrower account of the scope of

---

which requires a lawyer who withdraws to "take steps to the extent reasonably practicable to protect the client's interests," and adds that repugnant-client withdrawal is not permitted when the harm withdrawal imposes on the client "significantly exceeds" the harms that continuing in the representation imposes on the lawyer and others.

Accordingly, a lawyer who withdraws rather than aiding a client in pressing a repugnant claim must take steps to ensure that substitute counsel is secured quickly and that the change of lawyers harms the client's prospects as little as possible. Ordinary morality would often require the lawyer to take much more dramatic steps not only to disassociate herself from wrongdoing in which she has become implicated, but also actively to thwart or to stop it.

repugnant-client withdrawal. The narrower view distinguishes between lawyers' sensational and banal moral objections to their clients' conduct and, proceeding in the same spirit as the narrow, technical accounts of lawyers duties of truthfulness and fair play that I developed earlier, concludes that the rule allows lawyers to withdraw only in the face of sensational client immorality.[174] The narrower view of the repugnant-client withdrawal rule should be preferred because it better reflects the text of the rule, because it accords with the actual application of the rule to legal practice, and because it conforms (as the broader view of the rule does not) to the genetic structure of adversary advocacy (as reflected in the other rules by which the positive law limits the lawyerly vices within ongoing representations).

The textual argument in favor of the narrow view of repugnant-client withdrawal is straightforward. The Model Rules provision limits withdrawal to cases in which a lawyer considers her client's actions *repugnant* or finds herself in *fundamental disagreement* with them.[175] These are strong words: they probably apply only to ill-motivated and not just unreasonable client conduct, and they certainly do not apply merely because a lawyer concludes that her client ought, all-things-considered, to lose. Moreover, although other statements of the law governing lawyers, including earlier versions of the Model Rules, employ slightly broader language, even these do not allow a lawyer to withdraw simply because she concludes that her client has the weaker argument. The plain language of the repugnant-client withdrawal rule, especially in the version adopted by the Model Rules today but also in the most prominent alternative versions,[176] therefore limits withdrawal much too narrowly to offer lawyers general relief from their professional duties to lie and to cheat.

Moreover, the practice of adversary lawyering and the cases that apply the repugnant-client withdrawal rule also adopt a narrow view of the rule's limits, allowing withdrawal only in sensational and not in banal circumstances. There are literally no reported cases in which lawyers are permitted prejudicially to withdraw under the repugnant-client withdrawal rules (or indeed on any grounds) simply because their clients take positions that the lawyers would decide against as judges or jurors. And there are cases, although only a few, in which courts deny withdrawal requests from lawyers in such circumstances and insist the lawyers continue zealously to represent clients whose claims they privately reject. The case-law therefore confirms the textual reading of the repugnant-client withdrawal rule.

This is driven home most directly by cases in which lawyers conclude that their clients ought not to insist upon complete vindication of their positions but should instead abandon some of their contentions and accept a compromise resolution of the disputes in which they are involved—that is, in criminal cases involving plea-bargaining and civil cases involving settlement. When clients whose lawyers take this view reject compromise and insist on advancing their unmodified claims, lawyers sometimes seek to withdraw, citing personal beliefs in the repugnance of their clients' intransigence. They never succeed.

Thus courts have held, in the criminal context, that a lawyer who privately concludes that her client is guilty and therefore that his refusal to plea-bargain is repugnant may not withdraw for this reason.[177] Moreover, this holding is not merely an artifact of the special protections that the Constitution provides criminal defendants. Instead, the rule carries over to the civil context as well, where courts have long insisted that "the duty of an attorney to carry out an agreement to defend a case is not discharged because his advice to compromise it is not taken."[178] This has led them to conclude that a lawyer's frustration that a client rejects a settlement she recommends is not an ethical basis for withdrawal.[179] Moreover, the principle of client control enshrined in Rule 1.2 (including the Rule's express insistence that clients make settlement decisions) reaffirms that lawyers may not withdraw from representations on the ground that their clients' refusals to accept fair or even generous settlements are repugnant.[180] Indeed, courts have found that the principle that a lawyer may not withdraw because she regards her client's refusal to settle as repugnant is so central to the Model Rules that it cannot be waived by prior agreement.[181]

These cases reveal that courts do not regard the repugnant-client withdrawal rule as giving a lawyer general permission to abandon her clients whenever she banally disapproves of their actions but instead restrict the rule's application to much narrower and more sensational circumstances. Indeed, some courts have interpreted repugnance so narrowly as to hold that it presents grounds for withdrawal only when a lawyer's distaste for her client becomes so intense as to undermine the lawyer's effectiveness as an advocate.[182] In one case, a court denied a lawyer's motion to withdraw after a client in a child custody dispute demanded that she make unfounded and harassing complaints against the local commissioner of the department of human services and behaved toward her in an intimidating, hostile, and bullying fashion. The court acknowledged that the lawyer strongly disapproved of her client's conduct but concluded that the lawyer would be entitled to withdraw on this ground only if the dispute with her client had "resulted in a breakdown in the attorney-client relationship of such magnitude as to jeopardize the defendant's right to effective assistance of counsel."[183] The court determined that no such breakdown had occurred and therefore ordered the lawyer to continue in the representation.[184] Other cases repeat this insistence that a client's repugnance standing alone, and without any accompanying breakdown in the lawyer-client relationship, cannot justify withdrawal.[185] These cases clearly emphasize that repugnant-client withdrawal is permitted only in sensational circumstances and not on the banal ground that a lawyer thinks her client has the worse of the argument and should lose.

Nor are these outcomes surprising—they simply follow through, in a broader context, the same need for an adversary system narrowly to limit repugnant-client withdrawal that courts have explicitly recognized in the special case of settlements. An expansive right of repugnant-client withdrawal, which allows a lawyer to withdraw whenever she becomes privately unpersuaded of her client's case, is inconsistent with the deep structure of adversary advocacy. If a lawyer could prejudicially withdraw following even banal disagreements with her clients, this would undermine the principles of lawyer loyalty and client control upon which the entire edifice of adversary advocacy is built. Lawyers would be freed from the duty to serve their clients and could instead impose their private judgments on clients by prejudicially withdrawing when they found a client's claims unjustified. And (as the opinions that insist on clients' rights to reject even reasonable settlements emphasize) this would even threaten the background ideal of legal assertiveness. Clients who faced the threat of prejudicial withdrawal would lose effective control over the ends that their lawyers served and would instead be deprived of assistance in pursuing claims, including perfectly valid claims, that their lawyers privately rejected.

• • •

Although the law governing lawyers includes a host of secondary rules that constrain the lies that lawyers may tell and the ways in which they may cheat, the deeper principles of lawyer loyalty and client control bleed through these rules, so that lawyers remain professionally obligated to lie and to cheat on behalf of their clients in spite of the constraints.

The contrast between the genetic structure of adversary advocacy and the ideal of truthfulness makes plain why adversary advocates must necessarily lie. The truthful person makes up her own mind about what to believe and opens her beliefs up to others, to engage and to share. As a person departs further from this ideal, and betrays her own beliefs or disguises her beliefs to confuse others, she becomes increasingly involved in lying. Adversary advocates cannot, finally, avoid lying because the principles of lawyer loyalty and client control that constitute the foundations of their professional role require them to betray and to disguise their beliefs, in order to mislead others as their clients command.[186]

Similarly, the contrast between the genetic structure of adversary advocacy and the ideal of fair play makes plain why adversary advocates must necessarily cheat. Fair play requires not only mechanically following the rules, but also pursuing the independently justified substantive ends at which the rules aim. As a person departs from this ideal of fair play, and instead exploits the inevitable imperfections in a procedural system in order to thwart its substantive aims, she becomes increasingly involved in cheating. Adversary advocates cannot, finally, avoid cheating, because the principles of lawyer loyalty and client control that constitute the foundations of their professional roles require them to manipulate the gaps that inevitably open up between playing by the rules and playing fair, in order to exploit others as their clients command.

Chapter 3

THE SEEDS OF A LAWYERLY VIRTUE

THIS CHAPTER completes the account of the professional obligations of adversary advocates that I have been developing by introducing the ideal of professional detachment as an organizing idea for these obligations. The chapter serves two purposes with respect to the overall argument of the book. The first flows naturally from what has come before. The discussion of professional detachment returns the argument to the structural themes introduced in chapter 1, closing the circle around the more specialized rules discussed in chapter 2. This reinforces that lawyers' professional vices are not artifacts of any peculiar development of these specialized rules but are instead inscribed in the genetic structure of adversary advocacy. And in this way, the chapter completes the account of the lawyerly vices that will underwrite the effort, in Part II of the book, to elaborate the burden that lawyers' professional obligations impose on their ethical lives. The chapter's second purpose is more surprising and also more hopeful. When lawyer loyalty and client control are viewed through the lens of professional detachment, the seeds of a distinctively lawyerly virtue appear. This virtue, which I call *fidelity*, will figure prominently in Part III, where I discuss the possibility that the life of the lawyer may be worthy of commitment in spite of its attendant vices, so that legal ethics might be brought to a happy conclusion.

INTRODUCING PROFESSIONAL DETACHMENT

The basic doctrine of professional detachment is straightforwardly stated and appears openly on the face of the ethics codes. The interpretation of the doctrine is more complicated, however, and I develop an unconventional reconstruction of the ideal of professional detachment (indeed, the dual, or mirror image, of the more common view). This ideal captures the necessary connection between lawyer loyalty and client control on the one hand, and the lawyerly vices on the other.

The most prominent contemporary statement of lawyers' professional detachment appears in Model Rule 1.2, which declares that "[a] lawyer's representation of a client . . . does not constitute an endorsement of the client's political, economic, social or moral views or activities."[1]

(One might add that a lawyer's representation of a client does not constitute an endorsement of the client's factual or legal claims, either.) Nor is this principle of professional detachment special to the Model Rules. Instead, it also appears prominently elsewhere in the law of lawyering, for example in the ABA's Formal Ethics Opinions,[2] the Oaths of Admission to many State Bars,[3] and in the more informal lore of the legal profession.[4] Put simply, lawyers should not ordinarily be taken to endorse either the claims that their professional activities assert or the causes that these activities promote.

Now the principle of professional detachment's most practical purpose, and the reason for which it is insisted on by the bar, is to protect lawyers from certain forms of *legal* responsibility that they might otherwise bear for actions that they take in representing their clients. This aspect of professional detachment finds expressions in various doctrines outside the narrow confines of the ethics codes that, as I observed in an earlier discussion of legal assertiveness, protect lawyers from legal liability for some (but not, of course all) actions undertaken in furtherance of representing their clients. These doctrines, recall, grant lawyers immunity from tort liability for in-court statements (and often also for other statements made in connection with litigation) that would otherwise be defamatory,[5] shield lawyers from tort liability for actions (for example, breaching a contract[6]) that their clients take on the basis of good faith legal advice,[7] and exclude lawyers from various forms of statutory liability (for example, involving trademark and conspiracy) for their clients' acts.[8] Of course, the legal immunities that professional detachment secures for lawyers all have their limits. Most familiarly, a lawyer who knowingly aids clients in providing false information to others (and possibly even a lawyer who fails to correct client statements when she learns that they are false) may be liable for fraud.[9] And other less familiar limits on lawyers' legal immunities also exist, for example, that a lawyer who agrees in anticipation of a crime to defend a person in case he is caught may be guilty of conspiracy.[10] Neither the immunities nor their limits are surprising: without the immunities, lawyers could not function as adversaries at all; and without the limits, lawyers could undermine the adversary process whose value justifies their partisanship.

Lawyers also (commonly) assert an additional claim of professional detachment. They say that their professional role insulates them not just from legal but also from *moral* responsibility for the things that they do for their clients. Lawyers acknowledge limits to their moral nonaccountability, which again track the limits on partisan excess that the ethics codes impose. But lawyers insist that they are not morally accountable for their professional actions as long as they act within these limits, and it is common to hear lawyers, including through the organized bar, object to "public criticism of [a] lawyer because he has undertaken the representation of causes in general disfavor."[11] Indeed, the principle that "lawyers should not be held accountable for their clients" has been called "the most basic proposition about [adversary] advocacy."[12] This moral application of professional detachment is more surprising than the legal one, and certainly less secure. The argument for moral nonaccountability must translate the role understandings and subjective attitudes that directly constitute lawyers' professional detachment into propositions of generally applicable morality, and this movement of thought, although much attempted, has proved difficult to achieve.

Although both the legal and moral nonaccountability associated with lawyers' professional detachment belong among the mainstays of legal ethics, I shall not for the moment pursue either.* I have instead introduced professional detachment with a different, although complementary, purpose in mind, and with an eye more to the antecedents of professional detachment than to its consequences. This aspect of lawyers' professional detachment is much less remarked on than the alleged connection between detachment and nonaccountability, but it is no less important for going unnoticed.

In order for lawyers' professional detachment to have any hope of underwriting their moral nonaccountability, and indeed in order for detachment to be possible at all, professional detachment must be *required* of lawyers. If lawyers have a choice about how to stand with respect to their clients' claims and causes, then detachment will be foreclosed in every case. Lawyers who may choose whether or not to adopt a detached approach to particular representations cannot prevent decisions that are ostensibly about detachment from becoming, effectively, expressions of personal approval or disapproval of their client's claims and causes. A lawyer who purports to exercise her right to detach from a client will unavoidably express her personal disapproval of the client's case; and a lawyer who fails to exercise this right will unavoidably express her personal approval. Lawyers for whom professional detachment is a choice cannot avoid becoming personally implicated, in one way or another, in every representation they take on.

The mandatory aspect of professional detachment—and its connection to the complex of principles that culminates in lawyers' professional vices—is not generally made explicit in the ethics codes.†[13] This

---

* I discuss the argument about moral nonaccountability extensively in Part III.

† The old ABA Canons of Ethics provide the most important exception to this rule. Canon 5 expressly associated the "right of the lawyer to undertake the defense of a person accused of crime regardless of his personal opinion as to the guilt of the accused" with the duty, "having undertaken such defense" to use "all fair and honorable means . . . to present every defense that the law of the land permits."

is probably because professional detachment runs so deep in the self-understandings of an adversary legal profession that it is simply assumed. But a lawyer's obligation to remain professionally detached from her clients is insistently reasserted in the rare cases in which lawyers betray it. In these cases, lawyers who are overwhelmed by disapproval of their clients become unable to restrain their private views and, abandoning their professional obligations to advocate even for clients whose claims they regard as unjustified, instead repudiate their client's causes. Courts uniformly reassert the principle of professional detachment in such cases and, strikingly, insist that the breakdown of professional detachment has deprived the client of an advocate altogether.

The cases in which lawyers abandon professional detachment disproportionately involve lawyers appearing as defense counsel in criminal cases. (The natural explanation for this is that the degraded positions of criminal defendants, supported by other inequalities that commonly separate criminal defendants from their counsel, conspire to wear down lawyers' professional ethics.) The decisions that insist on professional detachment in these cases therefore invoke constitutional ideas concerning criminal procedure as well as ideas about the structure of adversary advocacy more generally. Nevertheless (as both the criminal cases themselves and a few, still rarer, civil analogs will show), the argument for demanding professional detachment—and insisting on the obligations to lie and to cheat that professional detachment necessarily involves—does not depend on the peculiarities of the criminal defense context.

The typical case arises when a lawyer who concludes that her client is guilty refuses, on the basis of this personal judgment, to present a vigorous defense and, moreover, instead undermines the client's legal position. A lawyer might refuse to ask a jury to acquit his client,[14] tell the jury in open court that he believes his client to be guilty,[15] tell an appellate court that although his client claims that the evidence at trial was insufficient to support a conviction, he does not agree,[16] or argue at sentencing that his client has a bad character and deserves a harsh punishment.[17] The retreats from adversary advocacy in these and similar cases involve more than just refusing to employ the prohibited adversary excesses discussed

---

A less important, because only partial, statement of the mandatory character of professional detachment survives to this day, in the rule that lawyers may not vouch for their clients in court—that they may not "assert personal knowledge of facts in issue . . . or state a personal opinion as to the justness of a cause, the credibility of a witness, the culpability of a civil litigant, or the guilt or innocence of an accused." A virtually identical command appears in the Model Code and in the Restatement.

Professional detachment is more familiar in the lore of the bar. MacMillan, for example, said not just that, "[i]n pleading a case, an advocate is not stating his own opinions" but added that "it is not part of his business and he has no right to do so."

in earlier chapters (for example, by refusing to proffer perjured testimony[18] or by refusing to assert frivolous defenses[19]), or even giving these prohibitions broader interpretations than the criminal context allows (for example by refusing to proffer a defendant's testimony based on a mere belief, unsupported by any firm factual basis, that it is false[20] or by refusing even to identify frivolous arguments for a court[21]). Rather, such cases involve a more fundamental rejection of the adversary process: they involve lawyers who abandon lawyer loyalty and client control and reject professional detachment in favor of its opposite. Far from setting aside their private views, these lawyers aggressively promote the outcomes that they privately regard as accurate and just.

Courts that confront this style of lawyering uniformly reject it and reassert the ideal of professional detachment against lawyers who deviate from it. Indeed, the courts reach this result through an argument that insistently places professional detachment at the very center of adversary advocacy, so that the path to this conclusion is as important as the result itself. Thus the courts all agree that a criminal defendant has a right to a lawyer devoted "solely to the interests of his client,"[22] who "set[s] forth all arguable issues"[23] and who certainly does not "argue the case against his client."[24] They insist that this right requires lawyers to serve rather than to judge their clients—that the lawyer's role does not "countenance disclosure to the Court of counsel's private conjectures about the guilt or innocence of his client" because "[i]t is the role of the judge or jury to determine the facts, not that of the attorney."[25]

Moreover, the courts insist that a lawyer who abandons professional detachment and judges rather than serving her client commits more than an ordinary dereliction of duty. She does not just fail to work for her client as effectively as she ought but instead, by "adopt[ing] and act[ing] upon a belief that [her] client should be convicted,"[26] she "essentially joins the prosecution's efforts in obtaining a conviction"[27] and therefore "suffers from an obvious conflict of interest."[28] Indeed, it is so profoundly improper for a lawyer to compromise a client's case because her conscience demands it that this motive *in itself* renders otherwise unobjectionable conduct impermissible: In the words of one court, "the failure to argue [a] case before the jury, while ordinarily only a trial tactic not subject to review, manifestly enters the field of incompetency when the reason assigned is the attorney's conscience."[29] And finally, the lawyer who abandons professional detachment and argues her conscience against her client thereby "fail[s] to function in any meaningful sense as the Government's adversary,"[30] so that her breach of professional detachment does not just contravene the law governing lawyers,[31] but also renders her performance constitutionally defective, even without the showing of prejudice that is usually required,[32] by bringing her conduct within the narrow range of cases in which a defendant suffers an "actual or constructive denial of assistance of counsel altogether."[33] Thus the courts have gone so far as to say that a loyal counsel (a counsel who remains professionally detached) is a "jurisdictional prerequisite" for a criminal trial.[34] In other words, the courts in these cases treat a lawyer who abandons professional detachment and judges rather than advocating for her client as being *no lawyer at all.*

The constitutional dimension of these cases, and in particular the insistence that defendants have an individual right to effective, and therefore detached, counsel obviously invokes the criminal context.* But although the consequences of finding an individual lawyer ineffective—in particular the client's (that is, the defendant's) entitlement to a new trial—depend on principles of criminal procedure and constitutional law, the account of lawyers' professional obligations that constitutes the core argument of the cases does not depend on any idiosyncratic features of criminal law but instead applies, quite generally, to all areas of legal practice. And although lapses of professional detachment are rarer in civil than in criminal cases—perhaps, as I have suggested, because lawyers generally respect their civil clients more than their criminal ones and, therefore, find the deference associated with professional detachment easier to sustain—such lapses do occur and receive, fundamentally, the same criticism from the courts as arises in the criminal context. For example, courts, drawing a direct analogy to criminal cases in which lawyers attempt to force clients to accept plea agreements, have held that lawyers who doubt the merits of their clients' civil cases may not impose their views by forcing resistant clients to accept settlements that the lawyers regard as reasonable.[35] Indeed, courts have even carried the internal workings of the argument for professional detachment into civil cases, suggesting that a lawyer who promotes her private view of a client's case too aggressively develops a conflict of interest with the client.[36] Like criminal lawyers, civil lawyers who allow private beliefs about their clients' causes too great influence abandon the principles of lawyer loyalty and client control that their professional ethics require. And professional detachment is as essential to adversary advocacy in the civil context as in the criminal.

When it is seen in this light—operating not as a shield but as a sword—professional detachment is revealed to reprise at a structural

---

* The distinctiveness of the criminal context should not be overstated, however. I argue in Part III that even if a civil litigant (unlike a criminal defendant) has no individual right to a loyal counsel who maintains professional detachment, the practice of civil adjudication owes its general authority to resolve disputes to lawyers who remain professionally detached.

level the commitments of adversary advocacy that the argument has been elaborating in more particular detail. The principle of professional detachment requires lawyers to *serve* rather than to *judge* their clients. And although the precise boundaries of lawyer loyalty and client control, and of the associated duties to lie and to cheat, will of course vary with the positive law, professional detachment rules out *eliminating* (rather than just constraining) these professional duties, because that would require lawyers to judge rather than serve.

Moreover, this connection between professional detachment and the lawyerly vices may be spelled out in greater detail.* With respect to the duty to lie, the idea that lawyers serve rather than judge requires lawyers to be more sympathetic to their clients' claims and more skeptical of opposing claims than a dispassionate commitment to truth would allow. For example, professional detachment appears in the lawyer's duty to present helpful evidence that the lawyer privately disbelieves and the duty to impeach damaging evidence that the lawyer privately considers persuasive.† Because "[i]t is the function of the trier of fact, not the advocate, to resolve the issue of reliability [of evidence]," lawyers must, as Hazard and Hodes say, give their clients "the benefit of the doubt"; any "more stringent rule [requiring greater candor] would have a chilling effect upon advocacy, and could make an advocate the guarantor of the actual truth or accuracy of matters presented on her side" rather than merely the client's loyal servant.[37]

Similarly, the basic principle that lawyers serve rather than judge their clients also influences the law of lawyering outside the immediate context of litigation, for example, by requiring lawyers to guard their clients' privacy more closely than a dispassionate commitment to truth would allow, and this is again recognized in connection with the rules through which the positive law limits the duty of confidentiality. A client must be able to take her lawyer into her confidence without exposing herself to the view of the wider world, or even just of the authorities.

---

* Here it is important that professional detachment applies, in its sword-like capacity, not just within ongoing representations, to prevent lawyers from working against their clients, but also at the points of entry and exit of the lawyer-client relation, to restrict lawyers' freedom to get and keep only those clients whose claims they personally endorse. This application of professional detachment is illustrated in the discussion, in the last chapter, of appointment and withdrawal.

† Similarly, the theme that lawyers serve rather than judge appears in the rules that forbid lawyers from revealing weaknesses in their clients' legal cases and, moreover, require lawyers to advance legal arguments that they privately think should lose. It is for courts rather than advocates to weigh up legal arguments, and a rule requiring lawyers to advance only arguments that they privately find legally persuasive would again chill advocacy and make lawyers into guarantors rather than just expositors of their clients' legal positions.

Otherwise, as one bar group has warned, lawyers, judging their clients, become "servants of the system rather than the bulwark between organized power and the individual."[38] In both respects, professional detachment requires lawyers (in the words of one prominent commentator) to "be disingenuous," that is, they must "make statements as well as arguments which [they do] not believe in."[39]

The idea that lawyers serve rather than judge clients also entrenches duties to cheat in lawyers' professional ethics. Eliminating the professional obligation to cheat, by forbidding lawyers from exploiting the legal process to promote outcomes that they privately think unfair or incorrect, would require that lawyers calibrate their litigation strategies with an eye to increasing the likelihood that the right result will be reached. And this would again require lawyers, abandoning lawyer loyalty and client control, to judge rather than to serve their clients—to determine what justice commands and then to promote the just outcome—which is precisely what no adversary legal ethics can require, or indeed even allow. The basic idea that neither side to a legal dispute is the other's keeper—that it is for courts rather than lawyers to balance the competing claims in a legal dispute and that advocates must remain partisan and "use legal procedure for the fullest benefit of the client's cause"[40]—makes it intolerable for lawyers in any adversary system to refuse categorically to exploit any undeserved advantages that their clients enjoy.[41] And, insofar as adversary advocates continue to exploit such advantages, they inevitably cheat.

Finally, the connection between professional detachment and the lawyerly vices is illustrated by the contrast between the ethics regime that governs lawyers generally and the special rules that the ethics codes develop to govern the conduct of criminal prosecutors, who are excluded from generally applicable principles of professional detachment and, concomitantly, forbidden to lie or to cheat. (This contrast also directly illustrates the qualitative difference between the secondary rules that merely constrain the vices required of ordinary lawyers and the more fundamental change, in primary rules, by which prosecutorial ethics eliminates these vices.)

Thus criminal prosecutors, as the ABA's Standards for Criminal Justice emphasize, come under a general duty to engage their own judgments as ordinary lawyers may not, and this underwrites more particular affirmative duties of honesty and fair play that do not apply to ordinary lawyers.[42] Most fundamentally, unlike ordinary lawyers, who must advance nonfrivolous claims when this serves their clients, prosecutors must form their own views of the merits of cases. Prosecutors should not institute charges "in the absence of sufficient admissible evidence to support a conviction"[43] or bring "any charges greater in number or degree than can reasonably be supported with evidence at trial or than are necessary fairly to reflect the gravity of the offense."[44] Indeed, prosecutors may "decline to prosecute, notwithstanding that sufficient evidence may exist which would support a conviction,"[45] including based on their private "reasonable doubts that the accused is in fact guilty."[46] Moreover, this general duty has more particular effects. A prosecutor may not mischaracterize the truthfulness of others: she "should not use the power of cross-examination to discredit or undermine a witness if [she] knows the witness is testifying truthfully," and she has only limited leeway to impeach even a witness whom she only *believes* to be truthful.[47] And finally, where ordinary advocates must pursue their clients' ends to the full limits of the law,[48] prosecutors must abjure forms of advantage-taking that belong to the stock-in-trade of ordinary advocates. For example, unlike ordinary adversary lawyers, a prosecutor must be proactively open about evidence: she "should not intentionally fail to make timely disclosure to the defense, at the earliest feasible opportunity [and quite apart from any discovery request], of the existence of all evidence or information which tends to negate the guilt of the accused or mitigate the offense charged or which would tend to reduce the punishment of the accused."[49] Prosecutors, in other words, must not lie or cheat.

These principles of prosecutorial ethics do not just moderate the adversary principles that would otherwise apply under the Model Rules; they instead abandon the adversary ideal entirely, or at least revise it wholesale. Moreover, they do so specifically by rejecting professional detachment for prosecutors and therefore also the principles of lawyer loyalty and client control that give professional detachment its most immediate expression. As the ethics codes acknowledge, "[t]he duty of the prosecutor is to seek justice, not merely to convict."[50] This is familiarly understood, from without legal ethics, as a concession to the constitutional rights of criminal defendants (so that the limits on prosecutorial zeal appear as another expression of the ideals that give criminal defense lawyers unusually broad duties of partisanship). But the distinctive professional commitments of prosecutors may also be understood from within legal ethics, as reflecting the fact that rather than representing an ordinary client before a neutral tribunal, the prosecutor represents one arm of the state before another. At least in principle,[51] the state has no proper interest in victory for its own sake because it should never pursue injustice; and the state does not need a bulwark against authority because it is in authority. The prosecutor's distinctive commitments to truth and fairness therefore elaborate a role whose genetic structure departs from the structure of adversary advocacy. Because of the special nature of her client, the prosecutor must judge the cases that she handles and allow the private judgments that she forms to guide her professional conduct.

• • •

Professional detachment, in its sword-like expression, requires ordinary lawyers (unlike prosecutors) to insulate the professional services that they provide their clients from their private judgments of the merits of their clients' claims—that is, to serve their clients equally regardless of their private judgments and to promote even client causes that they privately believe should fail. It requires, in other words, that lawyers abide by the principles of lawyer loyalty and client control that I have said establish the center of adversary advocacy, and that they accept the professional obligations to lie and to cheat that these principles engender. The cases that enforce the mandatory nature of lawyers' professional detachment—commenting that a lawyer who abandons detachment to judge rather than to serve is no lawyer at all—therefore reveal that the professional obligations to lie and to cheat elaborated earlier are constitutive of adversary advocacy. And finally, prosecutorial ethics, which simultaneously abandons professional detachment and eliminates the duties to lie and to cheat, further illustrates the organic connection between adversary advocacy and the lawyerly vices.*[52]

---

* The failed career of one proposal for reform is worth mentioning in this connection, because it illustrates adversary advocacy's structural commitment to the lawyerly vices. In 1975, Marvin Frankel proposed that the law governing lawyers be changed to impose on advocates a direct duty to pursue truth—the whole truth, as they judge it—and to place this duty above their duties to promote their clients' interests. In introducing his suggestion, Frankel claimed to wish merely to "modify (not abandon) the adversary ideal." But in his more reflective moments, Frankel acknowledged that his proposal might be inconsistent with "more fundamental ideals" that prefer "individual freedom and dignity above order and efficiency in government," and he added (more relevantly, given present concerns) that his proposal "certainly stretch[ed] out of existing shape our conception of the advocate retained to be a partisan." Frankel concluded by suggesting that if forced to choose between truth and these more basic ideals, he would sacrifice truth. Although he hoped that this would prove a false dilemma, which might be avoided, he did not explain why or describe how.

The subsequent history of Frankel's proposal more nearly reflects his fears than his hopes, and in doing so illustrates the structural (and hence ineliminable) connection between adversary advocacy and the lawyerly vices that I have made my theme. Although the proposal was discussed by scholars, it generally did not enter the positive law. Moreover the experience of the sole jurisdiction that adopted something like Frankel's proposal revealed its structural incompatibility with the broader commitments of an adversary conception of legal representation.

For roughly two decades, Rule 3.3(a)(5) of the New Jersey Rules of Professional Conduct departed from its analog in the Model Rules by requiring lawyers to not knowingly

The sword-like aspect of professional detachment therefore reprises the argument of chapter 2, although it sets aside the details that that argument emphasized and proceeds, instead, in broad strokes only. This approach has its drawbacks, of course. Even adversary advocates do not abandon their moral autonomy entirely, and, as Hazard and Hodes point out, they need not "slavishly engage in any immoral action that will benefit a client so long as it is legal."[53] And the argument from professional detachment therefore cannot substitute for the earlier, more detailed account of the metes and bounds of lawyers' professional obligations. But the sparer setting that professional detachment provides has advantages also. Most importantly, it emphasizes that lawyers' core professional obligations to lie and to cheat arise ineliminably out of the foundational commitments of adversary advocacy, so that "client objectives," as Hazard himself admits, will inevitably "impose substantial constraints on a lawyer's ethical autonomy."[54] These constraints include duties to promote a partisan view of fact and law in ways that deceive tribunals and to keep secrets in ways that promote false beliefs in third parties; and they include duties to exploit the legal process and the substantive law to gain benefits for clients who do not deserve them.

This direct emphasis on adversary advocacy's structural core is important. The more detailed accounts of the lawyerly vices developed

---

"fail to disclose to the tribunal a material fact with knowledge that the tribunal may tend to be misled by such failure." Even this rule fails completely to undo adversary lawyers' duty to lie, because it applies only to facts and not to law. Nevertheless, the rule does seem to aspire, within the realm of facts, to impose on lawyers an affirmative duty to assist courts in reaching the truth, as they see it.

The New Jersey rule was much criticized and little followed. Hazard and Hodes called it "a radical proposition indeed [that] begins to carry out a direct attack on the adversary system." Another commentator observed that "the rule seems to conflict with the basic premise that an advocate must present a client's cause in its best light." And the Chair of the New Jersey Supreme Court Disciplinary Review Board observed publicly that "I am satisfied, just from my knowledge of practice, that the rule is violated, grossly violated, by every lawyer who does trial work, because no lawyer can represent a client and comply with that rule."

The New Jersey Supreme Court finally retreated from the rule, observing that "the very nature of the rule makes compliance difficult." And although New Jersey law continues to cabin lawyers' obligations, and indeed permissions, to lie more narrowly than do the Model Rules, and New Jersey courts have begun to show some inclination to enforce New Jersey's higher standards, these practices self-consciously fall far short of imposing the generalized obligation of truthfulness (at least as to facts) that Frankel envisioned.

The Frankel proposal and New Jersey's experience with it, right down through the historical details, thus illustrate the organic connection between the adversary system's basic commitment to a structural separation between advocate and tribunal on the one hand, and the lawyerly vices on the other.

earlier are open to the objection that these vices may be eliminated by enhancing the secondary rules that already constrain them (for example, by narrowing to the duty to preserve client confidences, expanding the prohibition on asserting frivolous arguments or claims, and so on). Although these objections may be answered, as I hope that I have answered them, they have a tendency to demand individual attention and may be endlessly multiplied, so that the answers are unlikely to satisfy a skeptic. The sparer argument concerning professional detachment, by contrast, can cut through such quibbles and make plain why the technical restrictions on adversary advocacy that I address in earlier chapters (and all others like them) cannot possibly eliminate adversary lawyers' professional obligations to lie and to cheat. These obligations endure as long as lawyers must insulate their professional activities from their private views of clients whom they serve rather than judge—that is, as long as legal practice retains the commitments to lawyer loyalty and client control, and to professional detachment, that are fundamental to the adversary system. Adversary advocacy does not require lawyers to display the sensational vices that its critics denounce, to be sure, but it steadfastly insists that lawyers display the more modest vices that I have elaborated.

A LAWYERLY VIRTUE

Even as the turn to professional detachment reaffirms (and entrenches) the connection between adversary advocacy and the lawyerly vices, it also initiates a more hopeful development in lawyers' professional ethics. Perhaps surprisingly, the principle of professional detachment—the requirement that adversary advocates withdraw from their own judgments of their clients' cases—may *itself* be recast as a characteristically lawyerly virtue, which I shall call *fidelity*.[55] Fidelity is a complex virtue—quite different from loyalty *simpliciter* and its cognates and much more difficult to achieve. To understand both the distinctiveness and the difficulty of fidelity, it will be useful to develop the contrast between fidelity and more conventional virtues that lawyers have sometimes been thought to display.

Fraternity and Friendship

The suggestion that adversary advocacy involves characteristic virtues has been made before. Most familiarly, lawyers have been said to display distinctive and appealing forms of fraternity[56] or even friendship[57] toward their clients. But in spite of their prominence, ideals of fraternity or friendship cannot give a substantively satisfactory account of the lawyerly virtues.

Some of the difficulties that confront the suggestion that the lawyerly virtues are versions of fraternity or friendship are familiar. Indeed, even those who favor this suggestion acknowledge that the lawyerly virtues are at most *like* ordinary fraternity and friendship[58]—so that an account of the lawyerly virtues that departs from fraternity and friendship must travel some distance in order to produce a persuasive characterization of legal practice in which the likeness shines through obvious differences.

To begin with, the way in which lawyers associate themselves with their clients seems to depart radically from the virtues of fraternity and friendship, at least as these are commonly understood. Lawyers generally (and quite properly) insist on being paid for their services. But the demand for payment, as has been often remarked,[59] corrodes fraternity and friendship in any ordinary sense. Even those who reject purely other-regarding accounts of these values (for example, the familiar view that fraternity is measured in self-sacrifice and friendship in affection) must acknowledge that genuine fraternity and friendship cannot be bought. Lawyers also generally (and again, properly) accept and retain clients quite apart from any personal conviction in the merits of the clients' claims or the justice of the clients' causes.* But fraternity and friendship, at least in their common incarnations, must be embarked on with much greater discernment than this, so that lawyers, as measured by ordinary understandings, choose the wrong compatriots and make the wrong friends. Even those who reject moralistic accounts of these virtues (for example, Aristotle's view that true friends must be alike in virtue[60]) must recognize that the value of fraternity and friendship depends on the value of their objects.

Moreover, even if an appealing account of lawyerly fraternity or friendship could be constructed to overcome these familiar difficulties, it would face a still greater (if less familiar) obstacle. There is another important respect in which the attitudes associated with fraternity and friendship are fundamentally opposed to the lawyer's attitude toward her clients. The compatriot or friend characteristically serves the object of her affection on her own terms—she promotes his good as she sees it, and although she may respect his contrary views, and even adjust her behavior in light of this respect, she never completely *defers* to him.† In

---

* Of course, this does not entail that it is proper for lawyers to accept clients based narrowly on the clients' ability to pay fees, or for the legal profession to be structured around this method of allocating legal services.

† The true patriot, for example, does not endorse her country right or wrong but instead serves her country by insisting that it improve; and the true friend insists that her wayward comrade mend his ways.

this way, the compatriot or friend throws her entire self—including all her judgments and ambitions—into her relations. The lawyer, by contrast, must display precisely the deference to her client's purposes and objectives that the compatriot and friend reject.[61] Indeed, this deference—this refusal to apply personal judgments of a client's case—reprises the ideal of professional detachment (acting as a sword and not just as a shield) that, I have argued, organizes lawyers' professional ethics. Lawyers are therefore, in an important respect, the polar opposites of compatriots or friends. Rather than throwing themselves into the lawyer-client relation, lawyers *withdraw* important parts of themselves from it.

Fidelity

Although lawyers are like compatriots and friends in that they prefer their clients over others, the internal dynamics of lawyers' commitments to their clients differ from, and in important ways almost exactly oppose, the dynamics that drive true fraternity and friendship. Lawyers may look to their private interests in entering the lawyer-client relation (and even in negotiating its interstices[62]) in ways in which compatriots and friends may not; and lawyers must repress their private views of what is right for their clients in ways in which compatriots and friends should not. It is difficult to conceive how an account of lawyerly virtue that analogizes lawyer's attitudes toward clients (including the lawyerly version of loyalty) to fraternity or friendship could bridge these differences.

The root of the difficulty with the idea that lawyers are like compatriots or friends may be identified by returning to the basic structure of lawyers' professional ethics. These metaphors treat lawyer loyalty as an application of ordinary ideas of loyalty. But the basic principles of legal ethics are, as I have said repeatedly, lawyer loyalty *plus* client control, and the version of loyalty that lawyers display must be understood in light of the principle of client control. Moreover, the discussion of professional detachment elaborates just how client control intervenes to give the lawyer's loyalty to her client a distinctive character that the ordinary loyalty associated with fraternity or friendship does not share. In particular, lawyers must not just prefer their clients' interests over the interests of others but also prefer their clients' points of view—that is, beliefs about what is true and fair*—over other points of view, including especially their own. I call this attitude fidelity, in order to capture that it involves not just a concern for clients' ends but also, and indeed predominantly, a

---

* Here note that the principle of legal assertiveness gives clients substantial leeway in forming and pursuing these beliefs.

concern for deference and accuracy in identifying and representing clients' conceptions of what these ends are. As the arguments to come will reveal, the features that make fidelity distinctive account for a substantial part of fidelity's appeal, which makes the distinctiveness of fidelity essential to the more hopeful strands of lawyers' professional ethics.

The difficulty of fidelity, and also its virtue, may be appreciated by taking the argument in an unexpected direction, to develop an unlikely analogy between lawyers on the one hand and, on the other hand, poets. Although this comparison between lawyers and poets may seem strange and even misplaced,[63] it is in fact a species of the familiar analogy, most famously developed by Plato in Book IV of *The Republic*, between the state and the soul.[64] The analogy attempts to cast the lawyer's role in political life in the same mold as the poet's role in spiritual life. I take up the distinctively political side of the analogy, to display in detail the service that lawyerly fidelity provides political life, in chapter 8. The remainder of this chapter is more suggestive than systematic and deploys the analogy to poets in the service of elaborating on the nature of fidelity.

John Keats's ideas about the nature of poetic sensibility, specifically his idea of *negative capability*,[65] provide the starting point for this discussion of lawyerly fidelity. Keats proposed that the poet's negative capability provides a distinctive service to both the poet's subject and his audience. Each of these two elements of poetic negative capability has an analog in the professional life of the adversary advocate, and these analogs together elaborate characteristically lawyerly fidelity.

Begin with the service that the poet provides his subject. Keats argued that the negatively capable poet is unusually able to efface himself, maintaining "no identity" of his own, and (through this self-effacement) to work continually as a medium, "filling some other body—The Sun, the Moon, the Sea . . ."[66] and rendering this ordinarily mute body articulate. The lawyer is similarly required, by the sword-like component of professional detachment, to efface herself, or at least her personal beliefs about the claims and causes that she argues. And through this self-effacement, the lawyer becomes able to work continually as a mouthpiece for her client. Just as the self-effacing poet enables his otherwise insensible subjects to come alive through him, so also the lawyer enables her otherwise inarticulate clients to speak through her.

The analogy to poets therefore casts the deference that lawyers show their clients as an unusually selfless (in the literal sense) kind of empathy.* Ordinary good people acting in ordinary circumstances adopt the first-personal moral ambition to form their own opinions about the

---

* Such empathy should not be confused with warmer self-sacrificing virtues such as generosity, which is why it is not undermined by the fact that lawyers are paid and, indeed, for hire.

world that they confront and to express themselves in the service of
these opinions. But the good lawyer, acting in her professional capacity,
adopts the first-personal moral ambition to take her client's part and,
steadfastly suppressing her own ego, to speak her client's mind. The
good lawyer aims to address the world, negatively capably, through her
client's eyes.

Next, consider the service that the poet provides his broader audience. Although the poet can see through his subject, he does not see
only through his subject or become his subject's exclusive property. Instead, the negatively capable poet can occupy multiple points of view
simultaneously and therefore has a capacity "of being in uncertainties,
Mysteries, doubts, without any irritable reaching after fact & reason,"
a capacity of "remaining content with half knowledge"[67] that allows
insight, however uncertain, to which brighter but more uniform light of
their more positive capabilities leaves ordinary people blind. The lawyer, once again, has similar capacities. She is, as Hazard and Hodes observe, "trained in disbelief, or at least unbelief or suspended belief, and
[is] required to act in that frame of mind in many of [her] professional
duties," so that she "is not supposed to 'know' whether [her] client is
guilty in a criminal case, or whether he is entitled to prevail in a civil
case."[68] And the lawyer is therefore able to sustain all sides of an argument, to equivocate without any irritable reaching after a conclusion, to
remain content with persuasion rather than proof. The good lawyer follows Keats's dictum "to make up one's mind about nothing—to let the
mind be a thoroughfare for all thoughts. Not a select party."[69] This allows "the arguments of counsel to hold [a] case, as it were, in suspension between two opposing interpretations of it."[70] And because she can
do this, the lawyer sees more clearly and widely than ordinary people
see and can sustain resolutions to disputes that remain closed off from
those who insist, passionately, on substantive justice or right.[71]

The analogy to poets therefore casts lawyerly fidelity, and in particular
the suppression of lawyers' personal convictions that fidelity demands, as
a characteristically lawyerly version of the procedural virtues. Ordinary
good people acting in ordinary circumstances aspire, once they have
heard all sides to a question, to make up their minds and promote the all-
things-considered judgments that they have reached. But the good lawyer,
acting in her professional capacity, employs a distinctive subtlety of mind
and an unusual practical imagination to construct compatible possibilities where others see contradictory certainties, to distract attention away
from the deepest conflicts, to redirect energies toward shallower matters,
and in this way to achieve an accommodation among otherwise incompatible positions. Negatively capable lawyers cultivate, as Kronman has
observed, a distinctive blend of sympathy and detachment, which renders

them distinctively capable of containing, and even resolving, recalcitrant disputes.[72]

Fidelity, moreover, is not merely a theoretical curiosity. Instead, fidelity and negative capability join the ideals of lawyer loyalty, client control, and professional detachment in providing organizing principles for the doctrinal structure of the law governing lawyers. Most importantly, ideals of fidelity and negative capability can help to explain not just the partisan deference that that the positive law permits lawyers to display toward their clients but also the limits of their partisanship. Lawyerly fidelity is not a veiled invitation to completely unconstrained adversary zeal, but instead contains an implicit instruction to avoid such behaviors as would undermine negative capability itself. Most generally, fidelity and negative capability condemn forms of lying that help clients to *misrepresent* rather than to *express* themselves and forms of cheating that *close off* rather than *open up* the judicial process.

Moreover, this general principle may be given more fine-grained applications, so that fidelity and negatively capability can explain the balance between partisanship and its limits that the positive law imposes at a greater level of doctrinal particularity. The rules surrounding the duty to keep client confidences present a prominent case study,*[73] because both the duty of confidentiality and its limits may be explained in some detail in terms of fidelity and negative capability. The basic connection between fidelity and the underlying duty of confidentiality is clear enough: insofar as a lawyer is only negatively capable, client-lawyer communications are like purely internal reflection by the client (there being no other independent ego involved), so that the lawyer has no standing as an independent agent and therefore no right to reveal her client's confidences.†[74]

---

* Negative capability also helps to explain other limits on lawyers' partisanship. For example, the turn to negative capability helps explain why lawyers must reveal adverse legal authority to a court, but need not (and often may not) reveal adverse facts. This asymmetry is traditionally explained by saying that "revealing adverse precedent or other authority does not greatly damage the client-lawyer relationship, because the law does not 'belong' to the client in the same way that factual information does," but this claim (at least in its bare form) is conclusory. The ideal of negative capability makes it possible to replace the quotation marks around "belong" and to make the point theoretically precise: The negatively capable lawyer articulates her client's point of view, and although revealing adverse facts obstructs this process, revealing adverse law does not, because the law is not part of the client's point of view.

Similarly, the turn to negative capability helps to explain the law's prohibitions on filing frivolous claims—which prevent lawyers from helping clients who have nothing to say on their own behalves but aim merely to silence others.

† The same idea also helps to explain the attorney-client privilege, because it suggests that, as the lawyer has no independent practical capacities in respect of client communications,

Moreover, the idea of negative capability also helps to organize the exceptions to the duty of confidentiality that the law recognizes, such as the rules that the duty to keep client confidences runs out when clients use lawyers to perpetrate frauds and that lawyers may reveal such frauds as their services have (unwittingly) promoted.[75] If the duty of confidentiality is an expression of lawyers' negative capability, it should no longer apply insofar as lawyers are transformed from negatively capable exponents of client positions into positively capable coconspirators who employ *their own* reputations to assist clients in saying what the clients could not, no matter how articulate they were, say as persuasively themselves.*[76] This approach, by picking out as special cases in which the lawyer's personal credibility has been used by the client, also resolves the puzzle why not every assistance a lawyer gives to a fraudulent client (for example, by successfully defending a client against a meritorious claim of fraud or even just by relieving the client of some other burden that enables her more effectively to defend herself) involves the lawyer in the client's fraud in a way that triggers the exception to confidentiality. By

---

the state ought not to be able to compel revelations of things that the client has told his lawyer without going through the client.

This approach accounts for the otherwise surprising fact that the attorney-client privilege can be exercised to block attorney testimony with respect to communications whose content the client himself may be forced to reveal, for example, in a civil suit in which he may be deposed.

Insofar as communications between negatively capable lawyers and their clients are like the clients' own internal deliberations, the lawyers have no independent agency with respect to the communications, so that efforts to make their content public must work directly on the clients' wills.

Finally, the account explains why although the privilege generally does not extend to prevent the lawyer from revealing facts that she knows apart from privileged communications, it does so extend in criminal contexts when the client could refuse to reveal these facts by citing his Fifth Amendment privilege against self-incrimination. Once again, a negatively capable lawyer should not be a window into her client's affairs for the benefit of prying eyes, and certainly cannot be made to speak where her client would be silent.

* Another example, which proceeds by direct analogy to the explanation of the rule against promoting client fraud, is the rule, adopted in some jurisdictions, that lawyers may allow witnesses whose testimony they know to be false to proceed in narrative form (without the direction of questions from the lawyer). Whereas lawyers who direct witnesses inevitably lend their personal credibility to the witnesses' testimony and therefore may not elicit responses that they know to be false, a narrative presentation by a witness does not implicate the lawyer's positive capacities, and therefore does not trigger any duties affirmatively to tell the truth. (Note that this is a controversial rule and that only a minority of states allow narrative testimony when clients insist on giving evidence their lawyers know to be false. The majority view (adopted in the Model Rules, but made "subordinate" to State law) is that the narrative approach does not satisfy the duty of candor before the tribunal. A further minority of states forbids the narrative approach on the ground that it impermissibly discloses client perjury.)

contrast, more traditional approaches to the duty of confidentiality—which assess the duty according to its contribution to the accuracy and fairness of the legal process and therefore suggest that confidentiality's contours should be fixed however would best promote these values[77]—are less successful in this respect, because they depend on systematic evidence about the causal impact of confidentiality on the effectiveness of client fraud which cannot be had and would anyway be unlikely to line up with any clean doctrinal categories. (Indeed, even the background emphasis on participating in client fraud at the expense of other forms of conduct that contribute to inaccurate and unjust adjudication lacks empirical support.)

Nor are these the only areas of the law of lawyering that may be interpreted as expressions of lawyerly fidelity. And although it is not my purpose here to reconstruct all of the law governing lawyers in terms of fidelity, a brief mention of three representative examples from legal ethics more broadly will help to make the narrower use to which I put fidelity more compelling.

First, the ideal of lawyerly fidelity can explain the conflicts rule that lawyers may not represent clients that have adverse positions in the same litigated matter and that this conflict is nonconsentable.[78] The reason for the rule, and especially for its otherwise mysterious mandatory character, is that even if a lawyer might balance the interests of competing clients in a way that is fair to both, it is impossible to serve as a negatively capable mouthpiece for two incompatible positions at once. To do so would require a lawyer, as Lon Fuller observed, to "permit himself to be moved by a sympathetic identification sufficiently intense to draw from his mind all that it is capable of giving—in analysis, patience and creative power" in two inconsistent directions at once.[79] And that is too much to ask of anyone.[80] Second, the idea that lawyers are negatively capable explains the rule that a lawyer may not represent a client in a case in which she will be a necessary witness.[81] This rule is commonly defended by saying simply that "the two roles of lawyer and witness are incompatible,"[82] but that explanation merely repeats the rule, because it does not say *why* the two roles conflict so strongly. The answer is that whereas lawyers are negatively capable, witnesses are positively capable, so that the witness role requires precisely what the lawyer role forbids, namely that a person form and report her own characterizations of the events she testifies about.*[83] And third, negative

---

* Similar reflections explain the related rule that a lawyer may not express her personal opinions about a client's cause and in particular may not vouch for her client. Although this is an old rule (which already appears as Rule 5 in the 1887 Alabama Code of Ethics, the first U.S. ethics code), it receives a skeptical reception from theoretical legal ethics—Hazard

capability explains why it is so difficult for a lawyer to bring a retaliatory discharge claim against a client who fires her for doing her duty as
an officer of the court, for example for revealing a client fraud where
the ethics rules require her to do so.[84] Even if the lawyer is all-things-
considered justified in her actions—even if she is right to reveal the
fraud—she nevertheless violates fidelity when she does so. A lawyer who
reveals a fraud that her client would conceal necessarily speaks on her
own behalf. And even if she is all-things-considered right to do so, this
assertion of self renders the lawyer unsuitable to her client, thereby justifying her discharge.

This list of examples is obviously incomplete, and the discussion of
each example obviously foreshortened. But the three examples—which
involve the formation, conduct, and dissolution of the lawyer-client
relation—nevertheless help to illustrate the breadth of the explanatory
power that fidelity and negative capability possess in legal ethics.

• • •

Of course, to assert the importance of lawyerly fidelity is not yet to
demonstrate it; and the necessary arguments must abide Part III of
the book. This first part has been devoted more to description than to
evaluation—that is, to developing a detailed characterization of the content of lawyers' professional obligations. It is important, in this connection, to remember that in spite of the positive prospects opened up by
unorthodox ideas concerning fidelity, lawyers' professional ethics are
more conventionally, and more immediately, dominated by broad and
organic duties to lie and to cheat. And although secondary rules may
(and indeed do in the positive law) constrain adversary excess to eliminate the most extravagant expressions of these lawyerly vices, even the
more banal vices that lawyers necessarily display place adversary advocates in an ethically uncomfortable position. As the Model Rules admit,
the adversary lawyer faces a tension between her professional obligations and her "interest in remaining an upright person."[85]

The Rules go on to say that "The Rules of Professional Conduct prescribe terms for resolving such conflicts."[86] But although this may be
true as a matter of law, it cannot be true (at least it cannot be straightforwardly true) as a matter of *ethics*, because the lawyer's ethical sense

---

and Hodes, for example, say that it "is troublesome precisely because it protects less substantial interests and is not vital to the protection of the system itself." And even the rule's
defenders say little more in its favor than that it keeps lawyers from becoming too client-
centered. The current argument, by contrast, puts the rule on a firmer footing. The lawyer
who expresses personal opinions about her client's cause becomes positively and not just
negatively capable, and this offends against the organizing ideal of the lawyer's role.

of what it is to be an upright person cannot be stipulatively changed, even by the ABA. Moreover, the tension between a lawyer's professional obligations and her personal ethics also cannot be resolved by the suggestion, which dominates legal ethics and again appears in the Model Rules, that the *adversary system* in which the lawyer participates allows her to "be a zealous advocate on behalf of a client and at the same time assume that justice is being done."[87] Even if the adversary system defense can be established, so that the partiality that lawyers are charged with displaying is revealed to be a mere illusion, brought on by taking too narrow a view of the lawyers' activities,[88] this will not refute the separate charge that lawyers are vicious. The adversary system defense merely casts the lawyerly vices as necessary evils. But lawyers have good reason, as the remark in the Model Rules about "remaining an upright person" implicitly acknowledges, to want to understand themselves as not evil at all.

This rough intuition may be given a more careful philosophical development, moreover, which explains what it is like—what it is like ethically—to practice law subject to the professional obligations to lie and to cheat that the argument so far has identified. Part II is devoted to elaborating the ethical burdens associated with living subject to the professional vices that have dominated Part I, in order to complete the backdrop against which any more hopeful arguments that appear in Part III must proceed.

PART II

Integrity

Chapter 4

INTRODUCING INTEGRITY

PART I elaborated the lawyerly vices. It identified the professional obligations to lie and to cheat that are inscribed in the law of lawyering as it stands in the United States today, even in the face of the many ways in which the law reigns in adversary excesses. Moreover, Part I argued that these professional obligations are not just idiosyncrasies of some peculiar or extreme doctrinal development in the positive law but are instead immanent in the fundamental structure and everyday practice of adversary advocacy, *tout court.*

These professional obligations of adversary advocates constitute an ethical burden, which makes it doubtful whether a professional life that includes embracing the lawyerly vices and accepting this burden can nevertheless be worthy of commitment. The second part of the book explains the nature of the ethical burden imposed on lawyers by their professional vices. The main idea of Part II is that only an argument that addresses the lawyerly vices directly can relieve the ethical burden that they impose and so bring lawyers' professional ethics to a happy conclusion. A subsidiary idea, through which this chapter introduces the main idea, is that the form of argument that dominates traditional defenses of lawyers' professional ethics cannot satisfy this criterion. Part II therefore establishes the need for the unconventional approach to legal ethics whose possibilities, both in principle and in practice, I examine in Part III.

THE ADVERSARY SYSTEM EXCUSE

The dominant argument in legal ethics—especially among defenders of the legal profession but also, serving as a lightning-rod, among the profession's detractors—is the adversary system excuse. According to this argument, the common perception that lawyers come under professional obligations to do things that ordinary morality condemns is an illusion only, brought on by viewing adversary advocacy through too narrow a lens. A broader view reveals that locally partial lawyers play an essential part in an impartially justified moral division of labor, under which competition among partisan advocates concerned primarily for their clients produces, on balance, the best justice for all. Consequently, as the ABA announces in the Preamble to its Model Rules, "when an opposing party is well represented, a lawyer can be a zealous advocate on behalf of a client and at the same time assume that justice is being done."[1] The life of the lawyer is worthy of commitment, according to the adversary system excuse, simply in virtue of its place, within this division of labor, in the overall administration of justice.

In its standard application—that is, in the version associated with traditional conceptions of the lawyer's professional role—the adversary system excuse claims straightforwardly to underwrite a dramatic division of labor, in which lawyers' partisan commitments to their clients overwhelm their professional lives, arising regardless of their clients' ends and subject to only the thinnest and most formal constraint that they may not actually act illegally on their clients' behalves. This view was for a long time the conventional wisdom about lawyers' professional ethics: Hazard and Hodes, for example, simply assert that "lawyers administer justice in the broadest sense when they make available to all citizens whatever the law allows, without subjecting the law or their clients' objectives to any kind of 'moral filter' of their own design."[2] In fact, however, the details of the adversary system excuse are considerably more difficult to bring to a satisfactory conclusion than the conventional wisdom acknowledges.

To begin with, the factual predicates of the standard application of the adversary system excuse do not generally obtain. Even in an ideal legal system, in which the underlying substantive laws are just and access to legal services is fairly distributed, it remains uncertain precisely how much partisanship in fact best serves impartial justice in aggregate—and it seems sure that a lawyer whose aggressive partisanship was on the verge of *successfully* subverting justice would be required by impartiality to step back in ways that neither the bar's traditional self-conception nor its rules contemplate.[3] Furthermore, the application of the adversary system excuse to defend aggressive partisanship becomes more dubious still in nonideal legal systems (and therefore in every actual legal system), in which substantive laws are not perfectly just and legal services are not perfectly fairly distributed. As even the Model Rules acknowledge (recall their stipulation that the opposing party be "well represented"),[4] when adversary lawyers are more available to some persons than to others, for example, it becomes quite incredible that aggressively partisan advocacy will best serve justice for all, even only on balance.[5] The conclusions of the adversary system excuse—the precise forms of partisan lawyering that it actually excuses—must be adjusted and most likely narrowed to reflect these and related complications.

Moreover, the theoretical predicates of the adversary system excuse's standard application also stand on shaky ground. The aggregative conception of fairness on which the simplest versions of this argument rely faces challenges from competitor conceptions, associated with rights-based moral theories, that apply the demands of fairness separately to every relation between persons. The partisanship that adversary advocates display often harms third parties in ways that engage such rights-based considerations. (Lawyers may, for example, discredit truthful witnesses who have a moral right to be believed or interpose technical defenses to deny compensation to persons who have a moral right to receive it.) These rights violations cannot, as the standard application of the adversary system excuse would have it, be simply offset by benefits that arise elsewhere in the adversary administration of justice. And accordingly, even where the benefits of partisan lawyering are real and secure, they cannot relieve the lawyer of her obligations to the particular persons whom she wrongs. The adversary system excuse must therefore also be adjusted to reflect the constraints imposed by rights, once again most likely in ways that narrow the partisanship that it ultimately sustains.[6]

Critics of excessive partisanship have been pressing these and related arguments with growing confidence against a tradition of legal ethics that, although once satisfied that the simplistic account of the adversary system excuse can justify aggressive partisanship, has been increasingly in retreat. The positive law has taken notice, moreover. It has tightened the web of secondary rules through which it generally reins in lawyers' partisan excesses, for example to narrow the scope of the duty of confidentiality.[7] And it has made more narrowly tailored adjustments to the adversary process, for example to protect certain particularly vulnerable witnesses from ordinarily permitted forms of cross-examination, in areas where underlying inequalities render the standard division of labor that the adversary system excuse recommends locally unfair.[8]

These complications have engendered a lively debate—which dominates contemporary legal ethics—between defenders and critics of the standard application of the adversary system excuse and standard conception of aggressively partisan lawyering. But in spite of the debate's liveliness, it remains firmly contained within the paradigm established by the adversary system excuse at its inception, as defenders and critics of aggressively adversary advocacy argue about how properly to elaborate that argument and, consequently, about how much partisanship the adversary system excuse, taken in its best light, finally excuses. This shared commitment to the basic structure of the adversary system excuse entails that, whatever their intramural disagreements, the several views that together dominate legal ethics today all converge on two important points.

First, although defenders and critics of the standard conception of legal ethics disagree about the metes and bounds of lawyers' justified partisanship, even critics who propose a substantial retreat from the tradition of aggressive partisanship generally accept (at least their positions entail[9]) that *some* version of adversary advocacy is justified and should be retained.* Although the precise limits of the partiality required by the lawyer's adversary role may be open to question and will surely vary as the details of the adversary system excuse receive one or another development, "the partisanship principle remains" as a prominent commentator has observed, "at the core of the profession's soul."[10] Even those who would most restrain lawyers' partisanship nevertheless accept the structural separation between advocate and tribunal that constitutes the adversary system's central idea—the notion that lawyers should represent particular clients rather than justice writ large—and therefore also accept, at least in some form, the basic principles of lawyer loyalty and client control that give this idea its practical expression. Accordingly, even revisionists would subject lawyers to the professional obligations to lie and to cheat that, as Part I established, attend every form of adversary advocacy, no matter how modest.

And second, although defenders and critics of aggressively partisan lawyering disagree about the intricacies of the adversary system excuse, both sides agree that the division of labor, broadly understood, presents the right model for lawyers' professional ethics. This has important implications for the way in which the dominant tradition in legal ethics engages the vices that all parts of the tradition require lawyers at least in some measure to display. In particular, the lawyerly vices (in spite of their ineliminable place in adversary advocacy and their doctrinal prominence in the positive law) never receive direct attention from within the dominant paradigm. Arguments modeled on the division of labor never address the lawyerly vices head on, to *refute* the claim that lawyers are professionally obligated to lie and to cheat, but prefer instead (as the name under which the division of labor enters legal ethics indicates) merely to *excuse* the lawyerly vices on the grounds that although they remain immediately unappealing, it is ultimately for the best that lawyers display them. Accordingly, all sides in the current debate in legal ethics implicitly assume that the life of the lawyer may be all-things-considered worthy of commitment, even in light of the vices that it inevitably involves, simply in virtue of the contribution that it

---

* Here recall that I am using adversary advocacy broadly to refer to lawyering under the structural separation between advocate and tribunal rather than, in a usage that is perhaps more conventional, more narrowly in connection with the distinction between adversary and inquisitorial procedure.

makes, within the division of labor that the adversary system excuse describes, to the overall administration of justice.

This is a fatal flaw in the dominant tradition. Even within the range of its successful application (whatever this turns out to be), the division of labor that the adversary system excuse describes cannot vindicate lawyers' professional ethics, all things considered. In particular, the idea of a division of labor is by nature inadequate to sustaining the ethical appeal of any life that involves the lawyer's professional vices. Furthermore, the dispute about the outer extent of excused partisanship actually distracts attention from the question whether the proffered excuse can sustain a successful professional ethics for lawyers even within its limits, wherever they fall. This is a case in which a prominent and vigorous disagreement at the edges of an argument disguises a weakness at the argument's core.

The flaw in the dominant tradition is not hard to make intuitive, moreover, because the invocation of vice and virtue that the tradition ignores is not idle talk. Instead, such language and its effects are themselves important features of the ethical circumstances of adversary advocates—which express free-standing ethical burdens that lawyers' professional vices impose on their lives entirely apart from the considerations of partiality that the adversary system excuse makes its immediate focus. Accordingly, lawyers naturally and for good reason wish to conceive of themselves not only as beneficially or even necessarily vicious, but rather as *not vicious at all*. And insofar as lawyers wish this, the adversary system excuse cannot (even when it succeeds on its own terms) render the professional life of the adversary advocate worthy of commitment, at least from the points of view of the lawyers called on to live it.

This intuitively compelling thought receives practical expression in the stubborn resistance among good lawyers against the charges that they lie and cheat, for example in their oft-repeated insistence that only the most extreme forms of adversary advocacy require these vices and in their related tendency to emphasize exceptional (and therefore avoidable) cases of the lawyerly vices at the expense of more ordinary (and unavoidable) cases. The staying power of this denial in the face of the overwhelming evidence (elaborated in Part I) that even moderate adversary advocacy entails commitments to lie and to cheat demonstrates the importance that lawyers place on charges that they are professionally vicious. And the fact that even lawyers who embrace the adversary system excuse to answer claims that they are impermissibly partial nevertheless continue independently to reject charges that they lie and cheat demonstrates the free-standing ethical content that they ascribe to the lawyerly vices and the importance, for lawyers, of rejecting these charges head-on.[11]

Finally, lawyers are in a sense right so insistently to resist the suggestion that they are characteristically vicious. The desire in lawyers to refute this charge (rather than just excusing vices that they acknowledge) may be given a rigorous philosophical reconstruction. This reconstruction proceeds in terms of a philosophically precise conception of personal integrity, which lawyers sacrifice when they betray their personal conceptions of virtue and embrace professional obligations to lie and to cheat, including even when (as under the adversary system excuse) the betrayal is in the service of an impartially justified moral division of labor.

The idea of integrity therefore opens up a new front in lawyers' professional ethics, which deals in questions that the arguments that dominate traditional legal ethics have simply failed to engage. Insofar as integrity is a substantive value, the dominant tradition in legal ethics is inadequate to its problem and must at the very least be supplemented by a new form of argument, which addresses the lawyerly vices directly, in a way that allows lawyers to honor their professional obligations without sacrificing their integrity. Part III proposes just such an argument, which elaborates the virtue of fidelity introduced at the end of Part I and assesses that virtue's theoretical and practical potential for answering the charges that lawyers lie and cheat in a way that renders their professional lives worthy of commitment. But before turning to that argument, and in order to be certain that the new departure in legal ethics that it involves is really necessary, I develop a systematic and rigorous treatment of the shortcomings in the dominant tradition that I have so far described only informally and intuitively. This account explains the ideal of integrity and defends that ideal's ethical importance.

Two Approaches to Ethics

The adversary system excuse and the disputes about its structure and scope that dominate legal ethics today are all exercises in *impartial* moral argument. Such argument sets out from the idea that everyone's life is as important as everyone else's and, in particular, that each person is equally the source of independent, authoritative moral claims on others. Accordingly, impartial morality insists that an agent must justify her actions in terms that take into account—and indeed give equal consideration to—all persons whom they affect. Someone who does not grant equal concern and respect to all whom her actions affect denies those whom she fails to consider their equal status as sources of authoritative moral claims and to this extent she acts immorally.

Moreover, the dominant form of the adversary system excuse adopts what I shall call a *third-personal* approach to impartiality (although this is not, I shall argue, the only available conception of impartiality or the only possible version of the adversary system excuse). According to this conception, equal concern and respect requires counting all persons' interests equally as contributions to an aggregate or collective interest and then acting maximally to promote the collective interest. (The third-personal character of this approach arises out of its emphasis on the "they" who together make up the collective.) This conception of impartiality is evident in the conceit that the ethical difficulties that lawyers face may be resolved by taking the broader point of view associated with supervising the moral division of labor that adversary advocacy involves, and that legal ethics should focus single-mindedly on tailoring the law governing lawyers to produce the best outcomes overall, judged from this point of view.

The emphasis on impartiality in legal ethics belongs to a broader development toward impartialist reasoning in modern moral philosophy more generally. Impartiality is modern morality's characteristic ideal and also its greatest achievement. But a second set of ideas about ethics endures even in the face of this trend, ideas that the theme of impartial justification has not, in spite of its current dominance, quite obscured or erased. These ideas approach ethical justification from the agent's own point of view, in what I shall call the *first person*, although the precise sense in which such ethics are first-personal, and the precise relationship between first-personal ethics and impartiality, must abide further argument and will remain controversial in any event.* This more intimate approach to ethics elaborates the thought that ethically justified acts should promote the actor's success (writ large and not just his narrow self-interest)—that is, his efforts to live according to his own suitable life plan and to achieve his own admirable ends. This theme recalls the venerable Aristotelian tradition according to which morality is not just about the claims that others make against a person but instead serves, as Bernard Williams once helpfully put it, "as an enabling device for the agent's own life,"[12] so that virtue promotes the general well-being or flourishing (in Aristotelian terms, *eudaimonia*) of the virtuous.[13]

This idea—that a person's ethics and her first-personal success are intertwined, so that a person does well by doing good—has been thought natural (even self-evident) in many periods of human history; and the modern idea that a person's ethical duties are measured in the impartial currency of self-sacrifice may even, viewed historically, be the more unusual position. Indeed, although this claim is not necessary for my larger argument, the modern association between ethics and self-sacrifice may find its historical origins in certain forms of perversity—including notably

* I address these questions in chapter 6.

in early Christian asceticism (most extremely, in the asceticism of
St. Benedict and St. Simeon Stylites, but also, and more moderately, in
the thought of St. Augustine)—which sought to soften the pains of
worldly impotence by teaching that self-sacrifice in this world clears
the path to heaven in the next.[14]

Furthermore, even though the modern view of ethics in many respects
represents a substantial advance over earlier conceptions, most notably
in its outward-looking recognition that a large part of ethics involves respecting other people (equally) as self-originating sources of independent
moral claims, it also introduces certain still unresolved pathologies into
both ethical theory and ethical life. One of these pathologies accounts
for the complexity of the ethical circumstances of modern lawyers.[15]

On the one hand, modern ideals of human equality rightly emphasize
the impartial aspect of moral argument—the idea that each person must
justify her actions to others in light of the fact that her own life is
no more important than theirs. On the other hand, this emphasis leads
modern ethical thought to underplay certain first-personal elements of
morality that remain important. In particular, modern ethical thought
underemphasizes that a person's ambitions and the actions by which she
pursues them do not just produce external results but also determine,
and indeed constitute, the kind of person that she will be. Even with
equality and impartiality in place, each person therefore continues to
identify specifically with his own actions, to see them as contributing to
his peculiar ethical ambitions in light of the fact that he occupies a special position of intimacy and concern—of authorship—with respect to
his own actions and life plan. Moral persons form and carry out ambitions and plans with an eye not just to their effects but to the ambitions
and plans in themselves—they seek ambitions and plans that leave them
reflectively satisfied not just with what they have done to others, but
also with what they have made of themselves.[16] And, having adopted
such ambitions and plans, moral persons seek to live in a manner that is
true to them, to live lives, one might say, of moral *integrity*.

The modern hegemony of impartialist moral ideas has therefore given
rise to a new and distinctive form of subjugation, associated with understanding morality solely in terms of sacrificing oneself to satisfy burdensome duties owed others—as an external force in one's life, to which
one must *submit*.[17] It has also engendered a distinctive form of alienation, associated with identifying guilt as the principal moral motive.
Both difficulties are dramatically articulated in existentialist calls for
making authenticity the prime virtue of action. They are also dramatically illustrated by the ethical lives of adversary advocates, and in particular by the failure of impartialist accounts of legal ethics, including
most prominently the adversary system excuse, directly to address the

lawyerly vices that adversary advocates are professionally obligated to display. Even if the modern lawyer can justify her morally troubling actions to third parties in impartial terms (as part of a division of labor that produces the best justice overall), this does not enable her to avoid the sense that they are vicious or to cast them as components of a life she that can happily endorse, and she therefore cannot construct an acceptable self-image as their author. Even where the adversary advocate can justify her professional conduct to others, the justification that she offers leaves her alienated from her ambitions for her own ethical life. It deprives her of her integrity.

These remarks are suggestive, but they paint in broad strokes only. The argument will need to be developed more carefully if it hopes to make good on the suggestions that they contain—that is to demonstrate just how and why the impartialist justification of adversary advocacy presented by the adversary system excuse deprives lawyers of an ethically significant sense of authorship and undermines their integrity.

JIM AND THE INNOCENTS

It is possible to develop a philosophically precise conception of personal integrity and to defend this ideal against the insistent encroachments of impartial duty. The most promising effort in this direction was initiated by Bernard Williams, and I set out from the same thought experiment from which he began.[18] Imagine that Jim is confronted by a dictator who has captured twenty political prisoners and offers Jim the following choice: either Jim must kill one of the prisoners or the dictator will kill all twenty. What should Jim do?

Jim's situation has been constructed so that his killing an innocent will minimize the total number of innocents killed. Moreover, barring special circumstances—for example, that the person Jim has been asked to kill has grounds for specially objecting to being killed by Jim (perhaps because she is his friend)—Jim's refusing to kill the one is better for *nobody*. The dictator has not told Jim "You kill that one or I will kill these twenty" but has instead presented Jim with a circumstance in which even the one Jim might kill will be killed in any case. Indeed, there is a sense in which all the innocents are benefited by Jim's killing—one might even imagine that the innocents ask Jim to join them in adopting a (fair) procedure for choosing which innocent he will kill and that the chosen innocent accepts being killed by Jim's hand. An impartial concern for the lives of others therefore recommends that Jim kill.

Nevertheless, Jim may have a good first-personal ethical reason for refusing to kill the one. Jim, we may suppose, accepts the moral principle that one should not kill innocents. Indeed, this is probably something of an understatement—the ambition not to kill innocents is likely foundational, or at least comes very early, among Jim's first-personal ethical ambitions, in the sense that honoring this ambition is central to being the person that Jim aspires to be.

If Jim refuses to kill, then, as Williams has observed, the result will not be simply that twenty innocents are dead or even that Jim has caused twenty innocents to die, but rather that the dictator (and not Jim), pursuing her projects (and not Jim's) has killed twenty innocents.[19] This much, Williams points out, is made plain by the observation that if the dictator responds to Jim's refusal to kill by telling Jim, "You leave me no alternative but to kill twenty," then she is, straightforwardly, lying.[20] If Jim declines the dictator's offer and refuses to kill, then he is, in some measure at least, enforcing the distinction between his projects and the dictator's and insisting on the moral significance of this distinction, in particular with respect to the intimacy of each of their connections to whatever killings are committed.

On the other hand, if Jim accepts the dictator's offer and kills the one, then he allows himself to become a partner in the dictator's active malevolence. If Jim kills, then he must abandon, or at least betray, his own benevolent projects, which include (indeed begin from) the project to avoid killing innocents. Instead, as Thomas Nagel observed in a closely related context, Jim must come himself to aim at part of the dictator's evil—the death of the one—and must make this evil into his own end, so that if his chosen method of killing the one fails, for example, Jim must adjust his actions to eliminate or correct the failure and to accomplish the killing. If Jim accepts the dictator's offer, then he must "push[] directly and essentially against the intrinsic normative force" of his ordinary ends.[21] In accepting the dictator's offer, Jim allows his projects to be determined by her evil ends.

Now because of the numbers involved in this case, Jim may reasonably decide that he should, in the end, kill the one. He may conclude that when nineteen additional killings (or twenty times as many killings) are at stake, it is self-indulgent to refuse to kill; he may conclude that the badness of becoming implicated in the dictator's malevolence is simply outweighed by the nineteen lives that his doing so will save. But even if it is right, when the numbers are large enough, for Jim to think in this way, the numbers may not always be large enough, and the moral relevance of his having killed the one will in any case not be *erased* by these ideas and will continue to be felt by Jim. Once again, nothing in Jim's situation forces *him* to kill; if Jim refuses, then the dictator's evil plans will be pursued only by the dictator, acting alone. But if he accepts the dictator's offer, Jim must recognize that the dictator's malevolence has induced him to violate the principle—which he had previously held dear—that one should not kill innocents and to join in the dictator's project and to make a killing his own.

Changing the terms of the example slightly makes this side of the question stronger still. Imagine that the dictator tells Jim that to save the remaining prisoners, he must kill using some involved method, say a slow and deliberate torture, whose execution will command Jim's protracted effort and attention, requiring him to pursue debased skills and master dark arts that further conflict with his own benevolent ideals and ends.* Moreover, imagine that the dictator's offer applies not just to one set of prisoners but as an ongoing arrangement, so that the dictator is in effect offering to moderate her evil going forward if Jim will become her henchman.

Although it remains impartially best for Jim to accept the dictator's offer even in these modified circumstances (indeed, the impartial case for accepting may be thought stronger still), the first-personal arguments for rejecting the offer become even more robust than they were before. Indeed, looking ahead somewhat, one might say that if it is self-indulgent for Jim to refuse to kill when the numbers get large enough, accepting the dictator's offer can involve Jim in self-indulgence of another kind— the self-indulgence of believing that he can so signally betray his own ideals and yet somehow remain faithful to them. Certainly it would be grotesque for Jim to ignore this betrayal entirely—to deny that he has cooperated with the dictator or killed at all, and instead to congratulate himself on cooperating with the innocents in saving (some of) their lives. Jim *will* help the innocents and save lives by accepting the dictator's offer, but that's not *all* he'll do.

Jim's case illustrates broader ideas about the moral importance of the special relation, which I am calling the relation of authorship, that a person has to his own projects and actions, a relation the person does not have to other people's projects and actions, not even to those that he could have undermined or prevented. Someone who thinks it *straightforward* that Jim should kill the one (that Jim has *no* good reason for refusing) in effect insists that there is never a morally relevant distinction between pursuing a project himself and failing to prevent someone else from pursuing the same project and so denies the moral importance of authorship. Such a person—who takes whatever actions and pursues whatever projects will produce the best consequences overall—therefore

---

* In order to continue comparing likes, we may suppose that the dictator will employ the same method on all twenty prisoners in case Jim refuses.

places his own decisions at the mercy of other people's projects and thereby attacks his own moral personality. Such a person sees himself as merely a cog in a causal machine or, using Williams's metaphor, as nothing more than a "channel between the input of everyone's projects, including his own, and an output of optimific decision."[22]

This makes it unclear how someone who understands himself in this way retains a well-defined moral self—a sense of his own distinctive moral agency—at all. Such a person rejects the idea that certain actions and projects are peculiarly his, that he is their author and that they should bear an especially close relationship to his own ideals and ambitions. Indeed such a person's projects are so completely determined by other people's ideals—he adopts new interim projects so capriciously— that he measures his moral ideals and agency as the weather measures the wind and cannot recognize which projects and ideals are, finally and properly, his own. He therefore suffers, as Williams says, "in the most literal sense, an attack on his integrity."[23]

But this is precisely the approach to authorship that is implicit in the third-personal account of impartiality and in particular in its suggestion that Jim should accept the dictator's offer and kill *whenever* doing so minimizes the total number of innocents killed. That approach deprives Jim of any sense that it is *his* project not to kill innocents, or indeed that he has any distinctive principles on the subject at all, and instead leaves him wholly at the mercy of the contingencies opened up by the actions of others (most notably, the dictator). And Jim's integrity therefore depends on his resisting (at least in some measure) the demands of third-personal impartial morality and at least sometimes refusing to kill the one even when it would be third-person impartially best for him to kill.*

---

* Notice that this argument does not involve the suggestion that killing the one is in itself unpleasant or burdensome for Jim or involves a greater self-sacrifice than morality can require Jim to bear. Both elements of this suggestion are perfectly sensible: Jim's killing may do him considerable psychic harm (for example by leaving him haunted by images of a gun in his hand and a bullet striking home); and the prospect of this harm may justify, or at least excuse, Jim's refusing to kill the one (just as, if the dictator had presented Jim with a threat rather than an offer, the prospect of suffering physical harm might have justified or excused Jim's decision to kill). But even though this suggestion is sensible, it plays no part in the argument of the main text, whose theme is not that Jim cannot be required to sacrifice his *interests* to the common good but rather that Jim cannot be required to sacrifice his *ideals* to the common good. This difference, which is extremely important, is reflected in the thought that where the argument identified in this footnote focuses on the distinctness of persons as *patients*—on the idea that people have a special relationship to their own well-being—the argument developed in the main text focuses on the distinctness of persons as *agents*—on the idea that people have a special relationship to their own actions and to the ideals that guide them. I develop this idea at greater length in chapter 6.

Lawyers and Jim

Just as Jim could best serve his commitment to human life by killing, so adversary advocates can best serve their commitments to truth and justice by lying and cheating. And like the argument that Jim is impartially required to kill the one, so the adversary system excuse (no matter how modest the partisanship that it ultimately defends) defends lawyers' lying and cheating in terms that make a direct assault on their integrity. Adversary advocates, in other words, face ethical circumstances structurally analogous to Jim's. The analogy, moreover, is important enough to lawyers' professional ethics to bear closer examination.

Lawyers approach their professional lives with first-personal ambitions in favor of honesty and fair play that, like Jim's ambition not to kill innocents, figure prominently in their ethical self-understandings. But when lawyers acquire clients who assert claims and defenses that they privately reject, their professional role requires them to lie and to cheat, in violation of these ambitions. Just as Jim is drawn into association with the dictator's evil project, so lawyers are drawn into association with their clients' dishonest and exploitative projects. And just as Jim's accepting the dictator's offer in order to reduce aggregate killing involves a self-betrayal that threatens Jim's integrity, so lawyers who honor their professional obligations betray their personal ambitions and place their integrity under pressure.

Indeed, although the attack on lawyers' integrity is less sensational than the attack on Jim's, it is perhaps ultimately more damaging. To begin with, lawyers' integrity is more pervasively imperiled than Jim's. Whereas Jim's confrontation with the dictator involves a single action and is isolated from the rest of his moral life (in his initial presentation of the example, Williams even made Jim a tourist on a foreign vacation[24]), lawyers' professional obligations require them to lie and to cheat repeatedly and even to cultivate these vices and become skilled in their exercise. Indeed, the lawyer's case in this respect more nearly resembles the modified version of Williams's example, in which Jim must kill regularly and using involved means, and the threat to lawyers' integrity is correspondingly severe.

Moreover, the threat that lawyers' professional obligations pose to their integrity has deeper roots in their moral lives than the threat that Jim faces has in his. Whereas the circumstance that threatens Jim's integrity is forced upon him, lawyers invite the threats to theirs when they adopt (and persist in pursuing) a profession that they freely choose. Accordingly, although Jim's sense of being himself a victim of the dictator's evil scheme might perhaps temper the betrayal of his ambitions that accepting the dictator's offer involves,[25] lawyers are less able to dissociate themselves from professional vices that they have (at least indirectly) chosen. In this respect also, the analogy to Jim underestimates the damage that the lawyerly vices do to lawyers' integrity.

Nor, of course, can lawyers salvage their integrity simply by observing that they are impartially justified (under the adversary system excuse) in betraying their ambitions to honesty and fair play and adopting instead the lawyerly vices that their professional circumstances demand. Jim, after all, is similarly impartially justified in accepting the dictator's offer and killing the one, but this does nothing to protect his integrity against the self-betrayal that the killing involves. To the contrary, the fact that impartial morality aligns itself with lawyers' lying and cheating accentuates rather than decreases the attacks on integrity that these cases involve: it is precisely because the arguments in favor of the lawyerly vices are so weighty that lawyers cannot simply stand by their personal ambitions and abandon their professional obligations, but instead face a genuine dilemma.

Moreover, the analogy to Jim's case is not undermined (and the threat against lawyers' integrity that this analogy illustrates is not eliminated) simply because the impartial pressures toward the lawyerly vices are ineliminable, and in a sense impersonal, consequences of the structural separation between advocate and tribunal that characterizes adversary adjudication, whereas the impartial pressure for Jim to kill is more narrowly the product of the dictator's idiosyncratic evil, specifically of the manipulative choice that he imposes on Jim. This difference between the two cases would matter for the overall argument if the attack on Jim's integrity from which the argument begins depended on Jim's being made the dictator's pawn, or (more narrowly still) on the dictator's being motivated not just to kill innocents but also, and independently, to corrupt Jim. (Lawyers would face analogous situations only insofar as their clients brought dishonorable lawsuits at least partly out of an independent motive to corrupt them.) But the source of the attack on Jim's integrity lies not in the dictator's ambitions but rather in Jim's, and the attack endures as long only as impartial considerations require Jim to embrace a project that is inconsistent with his first-personal ethical ambitions, regardless of whether the dictator is independently motivated to encourage this embrace. And in this respect, adversary advocates whose clients pursue dishonorable claims (even without any independent motive to implicate or corrupt their lawyers) inhabit circumstances ethically like Jim's and therefore face analogous threats to their integrity.

•   •   •

Like Jim, adversary advocates best serve impartial morality by betraying their first-personal ethical ideals and ambitions. And the argument about integrity therefore begins to make rigorous the intuitive sense (from which this chapter began) that the adversary system excuse (in whatever form it settles into following the intramural debates that dominate legal ethics today) cannot be the last word on legal ethics. The lawyerly vices matter apart from the charge of partiality, and the value of integrity gives lawyers a reason to resist their professional obligations to display these vices even in the face of the success of the adversary system excuse and the suggestion that it would be impartially best for lawyers to lie and to cheat.

But this treatment of integrity remains in two respects incomplete. First, the argument up to this point has implicitly relied (both in its reconstruction of the adversary system excuse and in its presentation of the Jim example) on a third-personal, maximizing conception of impartiality, according to which it is straightforward that persons must abandon their first-personal ambitions *whenever* this best serves impartiality in aggregate. This is not, however, the only possible (nor even necessarily the most persuasive) account of impartialist morality, and it may be that an alternative account of impartiality can accommodate integrity, so that the threat to integrity from impartialist arguments, including from the adversary system excuse, is eliminated. And second, the argument has so far said nothing about the weight or importance that persons may reasonably attribute to their integrity, and it certainly has not defeated the plausible suggestion that it is simply self-indulgent for a person to insist on her integrity even to the point of persisting in first-personal ambitions that can no longer be impartially justified.

Thus, although this chapter has made progress toward the promised philosophically rigorous reconstruction of the intuitive dissatisfaction with the adversary system excuse from which it began, the reconstruction remains in both these respects incomplete. The next two chapters take up these unfinished matters in order firmly to establish the need for the first-personal legal ethics that I develop and discuss in Part III.

Chapter 5

AN IMPARTIALIST REJOINDER?

WILLIAMS INTRODUCED the Jim example and developed the arguments that I have just rehearsed as part of an extended polemic against utilitarianism—which Williams took, metonymically, to represent the third-personal approach to impartial morality more broadly. But the third-personal approach to impartial morality, which also dominates the traditional presentation of the adversary system excuse, presents a particularly immediate and crass threat to integrity, which may be cast in unusually stark terms. Moreover, the language in which the argument concerning integrity has so far been developed exploits these weaknesses to powerful effect.

This makes it natural to wonder whether the argument concerning integrity displays the limitations of impartial morality generally (and the enduring importance of older more intimate conceptions of ethics) or instead makes only a narrower point about the limitations of the peculiar utilitarian account of impartiality that Williams was, as a historical matter, addressing and that the traditional development of the adversary system excuse imports. Perhaps if this crude, third-personal conception of impartiality is replaced with another more sophisticated conception, impartial morality will no longer pose any threat to integrity, either in Jim's case or (once suitable modifications to the adversary system excuse have been made) in the case of lawyers. If so, then legal ethics could retain its purely impartialist character, and indeed remain focused on the adversary system excuse, and still succeed at rendering the legal profession worthy of commitment, all things considered.

In this case, the more radical departure in legal ethics that I pursue in Part III, which steps outside impartialist morality entirely to address the lawyerly vices directly in a first-personal register, would lose much of its motivation. The upheaval in legal ethics that I shall propose therefore cannot be justified until the more modest revision is shown to be inadequate. Moreover, although the underlying problem of integrity cannot, finally, be resolved from within the impartialist paradigm, the sophistication of the alternative to the third-personal account of impartiality means that some care must be employed to see just why not.

JIM REDUX

The third-personal conception of impartiality insists that value inheres fundamentally in states of affairs and that an action is morally justified if and only if taking it maximizes the value in the world, which is to say, produces the state of affairs that is overall best.*[1] This is a conception of impartiality because it weights all persons equally in determining the value of a state of affairs and therefore insists that in order to act rightly a person must give all others equal concern and respect, as under Bentham's dictum:[2] "everybody to count for one, nobody for more than one."† It is third-personal because (as I observed earlier) it focuses morality on the "they" who collectively constitute the world whose value is to be promoted.[3]

Third-personal impartiality, therefore, instructs Jim to decide whether or not to kill the one on the basis of an utterly mechanical reasoning process: first, Jim must recognize that killings are *ceteris paribus* bad and that more killings are *ceteris paribus* worse than fewer killings; second, Jim must conclude that impartial morality requires him, *ceteris paribus*, to adopt the course of action, of those available to him, that minimizes the number of killings the world contains; and third, Jim must recognize that causes and effects (including in particular the dictator's evil plans) have arranged themselves in such a way that his killing one will minimize the number of killings overall.

Similarly, the third-personal version of the adversary system excuse instructs lawyers to lie and to cheat through an analogously mechanical reasoning process: first, lawyers must recognize that miscarriages of justice (inaccurate or unfair resolutions of legal disputes) are *ceteris paribus* bad and that greater miscarriages of justice are *ceteris paribus* worse than lesser miscarriages of justice; second, lawyers must conclude that impartial morality requires them, *ceteris paribus*, to adopt the course of

---

* Philosophers generally call this third-personal approach to impartiality by the name *consequentialism*. There is nothing wrong with this term (indeed, the reasons for its adoption will become obvious in a moment), but the language I have been using better emphasizes the contrasts that I am developing, and (in order to avoid a confusing multiplication of terminology) I set the standard usage aside.

† Bentham, of course, subscribed to utilitarianism, which as Williams's metonymy emphasizes, is the flagship third-personal conception of impartiality. Utilitarianism adds to the formal structure of third-personal impartiality the substantive propositions that (roughly) the property in virtue of which states of affairs have value is the amount of well-being that they contain and that the amount of well-being a state of affairs contains is an additive (and not just any symmetric) function of the well-being of the several individuals in that state of affairs. According to the utilitarian version of third-personal impartial morality, therefore, each person ought always to adopt the course of action, of those available to him, that contributes the most well-being to the world.

action, of those available to them, that minimizes the miscarriages of justice that the world contains; and third, lawyers must recognize that causes and effects (the interplay between their clients' claims and the possibilities and limits of accurate dispute resolution) have arranged themselves in such a way that they will minimize the miscarriages of justice that occur overall by acting as partisan advocates even for clients whose claims they privately regard as unjustified.

These features of the third-personal approach to impartiality make it natural to elaborate the threat to integrity that impartial morality poses in terms of maximizing and causal metaphors. Williams could describe this threat in the language of inputs and outputs of optimific decision because such language figures so prominently in specifically utilitarian moral reasoning. Moreover, this is no mere accident of language, but instead reflects structural inadequacies in the third-personal approach to impartiality. On the third-personal view, the facts that Jim minimizes overall killings only by *committing a killing himself* and that lawyers minimize miscarriages of justice only by *lying and cheating themselves* appear only as afterthoughts, if they appear at all. Indeed, once the causal levers that exist in the world arrange themselves, as they have in Jim's case and also in the adversary advocate's, so that an ordinarily value-decreasing action becomes inexorably connected to an increase in total value, then the action's wrong-making properties are, from the third-personal point of view, simply *erased*. From the third-personal point of view, the innocent Jim kills and the persons against whom lawyers lie and cheat become, all things considered, bads rather than goods.

The third-personal conception of impartiality is therefore committed, as Christine Korsgaard has said, "to the view that it is *obvious* that Jim should kill" and (I add) that lawyers should lie and cheat, whereas in fact "few people can imagine themselves in Jim's position [or in an adversary advocate's] without some sense of dilemma."[4] Indeed, third-personal impartiality is structurally committed to the view of Jim's circumstance that I earlier characterized as grotesque, namely that, having killed the one, Jim might congratulate himself on saving nineteen lives. And the proponent of the third-personal version of the adversary system excuse must adopt the similarly grotesque view that adversary advocates who make false arguments and exploit unfair advantages should ultimately congratulate themselves for their truthfulness and fair play.

All of this makes the third-personal account of impartial morality an especially easy target for arguments about integrity. In particular, there is a connection between the threat that third-personal impartial morality poses to integrity, on the one hand, and, on the other, its peculiarly wooden insistence (brought on by its cumulative conception of value and maximizing conception of right action) that once Jim can save nineteen by killing one, and once lawyers can serve justice by lying and cheating, they have no remaining moral obligations to those whom they might kill, lie to, or cheat. This obtuse refusal to recognize a moral remainder in such cases makes the mechanistic metaphors through which Williams accuses third-personal impartial morality particularly apt and the threat to integrity that those metaphors expose particularly vivid, by rendering more particular personal projects—like not killing or truthfulness and fair play—ultimately contentless, at least as anything other than contingent summaries of more basic moral calculations. As Barbara Herman has observed, the third-personal conception requires that a person "not only be prepared to interrupt his projects whenever utility calls, but . . . also [that he] pursue his projects without the sense that what makes them worth pursuing is connected to the fact that they are his."[5]

But these features of the third-personal account of impartiality also suggest that the third-personal conception's failure to accommodate integrity may be too spectacular to support my broader claim about impartiality's general inadequacy in this connection. The third-personal conception's refusal to recognize a moral remainder—its insistence that Jim does no wrong to the one whom he kills and that lawyers do no wrong to those against whom they lie and cheat—does not merely pose a threat to integrity but also mischaracterizes the duties of impartiality that Jim owes the innocents and that lawyers owe those against whom they lie and cheat. This calls into question utilitarianism's standing as a representative impartial moral theory. And it remains possible that correcting this third-personal error of impartial morality will, simultaneously, undo the threat to integrity that impartiality poses.

The Second Person

The third-personal approach to impartiality can insist that Jim's killing and that lawyers' lying and cheating pose no moral dilemmas only because it denies that individual persons underwrite separate bilateral moral claims on others even apart from any contributions that they make to overall value. As John Rawls has said in a related context,*

---

* Rawls was criticizing utilitarianism for failing to recognize the demands of distributive justice—for being concerned exclusively with total well-being at the expense of every consideration about how that total is distributed (including especially whether the distribution is equal or unequal). And, indeed, this particular failure of utilitarianism arises most starkly in cases such as the ones Rawls envisions, in which utilitarianism too readily sacrifices some for the greater good of others. The distributive element is of course missing from Jim's circumstance, which has been constructed so that the one Jim is asked to kill would be killed in any case, and the sense of *sacrificing* the one for the good of the

"[u]tilitarianism does not take seriously the distinction between persons."[6] Furthermore, the threat to integrity that third-personal impartial morality poses may perhaps be traced back to this purely impartialist error: The inadequacy of the third-personal analysis of Jim's and lawyers' cases—the failure to recognize these cases' complex and conflicted quality—may perhaps be explained in terms of the third-personal failure to credit that Jim must justify killing, and that lawyers must justify lying and cheating, not just based on aggregate effects but also in terms that fully respect the separate demands for moral justification directed at them by the individual persons against whom they act. Perhaps, then, reconstructing impartiality to reflect the distinction between persons will enable impartialist morality to explain the full moral complexity of cases like Jim's and to protect the integrity of persons, including adversary advocates, who act impartially in the face of such complexity.

The most prominent impartialist effort in this direction seeks to cure the mistake in the third-personal conception of impartiality by abandoning the theory of value on which this conception is founded. That theory of value, it is alleged, lies at the root of both the sense that the third-personal approach leaves no room for the moral remainders that generate the dilemmas Jim and adversary advocates face, and relatedly, the compelled character of third-personal arguments that Jim should kill and that lawyers should lie and cheat and the threats to integrity that these arguments pose. For it is the fact that value is supposed to inhere, fundamentally, in states of affairs that makes it so difficult for the third-personal approach to impartiality to credit that there could possibly be a reason against producing a state of affairs that is not founded in its badness and is therefore equally a reason to prevent that same state of affairs from being produced by someone else or in some other way.[7] It is this difficulty that leads third-personal impartiality to ignore the moral differences between Jim's killing and the dictator's, and between lawyers' lying and cheating and other imperfections in the administration of justice, and so to conclude (contrary to all common sense) that Jim must *of course* kill the one and that lawyers must *of course* lie and cheat. And that is why third-personal impartiality threatens individual integrity in such stark terms.

---

others therefore does not arise. But in spite of this difference, the form of the utilitarian mistake—the failure to consider persons as individual, independent sources of moral claims—remains the same in both cases. This is not, of course, to suggest that the introduction of a distributive component to Jim's problem—say, by changing the terms of the dictator's offer so that the one Jim is asked to kill will be allowed to live if Jim refuses—is irrelevant to Jim's dilemma. Quite to the contrary, the absence or presence of this distributive component may, as I observe in a moment, determine what nonutilitarians think impartial morality requires Jim to do.

Observations like these appear prominently in the work of philosophers (such as Korsgaard) who reject the third-personal idea that value inheres exclusively or primarily in states of affairs and emphatically insist instead that moral value inheres, fundamentally, in relations among persons. On these views, "[t]he subject matter of morality is not what we should bring about, but how we should relate to one another."[8] Similarly, these views insist that the content of morality is not that we should maximize aggregate well-being (or some other similarly structured value*), but rather that we should relate to other persons always as ends and never as mere means. This requires, as Korsgaard says, that we treat persons only in ways to which they can consent,[9] or expressed a little differently (this time by T. M. Scanlon), that we act only in ways that no person could reasonably reject.[10]

This is a conception of impartiality because it insists that each person's entitlement to justification is equally compelling and therefore that each person be given equal concern and respect. But this conception of impartiality elaborates equal concern and respect in a new way and departs fundamentally—indeed, in its natural grammar—from the third-personal view. Whereas the third-personal approach to impartiality merely insists that moral justification must take others into account, this approach to impartiality insists that moral justification must be acceptable to them. It insists that moral justification must not only *count* others but rather must *address* them, so that one may say, speaking loosely, that it requires impartial morality to proceed not in the *third* but rather in the *second* person.

Proponents of the second-personal approach to impartiality—which, engaging in another metonymy, I shall sometimes call the Kantian approach[11]—have suggested that it can account for the complex ethical intuitions that cases like Jim's and the adversary advocate's generate, and preserve integrity in these cases, entirely from within impartial morality and without resorting to alternative more intimate moral schemes. Indeed, Korsgaard, whose Kantian ethics pursues this second-personal approach to impartiality particularly vigorously, seeks expressly to defeat the suggestion that the Jim example and the ideas about integrity that it generates require philosophy to contemplate any departure from impartial morality not only in its third-personal elaboration, but more generally.[12]

Korsgaard begins by observing, as I have done, the tinniness of the utilitarian failure to see a dilemma in Jim's circumstances and the sense that even though Jim is in a position to save nineteen lives, he is not being offered "a happy opportunity for doing some good."[13] Instead,

---

* Including, incidentally, morally good relations among persons.

Jim is being asked to stand, vis-à-vis his innocent potential victim, in the relation of intentional, and indeed deliberate, killer. The fact that Jim's killing the one will also save the other nineteen does not undo or eliminate impartial morality's concern with this relationship, including, in particular morality's insistence that this relationship be justified *to that one*. The Kantian principle that Jim must treat each person (one at a time) with respect and as an end rather than a means comprehends that Jim's obligations to the one whom he might kill are not simply extinguished by the fact that this killing will save nineteen lives. It, therefore, recognizes that Jim retains a special obligation to justify his killing (but not the dictator's killings) to this victim.

These observations similarly hold true, *mutatis mutandis*, for the adversary advocate. Even when her partisanship ultimately promotes justice, hers is not simply a happy situation but instead involves intentional, deliberate misuse of the persons against whom she lies and cheats. The fact that justice will be served overall does not eliminate or extinguish the lawyer's impartialist duties to these persons or her obligation to justify herself individually to them. And the lawyer therefore retains a special obligation to justify her own conduct (but not the miscarriages of justice that otherwise arise) to the persons against whom she acts. In each case, the Kantian view recognizes the sense of moral dilemma that the utilitarian view improperly ignores.

But even as it recognizes moral complexities in Jim's circumstance, and also in the circumstances of adversary advocates, that the third-personal approach to impartiality ignores, the second-personal conception of impartiality nevertheless recommends that Jim sometimes kill and that lawyers sometimes lie and cheat. In Jim's case, the demands of second-personal impartial morality turn on what the innocents themselves, and especially his potential victim, want him to do. Thus Korsgaard asks us to imagine that one of the innocents "steps forward and says, 'Please go ahead, shoot *me*, and I forgive you in advance.'"[14] Adding this feature to the example makes a substantial difference to the impartial moral case for Jim's killing the one,[15] at least on the Kantian conception of impartiality, because it includes that innocent in Jim's deliberations and addresses him—his individual point of view—in a way in which no utilitarian counting of total lives saved could ever hope to do. "*Very* roughly speaking," suggests Korsgaard, "[Jim is] not treating him as a mere means if he consents to what [Jim is] doing."[16]

Moreover, an analogous argument recasts the adversary system excuse to deliver a second-personal impartial justification of the ways in which adversary advocates lie and cheat. Thus although the lawyerly vices cannot be simply offset by the contributions that these vices make to the overall administration of justice, they may be squared with second-personal impartial morality in another way. Once again, although liars and cheats ordinarily use their victims merely as means, lawyers do not misuse persons who, perhaps because they are persuaded by the division of labor argument in the adversary system excuse, consent to practice of adversary adjudication.

These arguments show that the second-personal impartial justifications of Jim's killing, and of lawyers' lying and cheating, are possible, although the justifications are much more complex than the third-personal justifications and are subject to reservations that did not trouble the third-personal arguments considered earlier. It is always possible, for example, that no volunteer comes forward and asks to be killed and, quite to the contrary, that the innocents (perhaps because they are pacifists) unanimously express to Jim that they would rather die than ask him to commit an act of violence. And it similarly is always possible that the participants in a legal dispute (perhaps out of gallantry or graciousness) might unanimously sacrifice the accuracy or justice of adjudication to preserve ideals of individual truthfulness and fair play.* In such cases, the decisions that Jim should kill or that lawyers should lie and cheat, rather than addressing the innocents or the parties to legal disputes, now ignore their points of view and therefore suffer, as Korsgaard says (speaking of Jim's case), "a slight taint of paternalism."[17]

Of course, even when an innocent does volunteer to be killed, and even when the participants in a legal system do accept adversary procedure, these expressions of consent require, as Korsgaard herself observes, "*many* qualifications"[18] before they render ordinarily immoral actions consistent with the Kantian injunction to treat persons, individually, always as ends and never merely as means. Obviously, "[a]ctual consent—in the sense of saying yes—can easily be spurious."[19] And the circumstances of the cases at hand—in particular the threats of still greater misuse that mingle in the deliberations leading up to consent—justify taking an especially dubious attitude towards any expressions of consent that these cases produce.

But although this concern—about the validity of consent—is indeed troubling, it can perhaps be met by the recognition that, under the

---

* Here it is worthwhile to recall that all forms of adjudication that retain the structural separation between advocate and tribunal (including, importantly, forms more commonly called inquisitorial) count as adversary for purposes of my argument, because (as Part I demonstrated) they involve the lawyerly vices and therefore generate the complicated professional ethics that I am addressing. Without this point, which expands the category "adversary system" beyond the forms of extreme partisanship that it most immediately calls to mind, it might seem strange to imagine, as the main text does, that abandoning adversary advocacy to preserve lawyers' truthfulness and fair play involves sacrificing the accuracy or justice of adjudication.

(admittedly strained) circumstances of the cases at hand, the consent at issue is *reasonable*. Jim's killing does save lives, and the innocent, who will be killed in any case and regardless of what he says and of what Jim decides, is made no worse off by consenting to Jim's killing. This feature of the situation, the Pareto superiority of Jim's killing one innocent, makes it possible to say that even though it is not reasonable for the innocents to consent to being killed *absolutely*, it is reasonable to consent to being killed *by Jim*. Furthermore, even where no volunteer arises and actually consents to being killed, it may be reasonable for Jim, if he can develop a fair procedure for choosing which of the twenty innocents to kill, to apply the procedure and impute consent to the innocent who is chosen. As Arthur Applbaum has argued, it is surely reasonable for someone to accept a lesser violation of his person in exchange for avoiding a greater, and from an *ex ante* perspective Jim's adoption of a fair selection procedure does just this; it imposes on each innocent a chance (most likely a one-in-twenty chance) of being killed in exchange for relieving each innocent of the certainty of being killed.[20]

Similarly, insofar as adversary adjudication establishes a division of labor calibrated best to secure the rights of every participant in a legal system, even the persons against whom lawyers lie and cheat can expect (at least *ex ante*) their own legal rights to become less secure if lawyers are forbidden from adopting these adversary tactics. And accordingly, even if it is not reasonable to consent to being lied and cheated against in general, it may be reasonable for the participants in legal disputes to consent to being (in some measure) lied and cheated against by lawyers. The adversary system excuse, which is (as I have said) traditionally presented in the third-personal language of maximizing justice overall, may therefore be reconstructed to satisfy the second-personal conception of impartial morality.[21]

Of course, this Kantian reconstruction—which requires that the adversary system is not only most just overall but also most just to each person[22]—will substantially narrow the limits of partisanship that the adversary system excuse justifies.* In particular, it will focus attention all the more insistently on the various imperfections—unequal access to lawyers, unequal chances of becoming the victim of adversary tactics,

---

*This narrowing also figures in Jim's case, although the Jim example has from the start been constructed so that the practical difference between the third- and second-personal analysis of Jim's impartialist obligations is implicit only. Thus the third-personal account of impartial morality would recommend that Jim kill one even if, contrary to the example, the dictator would not kill Jim's victim in any event but would instead kill twenty *other* persons. This distinction is of course crucial for the second-personal argument in favor of Jim's killing the one, which would not apply in the revised example, in which the one could reasonably object to being killed by Jim, because he would not otherwise be killed at all.

and unjust substantive laws—that plague every actual adversary system. On the traditional (third-personal) development of the adversary system excuse, such imperfections undermine adversary advocacy only when they become so substantial that the adversary system becomes less just than its competitors in aggregate. Under the modified, Kantian adversary system excuse, by contrast, adversary advocacy loses its impartial justifications much more quickly, as soon as adversary tactics become less effective at securing justice for any individual person. But even as the Kantian reconstruction of the adversary system excuse justifies a narrower, more constrained form of adversary advocacy than its third-personal counterpart (especially in imperfect legal systems), it continues to justify the foundational commitments of the adversary process, including most notably the structural separation between advocates on the one hand and judges and juries on the other.[23] And as Part I argued in detail, as long as this structural separation endures, lawyers will remain professionally obligated sometimes to lie and to cheat.

No Solution

I introduced integrity in response to inadequacies in the third-personal approach to impartiality, in order to suggest that ethics, and in particular legal ethics, cannot be understood from purely within the impartialist tradition but must instead also elaborate alternative more personal ethical themes. But the question now arises whether the increased sophistication of the second-personal approach to impartial morality renders my invocation of this alternative to impartiality unnecessary and, indeed, misplaced—whether the second-personal account of impartiality, and the Kantian reconstruction of the adversary system excuse, can domesticate the ethical burdens associated with the lawyerly vices and solve the problem of lawyers' integrity and therefore, standing alone, render the legal profession worthy of commitment.

Kantian arguments, after all, recognize moral complexity—and indeed a moral dilemma—in Jim's and the adversary advocate's circumstances that the third-personal approach to impartiality obscures: even as the Kantian argument concludes that, under certain conditions at least, Jim should kill and lawyers should lie and cheat, it narrows these circumstances and denies that these choices are in any sense *obvious* or *easy*. The second-personal account of impartiality appears, therefore, to correct many of the inadequacies in third-personal impartial morality while remaining purely within the impartialist moral tradition.

The problem of integrity, however, endures. The third-personal account of impartial morality that Williams had directly in mind, and that the commonest versions of the adversary system excuse incorporate, presents a particularly crass threat to integrity, to be sure. And the Kantian insight that the dilemmatic aspects of these circumstances are connected to the relationships that the dictator's offer invites Jim to enter into with the one whom he kills and that lawyers enter into with those against whom they lie and cheat represents an advance in understanding. But even after the appropriately full subtlety and complexity of second-personal impartial moral analysis is brought to bear on Jim's and the adversary advocate's ethical circumstances, an ineliminable component of the dilemmas that they face endures and remains unaddressed. And the Kantian advance does not eliminate the threat to integrity that impartiality—including the adversary system excuse—poses or diminish the attractions of alternative, more personal approaches to ethics, including to legal ethics.

The second-personal approach to impartial morality calls on Jim and on lawyers to betray their personal ideals and ambitions less often and less aggressively than third-personal impartiality would do. But in appropriate circumstances, second-personal impartial morality still requires Jim to kill and lawyers to lie and to cheat and, moreover, continues merely to excuse such conduct rather than denying its viciousness directly. Accordingly, the second-personal reconstruction of impartial morality still demands persons who face such circumstances to betray their native ambitions in ways that blur the distinction between their own projects and other people's and therefore to alienate themselves from their personal projects and ambitions in ways that threaten their integrity.

Indeed, in spite of the Kantian's advance, she risks committing an error that is similar to the grotesque error that (I have suggested) is committed by the utilitarian who insists that Jim should kill and congratulate himself on saving nineteen lives and that lawyers who lie and cheat should congratulate themselves on their truthfulness and fair play. The character of this error is revealed in something Korsgaard says in the course of explaining why Jim might kill an innocent without violating the Kantian principle of respecting all persons, one-by-one, as ends in themselves. After admitting that any innocent Jim kills has been wronged absolutely—or, as she puts it, in the "larger moral world"—Korsgaard says that Jim and the innocents are forced by their circumstances to regard the dictator and their powerlessness before him as natural phenomena, and that there arises, therefore, a "smaller moral world within which the issue is between [Jim and the innocents]." And when an innocent agrees to be the one Jim kills, then, says Korsgaard, "in that world this [innocent] consents."[24] Similarly, when an adversary advocate whose client ought to lose lies or cheats, she wrongs the persons against whom she acts absolutely, that is, from the most general point of view. But the Kantian will claim that insofar as her victims unite with the advocate in believing that the adversary system is the best response to the inevitable immorality of some litigants and the inevitable imperfections of adjudication, then the advocate and her victims again inhabit a smaller moral world, in which the wrongness of her client's claim (and the imperfectness of the court's response) are givens, and the victims, because they support the adversary system, consent to being lied against and cheated.

In adopting this "smaller world" metaphor (and particularly in applying the metaphor in connection with characterizing the dictator and the wrongful client as part of the fixed background), the Kantian treats Jim as of necessity engaged in a noble cooperative project with the innocents, whose purpose is to respect persons' lives given the injustice imposed by the dictator's evil motives and their own inability simply to defeat him. And the Kantian similarly treats the lawyer as of necessity engaged in a noble cooperative project with those against whom she lies and cheats, whose purpose is to respect all persons' legal rights given the injustice imposed by her client's mistaken claims and the legal system's inability perfectly to adjudicate them. (These noble purposes are achieved, in each case, by the collective adoption of fair procedures for selecting the innocent who will die and for adjudicating the legal claims in dispute, procedures that require Jim to kill and lawyers to lie and to cheat.)

But this treatment is merely the Kantian analog to the utilitarian claims that Jim has a happy opportunity to save lives and that lawyers have a happy opportunity to promote truth and fair play. Like the utilitarian, the Kantian attempts to domesticate ordinarily immoral conduct by colonizing these activities for impartial morality, this time casting the argument not in the utilitarian calculus of beneficence but rather in the Kantian frame of respectful relations.

Moreover, Kantian ideas are no more persuasive on this point than their utilitarian counterparts. Even though second-personal impartial considerations concerning Jim's and the lawyer's circumstances are exhausted by describing the smaller world in which Jim pursues a cooperative venture with the innocent whom he kills and the lawyer cooperates with those against whom she lies and cheats, these impartialist accounts again incompletely characterize Jim's activities in killing and the lawyer's activities in lying and cheating. When Jim kills (even if Jim's victim consents), then he is *also* engaged in a second, debased collective project *with the dictator*; and when lawyers lie and cheat (even if their victims consent) then they are *also* engaged in a second, debased project *with their wrongful clients*. The goals of these projects, which arise in the larger moral world, are to kill an innocent and to promote a meritless legal claim, whose death and whose success are, from the point of view of this larger world, not necessary and not consensual. Accordingly, adopting them requires Jim and lawyers to betray their personal ambitions (against killing, and in favor of honesty and fair play) in precisely the manner that threatens their integrity.

The dilemmas that these cases involve arise because Jim's circumstances, and also the adversary advocate's, make it impossible to adopt one cooperative project without becoming implicated in the other, making it necessary to choose between participating in neither project or participating in both. And just as the utilitarian's exclusive focus on the lives that Jim saves and on the overall justice that the zealous advocate promotes grotesquely ignores the facts that Jim is also intimately involved in killing and that lawyers are also intimately involved in lying and cheating, so the Kantian's exclusive focus on Jim's noble collaboration with the innocents and lawyers' noble collaborations with their victims grotesquely ignores the fact that these decisions also involve Jim in a debased collaboration with the dictator and also involve lawyers in a debased collaboration with their undeserving clients. Even if Korsgaard's analysis is right, Jim's and the lawyer's decisions will determine how intimately they are connected to these debased projects; that is, will fix the authorship of the projects. The "smaller world" that second-personal impartial analysis invokes in such cases is therefore inadequate to the moral content of the cases, and this reflects a substantial limitation of second-personal impartial morality and not just a careless metaphor. Like the utilitarian, the Kantian in the end just ignores or even suppresses the fact that impartial morality requires Jim and adversary advocates, betraying their personal ideals and ambitions, to sacrifice their integrity.*

• • •

The Kantian innovation in analyzing the impartial component of the dilemmas that Jim and adversary advocates face has therefore left the

---

* The Kantian might try to resuscitate the smaller world metaphor by arguing that it produces insights into Jim's state of mind when he kills and lawyers' states of mind when they lie and cheat that dissolve the tension between these actions and their more personal ideals and ambitions. Specifically, the Kantian might argue (employing a distinction that is familiar in criminal law) that the smaller world metaphor reveals that although Jim and lawyers must *intend* for their debased projects to succeed, they are not principally *motivated* by the considerations underlying these debased projects, and that this creates a protective distance from these projects that helps preserve integrity. But while the distinction between intent and motive may be helpful in other contexts, it cannot usefully be employed here. The ordinary first-personal ambitions that the debased projects betray include the ambition to avoid intentional (indeed, probably even negligent) and not just ill-motivated killing, lying, and cheating. Moreover, and probably more importantly, the ambition to avoid only ill-motivated killing, lying, or cheating cannot properly be formulated as a

problem concerning integrity precisely where it was. Even on the second-personal account of impartiality, the all-things-considered, impartially most justified courses of action—the noble collaborations to save lives and promote justice—intimately involve Jim and adversary advocates in parallel courses of action—the debased collaborations with the dictator and the wrongful clients—that require them to abandon, and indeed to betray, ideals and ambitions that are near the core of their personal conceptions of the forms of life they aim to achieve.*

To be sure, the shape of the problem is rendered slightly different under the second- than under the third-personal conception of impartiality, and the metaphor through which the problem is developed has changed accordingly. Thus the Kantian's emphasis on individualized, intersubjective justification allows her to recognize that there can sometimes be a difference between a person's doing an act herself and failing to prevent someone else from doing the same thing. And this, relatedly, allows her to resist the unattractive, overtly mechanical characterization that Williams successfully imposed on utilitarianism, namely that it requires persons to see themselves as nothing more than "channel[s] between the input of everyone's projects, including [their] own, and an output of optimific decision."[25]

But although, unlike the utilitarian, the Kantian can recognize that (because of the dictator's supervening responsibility) Jim's refusing to kill the one is not *equivalent* to murdering nineteen and the lawyer's refusal to lie and cheat is not *equivalent* to subverting justice, she cannot adequately recognize that the difference between these two—the degree of intimacy of Jim's and the lawyer's connections to a course of action—*may properly matter more to Jim and to the lawyer than to third parties.*†[26]

---

personal ambition at all, at least not where (as the impartialist arguments would have it) ill-motivated is understood merely to mean inconsistent with the demands of impartial morality. As I shall argue in the next chapter, integrity requires forming ambitions at a greater level of particularity than the generic ambition to do what is impartially required.

* Here it is particularly striking, in light of her express concern for the possibility that the innocents may be pacifists, that Korsgaard never asks where *Jim's* pacifism would leave the argument.

† Korsgaard's proposal that in the smaller world in which they must think of themselves as acting, Jim and the adversary advocate are "forced" to view the dictator and the wrongful client as "natural" phenomena, suggests that the Kantian position may be even weaker in this respect than the main argument asserts.

Kant's own views introduce the difficulty. In particular, Kant famously claimed that it is always wrong to use deception or coercion, even in order to combat evil, and that such methods are anyway unnecessary because the evildoer retains entire responsibility for all his actions, leaving no place for blaming the person who might have prevented these actions through coercion but declined to do so. This view, which is the precise opposite of

And although, unlike the utilitarian, the Kantian can (because she recognizes the separate importance of all moral creatures and relationships) avoid the mechanistic cog-like account of individual agency of which Williams accused utilitarianism, she cannot adequately recognize the degree of independence each moral agent may properly claim from all others. For both these reasons, the person whose practical reasoning follows, exclusively, the Kantian conception of second-personal impartial morality once again displays an insufficiently secure relationship to his own moral ideals and ambitions. He may not quite measure his ideals and agency as the weather measures the wind, but he does nevertheless suffer, "in the most literal sense, an attack on his integrity."[27]

---

the utilitarian idea that the good person should adjust herself infinitely flexibly to others as she finds them, pursues moral purity and preserves integrity. But it does so only by insisting that it is obvious that Jim should *never* kill and that lawyers should *never* lie or cheat, so that the protection for integrity comes at the expense of wildly implausible claims about impartial morality.

Korsgaard accepts this criticism of Kant. She argues that Kant's tendency to respond to wrong in others by withdrawing into moral purity and attributing all the blame to the initial wrongdoers represents a misplaced rigorism, and she tries, within the Kantian frame, to explore the possibility of abandoning ordinary moral scruples in order to combat evil. Korsgaard proposes an analog of the smaller world metaphor as a way of treating the evildoer as a force of nature placed outside of the primary arena of moral concern, and in this way attempts to open up a space for the moral entitlement to use coercion and deception against evil and a space for limited moral responsibility for failing to do so. But, this approach to the dilemma of dealing with wrong in others again goes too far (and for the reasons that the main text identified). By treating wrongdoers as natural phenomena that reside outside of the agent's moral world and force the agent to respond, Korsgaard again abandons the sense of the difference between the wrongdoers' plans and the agent's own, and the sense of the wrongdoer's independent responsibility, on which integrity depends. Efforts to accommodate utilitarian intuitions about the need to be flexible in the face of evil into the Kantian view seem inevitably to go all the way over to the utilitarian view, ignoring the side of the question on which Kant himself insisted and joining in utilitarianism's sacrifice of integrity.

These cases are so difficult because the dictator and the wrongful client have made compromising offers *and* left Jim and the lawyer free to decline; and this imposes responsibility on both the initial wrongdoers *and* the persons who react to them. Fully understanding such cases requires coming to grips with both elements of each description and balancing them against each other. Purely impartial morality, in either its utilitarian or Kantian instantiations, cannot achieve this balance because it denies one or the other of the poles across which the balance must be achieved. And efforts, like Korsgaard's, to moderate an impartialist view's extreme position inevitably swing all the way to the other extreme, so that they are unable to sustain the sense that an agent can be both responsible for adjusting her actions in response to wrongs that others have initiated and less responsible than those who initiate the wrongs. By contrast, the first-personal moral ideas toward which I am arguing make it possible to recognize both poles at once and thus render the required balancing effort possible.

Perhaps Jim can, in the shadow of the dictator's threat and offer, justify his killing either in utilitarian terms, as minimizing aggregate killings, or in Kantian terms, including to the one whom he would kill. And perhaps lawyers can, in the shadow of their clients' meritless claims, justify lying and cheating, either in utilitarian terms, as promoting justice overall, or in Kantian terms, including to those against whom they lie and cheat. But while it may be that, in the shadow of the wrongs that confront them, Jim and adversary advocates are impartially justified in killing or in lying and cheating, they are not simply *subsumed* in the shadow of these wrongs. Moreover, such impartial justifications cannot resolve, and must make room for, the separate question how far and how fully Jim and adversary advocates should enter into the shadows of the wrongs that they confront.[28] And this is necessarily a more intimate, more personal question, because it involves considering whether to retreat (for the moment) from their own benevolent ideals and instead to implicate themselves in the wrongful projects of others, at least in the sense of making one of these projects—killing the one, or lying and cheating in the service of meritless claims—into their own.

The dilemmas that Jim and lawyers face are not dissolved by impartial moral analysis because the problems of the intimacy of Jim's connection to the killing and of lawyers' connections to lying and cheating—the problems of authorship—that the dilemmas pose are not dissolved, or indeed even addressed, by impartial moral analysis in either its utilitarian or Kantian forms. Nor, on reflection, could they be. Impartial moral analysis necessarily proceeds from the points of view of others, and the Kantian innovation was to focus this moral inquiry not on the third-person-plural point of view of aggregate value, but rather on the independent, second-personal points of view of individual agents, taken one at a time. The problems of authorship and integrity that lie at the core of these dilemmas, on the other hand, are *first-personal*. They must be addressed not from the points of view of others, but from the point of view of the agent herself—that is from *Jim's point of view, and from the lawyer's*.

Chapter 6

INTEGRITY AND THE FIRST PERSON

LAWYERS' PROFESSIONAL obligations to lie and to cheat threaten their integrity. Moreover, impartialist moral arguments such as the adversary system excuse—which justify the lawyerly vices only indirectly and as necessarily evils rather than directly refuting that adversary advocates display them—cannot relieve this threat. Indeed such arguments entrench the attack on lawyers' integrity by increasing the pressure on lawyers to honor the professional obligations at its source. Accordingly, insofar as integrity is a substantial value, the ethical burdens associated with the lawyerly vices require independent attention, of a sort that the impartialist tradition in legal ethics cannot provide, before the legal profession may be rendered all-things-considered worthy of commitment.

This makes it natural for legal ethics to develop the unconventional themes toward which I have been gesturing and which I take up in earnest in Part III. The idea of integrity suggests that living an ethical life involves more than responding impartially to the claims of others, whether these arise in the third person (through the contributions they make to overall value) or in the second person (through the demands they make for individuated justification). Instead, persons also have a deep and distinctively ethical interest in living a life that can be seen, from the inside, as an appealing whole and, moreover, a whole that is authored by the person who lives it. Insofar as integrity is ethically important, therefore, a person who forms ambitions and plans—who undertakes to author her own moral life—thereby (in a way) creates ethical reasons for herself. As I have been saying, integrity, and the plans and ambitions through whose recognition and pursuit integrity arises, involve not third- or even second- but rather *first-personal* ethical ideals.*

---

* A more common usage, which refers to "agent-relative" and "agent-neutral" instead of to first-personal and impartial reasons, tends to obscure the important point that first-personal ideals have as much claim to be called ethical as impartial ideals, instead making it natural (although not required) to associate agent-relative with prudential reasons and to reserve ethics for agent-neutral reasons. This natural association diminishes agent-relative reasons and elevates agent-neutral reasons and therefore makes it difficult to credit that the former may sometimes outweigh the latter in all-things-considered practical deliberations. My slightly unusual usage is designed to counteract this tendency and to emphasize that first-personal ambitions may involve serving others and can be as ethical as

An Insubstantial Ideal?

But although the book's overall movement of thought hinges on the importance of integrity, I have not said anything formal to establish that integrity is a substantial ethical ideal or indeed that it is appealing at all. The argument has instead proceeded purely intuitively on this point, emphasizing the powerful sense that lawyers (and also Jim) face a genuine dilemma—that lawyers who lie and cheat (and Jim if he kills) should experience considerable distress, and indeed that a truly good person facing such a dilemma might not always lie and cheat (or kill) simply because doing so is impartially required. But although it is surely difficult to imagine that lawyers can take lightly their professional circumstances (just as it is difficult to imagine that Jim might lightly kill), to identify the burdens that lying and cheating involves is not yet to take their measure. In particular, it is not obvious that the burdens associated with lost integrity are *ethical*, rather than merely *emotional*. Indeed, it is tempting to doubt integrity's ethical appeal—to say that although integrity would be a nice thing in a perfect world, it should not be sought in our imperfect world, at least not when integrity comes at a cost to impartial morality.

The very examples through which I have introduced integrity contribute to this doubt about integrity's ethical *bona fides*. The adversary system excuse entails that (no matter how noble their motives) lawyers who refuse to lie or to cheat act *unjustly*—that they do not only disappoint their clients but also promote legally and morally incorrect outcomes. (Jim would act similarly unjustly in refusing to kill even if he refused in the name of a benign ambition.) This is a serious matter, and I have accepted from the beginning that when the injustice becomes great enough (or, as I put it in connection with Jim's case, when the numbers get big enough) then it seems self-indulgent for a person to insist on his integrity and refuse to do what impartialist morality requires. Moreover, it is unclear why the sense of self-indulgence depends on the extent of the injustice—even smaller injustices involve failing to satisfy obligations to others, after all.

Accordingly, a person who insists on his integrity at the cost of doing injustice, no matter how trivial, seems to display an unappealing interest in his own moral purity.[1] At the very least, he appears utopian, which is to say not quite morally serious. Insisting on integrity in Jim's case

---

impartial ideals. (Agape, after all, is a first-personal ideal, as are any number of traditional virtues.) This is appropriate for an argument that seeks to unseat the hegemony of impartial ethics.

seems to wish away evil rather than to confront it.*[2] And insisting on integrity in the case of lawyers seems childishly to cling to naïve ambitions that must be outgrown in order to function as mature participants in complex, professionally specialized societies. Integrity, it seems, is nothing much to vaunt of, being unsuited to moral life in the world as it actually is.

These suggestions express a more basic idea, namely of the ethical hegemony of impartiality. This idea acknowledges that personal moral ambitions may conflict with impartiality and that insisting on impartiality in the face of such conflicts may threaten integrity. But the hegemonic view of impartiality insists that personal moral ambitions, and the ideal of integrity that frames them, are categorically less substantial than impartial values, so that the conflicts must, in every case, be resolved in favor of impartiality. Alternatively, such a view may bring the hegemony of impartiality within the agent's personal ambitions, as it were, proposing that a good person will look to impartiality in constructing his personal ambitions, and will in particular make it his ambition always to comply with the demands of impartial morality. Integrity may, of course, be emotionally important; but it is not, on this view, an ethically substantial value, in the sense that considerations concerning integrity carry vanishingly little free-standing weight in all-things-considered practical deliberations. Rather than indulging integrity, as I propose to do, practical thought ought to overrule it.

I shall argue, against this view, that integrity is an ethically substantial ideal—that insisting on integrity is not self-indulgent or frivolous. The argument proposes that the first-personal ideals and ambitions that establish the architecture of integrity are essential to the ethical personalities of creatures like us. If first-personal ambitions are not respected, and sometimes even held to outweigh impartial morality in all-things-considered practical deliberations, this attacks the very features of persons to which impartial morality latches on (and in particular their individual agency). Integrity and its associated first-personal ambitions are therefore not optional for ethics—not optional from the point of view of the agent who insists on them and also not optional for ethical theory, either, which cannot go about placing demands on persons that attack the personality in whose name it arises.

---

* These thoughts bring to mind the arguments of David Hare's reforming politician, who wishes to abandon his party's ideological purity in favor of a pragmatic approach: "Doing good is easy. The world needs people who'll fight evil as well. Yes, and that's a much dirtier business, much harder, it needs more discipline, it needs much more skill . . . it means being serious."

Hegemonic Impartiality

The pathologies of hegemonic third-personal impartial ethics are already familiar from the initial treatment of the problem of integrity. The third-personal construction of impartial morality does not just occasionally oppose particular ambitions—as these ambitions come into conflict with the common good—but instead always opposes *every* personal ambition, and indeed runs roughshod over the *very idea* of a personal ambition. To see why, recall Herman's observation that even when utilitarianism allows a person to pursue a personal project, "the utilitarian agent must accept as the justifying reason for his action that it turned out to be the impartially preferred path."[3] Utilitarianism insists, in other words, that the agent "must not only be prepared to interrupt his projects when utility calls, but he must also pursue his projects without the sense that what makes them worth pursuing is connected to the fact that they are his."[4] Utilitarianism, once again, fails to "take seriously the distinction between persons,"[5] and not just in the familiar sense of denying that persons, as patients, are free-standing sources of individual demands on others, but also in a second sense. It also denies that persons, as agents, may possess individual projects that are peculiarly theirs and for which they bear special responsibility.

The practical personality of an agent who accepts the hegemony of the third-personal conception of impartial morality thus falls apart, so that the third-personal view quite literally deprives morality of its subjects and reduces persons to being morality's many objects. (Third-personal morality represents, in this respect, an abstract generalization of the view expressed by Arthur Koestler's old Communist Rubashov, that "honor is to be useful without fuss,"[6] which similarly deprives honor of any persons who might display it.) Accordingly, it is neither self-indulgent nor utopian to resist the hegemony of third-personal impartial morality, because it cannot be morally self-indulgent for a moral agent to insist that she is, simply, a moral agent, even if this comes at some cost to the common good. It cannot be self-indulgent because the alternative—which is to abandon any sense of her individual and distinctive moral personality—leaves morality with no one to whom to apply, and so renders morality itself obsolete.

The hegemonic claims of third-personal impartial morality should clearly be resisted. But the third-personal, as is by now familiar, is not the only available account of impartial morality. And the argument has therefore not yet justified resisting impartiality generally in the name of first-personal ethical ambitions. Even if it is not self-indulgent to insist on integrity in the face of the extravagant demands of third-personal impartiality, it may yet be self-indulgent to resist even the more modest demands made by impartiality's second-personal elaboration.

The case against a purely second-personal view of ethical life is much less secure, and the arguments by which I make it traverse rough and treacherous terrain, so that I will necessarily step more tentatively than before. They begin from the observation that even second-personal impartiality can override an agent's first-personal ambitions. Second-personal morality is famously no cakewalk: Kantians admit that it "does involve a requirement that one be prepared to set aside one's deepest projects if they require [impartially] impermissible actions."[7] Moreover, Kantians celebrate this feature of impartial morality. They insist that impartial morality should play a special role in practical life—that whereas all other ambitions must yield in the face of conflicts with impartial morality, "the attachment to morality," as Herman says, "*is* supposed to be unconditional."[8] Put slightly differently, "[t]he Kantian argument is that at the limit, where the conflict with morality is serious and unavoidable, morality must win."[9]

But Kantians also claim that the second-personal elaboration of impartiality is nevertheless more modest, in respect of first-personal ambitions, than the third. Impartiality, on the second-personal view, does not attack the very idea of a first-personal ambition, but instead functions only to set the limits within which first-personal ambitions may flourish.[10] Instead of insisting that impartiality must subsume all of an agent's projects, the second-personal approach to impartial morality merely subjects these projects to a kind of appellate review based on an impartial standard.[11] Accordingly, second-personal impartial ethics allows persons to pursue their projects and plans in many cases, including even for the reasons that these are their projects and plans, and cuts a person off from her ambitions only when these ambitions come into conflict with the requirements of second-personal impartial justification.

Kantians claim that this modesty makes second-personal impartiality consistent with integrity. They observe that not every constraint on first-personal ambitions undermines integrity and propose that the discrete (rather than pervasive and continuous) sacrifices of first-personal ambitions that second-personal impartial morality requires merely limit the expression of an individual moral personality whose underlying endurance the second-personal view recognizes and even values. Thus although Herman recognizes that, "[f]or morality to respect the conditions of character (one's integrity as a person), it must respect the agent's attachments to his projects in a way that permits his actions to be the expression of those attachments," she insists that it need not "honor *unconditional attachments*."[12]

Indeed, Kantians go even further and propose that because second-personal impartiality allows agents to retain and promote a broad range of first-personal projects and ambitions, respecting the commands of second-personal impartiality might *itself* become a first-personal ambi-tion, whose adoption *promotes* integrity—that "an attachment to impar-tial morality can itself be a project that gives a life meaning."[13] Kantian morality proposes, along these lines, to sustain in persons "an idea of the whole: a project whose point is to shape and limit other projects so that they are compatible with an ideal sense of how a person ought to live."[14] For the Kantian, second-personal impartial morality "can be (and is meant to be taken as) defining of a sense of self" so that "in hav-ing a moral character, a person will not have given up something in the way of integrity that standing aside from impartial morality would allow."[15] And accordingly, the Kantian concludes that although it might not be self-indulgent or utopian to resist the (complete) sacrifice of integ-rity that the totalizing demands of third-personal impartiality impose, it is self-indulgent to resist the more modest restrictions on first-personal ambitions that second-personal impartiality requires.*[16]

The Kantian development of second-personal impartial morality there-fore accepts that integrity is important and squarely poses the right ques-tion, namely what limits on first-personal ambitions, and what sacrifices of integrity, it is reasonable for impartiality to require. Moreover, the Kantian position is surely right to insist that no first-personal ambition may be held *unconditionally*, so that when impartial considerations be-come important enough, they override *every* first-personal ambition. As I have said from the beginning, as the numbers get larger, it eventually does become simply self-indulgent for Jim to insist on his personal ambi-tions to benevolence and to refuse to kill the one. But there is a large gap between the irresistible and indeed banal idea that every first-personal

---

*The idea that impartial morality can serve as an organizing whole for a person's first-personal ambitions brings to mind a more radical view about the relationship between impartiality and integrity, which is often associated with Kant himself. According to this view, making second-personal impartiality into a first-personal project is not only consis-tent with integrity but *required* for integrity, because only ambitions that are consistent with impartiality can be autonomous and authentic (because all ambitions that are incon-sistent with impartiality involve the heteronomous capitulations of the agent's will to ex-ternal causes). The burden of this approach, of course, is to draw the necessary connection between autonomy and integrity on the one hand, and impartiality on the other. Kant himself believed the connection to be extremely intimate—when he claimed that the For-mula of the Universal Law ("Act only on that maxim through which you can at the same time will that it should become a universal law.") and the Formula of the Kingdom of Ends ("So act as if you were through your maxims a law-making member of a kingdom of ends.") are alternative formulations of the single principle he called the Categorical Im-perative, Kant in effect claimed that autonomy is *equivalent* to impartiality. Modern Kan-tians who follow this approach find the connection less close—even Korsgaard, who takes a particularly demanding view, connects autonomy to impartiality only by reference to ad-ditional ideas about the nature of Enlightenment practical identity and the public charac-ter of reflection and deliberation.

ambition must be sometimes overridable, including by impartial considerations, on the one hand, and, on the other, the much stronger and less obviously appealing claim that impartiality should *itself* be the limiting principle of first-personal ambitions, so that the boundaries of integrity are *precisely* established by the delicate balance of second-order impartial moral reasons. And this is the claim that Kantians who promote the hegemonic reconstruction of second-personal impartial morality assert.

Integrity and Practical Reason

Although persons should of course be attuned to impartiality and make it an important consideration in their practical lives, an unconditional attachment to impartiality, even in the limiting sense associated with the second-personal approach, is not appropriate for creatures like us. As both the Jim example and the case of lawyers illustrate, second-personal impartial morality is too broad-reaching in its concerns and consequently too fluid in its requirements for narrow and imperfect creatures like us to take it hegemonically as our own. Indeed, *every* first-personal project will sometimes conflict with impartiality in a way that can place integrity under threat, which is why the problem of integrity cannot be resolved simply by making impartiality itself into a first-personal ambition.* Forming first-personal ambitions that sometimes outweigh impartial morality, all things considered, is therefore constitutive of the kinds of creatures that we are, and indeed of our capacity to engage morality (including impartial morality) at all. Put slightly differently, our interest in integrity is not just an ordinary ethical failing (like petty selfishness), which we would do better to suppress (insofar as we can). Instead, if we lacked this interest we would be not better but rather so different that the ethical ideals we find familiar (including the ideals associated with impartiality) would no longer properly apply to us in the familiar way.†

Sustaining this view of integrity requires an argument that takes up the basic structure of human practical reason. This is a demanding condition.

---

* It may be helpful, in this connection to draw a loose analogy between the problem of integrity in practical reason and the problem of consistency in theoretical reason. According to this analogy, people cannot save their integrity by abandoning all independent first-personal ideals and aiming simply to do that which is impartially best for much the same reasons for which they cannot avoid inconsistent beliefs by abandoning all particular beliefs and adopting only a generic belief in "the truth."

† Our interest in status perhaps serves as a useful analogy in this respect. We could not lose this interest without totally transforming ideals concerning nonsubordination that are central to ethical life as, being creatures concerned with status, we now know it.

In particular, it will not do to proceed in a merely psychological mode, in the sense of addressing only the emotional rather than the rational structure of our first-personal ambitions. A psychological argument may be suggestive. But it cannot sustain the idea, on which the independence of first-personal morality depends, that our interest in integrity is constitutive of our moral personality and not just a regrettable (and resistible) weakness.

Both the suggestiveness and the shortcomings of the psychological approach are illustrated by an effort Williams makes to enlist the psychological structure of first-personal ambitions in resisting the hegemony of impartialist morality. Williams observes that certain projects—Williams calls them *ground projects*—are so central to a person's ambitions overall that "the loss of all or most of [these] would remove meaning [from that person's life]"[17] and therefore leave him "unclear why [he] should go on at all."[18] These projects therefore set the limits of persons' engagements with morality in any form,*[19] and Williams proposes that the hegemonic claims of impartial morality should be rejected because they make no room for these limits—either because, on the third-personal model, they refuse to acknowledge the very idea of a personal ambition or because, even on the second-personal model, they refuse to accord an ambition's status as a ground project suitable weight in deliberations about how to proceed.†[20] It is, Williams thinks, "quite unreasonable for

* Note that whatever else they may be, ground projects are not mere symptoms of petulant self-absorption. Persons do not act in accordance with ground projects for the sake of having a reason to continue (just as persons do not act in accordance with their ambitions for the sake of preserving integrity). Instead, they act because of that which would make them have no reason to continue (which would make them lose their integrity) were they to act otherwise.

† If the hegemonic idea that only impartiality is unconditional means anything, it means that persons must abandon even their ground projects whenever these transgress the limits that impartiality establishes. (Here recall that although Korsgaard asks how the *innocents'* possible pacifism might affect the Kantian analysis of Jim's situation, she gives no consideration to the question of *Jim's* possible pacifism or how this might affect the analysis of what he should, all things considered, do.)

To be sure, an ambition's status as a ground project may increase the suffering that the person who holds it will experience if he is required to give it up, and this may lead the Kantian (and indeed even the utilitarian) to conclude that the person should not give it up. But this suggestion cannot explain why the person's suffering should not be thought to express morally unjustifiable attitudes and therefore viewed as the person's own fault. Moreover, the suggestion also fails to capture the concerns reflected in the argument about integrity. It treats the person whose ground project is under threat as a patient and asks how much he may fairly be required to suffer, so that the dilemmas faced by Jim and by lawyers become exercises in the limits of self-sacrifice. The argument about integrity, by contrast, approaches the problem from an altogether different angle, and is concerned with ground projects not in order to protect their authors' interests as patients, but rather to preserve their integrity as agents.

a man to give up, in the name of the impartial good ordering of the world of moral agents, something which is a condition of his having any interest in being around in that world at all."[21]

Moreover, adds Williams, it is equally unreasonable to expect persons to avoid this extremity by placing impartiality itself at the center of their first-personal ground projects, acquiring, as he puts it, the disposition to promote the conclusions of casuistical argument.[22] This suggestion, he says, is inconsistent with "the psychological form in which ethical considerations have to be embodied"[23] in practical deliberations, namely that they can be effective only if they are incorporated into an agent's *character*.* Williams insists that the problem of character imposes a bound on people's responsiveness to the conclusions of impartial moral argument, including even in the merely limiting role proposed by the second-personal reconstruction of impartiality. The ethical dispositions that make up a person's character display, Williams says, "resistance or (to change the metaphor) momentum" and this is one reason why "we can have, and we need, more than the one ethical disposition of asking the question 'what ought [impartially] to be done?' and abiding by the answers to it."[24]

Williams seeks, through these observations, to resist the hegemony of impartiality, including in its second-personal incarnation, because it is inconsistent with the psychological structure of our engagement with morality. But although Williams's argument has some intuitive appeal, it is ultimately let down by its psychological nature.[25] Williams's psychologism undermines his conclusion that it is *unreasonable* for impartial morality to take a hegemonic turn, or at least confines this conclusion to giving "unreasonable" a philosophically less interesting meaning than the circumstances require. Although Williams's argument might establish that persons have only a fragile moral resolve and only a limited moral flexibility, it does not establish that these limitations are anything more than ordinary moral weaknesses, like greed or cruelty, which should be suppressed insofar as possible, although they will inevitably resurface. And although it may be unreasonable, in the sense of being unrealistically optimistic, for morality to ignore that we are, in respect of our integrity, flawed creatures, it is surely not unreasonable, in the sense of ignoring a form of value, for morality to seek to correct and constrain our integrity insofar as this is possible and to lament that we are flawed insofar as it is not.

*This reference to character reprises the idea of integrity in a new context. Thus, when a person acts *in character* we say that her actions and her character are *integrated* or, for short, that she has integrity. And when a person is required by impartiality to betray her first-personal ideals and ambitions (as Jim and lawyers are required to do), we say not just that her integrity is forfeit but also, and relatedly, that she acts out of character.

To sustain the view that our interest in integrity, far from being self-indulgent or reflecting moral weakness, defeats the hegemonic ambitions of impartialist morality requires developing a *practical* and not just a psychological elaboration of the idea that integrity gives ethical ambitions an inertial force capable of overpowering the shifting demands of impartialist morality (including even in its second-personal development). To this end, I borrow some of the intuitions that Williams's argument pursued but reconstruct these intuitions using ideas from the theory of bounded rationality rather than from moral psychology. Our practical rationality is bounded in ways that make it reasonable for us sometimes to insist on our integrity and to pursue first-personal ambitions even when this is not impartially best and that make it unreasonable for us to accept an unconditional attachment to impartialist morality (including even in its second-personal manifestation).[26]

The most familiar sense in which persons are only boundedly rational is that they possess limited deliberative capacities. Persons are not "frictionless deliberators,"[27] as Michael Bratman says, but instead "have limited resources for use in attending to problems, deliberating about options, determining likely consequences, performing relevant calculations, and so on."[28] These limits render persons open to the values of repose. The outcomes of persons' practical deliberations—the intentions or plans that these deliberations generate—must "resist[] reconsideration,"[29] so that they have "a characteristic of *stability* or *inertia*,"[30] which is, Bratman proposes, "appropriate for guiding the education and development of agents like us over the long run."[31] If they did not, persons would revisit their intentions in response to new reasons (or even just a new appreciation of old reasons) even when the increased accuracy of the conclusions that the additional deliberation generated could not justify its deliberative costs. In the extreme case, which is never far off, persons would be made practically impotent—literally paralyzed—by endlessly revisionary deliberation, being bankrupted (as it were) by the costs that such deliberation involves. Given the costs of deliberation, "the partiality of [our] plans is," as Bratman says, essential to their usefulness to us."[32]

The inertia of intentions necessarily has effects on practical reasoning going forward—"prior intentions not up for reconsideration *constrain* further intentions"[33]—so that a boundedly rational person who appropriately does not reconsider one of her intentions may depart from what, in a sense, she has all-things-considered most reason to do. Indeed, insofar as the friction associated with deliberation about whether or not to reconsider an intention makes it reasonable for an agent to apply the same dispositions of nonreconsideration across many cases, it can be reasonable for the agent to fail to reconsider even when the improvement in the accuracy of her intentions that reconsideration would have produced exceeds the frictional costs that the reconsideration would have involved specifically in the case at hand.[34] Moreover, it can be unreasonable, even from a point of view outside the agent and not subject to the inertial constraints associated with the agent's intentions, to criticize the agent in such a case. The criticism is unreasonable insofar as (because of the friction that deliberation necessarily involves) the habits and dispositions of nonreconsideration that the agent applies are reasonable for the agent to have, because they tend, over the long run and given the costs of deliberation, to promote the effectiveness and accuracy of the agent's practical deliberations.[35]

This analysis of bounded rationality suggests a practical reconstruction of the architecture of first-personal morality that resists the hegemony of impartial morality while avoiding the psychologism that undermined Williams's account. Insofar as it is reasonable for an agent not to reconsider her intentions, it can be reasonable from the agent's own point of view sometimes to persist in pursuing her first-personal ambitions—which are simply grandiose and highly general intentions—even when, as circumstances have developed, these ambitions have become inconsistent with impartial morality. An agent who persists in this way is not giving in to her shortcomings or being self-indulgent but, to the contrary, managing her unavoidable limitations as best she can. Indeed, it is unreasonable for others to criticize such an agent even though they perceive, as she does not, that she is in a sense departing from what impartiality requires—unreasonable because such criticism ignores the costs of the friction that unavoidably accompanies the reconsideration necessary for her to track impartial morality more perfectly in the case at hand.

This friction (and the unreasonableness of ignoring it) will of course be greater if impartial morality is given a third- than if it is given a second-personal interpretation, because the maximizing conception of impartiality that the third-personal view elaborates is much more fickle in the face of changed circumstances than the limiting conception associated with the second-personal view. But even the second-personal approach to impartiality is sensitive to circumstance (as both the lawyer's case and Jim's illustrate), so that the deliberative costs of tracking even second-personal impartiality cannot be ignored and sometimes underwrite retaining first-personal ambitions that transgress the limits that second-personal impartiality would impose under conditions of perfect rationality.* Integrity, rather than being self-indulgent, is revealed by

---

*Once again, insofar as the friction associated with deliberations about whether to reconsider makes it reasonable to develop general habits of nonreconsideration, the failure

this argument to be an expression of the necessarily inertial character of the intentions of boundedly rational creatures.

But even as these observations explain why it is in many situations unreasonable for a person always to sacrifice her ambitions to the demands of impartial morality, and unreasonable for others to criticize her for not doing so, they do not quite apply to circumstances like the adversary advocate's (or Jim's). The resistance to impartial morality that the argument so far supports depends on the reasonableness of not even reconsidering the first-personal ambitions under whose banner this resistance arises. But the one fixed fact about situations like the lawyer's (and Jim's), the fact to which the argument has returned again and again, is that these situations involve moral dilemmas. The impartial principles and the first-personal ambitions at stake in these cases are both so weighty, and the tensions between them are so great, that any reasonable person in the lawyer's position (or in Jim's) will experience an almost irresistible impulse to deliberate intensively about what she should do.* Given the stakes on both sides, nonreconsideration of the lawyer's ambitions not to lie and cheat (or of Jim's ambition not to kill) is in these cases unreasonable. And so the account of integrity developed in the previous paragraphs does not, by its very nature, quite apply in the cases at hand.

Nevertheless, the form of this approach to integrity—the idea that the grounds of integrity lie in our imperfect rationality—is broader than the specific development that I have so far presented. And it is possible to adapt this argument to explain why it is unreasonable hegemonically to make impartial morality into the limiting condition of first-personal ambitions even in dilemmas in which reconsideration is clearly appropriate. The necessary adaptation proposes a practical reconstruction to the intuitions concerning the limits of human motivation that Williams gave a merely psychological expression.

The deliberative frictions that the argument so far has emphasized do not exhaust the ways in which our practical rationality is bounded. Instead, we remain boundedly rational even after our deliberations have been concluded. Even after we have determined what we have most reason to do, we must still *intend* to do what we have identified as best,

---

to reconsider can be reasonable even when the benefits of reconsideration exceed its costs in the case at hand.

*I do not claim that every conflict between impartial morality and first-personal ambitions necessarily involves a dilemma or that nonreconsideration of first-personal ambitions that come to conflict with impartial morality is always unreasonable. For example, someone whose first-personal ambition to kindness causes her habitually to tell white lies (many of which may also be impartially justified) may reasonably fail to reconsider this habit even in cases in which impartial morality condemns certain lies that she tells.

and even once we have formed an intention, we must furthermore *endeavor* to do as we have intended. We may therefore trip over the bounds of our rationality not just during deliberations but also in the subsequent stages of our practical engagements: even when we have concluded our deliberations and decided, we may fail to intend; and even when we have intended, we may fail to endeavor.[36] Both phenomena are familiar from ordinary experience: we know that we have most reason to make generous charitable donations and yet never even intend to give; we intend to diet and yet never seriously endeavor to lose weight, instead abandoning our intention when we pass the first bakery.

Moreover, just as our deliberations are costly, so the subsequent stages of our practical engagements, in which we intend to do as we have decided and endeavor to do as we have intended, are also not frictionless. In order to act as we have decided rather than giving in to contrary temptations that subsequently confront us, we must shepherd our practical energies so that they stand behind the course of action that we have decided upon, to produce intentions and endeavors that conform to our conclusions. This process of marshalling our inclinations—which I shall call, adopting a usage that is only slightly unusual, by the name *motivation*—is the structural analog to deliberation's marshalling of reasons. Motivation employs what Richard Holton has called *will-power*, that is the faculty that allows us actually to endeavor to do what we have concluded is best.[37]

Like deliberation, motivation is costly, and we must often struggle to motivate ourselves to remain true to the conclusions of our deliberations in the face of temptations to depart from them, even going so far as to engage others—trainers, for example, or inspirational leaders—to help us to sustain our will-power. Indeed, one of the costs of motivation is paid in will-power itself, which is diminished when it is redirected from one undertaking to another (especially when the alterations and reversals come too frequently or too suddenly for whatever natural process of replenishing will-power we possess to keep pace). This is again familiar from our practical experience of the world. Donors, for example, become fatigued when confronted with a succession of humanitarian crises, so that they give progressively less even as they acknowledge that they have more rather than less reason to give. Similarly, it is a commonplace that soldiers become progressively less careful to avoid risks as a war continues, even though they acknowledge that the new risks that they ignore are as serious as the risks that they once evaded. Indeed, we are all susceptible to fatalism, which is just the state in which, perhaps because of the friction associated with repeated motivational efforts and perhaps for some other reason, our will-power has been completely depleted, so that we feel quite simply no longer able to direct our own lives.

Moreover, these costs of motivation have also been demonstrated in the laboratory. Experimental subjects given the opportunity to donate money to anonymous others increase their giving less than proportionally as the number of others increases.[38] And other experiments directly demonstrate, as Holton puts it, "that will-power comes in limited amounts that can be used up,"[39] for example when its exercise to resist one petty temptation makes experimental subjects less likely to resist a second temptation than their fresher counterparts.[40] Indeed, Holton, in summarizing the experimental literature, goes so far as to suggest that will-power "works very much like a muscle" in that it "takes effort to employ" and "tires."[41] This is of course just a biological alternative to the economic metaphor that I have employed.*[42]

Even if deliberation itself were frictionless, we could not continually translate the revisions brought on by reconsideration into action, because incessant revision would increase the costs of motivation and eventually cause us to run out of the will-power that we would need to resist temptation and act as we had concluded. The economy of motivation therefore elaborates another source of inertia in the practical reason of boundedly rational persons—another way in which the intentions and endeavors of such persons constrain their future intentions and endeavors—which answers the costs of marshalling persons' inclinations (of motivating them) so that they intend and endeavor to do the acts that their deliberations recommend.[43] This inertia survives reconsideration and therefore applies even when reconsideration would otherwise appropriately trigger revisions in an agent's beliefs about what she has most reason to do.

Thus it is possible to say that even a person who has (following reconsideration) discovered that his old intentions and endeavors are flawed, perhaps because they are no longer impartially best, may yet reasonably decline to change his intentions and endeavors in light of his economy of motivation.† Moreover, it may be unreasonable, in light of the economy of motivation, for someone else to criticize the agent in

---

* Holton's biological metaphor has one more element, namely that will-power, like a muscle, can be trained to become stronger (or, as I would say, that investment can increase the supply of will-power and perhaps even make motivation more efficient). But however well-trained the will becomes, it always eventually tires when stressed (the supply of will-power is never inexhaustible and motivation is never free). And this is all that my central argument concerning integrity requires.

† Indeed an agent who reasonably concludes that the economy of motivation would preclude changing her intentions and endeavors in response to revised beliefs brought on by reconsideration can reasonably decline even to reconsider for this reason. She can conclude that reconsideration that would be worth its direct costs ceases to be worthwhile, all things considered.

such a case. This will happen insofar as the inertial force that the agent gives his intentions and endeavors even in the face of revisionary reconsideration tends, over the long run and in light of his economy of motivation, to support the agent not just in identifying but in actually doing what he has most reason to do—that is, to motivate the agent to intend to do that which he identifies he has reason to do and to endeavor to do that which he intends.*

Like reconsideration (changing one's mind), remotivation (changing one's intentions and endeavors) involves friction, and this friction makes it sometimes unreasonable to require an agent to shift her intentions and endeavors even when otherwise reasonable reconsideration would cause her to change her mind. Moreover, the practical effects of motivational friction will naturally grow as an intention and endeavor comes to occupy an increasingly central place in an agent's practical personality, and in particular as it matures into what I have been calling a first-personal ambition or project. Ambitions and projects, in their place in the economy of motivation and therefore also in their inertial properties, resemble what Jed Rubenfeld, writing in a similar vein, has called *commitments*. They are cases in which "the self permits itself to be *thrown* into its own engagements,"[44] making "investments and attachments . . . deliberatively and motivationally."[45] The physical metaphor is again helpful here, because, like Bratman's metaphor of friction, it emphasizes the energy that motivation requires and the possibility that changing course involves loss.

The motivational loss people experience after shifting away from basic and important ambitions is again familiar from ordinary experience, for example in the tendency (which people often described as being at loose ends) to drift aimlessly from temptation to temptation that commonly follows the breakup of a marriage, the abandonment of a career, or even the sacrifice that inevitably accompanies action in the face of a moral dilemma. Indeed, Williams's idea of a ground project, and his insistence that a person cannot effectively shift away from his ground project, may now be read (setting aside its narrowly psychological roots) as simply the most extreme case of the marshalling of inclination that motivation involves. A ground project arises when so much of a person's will-power is thrown into an ambition that shifting from the ambition

---

*Note that these arguments cast first-personal ambitions as more than just rules of thumb, which enable persons who apply them more nearly to conform to impartiality over the long run than persons who apply impartial morality directly. Rules of thumb have no inertia but instead give way entirely as soon as it is known that they do not apply to a particular case. But first-personal ambitions, especially because of the motivational element of bounded rationality, retain their inertia even in such circumstances.

to another would involve such friction that the person would have too little will-power left over reliably to pursue a new project, which is why he literally could not (at least for the moment, until the reservoir of will-power is replenished) carry on.

Finally, although first-personal ambitions, being path-dependent products of an agent's deliberative and motivational history, are in a way self-given,[46] they are neither fundamentally self-regarding nor purely private (in the sense of being absolutely inaccessible to persons other than the agent whose ambitions they are). After all, the reasonableness of first-personal ambitions (including in respect of their departures from impartial morality) may be judged by others as well as by those who have them, in both cases attending to the same ideas concerning the economies of deliberation and motivation. The idiosyncrasy of first-personal ambitions and the reasons that they generate comes, on my account, not from some fundamentally self-regarding or private domain of normativity but rather from the ways in which boundedly rational persons incorporate the public reasons to which they all have access into forms that can sustain actual practical engagements: the economies of deliberation and motivation that govern persons' practical lives require them to organize the public normative realm that they all share into personal (first-personal) ambitions, which are only imperfectly revisable, including in response to changes in the public norms out of which they were formed.[47] Instead of involving an unappealing (and perhaps incoherent)[48] inward-looking retreat from the idea that normativity is fundamentally public and impartial, concerns for integrity and first-personal morality reflect a clear-eyed appreciation of the limits, as well as the possibilities, for ethical action in persons who are only boundedly rational and therefore cannot always attend to impartial morality directly but must instead marshal moral reasons through their own deliberative and motivational processes, to produce ambitions that have free-standing influence over them and are distinctively theirs.[49]

If persons were perfectly rational—if they enjoyed frictionless deliberation, so that to consider was to conclude, and frictionless motivation, so that to conclude was to intend and to endeavor—then their integrity would not clash with impartial morality. They would have no need to throw themselves inertially into their ambitions or indeed to have any sense that these ambitions were distinctive to them, as opposed simply to tracking impartiality. In this case, morality would be a much simpler thing for persons: much of the skill involved in living morally would become unnecessary, and being fair-minded—which is to say, adopting the deliberative stance that proponents of impartiality champion— would be enough to secure living a good life. But persons are only boundedly rational, so that it is reasonable, in light of their economies of deliberation and motivation, for them to endow their ambitions with inertia and, moreover, unreasonable for others to criticize such inertia, including even in circumstances in which it causes persons' actions to depart from what impartiality would ideally require. In particular, it is unreasonable to insist that persons form the overriding ambition to conform to the demands of impartial morality, because these demands (even on the second-personal approach to impartiality) shift too capriciously for it to be efficient for persons to track them, either in their beliefs (given the economy of deliberation) or even (given the economy of motivation) in their intentions and endeavors.

The ideal of integrity is the natural consequence of these features of persons' practical rationality, stated in terms of the boundaries of their moral personalities. Integrity expresses, practically, and not just psychologically, the inertial qualities of persons' ambitions—the fact that persons can understand and engage the world most effectively in terms of beliefs and through intentions and endeavors that are distinctively theirs, both in the sense of being holdovers of their prior deliberations, intentions, and endeavors and also in the sense of themselves introducing an idiosyncratic path-dependency into their future practical lives. Far from being self-indulgent, the interest in integrity, and the related idea that first-personal ambitions might sometimes resist the hegemonic claims of impartial morality, reflects deep features of human nature—features that are intimately involved in the ways in which morality applies to human persons, *tout court*, from the practical stance to which such persons, given human nature, should aspire. One might say, simply, that persons, being boundedly rational, are *examples* only and not *representatives* of the moral point of view.

• • •

The argument is ready to return to specifically legal ethics, which, it is now clear, cannot limit itself to the impartialist adversary system excuse (no matter how refined). Instead, the professional life of the lawyer may be rendered worthy of commitment, if it is worthy of commitment at all, only through a first-personal legal ethics, which confronts head on and refutes the charge that lawyers necessarily display characteristic vices. Such a first-personal professional ethics proposes to replace the first-personal ambitions to honesty and fair play that good people ordinarily pursue with idiosyncratically lawyerly first-personal ambitions, which recast the professional conduct ordinary people consider lying and cheating as virtuous.

The raw materials out of which to achieve this transformation are already to hand—in the form of ideals of lawyerly fidelity and negative capability introduced at the end of Part I. Part III asks whether these raw materials may be refined into a successful first-personal legal ethics. The inquiry has three stages, asking: first, how idiosyncratic professional ambitions may be formally incorporated into a lawyer's first-personal ethics; second, whether fidelity and negative capability are substantively suited to supplanting the ordinary first-personal ethical ideals that generate the sense that lawyers are professionally vicious; and, third, whether lawyers might in practice gain access to and sustain such idiosyncratically professional first-personal ambitions as are in principle available to them. The first two questions may be answered to lawyers' ethical advantage, but the third involves complications that lawyers' professional ethics likely cannot overcome.

PART III

Comedy or Tragedy?

Chapter 7

INTEGRATION THROUGH ROLE

THE ADVERSARY system excuse that dominates academic debate in legal ethics today, in keeping with the broader tradition of impartialist moral thought to which it belongs, devotes no independent attention to charges that lawyers lie and cheat. Instead of refuting these charges directly, it merely excuses vices that it (implicitly) acknowledges lawyers display, citing the impartially justified division of moral labor that requires lawyers to display them. But this approach cannot satisfy lawyers, who naturally resist these charges and wish not just to excuse the lawyerly vices but rather to deny that they display them at all. Moreover, lawyers' natural resentment may be given a philosophically rigorous reconstruction, in terms of the idea of integrity. The adversary system excuse fails to sustain lawyers' integrity, and indeed contributes to placing lawyers' integrity under threat. Accordingly, a successful professional ethics for lawyers—one that renders the legal profession worthy of commitment— must look beyond the adversary system excuse and indeed beyond impartial morality more generally, to revive the first-personal themes in ethics toward which I have been proceeding.

An alternative tradition in legal ethics, largely developed by practicing lawyers and often stated informally (for example, in memoirs), begins to move in the right direction. This approach takes on the lawyerly vices directly, by means of an argument, involving the ethics of role, that departs radically from the impartialist tradition preferred by scholars. The role-based approach to legal ethics has received a skeptical, even scathing, reception in academic circles, where it has been cast as an effort to supplant impartial moral analysis entirely in favor of self-serving self-reference. But although such skepticism is sensible as far as it goes, it involves a fundamental misunderstanding of the possibilities of role-based ethical arguments. These arguments are most profitably deployed not to compete with but rather to support impartial moral analysis. Rather than seeking to supplant impartial morality, role-based argument proposes to protect the integrity of lawyers against the threat that charges of lawyerly vices continue to pose even when they can be impartially justified, for example by the adversary system excuse. This chapter elaborates the ethics of role and introduces its relation to lawyers' professional ethics. It sets the stage for the final phase of my larger argument, in which I assess, on their own terms, whether these role-based arguments can possibly succeed at preserving the modern adversary lawyer's integrity and thereby rendering the legal profession worthy of commitment, all things considered.

THE ETHICS OF ROLE

Practical lawyers often respond to moral criticism of their professional activities by pointing out that when lawyers act in their professional capacities they act not as ordinary people but instead as *occupants of a role* and by insisting that this fact is essential to evaluating the things that they do as lawyers.

In one not very interesting sense, this is what the adversary system defense has been saying all along. Lawyers perform functions (and are subject to regulations) which, given the moral division of labor, mean that they may do certain things ordinary people may not do (and also, of course, that they have certain duties other people do not have). The things lawyers may do when they act in role, the adversary system defense says, turn out to include being partisan and therefore also lying and cheating. But, critically, this conclusion of the adversary system defense is itself part of a larger impartial moral argument; it depends on the fact that everyone's rights are best protected when lawyers may do these things. Understood in this way, remarks about the lawyer's role are just a short-hand for ideas about the moral division of labor and the adversary system defense—they offer a plausible route into these arguments, but they do not do anything more. Most importantly, role-based arguments understood in this limited way do not provide any direct defense against the charges involving the lawyerly vices, which arise independently of the question of lawyers' partiality and therefore continue to threaten lawyers' integrity even after the charge of partiality has been defeated.

And indeed, those who engage the ethics of role, who point out that lawyers act not as people *simpliciter* but rather as the occupants of a distinctive social role, generally go on to make another rather more substantial claim. They add that the fact that lawyers are acting in role, instead of being merely a part of ordinary moral affairs, *insulates* them from certain forms of ordinary moral evaluation, so that their actions cannot be assessed by the standards of ordinary morality but only in terms of the principles and rules that make up the lawyer's role. At the root of this suggestion is the idea that because lawyers act in roles, the only accurate descriptions of what they are doing proceed in terms of these roles. Accordingly, the descriptions on which ordinary moral evaluations of the lawyers' actions depend are inadequate, and the moral evaluations in question do not apply. The lawyer simply has not done what ordinary morality seeks to evaluate him for doing, and what he has done cannot be described in terms that ordinary morality can evaluate.

This form of argument, which I shall call *role-based redescription*, has for centuries been employed by lawyers to defend their morally questionable actions. For example, David Luban reports the case of the eighteenth-century lawyer James Giffard, who sought to protect his client's illegitimate possession of an estate by commencing a fraudulent murder prosecution against the rightful owner. Although Giffard proposed to have the innocent owner falsely convicted and hanged, he refused to accept that he had done anything blameworthy. When Giffard was asked, "[d]id you not apprehend it to be a bad purpose to lay out money to compass the death of another man?," he answered, "I make a distinction between carrying on a prosecution and compassing the death of another man."[1] Giffard claimed that because he had acted in role, only role-based descriptions of his actions could possibly be accurate. In particular, the description that the *person* Giffard had sought to have a man killed was not accurate; the only accurate description being that the *lawyer* Giffard had carried out a prosecution. And the only evaluative question to ask about Giffard's action described in this way is whether he prosecuted well or badly, whether he was good or bad as a lawyer. On Giffard's view, the question whether he had acted morally well or morally badly in the ordinary sense simply does not apply.

Modern lawyers also defend their professional activities by precisely analogous, if somewhat less shocking, versions of this argument. When they are accused of lying and cheating, they insist that the criticism does not apply because they simply have not done the things the criticism describes. Instead, lawyers say, their actions must be described in the context of their roles, so that lawyers who make arguments that they do not themselves believe and lawyers who take advantage of unfair bargaining power should be evaluated according to the forensic and tactical standards of partisan advocacy. Furthermore, lawyers insist, these role-based descriptions are the only ones that accurately capture what it is that the lawyers are in fact doing. They argue that the role "lawyer" is logically prior to—one might say constitutive of—the things lawyers do.[2] And they claim, therefore, that there is simply no way to understand cross-examination, for example, except by reference to the adversary judicial process and the lawyer's role in it, including the requirement that she must seek to undermine the testimony of hostile witnesses even when they are telling the truth.

In particular, lawyers argue, such activities cannot be accurately understood in ordinary moral terms. Because moral descriptions do not begin from the lawyer's role, they cannot accurately capture actions that are possible only in terms of the role. Thus, lawyers who focus on the lawyer's role seem to suggest, the only evaluations one can sensibly apply to lawyers' role-based activities are lawyerly evaluations.[3] The ordinary moral criticisms that lawyers lie and cheat must therefore be misplaced.

It is clear at once that this version of the argument involves a very different conception of role from the one that appeared in the adversary system excuse. There, the lawyer's role was merely a placeholder, or stepping-stone, in an argument involving ordinary moral evaluation, a part of the moral division of labor. Here, the lawyer's role rests on its own bottom, as an independent evaluative scheme that competes with ordinary moral evaluation. This makes it important to ask how the competition between the two schemes should be decided. Can role-based redescription enable the lawyer successfully to resist ordinary moral ideas, in particular the ordinary moral idea that she displays the lawyerly vices?

The resolution of this question depends on how the lawyerly vices are understood. On the one hand, accusations that lawyers lie and cheat might be understood as merely further specifications of the impartial charge that lawyers are impermissibly biased in favor of their clients. In this case, no effort to resist such charges through role-based redescription can possibly succeed. On the other hand, these accusations might be understood, in the light of the earlier argument concerning integrity, as invoking independent moral ideals that survive the defeat of the charge of partiality and sound in first-personal morality. In this case, efforts at role-based redescription stand a chance of success. I consider each possibility in turn.

A Substitute for Impartial Morality

I have already indicated that academics writing about legal ethics generally emphasize impartial moral argument. They consequently approach the suggestion that lawyers lie and cheat not as making an independent moral claim but instead as elaborating the one important moral claim, namely that lawyers are unacceptably partial, by identifying prominent forms of lawyers' bias. (On this view, such charges function as a rhetorical shorthand—or perhaps a rhetorical thrust—developed in connection with the fundamental claim that lawyers promote their clients' interests more extensively than impartiality allows.) Accordingly, academics typically take a dim view of practical lawyers' attempts at role-based redescription, which they see as a self-serving and antiegalitarian effort to escape impartial morality by hiding behind what amounts, in the end, to no more than a club.[4] Unsurprisingly, the academics conclude that this effort cannot possibly succeed; they reject the very idea that a role could ever insulate its occupant from impartial moral evaluation, that impartial morality could ever be replaced by F. H. Bradley's ideal of "my station and its duties."[5]

One reason academic legal ethicists give for adopting this dismissive stance is that roles are themselves in need of impartial moral justification,[6] justification that cannot possibly proceed in terms of role-based concepts (which would be circular) but must instead be independent of the roles at issue, addressing people not as occupants of roles but as moral agents *simpliciter*. There are some roles, for example torturer, that no moral person may ever accept; and there are other roles that every moral person must renounce whenever they impose certain requirements on him, as a person must renounce being a soldier whenever this role requires that he commit a war crime. Thus it is always a sensible, and furthermore a moral, question to ask of someone whether she ought to be in her role—whether a role that requires her to act as she does is justified. And this question cannot be asked without describing what the role involves not just in the role's own terms but in terms of impartial morality. Lawyers cannot employ role-based redescription to avoid the charge of partiality because the very role on which such redescription is based is itself in need of impartial moral justification.

Furthermore, and in the present context also more importantly, role-based redescription's insistence that only role-based descriptions accurately capture what role-inhabitants are in fact doing is simply mistaken. It is a familiar observation that all actions may be described in many different terms and also that the answer to the question which of an action's many descriptions is accurate turns on the context in which the action is described. Thus, for example, when a young man asks a woman to marry him and gives her a gemstone ring, he may say he is demonstrating his love, a sociologist who is skeptical of marriage may say that he is marking her as his property, and a tax collector may say that he is transferring wealth. And indeed, the man may be doing all of these things—all three descriptions might be accurate and appropriate answers to certain forms of the question "what is the man doing?" The man will say that he is in fact demonstrating his love; the sociologist will say that the man's species of sexual love involves a possessory instinct; and the tax collector will say that, love or no love, the woman is richer than she was before. Furthermore, and this matters crucially, people who are interested in one of the three descriptions need not care that this description is rejected by people who are interested in another description (although they may of course care nevertheless). The fact that the young lover refuses to think of the ring in economic terms will not, for example, deter the tax collector from imposing her tax (although it might matter to the sociologist).[7]

A lawyer who wishes to employ role-based redescription to defeat the charge of partiality must, therefore, explain why people whose primary interest is in impartial moral evaluation should care about the fact that descriptions of the lawyer's actions that stand outside the lawyer's role and proceed in impartial moral terms cannot adequately comprehend these actions' lawyerliness. But impartial morality simply does not defer to role-based descriptions in this way—it does not care that its evaluations fail to do justice to the role-related elements of what lawyers do. This is because impartial morality forms a background that roles can never obscure or, as Williams puts it, because a role is something a person is, but never what he is.[8] Indeed, philosophers attacking role-based redescription have introduced the idea of the persistence of impartial morality in precisely this connection.[9] When impartial morality asks whether a lawyer impermissibly prefers her clients' interests over other people's by undermining a truthful but vulnerable opposition witness, it simply does not care whether these descriptions miss the fact that the lawyer is cross-examining. This term may indeed be central to describing accurately what the person is doing as a lawyer, but it does not matter to whether or not the person is (impartially) moral.

The central point behind all this, the reason for which lawyers cannot in the end escape the charge of partiality by hiding behind their role, has to do with the *audience* to which lawyers must address their defense against this charge. Role-based redescription cannot succeed as a defense against the charge that lawyers are impermissibly partial because this charge calls for a defense that is addressed to all people (in either the third- or second-person, depending on which account of impartiality is correct), because all people are entitled to the benefits of impartial treatment. But role-based redescription appeals to values and ideals that only role-inhabitants themselves recognize, to first-personal values and ideals, and those who do not recognize the values inherent in the lawyer's role will not find it any cost that impartial moral evaluation and the descriptions it involves ignore these values. Accordingly, lawyers must answer the charge that they are unacceptably partial—whether made nakedly or elaborated by reference to the lawyerly vices—in terms whose currency remains good even outside of the lawyer's role and can be converted into the universal language of impartial morality, for example, by means of the adversary system excuse.

These arguments demonstrate that academic legal ethicists are, in a sense, right to dismiss the impulse to defend lawyers' professional activities by means of role-based redescription. Efforts to use role-based redescription to defend against the charge that lawyers are impermissibly

partial, including efforts to defend against the charge of partiality articulated in terms of the lawyerly vices, cannot *possibly* succeed. The two
structural features of role-based redescription that I have just rehearsed
render it unsuited to impartial moral argument: first, roles are themselves in need of impartial justification, something internal-to-role arguments cannot provide; and, second, the concerns that impartial moral
argument addresses ensure that the descriptions it employs will persist,
regardless of their ability to capture the essence of social roles. In both
cases, role-based redescription's fundamental shortcoming involves a
mistake of audience. Insofar as the lawyerly vices are understood in
terms of impartial morality, lawyers must address them by means of arguments that appeal to everyone, including people who have no interest
in, or sympathy for, the lawyer's role. But this is a service that role-
based redescription, by its very nature, cannot ever perform.

A Complement for Impartial Morality

Although the ethics of role can never *displace* impartial morality, role-
based ideals may *complement* impartiality. Role-based arguments may
stand beside impartialist morality, to complete all-things-considered
practical deliberations. When practiced in this way, the ethics of role
often confirms impartiality's recommendations, and even when it departs from impartiality, it does so respectfully.

As long as the accusations that lawyers lie and cheat are understood
as surrogates or even synonyms for the charge of partiality, role-based
redescription cannot answer them. But, as I have been suggesting all
along, this is not the only sense in which these accusations may be understood; nor, I suspect, is it the only sense in which the lawyers against
whom the accusations are directed do understand them. Even after the
charge that lawyers are impermissibly partial has been defeated, perhaps
by the constellation of arguments that make up the adversary system
excuse, the accusations involving the lawyerly vices, now playing in the
register of *first-personal* morality, retain their sting. Understood in this
way, these accusations insist that even if the lawyer's professional activities are impartially justifiable, they involve a betrayal of the first-
personal ends and ideals—involving honesty and fair play—that good
people ordinarily make their own. Accordingly, even if it is impartially
justified or indeed required for lawyers to lie and to cheat—just as it
was impartially justified for Jim to kill an innocent—doing so involves a
betrayal that the good lawyer's integrity cannot, for now-familiar reasons, withstand. And insofar as role-based redescription plays in the
first person and aims to resist this movement of thought, the academic

attack on role-based redescription, although quite sensible as far as it goes, misses that argument's natural point.

Does role-based redescription succeed at this more limited, integrity-preserving task? Common experience, and also some of the ideas I have been developing here, suggest that it might. Certainly, role-based redescription is a familiar means by which people avoid first-personal moral criticisms in contexts other than the law. Prizefighters, for example, think of themselves as boxing rather than as assaulting their opponents; and executioners think of themselves as administering (executing) legal punishments rather than as slaughtering defenseless people. Of course, redescriptions like these will never evade the demands of third-personal impartial morality (the lesson that academic legal ethicists quite rightly insist on driving home[10]), but they are not necessarily meant to. Instead, *if* the practices in question can find their impartial justifications elsewhere (perhaps in a theory of voluntariness—boxing—or in a theory of just punishment—executions),* then role-based redescriptions, serving as complements rather than substitutes for impartial morality, can allow good people who inhabit these roles to preserve their integrity.

The effort to preserve integrity by means of role-based redescription proceeds in two stages.†[11] First, role occupants replace the first-personal ideals and ambitions that good people ordinarily have—ideals that their roles require them to betray—with new first-personal ideals and ambitions supported by their roles. Prizefighters, for example, replace ideals that condemn physical violence (especially hand-to-hand violence) with ideals that organize and distinguish among kinds of violence by reference to values such as courage, athletic grace, technical skill, and fair play;‡

---

* It goes without saying that these catch-phrases do not provide the required justifications, and indeed that none might be available.

† The description that follows makes plain that role-based redescription—which begins by acknowledging the tensions between role-obligations and ordinary moral ambitions—should not be confused with simple self-deception about first-personal morality. It is, to be sure, always possible to preserve the appearance of integrity simply by denying any tension between one's actions and ambitions. This technique may be common among lawyers, who can be shockingly, and even willfully, resistant to recognizing the weaknesses in their clients' claims and the ethical dilemmas that their work involves. For example, when corporate lawyers were asked about ethical dilemmas in their work, 75 percent reported that they had experienced none.

But this is not, of course, a serious form of moral argument. And the intensity with which lawyers, as I earlier observed, resent the charges that they lie and cheat suggests that these charges penetrate such self-deception.

‡ That these principles of boxing may be genuine ethical values, rather than merely excuses for brutality, may be seen from the fact that living up to them involves condemning violence outside the ring and even condemning certain forms of violence within the ring—for example, the blow below the belt. Indeed, boxers may find such forms of violence more abhorrent than do ordinary people, whose ethical responses in these areas are less finely developed.

and executioners replace ideals that condemn killing the defenseless with ideals of unflinching, dispassionate, and efficient service to the administration of justice.* And second, role-occupants redescribe certain of their actions through their roles, using terms that lead these actions to be judged (in the first person) through role-specific rather than generic first-personal moral ideals. Thus, prizefighters describe their punches as exhibitions of the sweet science rather than simply as battery; and executioners describe their killings as the administration of just punishment rather than as attacks on the defenseless.

The lawyer's effort at integrity-preserving role-based redescription, which in its proper form accepts that the lawyer's role must address the demands of impartial morality (perhaps by offering up a variant of the adversary system excuse), proceeds along structurally analogous lines. First, lawyers replace certain of the first-personal ideals and ambitions that good people ordinarily have (ideals and ambitions that are incompatible with the demands that impartial morality places on those who occupy the lawyer's role) with specifically lawyerly ideals and ambitions. And second, with these ideals and ambitions in place, lawyers recast their professional activities in terms of the lawyerly role-ethic and the lawyerly virtues this ethic describes. When it is employed in this respectful manner, role-based redescription allows role-occupants who recognize the demands of impartial morality to address these demands without having to betray their first-personal ambitions and sacrifice their integrity.[12]

This, as the last chapters have established, is no small service: the threat to integrity that impartial morality poses simply cannot be answered from within impartial argument (no matter how sophisticated that argument becomes), and integrity is neither self-indulgent nor superficial, but instead captures fundamental features of our practical engagement with the world. Indeed, one might even say that role-based redescription, insofar as it helps to square integrity with impartial morality, renders ethics as a whole suitable to imperfectly rational creatures like us. Roles are necessary to mediate between our cultural and social particularity on the one hand and our universal humanity on the other, not just in some vague way, but for the specific reason that we cannot sustain an integrated practical personality, especially in the face of the moral division of labor that a complex society demands, without resorting to role-based redescription.

---

*That these may be genuine ethical ideals, rather than merely excuses for slaughter, may be seen from the fact that living up to them involves condemning unofficial killings. Indeed, executioners may condemn some killings—for example, private revenge killings— on an unusually subtle moral register, finding them particularly unpalatable.

A New Hope for Lawyers?

The promise of the ethics of role makes it natural to ask when exactly role-based redescription can salvage the integrity of persons, including lawyers, whose circumstances place ordinary first-personal moral ambitions into conflict with impartial morality. Two conditions in particular must be satisfied in order for integrity-preserving role-based redescription to succeed. I take up each separately, and in earnest, in the next two chapters. In the remainder of this chapter, I briefly introduce the two conditions together, in order to provide a framework to organize the more careful and detailed arguments that follow.

The first condition involves the *substance* of the ethical ideals that a role can marshal in its defense. The first-personal ethical ambitions to which an agent turns to preserve her integrity must be appropriate and appealing, in the sense that their attraction, for the agent, can survive sustained critical attention. This does not require that the agent can convert everyone to her peculiar ambitions—which remain first-personal and therefore will hold an appeal for her that others do not share. But it does require, at the very least, that these first-personal ambitions may be employed, by the agent, to provide relief from the negative judgments that ordinary first-personal morality would apply to her circumstances, and also that they are internally consistent and connected to a recognizable vision of human flourishing. These ambitions must, to return to Williams's form of words, be capable of serving as "enabling devices"[13] for the lives of persons who adopt and pursue them, specifically by recasting the actions of these persons in terms that allow them enthusiastically, or at least comfortably, to claim authorship of their lives. Lawyers have grounds for optimism in this respect. Indeed, the ethical resources with which lawyers might give substance to their efforts at role-based redescription are already to hand, specifically in the ideal of lawyerly fidelity that I introduced at the end of chapter 3 and in the negative capability that lawyers display in service to this ideal.

Certainly these raw materials are well-suited to constructing distinctively lawyerly understandings of lying and cheating, under which lawyers' professional activities no longer embody these vices. Thus lawyers can connect the ordinary person's broad sense that deceit generally involves lying and that unfair manipulation generally involves cheating to all-things-considered substantive judgments and assertions of self (necessary for deciding what is deceptive and unfair) that are incompatible with the negatively capable self-effacement and plasticity of mind that lawyerly fidelity demands and that lawyers aspire to display.

Lawyers can elaborate, out of this observation, narrower lawyerly accounts of lying and cheating to replace the commoner constructions in their first-personal ethical ambitions. These narrower accounts exchange the conclusions about truth and fairness on which the ordinary person's judgments rely for ideas about possibility, procedure, and ambiguity that are more compatible with the negative capability at the root of lawyerly fidelity. Thus, the lawyer will say that when she presents an argument she does not personally believe she proceeds not as liar but as mouth-piece, which is consistent with her negatively capable commitment ac-curately to articulate what clients claim rather than to determine what she (privately) thinks is true. And the lawyer will say that when she pro-motes an outcome that she personally regards as unfair she proceeds not as cheater but champion, which is consistent with her negatively capable commitment to opening the processes of conflict resolution to all sides rather than determining which side should finally prevail. In these and related ways, lawyers can turn to their distinctive role ethic directly to defeat, at least in their own minds, the charges of professional vices that are leveled against them.*

Moreover, the ideal of fidelity is also well-suited to developing a distinc-tively lawyerly conception of *virtue* that lawyers' professional activities embody instead. Lawyerly fidelity is no makeshift construction, cobbled together out of sealing wax and string to put a brave face on a fundamen-tally dismal form of life. To the contrary, a return to the analogy to Keats's view of poets suggests that lawyerly fidelity is an essential virtue in any political order. "[L]ife and liveliness," Stuart Hampshire says, "within the soul and within society, consists in perpetual conflicts between rival im-pulses and ideals," so that a steward is required to "preside[] over the hostilities and find[] sufficient compromise to prevent madness in the soul, and civil war or war between peoples."[14] Poets, according to Keats, are keepers, guardians, and expositors of our inner sensibilities, of our spiri-tual relationship to the world around us, because their self-effacement

---

* Notice that the lawyerly versions of lying and cheating, even as they are in many ways narrower than their counterparts in ordinary morality, also impose obligations of truthful-ness and fair play on lawyers, some of which were discussed when fidelity and negative capability were introduced at the end of chapter 3.

Moreover, although the lawyerly conceptions of lying and cheating are generally less strict than their analogs in everyday morality, they do impose some constraints on lawyers that the ordinary morality of lying and cheating probably would not require. Thus it seems unlikely that ordinary persons who have been drafted unwittingly into the lies of others would feel obligated to correct these lies, as lawyers are often required to do. Simi-larly, a lawyer is more likely to be sensitive to the vices involved in suborning perjury and obstructing justice than an ordinary person and will regard conduct that falls under these headings as lying and cheating even when ordinary morality might not. (For example, the lawyerly reconstructions of lying and cheating are much less likely than ordinary morality to think it a justification for destroying damaging evidence against a person that the per-son is ultimately in the right.) As in the cases of boxers and executioners, these reflections help to establish the ethical bona fides of the lawyer's distinctive first-personal ambitions.

and tolerance of uncertainty allow them to speak on behalf of things in all their variousness, and not merely for themselves. And just as poetic negative capability preserves the intellectual imagination and promotes accommodation among inconsistent beliefs, so lawyerly negative capability preserves the practical imagination and promotes accommodation among incompatible interests. This makes lawyers into guardians of our outer sensibilities, and in particular of our political culture, because their fidelity enables them to state claims for clients who would otherwise be inarticulate and their procedural skills enable them to forge and sustain compromises that escape more judgmental ordinary people. In this way, lawyers administer the processes that legitimate (at least provisionally) resolutions to otherwise intractable political conflicts.[15]

The second condition for the success of integrity-preserving role-based redescription involves the *context* in which the resort to role arises. An agent cannot simply choose an integrity-preserving role-ethic but will instead typically require certain forms of cultural and institutional support in order to sustain her commitment to the idiosyncratic ambitions on which her integrity depends and resist backsliding into the more ordinary first-personal ambitions that place her integrity under threat. Few, if any, people can invent idiosyncratic first-personal ambitions out of whole cloth and support them standing alone, which is why I have emphasized the integrity-preserving properties not of redescription *simpliciter* but of *role*-based redescription.

The importance of this condition may be illustrated by returning to the Jim example to ask why integrity-preserving role-based redescription is not available to him. I have said that it would be grotesque for Jim to try to preserve his integrity by redescribing the act the dictator requires as "saving nineteen lives" or "cooperating with the innocents," or indeed to proceed under any description that ignores the conflict between the dictator's demands and Jim's own first-personal ethical ideals. But this claim, as it stands, is conclusory. To be sure, the argument of Part II shows that the demands of integrity cannot be satisfied by redescribing actions as generically "serving impartial morality," because that is not an ambition that can sustain the integrity of boundedly rational persons. But more particular (more local) redescriptions can sustain integrity in some cases (including in cases whose impartial bona fides may seem weaker than Jim's)—just think of the prizefighter who boxes rather than batters and the poker player who bluffs rather than lies. I have not said *why* analogous redescriptions cannot be persuasive for Jim.

Here it is necessary to proceed carefully, attending to the peculiar circumstances surrounding Jim's choice, including Jim's own ethical and in particular cultural circumstances. To be sure, insofar as Jim's first-personal ambitions are like ours, they do not *already* include any first-personal ethical ambitions in terms of which accepting the dictator's offer can be adequately redescribed. But beyond this, insofar as Jim's ethical culture is like ours, it also lacks the resources that Jim would need in order to *adapt* his first-personal ambitions in light of what impartiality now requires him to do. Jim finds himself in foreign circumstances, something Williams emphasized by making Jim literally a foreigner—a European tourist in South America. And just as Jim's body is ill-suited to protecting his health against local diseases, so his culture is ill-suited to protecting his integrity against local dilemmas. Jim belongs to a culture that has developed to suit the moral conditions of its own natural habitat (and that sustains his integrity in this habitat), not in the strange and distant place that has engendered the dilemma he now faces, in which the unsentimental logic of impartial morality (based on either a utilitarian calculus of human lives or a Kantian ideal of individual justification) requires him to kill.*

The ways in which these features of Jim's ethical ambitions and culture limit his access to integrity-preserving role-based redescription may be emphasized by contrasting Jim with someone whose ethical ambitions and culture are better adapted to the local ethical climate and who might be able to accept the dictator's offer, and do what impartial morality recommends, without sacrificing her integrity. Imagine, for example, that the dictator offers Jane the same choice he earlier offered Jim—that he brings twenty more innocents into the prison courtyard and tells Jane: "You kill one or I'll kill twenty." Furthermore, imagine that Jane (unbeknownst to the dictator) is not a stranger to the situation but is instead the leader of an organized and cohesive underground opposition to the dictator's rule. Although Jane despises killing innocents and aspires never to do so, her ethical circumstances do not place "never kill innocents" so centrally among her ethical projects. Instead, Jane's ambitions are much more hard-hearted than this, and favor the executory virtues. They include securing freedom for her people and overthrowing the dictator by whatever means are available (or at least by such means as do not sink to the dictator's level). And, more specifically, they include maintaining the ruthlessness and self-control needed for making difficult and unpleasant choices, including the choice to sacrifice innocents, in pursuit of these goals.

* Even if Jim refuses to kill the one, he will, of course, have a great deal to reproach himself for—specifically, nineteen unnecessary deaths—and so it is tempting to say that Jim's ambitions are so poorly suited to his circumstances that there is no way for him to escape the situation with his integrity intact. But to say that Jim cannot escape the situation without grounds for self-reproach falls short of saying that these grounds must always sound in a loss of integrity. Indeed, if Jim refuses to kill the one, the most natural thing to say about this decision will not be that he *sacrificed* his integrity but rather that he valued his integrity *too highly* (more highly than the impartial values that recommend that he kill).

Accordingly, Jane could accept the dictator's offer and kill the one and nevertheless develop an account of her actions that made them consistent with the most important of her first-personal ambitions and that did not require her to see herself as abandoning her own ideals in favor of the dictator's simply because impartial morality recommends it. Although she would, regrettably, be killing an innocent, Jane would also be pursuing political liberation with the courage and self-command she admires and aspires to display; and she could therefore recast the dead innocent as a casualty of a guerilla war to which she is committed, and recast her part in the killing as a battlefield decision that displayed the steely virtues of effective command. Although killing the one would represent a *defeat* for Jane because, against her ultimate purposes, another innocent had been killed, the killing would not represent a *betrayal* of Jane's first-personal ideals, and her integrity would remain intact.

Moreover, and critically, Jane has not simply invented the ambitions that would sustain her integrity in such a case out of whole cloth, or even chosen them in a single moment. Instead she has acquired them by inserting herself into a revolutionary culture of guerilla resistance and coming, over time, to take the methods and ambitions of this culture as her own. Jane's case therefore illustrates that role-based redescription involves not so much choice or simple assertion as education, complete with texts, teachers, fellow students, and even training and practice.

Indeed, the need for such cultural framing and support in order for role-based redescription effectively to preserve integrity is rendered more vivid by noting that when Jim and Jane face the dilemmas posed by peacetime political action, their positions with respect to integrity will likely be reversed. Jim, for example, finds no threat to his integrity when impartial morality requires acceding to the results of an election his side has lost. Being well-schooled in the democratic virtues, he does not view this defeat as a betrayal of the ideals that led him to vote for the losing side, but instead redescribes his acquiescence as part of pursuing another of his ideals, namely the self-possessed, calm, and steady practice of legitimate politics. But Jane will find these demands of impartiality enormously threatening to her integrity in such a case. Jane now confronts a circumstance—the mirror image of the one confronted by Jim— in which her cultural context lends no support to the course of action that impartiality requires of her, so that if she accepts her impartial obligations, and acknowledges the outcome of the election that she has lost, she betrays her commitment to executory effectiveness and sacrifices her integrity.*

---

* This, presumably, is one reason why just as successful democrats make poor freedom fighters, so successful revolutionaries famously find it difficult to adapt to peaceful politics.

Nor, finally, should the connection between cultural education and role-based redescription that arises for both Jim and Jane be surprising. Instead, it is just a concrete application of the abstract argument, made in Part II, that the first-personal ambitions of boundedly rational creatures necessarily possess an inertial quality. That argument entailed that persons whose first-personal ambitions are suited to preserving integrity while satisfying the demands of impartial morality in one political environment cannot *simply choose* new ambitions in order to preserve integrity while satisfying impartiality in a very different environment. Of course, the fact that first-personal ambitions have inertia does not make this inertia infinite or mean that it cannot be overcome—Jims do become Janes when dictators come to power (indeed, this is how resistance movements begin), and Janes do become Jims when their revolutions succeed (which is how democracies get going). The reflections concerning education and culture presented here identify the factors beyond simple choice that might make integrity-preserving role-based redescription a success.

These reflections are relevant to lawyers' circumstances. Certainly lawyers do not simply choose to replace ordinary first-personal moral ambitions with the ideals of fidelity and negative capability that might render their professional obligations consistent with their integrity. Instead, lawyers expose themselves to these ideals over time through systematic and rigorous professional education and practice. Moreover, unlike Jim, but like Jane, lawyers do not face the dilemmas of their professional circumstances alone. Instead, they may seek support, throughout the process of their role-education, from the legal profession, and in particular from the culture and institutions of the organized bar.[16] For both reasons, lawyers have grounds for hoping that they can satisfy the second, contextual, requirement of successful integrity-preserving role-based redescription also.

• • •

When confined to its proper context, as a complement rather than substitute for impartial moral argument, the ethics of role appealingly sustains the integrity of persons whose circumstances require conduct that betrays ordinary first-personal moral ambitions. Accordingly, a lawyerly role-ethic may be deployed as a friendly addition to the adversary system excuse, in a joint effort to render the legal profession all-things-considered worthy of commitment. Moreover, lawyers seem well placed to develop and embrace this type of role-morality. Their role contains raw material that may be fashioned into substantial and appealing ethical ideals; and the institutional structure of the legal profession offers a context to support lawyers who seek to embrace these ideals as their own.

But although these are hopeful suggestions, they remain suggestions only, and they cannot be properly evaluated without further theoretical and factual inquiry. With respect to substance, it remains to elaborate in detail an account of lawyerly fidelity that establishes fidelity as an essential political virtue and so redeems the initial promise suggested in the references to Keats and to Hampshire. And with respect to context, it remains to vindicate the hypothesis that the cultural and institutional structures of the legal profession can in fact sustain an idiosyncratic role ethics that insulates lawyers from the judgments of ordinary first-personal morality.

The next two chapters address each of these questions in turn and therefore complete the overall argument of the book. The answers that these chapters give provide more comfort to lawyers in connection with the first question than with the second. The book therefore ends on a bittersweet note, namely that although the lawyer's professional life is worthy of commitment in principle, contemporary lawyers lack the contextual support that they would need in order to sustain this commitment in practice.

Chapter 8

LAWYERLY FIDELITY AND POLITICAL LEGITIMACY

LAWYERS CAN successfully employ the ethics of role to preserve their integrity against the charges that they lie and cheat only, as I have said, if two conditions are met. First, the substantive content of the lawyer's role must support an appealing role-ethic that can rationalize the ways in which lawyers' professional morality departs from ordinary first-personal ethical ambitions (including, in particular, in respect of their professional obligations to lie and to cheat). And second, this role ethic (whatever it is) must be practically accessible to lawyers, who must be able to adopt the idiosyncratic ambitions it elaborates as their own and to sustain these ambitions against the insistent encroachments of ordinary first-personal ethics.

The next and final chapter of the book casts doubt over whether contemporary lawyers can meet the second condition, given the state of the bar today, and therefore doubts whether integrity-preserving role-based redescription is ultimately of much practical use to modern lawyers. This chapter, however, takes an initially more positive view of lawyers' ethics, arguing that there exists a powerfully appealing role-ethic for lawyers, which can more than carry the burden of meeting the first, substantive, condition for successful integrity-preserving role-based redescription. In principle, at least, the legal profession is morally worthy of commitment, all things considered. If legal ethics comes, finally, to an unhappy end, that is only because this is a commitment that modern lawyers, given the way things are with them, cannot bring themselves to make.

The centerpiece of the chapter is an effort to redeem the promise that I have earlier attributed to the lawyerly virtues—in particular to fidelity and its attendant negative capability—by setting these virtues in a political context. I seek, in this way, to demonstrate the importance and even grandeur of these virtues, by explaining just how it is that they allow lawyers to function as the political analogs of Keats's poets, presiding (as guardians of our outer sensibilities) over the inevitable conflicts that arise in complex, pluralist societies in a way that sustains political order and forestalls civil strife. More specifically, I place lawyerly fidelity and negative capability within a complex of ideas about political legitimacy and in particular about democracy (on whose contributions to political legitimacy the ethical appeal of the lawyerly virtues will ultimately be modeled). This approach has its costs, to be sure, in particular insofar as the emphasis distinctively on legitimacy will sometimes undermine (at least in respect of their first-personal ethics) the more traditional connection between lawyers and justice. Nevertheless, legitimacy remains a substantial value, so that if the argument that I propose succeeds, then lawyers may (at least in principle) comfortably and indeed proudly embrace a professional life that is integrated by the pursuit of lawyerly virtue. Fidelity and negative capability, which arose organically out of the interpretive engagement with professional detachment in chapter 3, will have found their place in the book's larger argument.

Before taking up the lawyerly virtues in earnest, however, it is important to return briefly to address the scope of their application and in this connection to repeat a familiar point and to add a new one. The partisanship associated with the lawyerly virtues is not, as I have said from the start, equally appropriate for all lawyers, but is instead better suited to lawyers in certain circumstances than in others. This is familiarly because the division of labor argument employed by the adversary system excuse does not apply to all circumstances in which lawyers work, so that partisan lawyering cannot always be impartially justified. (The degree of partisanship permissible in *ex parte* proceedings, for example, is narrowly cabined for precisely this reason.) Moreover, the connection between lawyerly fidelity and political legitimacy developed in this chapter underwrites an additional, first-personal argument for limiting partisanship, and the associated lawyerly virtues, to certain contexts. Insofar as fidelity derives its appeal from its contribution to political legitimacy, it ceases to be a virtue (even an idiosyncratic one) when displayed in circumstances in which political legitimacy is not needed, or even at issue.

This suggests, first, that the appeal of the lawyerly virtues will become stronger as lawyers' activities move nearer to addressing state-imposed resolutions of their clients' legal claims—because this is when the legitimacy of such resolutions is most insistently in need of a defense. Litigation, of course, represents the central example of such a case. But, as I have pointed out before, other activities, including even those at some distance from litigation, also implicate the authority of the state's mechanisms for applying law to resolve disputes. Settlement negotiations most obviously proceed in the shadow of litigated outcomes, as do many regulatory matters. And even when lawyers are engaged as counselors, before any specific dispute has been joined, clients arrange their affairs against the backdrop of what they believe the law will allow, so that even here the law's legitimacy is implicated.

Nevertheless, the shadow of litigation is not all-consuming, and fidelity is not a virtue in everything a lawyer does, for example, when a lawyer advises a client who has asked about the law's internal purposes. Nor, more importantly, is fidelity a virtue when lawyers assist clients to intervene in the political process whereby laws are made rather than in the legal process wherein they are applied.* Put crassly, insofar as the lawyerly virtues are connected to the authority of adjudication, lawyers who lobby on behalf of their clients cannot plausibly appeal to the same role-ethic as lawyers who litigate.

And second, and especially importantly in light of recent events, the lawyerly role ethic that I elaborate here does not apply in any natural way, and probably does not apply at all, to lawyers for the government. Once again, this is a consequence of the fact that the lawyerly virtues are appealing because of their contribution to the authority of adjudication. The government, after all, is not an ordinary disputant who confronts the authority of the state (through litigation or in some other way) but is, rather, itself *in authority*. Accordingly, an argument that bases the case for partisanship on the contribution loyal advocates make to legitimating the law in application does not extend to cases in which the law is applied to the government. Government lawyers, it seems to me, should more or less always seek positively capably to promote justice rather than negatively capably assisting the government in pursuing its idiosyncratic ends as effectively as it can.†[1]

These brief observations of course merely identify exceptions to the first-personal role-ethic that I develop for lawyers in general—they cannot hope to fix the boundaries between exceptional and more conventional forms of legal practice. I shall say no more about such matters here, however, because (in spite of their admitted importance) they should not distract attention from the ethical condition of lawyers whose practices fall within conventional forms.

POLITICAL LEGITIMACY

The fundamental problem of politics is that people come into conflict about how their collective affairs should be arranged. People have

---

* One might say, foreshadowing an analogy that I develop below, that lawyers who serve clients in the political process participate in the forms of legitimation associated with democracy rather than adjudication.

† This is recognized by the positive law in the narrow context of criminal prosecutions, on the ground, roughly, that the prosecution function is a special case of lawyering, made so in virtue of the special rights of criminal defendants. But if the argument that I propose is correct, then almost every form of lawyering on behalf of the government is a special case, and restrictions on the partisanship of government lawyers much more broadly are in order. This is implicitly recognized in the motto of the United States Department of Justice, that "the United States wins when justice is done."

incompatible interests, and insofar as they each pursue these narrow self-interests, this generates conflict. Moreover, although it is often thought that morality—and in particular the impartial idea that all people's interests are in some sense equally important—will eliminate or at least dampen political conflict, this is a mistake. Even people who all display an impartial regard for one another will continue to disagree about their collective affairs, and to come into conflict with one another, insofar as they have inconsistent beliefs about what their several interests consist in or about what balance among these competing interests is fair.[2] Secular humanists and religious fundamentalists, for example, may both care deeply about promoting the good life for everyone on equal terms. But they will disagree about the most basic features of the good life (including even about whether it may be found in this world or in the next[3]) and about the most basic structure of equality (including even about whether fairness requires concern for all or for only the faithful[4]). In this and myriad other analogous cases, morality, and in particular the impartial concern for others that thinking morally involves, does not promote harmony, but in fact itself presents an independent source of conflict, which is an *expression* of persons' moral commitments and not a *retreat* from them.

These conflicts are, moreover, ineliminable. They are inevitable expressions of the competition for scarce resources and the fact that the diversity of human experience and the complexity of human reason make pluralism the natural state of ethical life.[5] Collective life (and indeed peaceful coexistence) therefore requires people who are naturally free and independent, and capable of objecting and resisting against collective decisions, to accept and obey collective decisions even when they remain unpersuaded of the decisions' merits. Politics takes as its central task elaborating and marshalling reasons to obey.

The most obvious reasons for obeying collective decisions, in almost every case, arise in virtue of the collective's power to coerce compliance with its directives (including most familiarly by threatening, credibly, to punish those who disobey). But there are good grounds for hoping that other reasons for obeying collective decisions also exist, and indeed that these other reasons take the lead in persons' practical deliberations about whether or not to obey. To begin with, collective government that is experienced by the governed as coercive at every turn, or even just as principally coercive, will unlikely remain stable for long, because the opportunities for resistance tend to outstrip the means of coercion. Moreover, even if government could sustain stability through coercion alone, this would offend against the many and deep connections between individual freedom and human dignity. For both these reasons, government naturally (indeed almost universally) aspires not just to acquire the power to enforce collective decisions but also to generate voluntary compliance by sustaining an agreement about which decisions to obey, even in the face of disagreement about which decisions to adopt. Government aspires to achieve *political legitimacy*, which is to say to attain a distinctively political kind of authority over the governed.

Although some—philosophical anarchists[6]—have insisted that in spite of this natural aspiration, political legitimacy is impossible, so that government can never rise above brute coercion, the dominant traditions in political philosophy (especially in its liberal development) have resisted this despairing counsel and proposed routes by which governments might achieve legitimacy.* These proposals fall into two camps. The first approach, exemplified in the work of John Rawls,[7] articulates a free-standing conception of political (as opposed to moral) equality that claims to underwrite political legitimacy. According to this approach, political power is "proper and hence justifiable only when it is exercised in accordance with a constitution the essentials of which all citizens may reasonably be expected to endorse,"[8] specifically because it is "consistent with their freedom and equality."[9] Insofar as a government abides by this "liberal principle of legitimacy,"[10] which establishes the ground rules for political life, it may be justified to each citizen, from that citizen's own point of view, even in the face of intractable first-order disagreement about what political policies are best and even when government pursues (within these ground rules) particular policies that some citizens find unappealing. This approach to legitimacy places the understanding at the center of politics, proposing to achieve legitimacy by generating an agreement on abstract propositions about political essentials that may be sustained based on reason alone and entirely apart from any participatory engagement with the actual political process.†[11]

This theoretical approach to political legitimacy has been given powerful developments, including of course by Rawls himself. But these several theoretical elaborations of political legitimacy, indeed through their very appeal, emphasize a structural (and therefore ineliminable)

---

* Indeed, political philosophy might be thought of as the field devoted to resisting the anarchist, much as moral philosophy is the field devoted to resisting the egoist.

† Process plays a role in Rawls's theory, to be sure. In particular, the Original Position through which Rawls's theory of justice arises presents a case of what he calls pure procedural justice, in the sense that principles of justice adopted using the procedure of the Original Position are "correct or fair, whatever [they are], provided that the procedure has been properly followed." But the Original Position remains, as Rawls stresses, a "purely hypothetical" situation, and the appeal of the principles of justice that arise out of the Original Position depends on the theoretical appeal of the Original Position as a device for *representing* the problem of justice and not on any affective engagements that result from actually *inhabiting* it.

shortcoming of theoretical approaches to legitimacy.[12] Even as each theory of legitimacy purports (credibly) to regulate political power in ways
that fairly resolve disagreements among citizens about what first-order
ends power should serve, and therefore to justify power to every citizen
from her own point of view, the theories of legitimacy themselves remain inconsistent with one another. The several theories of political legitimacy propose incompatible answers to the question which uses of
power are in fact legitimate, so that as long as each retains adherents
(as it inevitably will) none succeeds at persuading all citizens to accept
the applications of power that it sanctions.

To be sure, a lack of unanimity does not in itself undermine the universalist aspirations of the theoretical approach to legitimacy: justification is a normative concept, after all, so that a theory of legitimacy
may *justify* political power to someone even though (perhaps because
of cognitive errors or self-dealing) she remains, as it happens, *unpersuaded.*[13] But, as the enduring liveliness of the field of political philosophy directly illustrates, the inevitable disagreement among theories of
political legitimacy is not disagreement *simpliciter* but rather *reasonable* disagreement: it does not reflect simple cognitive errors or failures
of respect or concern for other persons but (like moral disagreement)
instead arises inexorably out of the diversity of perspectives and experiences of free and equal participants in any shared political life.[14] And
even though brute disagreement does not necessarily undermine justification, reasonable disagreement does. The theoretical approach to legitimacy therefore cannot actually legitimate the exercise of political
power.

Perhaps for this reason, governments do not restrict their exertions
toward legitimacy to the theoretical model (although almost all governments do assert their legitimacy in theoretical terms) but instead apply
a second, practical approach to sustaining their legitimacy, which at
least complements the theoretical account of legitimacy and might even
harbor aspirations to substitute for the theoretical account. This approach is practical because it replaces the theoretical approach's emphasis on abstract propositions about justified political power with an
effort to elaborate a set of political institutions and practices through
which the participants in politics might come to take *ownership* of political outcomes, including even outcomes that they find substantively
unappealing and that their political participation sought to oppose.[15]
Whereas the theoretical approach seeks substantive principles of legitimacy that may be appreciated apart from any participation in political
practice, this practical approach emphasizes the affective consequences
of actual engagement with political practice—that is, the influence that

political participation aspires to have on the political attitudes of the participants.*¹⁶ One might say, as a short-hand, that the practical approach to legitimacy replaces the theoretical approach's emphasis on the understanding with an emphasis on the *will*.

Unlike theoretical principles of legitimacy, which attempt (and promise) principled resolutions to political disagreements that establish settled limits on the exercise of political power, the practical approach to legitimacy seeks to stave-off rather than to resolve political disagreements. The practical approach aspires to establish a provisional, although hopefully renewable, holding-pattern, in which disputants must actually go through the political process in order to accept the authority of the political outcomes that the process generates. Elaborating the practical account of legitimacy therefore requires identifying the political practices and institutions that sustain this holding-pattern and the individual ownership of political outcomes that it sustains in turn.

I shall argue that the adversary process, including in particular through the contributions of negatively capable adversary advocates who keep faith with their clients,† is central to the legitimacy of adjudication along the practical model. This argument has its limitations, of course. Most immediately, its practical character, and its focus on legitimacy, entail that the forms of adjudication that it describes will fall short of producing justice, especially when measured by the more exacting standards of theoretical models. This gap calls for a response: it may be (as I shall in various ways suggest, although never by sustained argument) that

---

* Substantive constraints on legitimate government also play a role in the practical approach to legitimacy, to be sure. Certain political practices, for example, policies that abuse some citizens, cannot sustain a sense of ownership among citizens generally simply in virtue of their substance, because those who are abused will experience the policies as alien and hostile, no matter how they were adopted. But this condition rejects a much narrower class of policies than the principles of justice associated with the theoretical approach. Instead of imposing a test of justice—for example, that political practice must be consistent with the idea that citizens are free and equal—the practical approach to legitimacy imposes only the test of critical theory. This is, roughly, that political practices must be capable of sustaining a sense of ownership even in the face of rational and critical reflection by citizens, employing whatever critical faculties they possess or can develop.

† Note that I am once again speaking of "adversary advocates" in the broad sense that I elaborated at the very start of the argument—that is, to refer not just to lawyers who conform to one or another positive code of legal ethics but rather to the general class of lawyers who work in the shadow of the structural division of labor between advocates and judges and who therefore come under some form of the professional obligations to lie and to cheat that this division of labor engenders. This means, once again, that legal systems that are commonly called inquisitorial may nevertheless include adversary advocates in my sense.

legitimacy is an independent value that sometimes outweighs justice, all things considered; or it may be that the gap between legitimacy and justice makes it proper for others to constrain lawyers who seek to pursue a legitimacy-based adversary role ethic.

But however these matters are best decided, they are in a way beside the present point: this, remember, is not to develop an impartialist defense of adversary advocacy, or even a defense that is independently sufficient, but rather to elaborate a set of ideals that can supplement impartial moral argument to help sustain the integrity of adversary advocates who do their impartial duty. And if I succeed in drawing a practical connection between adversary advocacy and the legitimacy of adjudication, this will give lawyerly fidelity and negative capability the ethical weight necessary for sustaining integrity-preserving role-based redescription, at least among lawyers who can adopt a role-ethic that involves these virtues as their own.

THE EXAMPLE OF DEMOCRACY

I take up the specific connection between adversary advocacy and the authority of adjudication in a moment. But before doing so, it will be useful to take a brief detour through democratic theory, both because democratic politics presents a more familiar illustration of the practical approach to legitimacy and because the example of democracy will serve as a template for identifying the contribution to legitimacy made by the adversary legal process.

Lived experience suggests that democracy is a substantial legitimating force in political life. Certainly, international law and politics treat democracy as a freestanding source of political legitimacy. The United Nations Universal Declaration of Human Rights, for example, does not just guarantee individual liberties and equal treatment before the law but also includes a right to democratic self-government.[17] Moreover, the freestanding authority of democratic politics may be discerned not just directly but also indirectly, through the experience of dissenters in democratic states who find that they cannot avoid personal responsibility for their governments' policies through dissent alone but only by taking more drastic steps to dissociate themselves from the governments, for example, by disobeying the policies (denying their authority) or renouncing their citizenship. The connection between democracy and political legitimacy is, one might say, a phenomenon in search of an explanation, and both main traditions of philosophical thought about political legitimacy have sought to provide one. A brief discussion of the drawbacks of theoretical accounts of democracy's contribution to political legitimacy and the advantages of practical accounts will lay the groundwork for a more intensive investigation of the contributions to political legitimacy made by the adversary legal process.[18]

Theoretical accounts explain democracy's legitimating character by reference to a special application of the broader ideals out of which they construct the general principles of political legitimacy that they champion, for example by casting democracy as the political branch of a more general ideal of equality. But although this approach is familiar, it is not adequate to the lived experience of democratic politics. In particular, the theoretical approach cannot credit the wide range of disagreements to which the authority of democratic practice—the legitimacy of democratic decision—extends.

The effort to connect democratic legitimacy to political equality appears in Rawls's early work, for example in the observation that "[p]erhaps the most obvious political inequality is the violation of the precept one person one vote."[19] But it is most fully developed by Ronald Dworkin, who elaborates an account of democracy expressly in response to the question, "How would a community based on equal concern [for all its members] choose its representative officials?"[20] Dworkin considers procedural answers to this question—which would equate democracy with the equal distribution of political power—but quickly and persuasively rejects these answers as unappealing or indeed incoherent.[21] Instead, he observes, the ideal of political equality leads inevitably to a broadly substantive conception of democracy that identifies democracy as the form of government "most likely to produce the substantive decisions and results that treat all members of the community with equal concern,"[22] or, put slightly differently, to "improve the accuracy" of political decisions, by making them more consistent with the demands of equality.[23]

This account of democracy places democratic decision making, in the intuitive sense associated with elections and majority rule, at the mercy of the substantive equality-principle out of which democracy derives, so that voting must give way to equality's demands whenever the two conflict. And Dworkin would indeed limit majoritarian decision to the narrow class of what he calls choice-sensitive issues, that is, issues "whose correct solution, as a matter of justice, depends essentially on the character and distribution of preferences within the political community."[24] Not many issues (and certainly not many politically vital issues) are choice-sensitive, so that this approach to democracy is far removed from the majoritarian and procedural elements that dominate everyday democratic understandings—so far removed that the idea that democracy arises when equality is applied to politics turns out not to generate a practice of democracy, in the ordinary sense, at all.*[25] Certainly this approach cannot explain the broadly legitimating force of democratic processes in ordinary political experience.

The theoretical approach to democratic legitimacy, by denying that democracy in its common procedural sense can legitimately resolve deep disagreements about political principles or even justice, converts the democratic process into a residual category, to be employed only in the narrow range of cases in which the liberal principle of equality produces indeterminate results. This approach, as Rawls admits, "submit[s] our conduct to democratic authority only to the extent necessary to share equitably in the inevitable imperfections of a constitutional system."[26] Democracy's broad contribution to political legitimacy must therefore be explained by other means. Indeed, what is needed is not an *abstract principle* but a *way of proceeding*, and the practical traditions of political legitimacy that I introduced earlier naturally suggest themselves.

These traditions explain democracy's contribution to political legitimacy in terms of the affective consequences of engagement with the democratic political process—that is, in terms of the influence that democratic politics aspires to have on the political attitudes of the persons who participate in it. Democracy functions, as Alexander Bickel said in elaborating a version of the practical view, "not merely as a sharer of power, but as a generator of consent."[27] This account of democracy is naturally suited to explaining the breadth of democracy's legitimating capacities in ordinary political experience. Because it accords the democratic process a free-standing political authority that does not depend on democracy's convergence on antecedent ideals—such as equality—the practical approach to democracy promises an expansive account of legitimate democratic decision, which may reach even cases in which democratic choices conflict with such ideals.[28]

The practical account of democracy proposes that the democratic process, properly constructed and managed, transforms citizens from isolated individuals into members of a democratic *sovereign*, with which they identify and whose will they take as their own even when they have been outvoted. It proposes that a well-functioning democratic process induces those who participate in it to take *ownership* of the collective choices that the process generates.[29] This proposal underwrites a practical theory of democratic political legitimacy because the sense of

---

* Nor are Dworkin's views idiosyncratic in this respect among philosophical liberals. Rawls's theory of justice similarly restricts the democratic process by imposing substantive requirements on policy concerning not just basic liberties but the distributions of all primary goods, including income and wealth, powers and opportunities, and even the social bases of self-respect.

individual ownership of collective decisions that the democratic process sustains gives these decisions the authority over individual citizens that political legitimacy requires. The practical view of democracy proceeds, one might say, in the spirit of Rousseau, defusing the problem of political legitimacy by proposing that democracy presents a political mechanism through which each person "uniting with all, nevertheless obeys only himself and remains as free as before."[30]

The great question for the practical approach to democratic legitimacy is just how an affective engagement with the democratic process sustains this sense of ownership even of outcomes that a person opposed. Rousseau's own view seems to have been that in properly functioning democratic systems, the democratic process simply *subsumes* citizens' political agency. Thus he claims that "[t]he citizen consents to all the laws, even to those passed against his will, and even to those that punish him when he dares to violate one of them."[31] And he adds, imagining a conflict between his private will and the democratic (general) will, that "[i]f [the] private will had prevailed, I would have done something other than what I wanted. It is then that I would not have been free."[32] This is at once implausible and sinister—it carries the deference to the collective that political legitimacy necessarily involves over into a denial of the individual self that cannot be had and should not be sought.

But the idea behind the practical approach should not be tarnished by Rousseau's excesses in developing it. Joint action has intrinsic and not just instrumental appeal for people, whose natural state is therefore not solitariness but rather engagement with others. And although politics is not the only way in which people can engage one another,[33] it is a properly prominent expression of the human instinct in favor of community. People therefore join in politics not merely to coordinate their conduct better to serve prepolitical ends but also (and perhaps even principally) to associate themselves with one another through collective action (to belong to a group), so that politics is an inner need for them, and not just a technological necessity.[34] This expresses itself most immediately through what Jeremy Waldron has called a "felt need . . . for a common framework or decision or course of action on some matter, even in the face of disagreement about what the framework, decision or action should be."[35] And democracy appears, at least in the shadow of the Enlightenment's rejection of the narrower forms of community associated with caste and class, as a natural way of satisfying this need.

The democratic politics that answers the need for community, and that generates a democratic sovereign whose decisions command the allegiance even of dissenters, must involve more than the aggregation of

antecedently held preferences associated with simple majoritarianism.*
Instead the democratic political process must generate engagements that
break through, that penetrate into, the preferences to be aggregated.

Most familiarly, democratic deliberation and the institutions that support it—in particular, for a for public debate such as a free press—
encourage political engagements among citizens once political debate
has been joined and underwrite forms of respect and loyalty that support the political legitimacy of outcomes even vis-à-vis those who have
lost the debate.[36] Democracies also encourage deliberation through political mechanisms—for example, the separation of powers in the United
States and proportional representation on the European continent—that
force coalition-building at various stages in the political process and
that therefore demand the forms of political debate and engagement
that are necessary for sustaining coalitions. And, finally, the formal and
informal structure of elections integrates ordinary citizens into the ap-
paratus of government in legitimacy-sustaining ways. "Voter," after all,
is a public office, and a citizen can be a voter, as opposed to a revolutionary who participates in an election because it suits her, only if she
acknowledges the legitimacy of the election's outcome, so that democracies that encourage their citizens to conceive of themselves as voters
therefore already sow the seeds of their own practical legitimacy. Similarly, the mass political parties that accompany democracy implicate
their members in the legitimacy of the political processes they seek to
influence. Political parties naturally evolve to pursue not raw power
(that is, the direct capacity to implement policy) but rather the intermediate end of political office, narrowly understood. And political offices,
being creatures of the wider political system in which they appear, can
be obtained only against the backdrop of the legitimacy of the procedures that this system employs for allocating them. (Revolutionaries
may implement policy when they overthrow a government, but they
cannot become senators.)† This once again encourages party members
to recast their political ambitions in forms that implicitly accept the

---

* Mere aggregation, even when it is fair, cannot sustain the authorship of its results on
which democratic political legitimacy depends. Certainly the most familiar forms of aggregation—lotteries, for example, or markets—do not do so. And voting separated from
the thicker forms of democratic engagement—public deliberation, political parties, a free
press—would fare no better.

† Thus, although it might be thought that political parties are important primarily because they connect parliamentarians to the masses (serving to keep ruling elites informed
of the wishes of the people), political parties' greater contribution to politics may be
rather to connect the masses to the parliament, in the sense of channeling political ambitions into forms that implicitly recognize government authority. This is probably especially
true in democracies, because although parties can exist under many political regimes, they
are most broadly appealing in democracies.

authority of the wider political system, including even the authority of competing parties when they win elections.[37]

These features of democratic elections penetrate individual citizens' political preferences in legitimacy-reinforcing ways even before what is ordinarily thought of as politics—that is, competition over whose preferences will dictate policy—has begun. And they therefore contribute to shaping the preferences of democratic citizens in ways that encourage the citizens to take authorship of democratic outcomes and acknowledge their legitimacy. The democratic process will not, of course, exercise an equally transformative power over the political attitudes of every citizen on every subject. The intensity of political interest, after all, will inevitably rise and fall from citizen to citizen, and no democratic process, no matter how intensive, will sustain maximal engagement from every citizen on all issues.

Such consumptive politics is not, however, necessary for legitimacy.*[38] After all, the demand for legitimation waxes and wanes with the political interests of the citizens over whom the state asserts its authority: As a citizen cares more or less about an issue she will be more or less inclined to resist her government's policies concerning the matter. Democracy, therefore, need not provide infinite, or even maximal, engagement and legitimation with respect to each citizen and every government policy. Political engagement may instead vary from citizen to citizen and, within each citizen, from issue to issue, so that citizens are drawn into the political process in proportion to their inclination to oppose or resist its outcomes, and democracy's transformative powers are concentrated where they are needed most. It is enough that the supply of legitimation be sufficient to meet the demands for legitimacy that citizens actually make.

Much more would have to be said, of course, to convert these rough reflections into a mature account of the practical legitimacy of democratic politics. The ways in which democratic institutions and political engagement penetrate citizens' preferences would have to be explained in greater detail. And it would be necessary to demonstrate that the feelings of authorship that democratic politics produces are justified (or at least that they can withstand rational reflection) and not mere ideology. (Here there is room for reintroducing some of the concerns that generated the theoretical treatment of legitimacy, although not in the expansive form that the theoretical treatment gives them.) But although these

---

* Nor, incidentally, is it desirable, all things considered. Legitimacy is not the only value, nor politics the only practical pursuit. And Rousseau's suggestions to the contrary notwithstanding, the society whose members spend the most time on politics is decidedly not the best.

are important topics, they can be set aside for now. What has been said so far is enough to establish a template for the account of the adversary system's contributions to political legitimacy that follows.

The Legitimacy of Adjudication

The example of democracy illustrates, in familiar circumstances, both the shortcomings of theoretical approaches to political legitimacy and the appeal of an alternative practical approach. Moreover, the legal process presents a problem of political legitimacy that runs parallel to the problem of the legitimacy of the political process, although at a different point in a society's overall structure of government. Finally the adversary system sustains the legitimacy of the legal process in much the same way as democracy sustains the legitimacy of the political process. The analogy to democracy therefore promises to generate a reconstruction of the adversary system excuse that can underwrite a rich and appealing political account of the distinctively lawyerly virtues.

Citizens may naturally object to their governments' authority at two places: first, when the government, most characteristically through legislation, decides disagreements about which general rules it should employ to structure how it will exercise its power; and, second, when the government, most characteristically through adjudication, decides disagreements about how to apply these general rules to particular facts in particular cases. The democratic process engages only the first of these, so that although democracy is a powerful legitimating force in politics, it cannot complete the legitimation of political power by itself. Nor does democracy in fact stand alone in the theories of political legitimacy in which it figures so prominently. Instead, political philosophy typically pairs the arguments about democratic legitimacy through which it explains the general authority of governments with arguments about the legitimacy of adjudication, typically proceeding under the heading "the rule of law," that sustain the authority of a government's specific applications of its powers to particular cases, including even over persons who continue to insist that the applications in question are unjust or otherwise unwarranted.*

It is, as Karl Llewellyn said, one of the "law-jobs" to sustain authoritative resolutions of "trouble cases"—cases in which general principles do not straightforwardly resolve themselves into consensus outcomes.[39] And

---

* This is the difference between adjudication proper (whose outcomes are imposed even on disputants who remain unpersuaded) and mere mediation (where decisions are enacted only if the disputants affirm them).

the process of adjudication, both directly and in the shadow that it casts over disputes that are resolved in more informal ways, establishes the context in which lawyers go to work. One might say, then, that what democracy is to political legitimacy at wholesale, adjudication is to political legitimacy at retail.*⁴⁰ And the professional habits of adversary advocates therefore gain in stature insofar as they contribute to the retail legitimation of political power that the legal process is called on to provide.

Accounts of the legitimacy of adjudication naturally proceed in parallel to the accounts of democratic legitimacy just discussed. Thus, the traditional elaboration of the adversary system excuse might, pursuing

---

* This idea, that even laws that have been adopted by legitimate political processes face a separate and independent challenge to their legitimacy when they are actually applied, is essential to the argument to come. It is also far from universally accepted. Thus it is often said that lawyers, especially in a democratic society, should respect the legitimate authority of the law, by which is meant the wholesale authority of lawmaking, and that this requires lawyers, in their work, to attend to and promote law's broader purposes (which are of course distinct from the lawyers' own moral ideals, including their views about what purposes it would be best for the law to have).

W. Bradley Wendel, for example, has recently argued that "lawyer[s] must respect the achievement represented by law: the final settlement of contested issues (both factual and normative) with a view toward enabling coordinated action in our highly complex, pluralistic society," and that this requires them to constrain their partisanship according to (their views of) the law's underlying purposes (even as it also entails that they may not constrain their partisanship according to their private moral beliefs, which would undermine the settlement that the law represents). And Robert Gordon has similarly suggested that the ethics of advocacy must be approached against the backdrop of a rebuttable "presumption that the law very imperfectly sets forth an approximately agreed-upon minimal framework of common purposes, a social contract."

I do not of course deny that in many cases disputes can be settled by applying general principles to particular cases in broadly accepted ways. Indeed, especially in close-knit communities, variations on this theme will likely be the dominant form of dispute resolution. But it is important not to ignore the difference between cases in which a law's meaning even in application is generally agreed upon and cases in which the meaning of a law is more contentious, so that its application, at least in some circumstances, meets with greater resistance. In the second type of case, the problem of the authority of law arises not just in respect of its adoption but also, and separately, in respect of its application.

Moreover, although such cases may be rare in close-knit and organic communities—and may even be confined to circumstances involving disputants whom well integrated people think of "as 'bad apples,' 'odd ducks,' or otherwise as people not aware of the natural working order"—they will be much more common in complex, pluralist societies in which the terms of the natural working order are themselves essentially contested. Legitimacy in application must be separately achieved in such cases, so that lawyers must also respect the free-standing authority of law in its retail application, in and around adjudication. And this, I shall argue, requires that they restrain, in some meaningful measure, not just their personal moral beliefs about what laws should be enacted but also their professional beliefs about the internal purposes of the laws that have been enacted. The retail legitimation of law requires, in short, that lawyers adopt client- rather than justice-centered conceptions of advocacy.

an analogy to the familiar theoretical claim that the democratic process is legitimate because it best serves antecedent ideals of equality, be redeployed to explain the legitimacy of adjudication. According to this approach, the balance between partisan lawyers that the adversary system establishes legitimates the retail application of political power insofar as it best serves antecedent ideals of truth and justice. But in spite of its initial appeal, this approach suffers shortcomings that are directly connected to its theoretical structure, as analogs of the familiar shortcomings of the theoretical account of democratic legitimacy. Thus it is natural to wonder, as I discussed in greater detail in chapter 4, just how much adversariness in lawyers *really* best serves truth and justice overall, especially given inequalities and imperfections that inevitably surround adversary adjudication in actual legal systems.

And as happened in the case of democracy, such considerations press inexorably toward turning adversary advocacy into a residual category, so that lawyers may act as partisans only (in the words of a prominent reformer) insofar as doing so, "considering the relevant circumstances of the particular case, seem[s] likely to promote justice," meaning resolution on the "legal merits," to be established by reference to the broader ideals of truth and justice from which the theoretical argument sets forth.[41] Indeed, just as the theoretical approach to democracy reaches its apogee in Dworkin's view that the ordinary democratic process should be confined to deciding questions in which majority rule is *constitutive* of equality, so the theoretical approach to adjudication proposes that adversary advocacy reaches its highest expression when lawyers "think like judges in determining what the relevant law is"[42] and, moreover, act like judges (and avoid ordinarily adversary advocacy) except in cases in which adversary advocacy is anyway ineffective, because there exist real judges who are capable of effectively imposing this judicial sensibility largely uninfluenced by lawyers' adversary efforts.[43] The theoretical approach to the legitimacy of adjudication therefore does not support, but rather undermines, the lawyerly virtues of fidelity and negative capability, which require partisanship well beyond what the theoretical argument countenances and certainly require lawyers to think and to act very differently from judges and to impose outcomes that reflect these differences.

Nevertheless, the folk practice of adversary adjudication, and the common experience of parties who subject their disputes to this practice, attributes legitimacy to adversary adjudication even when lawyers display partisan fidelity to their clients that substantially exceeds what the theoretical approach to legitimacy countenances.*[44] Moreover, a

---

* To be sure, dissatisfaction with adversary adjudication, especially among those who have just gone through it, is one of the banalities of contemporary legal culture. But the

practical account of the legitimacy of adversary adjudication, which closely parallels the practical account of democratic legitimacy, naturally presents itself.

The theoretical approach fails to take advantage of the legitimating powers of affective engagement with the legal process (just as the theoretical account of democracy fails to exploit the legitimating powers of affective engagement with the democratic process). In particular, the theoretical version of the adversary system excuse approaches the legal process as a technology for satisfying process-independent claims (just as the theoretical approach to democracy treats the democratic process as a technology for producing process-independent justice). The theoretical approach treats process, to borrow a word from legal sociology, as *transparent*, in the sense that it has "no effect on the values, goals, and desires of those who use the system,"[45] so that one can look backwards through a legal process, from its end to its beginning, and see the same claims asserted throughout, in undistorted form. But this is, as sociology points out, a mistaken account of legal process, associated with the formalism of classical jurisprudence and now discredited. Instead, "the relationship between objectives [in a dispute] and mechanisms [of dispute resolution] is reciprocal; not only do objectives influence the choice of mechanisms, but mechanisms chosen may alter objectives."[46] And this fact about the legal process opens up the way to a practical reconstruction of the legitimacy of adjudication, which (again analogizing to the practical account of democracy) emphasizes the affective consequences of engagement with the legal process—the transformations wrought by the process.

Finally, this practical account places lawyerly fidelity and negative capability at the center of the transformative power of the legal process and therefore at the foundation of its legitimacy. And in this way, the practical account of the legitimacy of adjudication gives these lawyerly virtues the ethical weight that they need to underwrite integrity-preserving, role-based redescription applied to the adversary practices in which they actually engage.

---

acceptance of adjudication's legitimate authority in spite of this dissatisfaction is equally entrenched in the culture. Disputants commonly satisfy verdicts without the need for separate enforcement proceedings (and often with little credible threat of sanctions should they resist). Even when voluntary compliance with adjudication breaks down—as, for example, in connection with the collection of child support from absentee fathers, although even here there is some reason to believe that delinquency is caused by inability rather than unwillingness to make payments—the success of resistance against judgments only emphasizes the extent to which compliance with the legal process more generally exceeds whatever compulsion legal institutions could credibly assert. And although the dissatisfaction is more discussed, the degree of acceptance of the legitimacy of adjudication is *much* more striking, as it requires losing disputants to accept the authority of decisions that they (reasonably) believe mistaken on the merits.

The Transformative Legal Process

The legal process does not achieve legitimacy by reaching settlements that satisfy the aims that the participants bring to the process, nor even by employing detached and purely theoretical arguments to persuade the participants that its outcomes are just or otherwise desirable. Instead, like democracy, the legal process legitimates the application of political power through the participatory engagements that it requires of the parties to legal disputes. These engagements penetrate the ideals and preferences of the parties in ways in which nonparticipants cannot share, so that the parties come, through their engagements with the legal process, to take ownership of the resolutions that the process produces, including even resolutions that they continue to dispute on the merits.

As the sociology of law observes, the legal process and the activities of the lawyers who administer it penetrate the attitudes of the disputants at several depths and therefore transform their attitudes in several different ways. Most shallowly the legal process "translates [disputants' private complaints], and reconstitutes the issues in terms of a legal discourse which has trans-situational applicability."[47] Lawyers "objectify" their clients' arguments and "set them apart from the particular interests they represent,"[48] so that the clients' positions come to be seen as participating in broader principles "in terms of which . . . binding solutions [to disputes] can be found."[49] In this way, the lawyers who administer the legal process serve as "culture broker[s]" for their clients,[50] organizing and transforming their clients' claims in terms of this discourse in order to render them more persuasive.[51] At an intermediate depth, lawyers and the legal process "test the reality of the[ir] clien[ts'] perspective[s],"[52] piercing unreasonable hopes and inaccurate perceptions[53] and, by contrast, legitimating the other elements of their clients' positions that are not pierced.[54] And at the deepest level, an engagement with the legal process does not just translate or test disputants' claims but fundamentally reconstitutes them,*[55] specifically by transforming brute demands

---

*Sociologists typically suppose that the legal process reconstitutes claims principally by "narrow[ing] . . . disputes . . . in order to produce a construction of events that appears manageable." Thus it is common to read that the process "transform[s] a putatively moral issue, which has strong substantive tones, into a technical-legal issue." Similarly, it is said that adjudication replaces "highly personal and idiosyncratic" perceptions with a blinkered emphasis on what can be proved objectively to have occurred.

But this narrowing is far from inevitable in the legal process, which can also broaden and contextualize disputes in an effort to find authoritative resolutions. An example of this broadening tendency, discussed in greater detail below, is the legal process's transformation of the individual injury associated with sexual harassment into a broader claim concerning sex discrimination at work.

into assertions of right, which depend on reasons and therefore by their
nature implicitly recognize the conditions of their own failure (namely
that the reasons do not support the claims in the case at hand).[56] Indeed,
the legal process can sometimes even induce disputants to recognize a
still deeper contingency in their demands, as they come to see a "problem as an adjustment between competing claims and interests, rather
than as one warranting a fight for principle."[57]

These transformations, taken collectively, can have real staying power.
When it is successful, the legal process, to borrow Lon Fuller's form of
words, has the "capacity to reorient the parties toward each other, not
by imposing rules on them, but by helping them to achieve a new and
shared perception of their relationship, a perception that will redirect
their attitudes and dispositions toward one another."[58] Indeed, the transformative effect on a dispute of the legal process is potentially so powerful that "the transformed dispute can actually become *the* dispute,"[59] so
that the parties abandon any of their demands that cannot be accommo-
dated within the transformation. When this happens, the legitimacy of
the legal process follows, because the reconstructed disputes and the resolutions that the legal process proposes have been tailored to suit each
other, so that parties who come (through their affective engagements
with the legal process) to see their disputes as the legal process proposes
also come to accept the resolutions that the legal process recommends.

These suggestions concerning adjudication's power to legitimate
through transformation find support, moreover, in empirical work on
procedural justice (although the empirical studies do not address the
precise mechanisms of transformation that I have proposed).*[60] Thus
there exists substantial evidence that people's compliance with the law,
as it is applied to them, depends significantly on their judgments concerning the legitimacy of the authorities who apply it,[61] and that judgments concerning legitimacy, in turn, depend on judgments concerning
the procedures that the authorities employ in determining what the law
requires, and especially in resolving disputes about this.[62] Furthermore,
people's judgments concerning procedures are practical and affective
rather than theoretical and detached: when people make such judgments, "they focus more on their opportunities to state their case than
they do on their influence" in producing decisions that they regard as
accurate.[63] Finally, although people do not require direct influence, they
do insist that their opportunities to be heard are genuinely participatory
rather than merely formal: "providing structural opportunities [for dis-
putants] to speak is not enough [to promote the legitimacy of a process

---

* These studies do, however, suggest that the importance of process for legitimacy is not
confined to trivial disputes but instead increases when the stakes are high.

of dispute resolution]";[64] instead disputants "must also infer that what they say is being considered by the decision-maker."[65] Of course, insofar as processes of adjudication possess a formal or technical character that makes a tribunal's willingness and indeed capacity seriously to consider disputants' views depend on their receiving a particular and (literally) extraordinary expression, lawyers (as specialists in this form of expression) will play a central role in adjudication's legitimacy, which the argument will in a moment take up in earnest.

One might say, by way of summary (and using words that would be conclusory but for what has come before), that someone who engages the legal process to resolve a dispute but denies its legitimacy when her claims fail on their legal merits commits bad faith against her opponent and against the legal process itself—she in fact retains unreconstructed and perhaps even unreasonable brute demands even as she purports to be asserting reconstructed, reasonable, claims of right. And she therefore escalates the dispute from a simple disagreement into a case of deception and manipulation—one might even say fraud. Disputants (who believe, after all, that they are in the right) naturally shrink back from such an escalation, and the legal process leverages this attitude—the natural good faith of disputants—in support of the legitimacy of its outcomes, including outcomes that disputants initially opposed.

Legitimacy and Justice

This account follows in a long tradition that emphasizes the legal process's contribution to political cohesion. It is as old, at least, as Tocqueville's impressed assessment of the lawyerliness of Americans, who, even in "their daily controversies," tend to "borrow . . . the ideas and even the language peculiar to judicial proceedings."[66] But the account is not yet complete, because stability is not the only value and even peace is not worth every price, so that the transformative effects of the legal process remain in need of justification. Indeed, the dominant view among those who emphasize the transformative character of the legal process also criticizes adjudication in this respect. According to this view, the transformations that the legal process induces in disputants' attitudes, and therefore resolutions to disputes that depend on these transformations, cannot be justified in a principled way. The legal process, on this view, is merely a tool of ideology—a way of manipulating litigants to get them to accept being cheated.

This happens most dramatically when lawyers persuade their clients simply to abandon claims or defenses that are justified, as when public defenders "cool out" criminal defendants and get them to accept punishments that they do not deserve,[67] or when lawyers "manipulate[] and fool[]"[68] consumer-clients about their rights under consumer protection laws and in this way "lead the client[s] to redefine the situation so that [they] can accept it."[69] It also happens, although more subtly, when the transformations wrought by the legal process deprive even claims that survive of their principled content, for example, when engagement with the legal process that administers worker's compensation in the face of industrial accidents, "convince[s] workers to rely on employer paternalism to ensure their safety and relinquish claims to control the workplace."[70]

In these ways, and in myriad others, lawyers and the legal process support transformations in disputes that "create ends so that clients come to want—or at least accept—what the system is prepared to deliver."[71] Most generally, the "social construction of the self through ideology and language" that the transformative legal process involves, causes "depoliticization, apathy, anomie"[72] and so "suppresses the full potential of the self."[73] The legal process, to put it bluntly, secures peace only by abandoning justice.

There is much in this view, to be sure, and the peaceful resolutions to disputes that the transformative legal process sustains certainly can come at an unacceptable cost to justice, including perhaps in some of the cases just mentioned. But this argument should not be taken too far. To begin with, the empirical question how commonly lawyers betray their clients in the ways suggested is complex and difficult. Although some lawyers undoubtedly sometimes do sacrifice their clients in the service of order or even other powerful interests, there is evidence that lawyers overall represent their clients more assertively than critics suggest, not least because clients are less easily fooled by their lawyers than critics suppose.[74]

Moreover, and in a sense more importantly, the view that lawyers improperly "sell-out" their clients makes a theoretical mistake about the normative structure of legitimacy. In particular, it is wrong to conclude that every time engagement with the legal process induces disputants to accept outcomes that are less than perfectly just this should be resisted, or that disputants who accept less than just outcomes are being exploited or made victims of an ideological sham. Such an extreme conclusion neglects the *political* character of legitimacy and the *practical* character of the legitimation that the adversary process sustains, which together entail that legitimacy necessarily stands apart from moral values, including even justice and its cognates, and can sometimes outweigh them, all things considered. The analogy to the democratic process is again apt: as the practical conception of democracy entails that some political outcomes can be legitimate even though they are not perfectly just, so the practical conception of adjudication entails that some legal outcomes can be legitimate although not quite just. Each process properly aspires not to persuade participants that its outcome is right on the merits, but only to sustain their ownership of these outcomes, so that they accept an obligation to comply, even when they remain unpersuaded on the merits. Each process aims, that is, to exclude disputants' independent judgments of the merits from their grounds for resisting, and in this sense to achieve authority.

Indeed, insofar as procedure is transformative, then the outcomes that disputants are prepared to accept after having engaged the legal process *necessarily* differ from the outcomes that they set out to pursue through this process or that they regarded as antecedently just, and disputants who have come through the legal process will prefer these outcomes to alternatives that they initially rated more highly. And unless one is prepared to cast the legal process's transformative powers as absolutely and irredeemably oppressive, so that the aims parties bring to a dispute are necessarily more worthy of respect than the aims that they take from it, one must approve some portion of the inevitable departures from antecedent notions of justice that the process generates.

Moreover, there is no good reason to take such a skeptical view of the transformations that the legal process induces in disputants—no reason to think that the consequences of affective engagements with the process are necessarily manipulative or exploitative. And there is an excellent reason for embracing the transformative powers of adjudication instead and thinking it unreasonable to evaluate postprocess outcomes based exclusively on preprocess attitudes and standards. As with democracy at the wholesale level, so also (if less familiarly) at retail, legitimacy is the most that can be hoped for in the shadow of the deep and intractable theoretical disagreements that disputes involve—including disagreements not just about the facts or the legal and moral values that are at play but also about how justly to resolve disagreements concerning these facts and values. Transparent procedures that answer to theoretical ideals of justice simply cannot sustain orderly dispute resolution in these circumstances, because they inevitably become themselves subjects of disputes. This is simply another way of saying that the problem of political legitimacy arises not just at wholesale but also at retail, because there is intractable reasonable disagreement not just at wholesale, about which general principles to adopt, but also at retail, about how general principles should be applied to govern particular cases. Only transformative procedures, which answer to practical conceptions of legitimacy, can hope to sustain a stable political life, and both democracy (at wholesale) and the legal process (at retail) must be approached keeping these basic features of politics in mind. It is therefore a piece of good fortune—and not a thing to be lamented—that our practical nature leaves us susceptible to the transformative effects of procedure, for if we were not so susceptible, collective life would not be possible for us.*[75]

ADVERSARY ADVOCACY REDUX

Of course, this practical account of retail political legitimation and the legal process depends on the effectiveness of the legal process at penetrating disputants' attitudes and at sustaining the transformations in these attitudes, and the attendant sense of ownership of outcomes, to which it aspires. These legitimating attitudes are not easy to sustain.

To begin with, the legal process necessarily answers not only to the need for retail political legitimation but also to a series of imperatives associated with the need to provide more or less efficient, accurate, and fair settlements for a large class of disputes, whose subject matters and party structures vary widely. (That efficiency, accuracy, and even justice, are not *sufficient* for retail political legitimacy, and that the structure of adjudication cannot be understood as determined by these ideals, is perfectly consistent, after all, with the ideals' being in some measure *necessary* for legitimacy.) These imperatives require the legal process to adopt practices and arrange itself into patterns that appear technical, unfamiliar, and indeed alien to disputants who are not schooled in law or its methods. Thus it is familiar to social psychologists that there exists a "sizeable gap" between the processes of dispute resolution recommended by the ordinary psychology of procedural legitimacy and those that the law provides, and that this gap threatens to cause disputants to regard even ideal legal processes as illegitimate.[76]

*This idea is more emphasized in political literature than in political philosophy. A particularly forceful example is Robert Bolt's treatment of Thomas More, whose central theme is to celebrate the political possibilities brought on by human impurity. Bolt's More insists, for example, that even imperfect laws must be respected, because to do otherwise invites catastrophic conflict: "This country's planted thick with laws from coast to coast—Man's laws, not God's—and if you cut them down—and you're just the man to do it—do you really believe you could stand upright in the winds that would blow then." And he emphasizes how unsuited persons are to standing on principle: "God made the *angels* to show him splendour—as he made animals for innocence and plants for their simplicity. But man he made to serve him wittily, in the tangle of his mind! If he suffers us to fall to such a case that there is no escaping, then we may stand our tackle as best we can and . . . we may clamour like champions . . . if we have the spittle for it. And no doubt it delights God to see splendour where he looked only for complexity. But it's God's part, not our own, to bring ourselves to that extremity! Our natural business lies in escaping."

The historical More, by contrast, probably took quite the opposite line on these matters, and seems to have gone to his death convinced that martyrdom would bring him closer to God.

Moreover, because legitimacy is a normative and political ideal rather than just a matter of positive psychology, not every way of bridging that gap and establishing the *perception* of legitimacy will *actually* legitimate. Even if the argument succeeds in demonstrating that justice is an inappropriate standard for judging the legal process (as it is an inappropriate standard for judging the democratic process), the practical approach to the legal process cannot rest on the bare fact that disputants accept ownership of the resolutions that the legal process proposes. A merely subjective experience of ownership of an outcome may be manufactured in ways that undermine its capacity to legitimate, even on the practical view. Thus, the sense of ownership may be secured by deception, for example, about the relative benefits and burdens that a particular way of resolving a dispute imposes on the disputants, or by coercion, as when the accused at show trials come to believe their confessions. More broadly, such ownership may belong to larger patterns of ideological manipulation designed to cause disputants to accept burdens that they should reject, as, for example, when victims of sexual violence internalize norms of chastity that cause them to blame themselves. In all these cases, the experience of ownership that the legal process engenders is a kind of alien attitude, which overwhelms rather than expresses disputants' native practical personalities, and it therefore cannot sustain the practical political legitimacy to which the legal process aspires.

In order for the legal process to legitimate the retail application of political power, the ownership of outcomes that follows engagements with the process must be more durable and more secure than in the examples just discussed: it must be assumed freely rather than through fraud or force, and it must be authentic rather than ideological. These requirements are, to be sure, weaker than the requirement, associated with the theoretical approach to the legitimacy of the legal process, that adjudication must secure substantive justice. But they nevertheless have real bite. Thus the practical legitimacy of the legal process requires that the sense of ownership of outcomes that the process produces survives even when disputants learn whose interests it serves, for example, or how (that is, by what methods) the legal process has established this sense of ownership in them (and how the transformations that follow their engagements with the legal process fit into their broader ethical and political attitudes). In short, the practical political legitimacy of the legal process requires that the experience of ownership that the legal process engenders remains stable in the face of the rational reflection of those who experience it, when they apply the critical faculties that they have or can develop.*

---

*The practical account of political legitimacy follows a middle path between insisting on justice on the one hand and affirming whatever people can be made to accept on the

These considerations naturally return the argument to adversary advocacy and, in particular, to the lawyerly virtues, to cast these virtues as ethically substantial—substantial enough to underwrite a first-personal lawyerly role ethic that supports integrity-preserving role-based redescription. The practical approach to adjudication proposes that (whatever its connection to justice) distinctively adversary advocacy lies at the center of the legal process's retail legitimation of political power. According to this argument, adversary advocacy is essential to the legal process's capacity to transform disputants' attitudes so that they take ownership of its outcomes even in spite of its initial strangeness, and, moreover, to ensuring that this sense of ownership remains stable in the face of rational reflection among those who experience it. Lawyers, as even the harshest critics of the legal profession observe,[77] serve as experts who "mediate between the universal vision of legal order and the concrete desires of [their] clients."[78] In short, "the lawyer's job," as Robert Gordon says, "is selling legitimacy,"[79] not at wholesale but at retail, one client at a time. And in order to be an effective salesman— one who has (appropriately) satisfied customers—the lawyer must display fidelity and cultivate negative capability.[*80]

It is not surprising that the practical approach to legitimating the legal process should emphasize the lawyer-client relation. This relation, as Talcott Parsons observed, "is focused" on the "smoothing over" of "situations of actual or potential social conflict."[81] Certainly the connection

---

other. In this way, the practical account proposes a decentralized and also naturalized approach to political philosophy: the practical account of political legitimacy replaces elaborate theorizing about which political arrangements are best or most just with a much sparer account of what people whose reasoning is functioning normally (but not necessarily ideally) are willing to accept.

[*] This does not mean that partisan lawyering is appropriate in connection with all disputes. Applying adversary methods to shallow disputes, in which parties' differences result from mere misunderstandings which may be cleared up without any deep transformations in their attitudes, may be not just inefficient but counterproductive. Adversary advocates may misconstrue their roles or perhaps look for deeper disputes to which to apply their distinctive (negative) capabilities and in the process create disputes that did not previously exist. Thus Mirjan Damaska has observed that when a professional ethic of lawyer loyalty and client control is coupled with a procedural regime that gives parties control over the evidence, this exerts an inflammatory pressure on disputes.

The possibility that applying adversary advocacy to shallow disputes might deepen them suggests encouraging lawyers (in an adversary system) to distinguish shallow from deep disputes and to adjust their conduct depending on the kind of dispute in which they are involved. The positive law of lawyering contains the seeds of this approach, in the regimes that govern lawyers who function as intermediaries or third-party neutrals. The intermediary role had been the subject of its own rule, Model Rule 2.2, which was deleted from the Model Rules in 2002. This change did not reflect any disapproval of the role but rather the sense that it was "better dealt with in the Comment to Rule 1.7."

between disputants' *perceptions* of legitimacy and their lawyers' activities has empirical support. A study of felony trials, for example, reported that defendants' attitudes toward the legitimacy of their trial courts were substantially determined by the intensity of their interactions with their lawyers, measured by factors "such as how often their attorney had consulted with them in deciding how to resolve their case."[82] Indeed, the subjective experience of legitimacy seems to have been more influenced by the intensity of defendants' interactions with their *lawyers* than by the intensity of their interactions with their *tribunals* (for example, whether their cases were resolved by plea bargain or trial).[83] Results like these probably should not surprise. After all, the transformative engagements with the legal process that generate the experience of ownership of outcomes on which practical legitimacy depends are administered directly through the lawyer-client relation.

Moreover, lawyers play a central role not only in sustaining *positive perceptions* of legitimacy but also in establishing *actual* legitimacy, understood as a *normative* ideal. The *adversariness* of lawyers should figure particularly prominently in this context. The lawyerly virtues associated with adversary advocacy, specifically through their contributions to lawyers' negative capability, come into their own as supports for the transformative influence of the legal process. The lawyer, Gordon observes, "cannot deliver unless she can make plausible arguments rationalizing her client's conduct within the prevailing terms of discourse,"[84] and she can do this only insofar as she is able, negatively capably, "to understand the day-to-day world of the client's transactions and deals as somehow approximating, in however decayed or imperfect a form, the ideal fantasy world of the legal order."[85] Adversary advocacy—including lawyerly fidelity and negative capability—is therefore a necessary condition for the transformative power of the legal process, without which the legal process could not appropriately penetrate disputants' attitudes and certainly could not underwrite transformations that remain stable in the face of disputants' rational reflection.*[86]

---

*It is worthwhile expressly to distinguish my approach from another, very different claim about the contributions that lawyers make to resolving disputes, which gives lawyers a role in dampening disputes while holding on to a transparent view of procedure. According to this claim, lawyers (unlike most clients) are repeat participants in the legal process and (unlike clients) can therefore establish reputations for cooperative dispute resolution that can help clients to avoid the prisoner's dilemma aspect of much litigation and can therefore improve the efficiency of outcomes.

Although I do not deny that cooperative lawyers can have this effect, the efficiency gains associated with cooperative lawyering will come at some cost to the legitimacy of the legal process, at least on the practical account of legitimacy that I am proposing. Lawyers can exploit reputations for cooperation only if they can resist when clients (who are not repeat players and have no reputations to defend) issue instructions to defect.

The adversariness of lawyers is necessary for sustaining all the transformations that the legal process engenders—from the shallowest to the deepest. Even the most superficial transformations, associated with the mere translation of claims from ordinary into legal language, will be stable only if clients place a high degree of trust in lawyer-translators. Specifically, clients must trust in lawyers' capacity to *understand* their claims and, moreover, in lawyers' commitments to fidelity in translation (even when fidelity requires lawyers to ignore their own assessments of the clients' claims).

Only negatively capable lawyers can earn and sustain such trust, because only negatively capable lawyers have the empathy necessary for understanding their clients and the open-mindedness necessary to avoid judging them. If lawyers retreat from adversary ideals of lawyer loyalty and client control and abandon the fidelity that adversariness involves, their efforts at translation will come to be experienced by clients as judgmental, and hence foreign and hostile, so that they disrupt rather than enhance the clients' engagements with the legal process. Insofar as lawyers reject fidelity in favor of a more positively capable conception of their professional roles, lawyers' professional behavior "grows introverted, preoccupied with its own norms and activities,"[87] so that the "institution [of the legal profession] develops a carapace, impermeable to external information, prescription, or influence."[88] And when this happens, lawyers' efforts at translation inevitably fail, and "the problems [the legal profession] handles are the problems defined by the institution, not the society; the solutions it generates are solutions for the institution, not the society."[89] Rather than serving as intermediaries whose interpretive efforts connect clients to the legal process, nonadversary lawyers confront clients as an unmediated part of the process. And rather than bringing clients into the legal process in ways that support its legitimacy, nonadversary lawyers alienate clients in ways that undermine the legal process's authority.

Moreover, lawyers' ability to dampen disputes by encouraging clients to abandon or modify their most unreasonable positions—the intermediate of the three transformations in client attitudes that sustain the practical legitimacy of the legal process—also depends on their commitment to fidelity and on the negative capability that follows from this commitment. This is, to begin with, a matter of psychology and even of

---

As has been observed, "client-centered advocacy presents a serious problem for the lawyer seeking to establish or to maintain a reputation for cooperation." And insofar as such resistance undermines the adversary lawyerly virtues, it may also undermine lawyers' capacity to connect clients to the transformative legal process in ways that can sustain that process's legitimacy.

emotion. Disputants' most unreasonable positions often reflect frustration and anger rather than considered judgments, so that they are open to being talked down and may even seek it out. But only a sympathetic and nonjudgmental counsel will inspire the trust needed to cool passions in this way. As Parsons says, "In order to be capable, psychologically, of 'getting things off his chest' a person must be assured that, within certain limits . . . sanctions will not operate . . . . The confidential character of the lawyers' relation to his client [and, Parsons might have added, the lawyer's loyalty and deference more generally] provides such a situation. The client can talk freely, to an understanding and knowledgeable ear, without fear of immediate repercussions."[90]

In addition, the adversary lawyer's unique capacity to deflate her clients' most extreme claims has an ethical component. Both ethical theory[91] and empirical research[92] suggest that disputants have a natural ethical inclination in favor of resolving disputes through reasonable reciprocal concessions. But most clients, being inexperienced in the disputes in which they are engaged, will be uncertain which concessions are in fact reasonable. Lawyers have experience and expertise that clients do not and can therefore help to resolve this uncertainty. But lawyers will be trusted to do so only when clients are confident that they remain faithful in spite of giving deflationary advice and that the advice they give reflects a refined and sympathetic understanding of the clients' positions—only, that is, when lawyers accept the adversary obligations associated with fidelity and display the negative capability needed sensitively to discern what fidelity requires.

In these ways, adversary advocates support both the psychological and ethical mechanisms through which engagements with the legal process persuade disputants voluntarily to abandon their most aggressive and unreasonable demands. And adversary advocates therefore transform disputants' attitudes in legitimacy-enhancing ways, whereas lawyers who abandon their adversary obligations, and judge their clients rather than serving them, undermine trust and therefore have an opposite, delegitimating effect.[93]

Finally, lawyers' adversary commitments are especially important for transforming clients' claims from brute demands into assertions of right whose implicitly defeasible character makes the deepest contribution to the legitimacy of the legal process. Once again, "a high degree of trust and confidence are usually necessary [if lawyers are] to 'sell' [the] new definition of the situation" that the conversion of brute demands into claims of right involves,[94] and lawyers' adversary commitments justify their clients' trust. Furthermore, the internal logic of the legal process (and not just the willingness of clients to go along) also emphasizes the importance for legitimacy of using adversary advocates to convert disputants' brute demands into assertions of right. The legal process insists that disputants frame their demands as assertions of right because of a commitment, on which its legitimacy depends, to address every assertion of right that can be made in support of a disputant's position. Accordingly, the lawyers who help disputants to transform their brute demands into assertions of right must not fail to assert any rights that are immanent in their clients' positions. (Such unasserted rights cannot be addressed in adjudication and therefore threaten to undermine legitimacy by coming between disputants and the resolutions to disputes that the legal process proposes.) And lawyers can do this only if they keep faith with their clients and, negatively capably, amplify and refine all their clients' reasonable claims rather than evaluating and choosing among them.

Lawyers who abandon their adversary role in favor of positively capable personal assessments of their clients' claims quite literally prejudge these claims. And when this happens, the legitimacy of the legal process becomes dependent on the legitimacy of the lawyers' judgments. But these judgments, being creatures of the lawyers' individual minds, are virtually impossible to legitimate and certainly cannot be legitimated by reference to the transformative powers of a legal process that has not yet begun. Lawyers who abandon their adversary role merely shift the burden of legitimation forward to their own assessments, which necessarily address their clients' demands in an untransformed, and hence intractable, state.*[95]

ADJUDICATION'S REACH AND GRASP

This is, to be sure, a demanding account of the authority of adjudication—demanding specifically with respect to the scope and intensity of client participation in the process of dispute resolution (and hence also of lawyer involvement as a means of drawing clients into this process) on which it makes adjudication's authority depend. It is therefore important not to take an unrealistic view of the degree of disputant participation that adversary adjudication as actually practiced invites or indeed permits.

The transactions costs of disputing inevitably entail that routinized methods of dispute resolution will evolve in any legal system, in which experts quickly determine the value of many claims, without any affective intervention from the claimants themselves.[96] Moreover, such pressures

---

* This is vividly illustrated by the alienation that arises between lawyer and client in totalitarian legal systems in which, as a Bulgarian lawyer once said, "'there is no division of duty between the judge, prosecutor, and defense counsel. The defense must assist the prosecution to find the objective truth in a case.'"

figure prominently in the practice of dispute resolution in the United States today, where the costs of full-fledged adversary adjudication are overwhelming the legal system's capacity to supply it, so that the highest form of adjudication—the trial—is said to be vanishing, to be replaced by less participatory forms of dispute resolution, ranging from summary judgment, to settlement, to arbitration.[97] In many cases, then, the party participation permitted by full-fledged adversary adjudication is merely counterfactual, taking the form of the possibility that any given dispute may be taken out of the cost-saving routine and addressed in a more participatory way.

It is not clear what the consequence of this is for the legitimacy of retail dispute resolution as it is actually practiced. As at wholesale, so also at retail, the supply of legitimation need only be adequate to meet the demand for legitimacy, so that a system of adjudication, like a democratic system, need not direct its full energies equally at every dispute but may instead concentrate its transformative powers where they are needed most, that is, on the most recalcitrant disputants. Some disputes, most immediately those that are mere misunderstandings, may be authoritatively resolved from within existing attitudes and preferences and so require only clarificatory and not transformative processes of dispute resolution. Moreover, even when disputes are deeper than mere misunderstandings, so that their legitimate resolution requires some measure of transformative procedure, the participation needed to sustain these transformations involves a sliding scale: not every transformation requires the participatory engagement of full-blown adversary adjudication, and motion practice, settlement negotiations and even arbitration proceedings may all be sufficiently participatory to sustain the legitimate resolutions of certain disputes between parties who are amenable to these methods. (Repeat disputants, including in particular firms for whom disputes are endemic in ongoing business relations, present a particularly important example of this general possibility. Such disputants are naturally concerned less for seeking favorable outcomes in individual disputes and more for reducing the costs of dispute resolution in aggregate.)

A system of dispute resolution can therefore sustain retail political legitimacy while rationing participatory resources as long, first, as the total resources it provides are sufficient to support the total transformative engagements that the disputes it handles require and, second, as it allocates its transformative resources efficiently, so that each dispute receives resources sufficient for its depth and hence its needs. Unlike more immediately bureaucratic administration (which may be more rational and accurate than adjudication on balance but cannot provide even the possibility of individualized participatory decisionmaking), adjudication can concentrate its efforts toward legitimation on the disputes in which—because the disputants most insistently clamor to be heard—legitimation is most needed. Also, the counterfactual possibility of leaving the routine casts its shadow over all disputes and so changes the character of disputants' engagement with the system, even in the disputes that remain subject to the routinized part of the practice.

This theoretical possibility does not, of course, entail that adjudicative resources are either adequate in toto or appropriately distributed in any particular legal system, including of course in the United States today. Whether they are or not—and hence whether adversary adjudication as actually practiced is sufficient to sustain retail political legitimacy or whether, instead, the reach of this approach to legitimacy exceeds its current grasp—is an empirical question. (It is also, in the current context, in a way beside the point, since the issue here is not whether adversary advocacy is *sufficient* for retail legitimacy but whether it is *necessary*.)

There certainly exist good grounds for criticizing the legal system's current practice of adjudication from the perspective of the theory of retail legitimation. Many disputes are deeper than they may at first appear so that, as has been prominently observed, "[T]he transformative perspective suggests that there may be too little conflict in our society."[98] Moreover, there is good reason to suspect that the legal system misallocates such transformative resources as it does provide, at least for purposes of legitimation, so that they are inefficiently concentrated on disputes involving wealthy parties and especially economic firms. Thus it is a commonplace that some disputants receive no legal assistance and even disputants who manage to hire counsel do not always receive the same level of attentiveness or loyalty from their lawyers.[99] And because disputants who are not led to the legal process by loyal counsel are unlikely to experience the transformations in their attitudes on which the legitimacy of the process depends, and are doubly unlikely to experience transformations that can survive rational reflection, an unequal distribution of lawyers threatens the legitimacy of the legal process. Familiar concerns about equal access to justice therefore apply, *mutatis mutandis*, to generate concerns about uneven legitimation.* (And if there is no

---

*This difference in emphasis—which replaces traditional concerns for unequal justice with a concern for unequal legitimation—has policy implications. There is a tendency, in traditional criticisms, to respond to inequality in legal services by recommending a retreat from adversary advocacy, on the grounds that less partisan lawyers will have fewer opportunities to exploit opponents who lack legal representation and will therefore be less able to secure unjust advantages for their clients.

But the argument here reveals that this is a mistake: Insofar as the legal process's transformative powers are essential to its legitimacy and adversary lawyers are essential to the legal process's transformative powers, abandoning adversary advocacy will undermine the

epidemic of noncompliance then this is primarily because those deprived of legitimation tend also to be powerless.)

These last remarks are of course almost entirely speculative and clearly lack the systematic empirical foundations needed for offering reliable guidance concerning policy in this area. But the questions that they address—concerning the optimal provision and adequate distribution of adjudicative resources—are (again) beside the present point. That point, recall, is to elaborate the role that adversary advocates play in retail political legitimacy when they are employed. And the possibilities that our legal system undersupplies adversary advocacy, and even that it misallocates such adversary advocacy as it does supply, leave this basic normative connection between adversary advocacy and political legitimacy—between lawyerly fidelity and the authority of adjudication—intact.

• • •

These arguments do not, to be sure, countenance untrammeled partisanship in lawyers. As I have repeatedly observed,* both the adversary system and the ideals of fidelity and negative capability that govern the conduct of adversary advocates are self-limiting, in the sense of imposing boundaries on the partisanship that they countenance. Even as these ideals require lawyers to be partisan champions for their clients, they contain within them the seeds of restrictions against partisan excess. (For example, even as a negatively capable lawyer must preserve client confidences, she may not allow her own reputation to be used, positively capably, in the service of a client's fraud.) Moreover, this self-regulating tendency reappears in the present context as well, because just as a disputant may become alienated from adjudication if her own lawyer judges rather than serves her, so she may also become alienated if left at the mercy of an opposing lawyer whose partisanship in favor of his client is too aggressive and succeeds at subverting the legal process into a one-sided tool of his client's will.

---

authority of adjudication. Justice is secondary to legitimacy in political life, and there can accordingly be no substitute for securing adversary representation for all disputants.

It is, moreover, a surprising mistake. Most of those who condemn the unequal distribution of legal services also reject the transparent approach to procedure that is incorporated into the traditional adversary system excuse. But when these critics say that unequal access to lawyers produces unjust outcomes and address this injustice by cabining lawyers' adversariness, they adopt a process-independent conception of justice and ignore the imperative to sustain the authority of the legal process by engaging disputants, and they therefore implicitly revert to the transparent conception of procedure that they earlier rejected.

* In chapters 2 and 3, and most recently in chapter 7.

But although excessive partisanship undermines the legitimacy of adjudication, some partisanship—that is, legal representation by advocates who are recognizably adversary and therefore expose themselves to the lawyerly vices that render their ethics so difficult—remains essential for legitimacy. In order to legitimate its outcomes, the legal process must welcome rather than estrange the disputants who might engage it. If, as Lon Fuller observed, "the distinguishing characteristic of adjudication lies in the fact that it confers on the affected party a peculiar form of *participation* in the decision,"[100] then "whatever heightens the significance of this participation lifts adjudication toward its optimum expression," which is to say, increases the legal process's legitimacy.[101] And because lawyers provide the principal connection between disputants and the legal process, the burden of inviting disputants to engage the legal process, and of sustaining disputants' participation, falls principally on them.

In order successfully to shoulder this burden, lawyers must deny the potentially alienating features of adjudication (in particular, the legal process's divided sympathies) any foothold within the lawyer-client relation itself; instead, they must structure the lawyer-client relation so that they are able, through it, to "bring[] the client's case in a nonjudgmental way to the authoritative institutions of society."[102] Only adversary advocates, who practice the negatively capable lawyerly virtues that I have elaborated, can achieve this. And these virtues therefore carry all the ethical significance of being necessary for sustaining the transformations in disputants' attitudes on which the legitimacy of the legal process depends.

An Illustration

The transformations that engaging the legal process produces in disputants, and the place of lawyers in producing and sustaining these transformations, may be illustrated through case studies.

One particularly striking example—striking because its newness casts the transformative power of the legal process into sharp relief—is the adjudication of disputes that involve what is now understood as sexual harassment. These disputes begin when an employee experiences unwanted treatment in her job—unwelcome sexual advances, for example, or hostility and abuse.* She is insulted, perhaps even frightened and

* Although I initially represent complainants as female and harassers as male, the capacity of sexual harassment law to accommodate male claimants and female harassers, as well as cases in which complainants and harassers have the same sex, itself belongs (as the argument will show) among the features of such disputes that come under the transformative powers of the legal process.

humiliated; her career suffers; and she complains of her treatment and
seeks redress.

Initially, the complaint is likely to be informal and remain addressed
within her workplace. But if the employee finds no satisfaction there,
because her colleagues and employer reject either her account of what
has happened to her or her assertion that it is wrongful, and especially
when her employer fails to provide adequate internal procedures for reviewing her complaint,*[103] the employee may seek redress outside her
firm, by suing her employer and engaging the more formal process of
the law.†

When this happens, the legal process faces the burden of transforming the previously intractable dispute to give it a more manageable
structure—of recharacterizing the dispute into terms that allow a resolution that both the employee and those whom she accuses can come
(through engaging the legal process) to regard as authoritative. The law
achieves the required transformation through adversary advocates, who
depersonalize the dispute, replacing the emotional registers of manage-
rial independence, honor, and fear in which the dispute initially plays
out with the more dispassionate, and hence more tractable, register of
workplace sex discrimination.[104]

The transformation of these disputes from the personal and emotional
registers in which they naturally play out into the cooler registers of
workplace sex discrimination that now dominate the law of sexual harassment is a complicated and demanding task, requiring several doctrinal developments (some of which are not yet completed). To begin with,
the law declares it unlawful workplace sex discrimination for superiors
to make gender-based demands of subordinates—paradigmatically involving sexual advances—as a condition of continued employment or
advancement, in what the law calls quid pro quo sexual harassment.[105]
But although the quid pro quo paradigm covers many cases, it cannot accommodate all the disputes that the legal process must adjudicate in this
area. Instead, the central role that exchange plays in quid pro quo sexual
harassment threatens to "exclude from legal understanding many of the
most common and debilitating forms of harassment faced by women

*The law of sexual harassment actively encourages employers to internalize its substan-
tive norms by connecting employer liability to the absence of adequate internal procedures
for resolving complaints. In this way, the law in this area includes in its substance a commitment in favor of the transformations that I am proposing the process of adjudication
encourages generally.

†Note that the employer (rather than the immediate harassers) will generally be the
defendant in such a lawsuit and that this already reflects the outcome of a legal engagement, managed partly by adversary advocates, concerning the scope of an employer's responsibility for the actions of his employees.

(and many men) at work each day."[106] These forms of harassment arise when employees face gender-based *hostility* in the workplace—ranging from uncooperative or obstructionist conduct to psychological or even physical intimidation—that "undermine[s] [their] perceived competence as workers"[107] and, ultimately, their capacity to do their jobs successfully, but that is not connected to threats or offers of tangible employment actions. Accordingly the law pursues a second doctrinal development to accommodate these claims. This doctrinal strand—known as hostile work environment sexual harassment—observes that selective workplace hostility may be legally actionable discrimination based on sex even though it does not possess the conditional structure or involve the type of harm associated with the quid pro quo model.[108]

Faithful and negatively capable lawyers, moreover, play critical roles in sustaining the legitimacy of this legal frame, bringing the law's doctrinal categories and the concerns of clients into equilibrium, so that defendants come to accept the liability that the law imposes and plaintiffs come to accept that this liability is sufficient to give them satisfaction.

On the one hand, lawyers help employers to see that sexual harassment (on both the quid pro quo and hostile work environment models) is more than simply a private insult and that recognizing such sexual harassment at law will not overwhelm management discretion or colonize workplace social life for legal regulation.[109] Instead, because these behaviors impose harms based on gender, they constitute a form of public employment discrimination "because of sex" within the meaning of traditional antidiscrimination law,[110] and hence belong to a familiar, and narrowly cabined, class of legally redressable wrongs that employers already acknowledge.[111]

And on the other hand, lawyers help plaintiffs to look past the broad and personal feelings of disgust and anger that naturally dominate their immediate responses to being harassed and to focus instead on the gender-based unfairness that sexual harassment introduces specifically into the workplace, so that this unfairness, rather than their more visceral (and perhaps initially more forceful) responses, becomes appropriately central to their legal claims. Thus even as employees win legal protection against harms that constitute affronts to gender equality, they abandon hopes of redress for the other more individualistic and personal elements of the harms that they have suffered (involving, for example, betrayed friendship and trust or simply encroachments on privacy) and accept that other types of hostility, which lack the connection to discrimination, may not be actionable at law.

In both respects, sexual harassment doctrine is the result of an effort, by negatively capable lawyers, to elaborate disputants' concerns to render disputes more tractable and to propose resolutions to the reconceptualized disputes that may be legitimated to all sides. Together these doctrinal adaptations—sustained by negatively capable lawyers' imaginative reconstructions of their clients' claims—have expanded the authority of the legal process into an area of dispute resolution that it had not previously addressed.

The development of sexual harassment law is, moreover, an ongoing enterprise in which negatively capable lawyers remain actively engaged. In particular, they are active in expanding the scope of sexual harassment law by adapting the workplace discrimination model to include cases that involve no sexual desire and indeed include no overt sexual content. The hostile work environment prong of sexual harassment doctrine is particularly open to innovations in this direction, because it invites plaintiffs to characterize even nonsexual abuse that they experience in the workplace as a form of discrimination that, although it involves no sexual desire, nevertheless takes aim against women's professional ambitions.* It seems possible, and perhaps even natural, to expand the doctrine to encompass all forms of workplace abuse that are designed "to perpetuate the workplace as a site of male control, where gender hierarchy is the order of the day and masculine norms structure the working environment,"[112] specifically by "maintain[ing] work—particularly the more highly rewarded lines of work—as bastions of masculine competence and authority."[113] This reasoning suggests that it can be sexual discrimination to coerce nonconformists into traditional gender stereotypes,[114] and indeed that unlawful sexual harassment may arise between harassers and harassed of the same gender.[115] Finally this doctrinal model, through its emphasis on discrimination that enforces stereotypes and not just that disadvantages groups, might apply even in cases of reprisals against those who make common cause with coworkers of the other gender who have been harassed.[116]

Of course, this expansion of sexual harassment law will eventually exhaust itself, most likely when negatively capable lawyers cease to be able to persuade employers that the newly proposed classes of proscribed behavior fall within their antecedent commitments against sex discrimination and without the sphere of their freedom to manage their firms as they see fit.[117] (It would, for example, be surprising if sexual harassment were ever expanded to include hostility to efforts to arrange work-place childcare.) At this point, the question arises whether negatively capable lawyers, armed with the doctrinal expansions that defendants can be persuaded to accept, can capture for the legal process the

---

*Quid pro quo sexual harassment, in spite of paradigmatically involving demands for sex, may also arise apart from desire, as when a boss makes performing domestic chores at work a condition of employment for female but not male subordinates.

full range of claims that plaintiffs in such cases insist on bringing. This question investigates the boundaries of sexual harassment law's transformative powers. Its answer determines the ultimate authority of the legal process with respect to this class of workplace disputes.*[118]

These remarks of course present only a stylized and foreshortened account of the legal treatment of sexual harassment. They undoubtedly gloss over many important features of the legal doctrines, and also of the underlying human dynamics, that drive the adjudication of such disputes. But they nevertheless vividly illustrate the capacity of the legal process to recast intractable disputes into more manageable forms—and also the role of adversary advocates in developing and sustaining this transformative power. Moreover, the adjudication of disputes involving sexual harassment is not unique or even unusual in this respect, although the relative newness (even incompleteness) of this area of law makes the transformations that it engenders particularly visible.

Thus, I might have cited to many other examples, besides sexual harassment, in which engaging the legal process, through the adversary advocates that administer this process, transforms disputes in ways that can be identified in considerable detail. Indeed, in some of these examples, the transformative powers of the legal process are so effective that they are taken for granted. One such case is tort law's treatment of disputes involving accidents, especially accidents that harm persons. This case "epitomize[s] [the] transformation of disputes over injuries into disputes over money,"[119] and in this way translates "a dispute over complex issues . . . into the terms of a currency . . . which allows the issues in dispute to be quantified,"[120] and, moreover, "transforms" the victims' "concept of an acceptable outcome" in a way that renders the disputes more easily resolved.[121] The monetized view of tort law is far from inevitable: why should defendants be obligated not just to acknowledge their wrongs and seek forgiveness but to pay money damages; and why should plaintiffs be satisfied with damages that cannot restore their security or

*Although this short history of sexual harassment law portrays a trend toward increasing legitimation, nothing in the nature of the legal process requires that its efforts in this direction succeed. Negative examples, in which the legal process proves unable to recast disputants' claims into tractable forms, are also available. One increasingly prominent source of such negative examples is the dispute over the proper place of religion in American life, not just in its grand expressions (for example, the battle over abortion) but also as it plays out in countless more humble conflicts.

A Colorado case, Cole v. Lehman, presents a typical example. A new age teacher encouraged meditation in her class, and fundamentalist parents sought to have her fired for Satanism. The teacher filed a lawsuit, claiming defamation. The parents remained intransigent, and their lawyers took a back seat to their religious advisors. The dispute therefore remained intractably a contest between intransigent ethico-religious outlooks, and no party was satisfied with the outcome that the court imposed.

honor? But the monetized approach to tort is so long-established and so deeply entrenched that little new effort is required to sustain it on a case-by-case basis. Instead, even before they engage the legal system as defendants and plaintiffs in particular cases, persons acknowledge that their obligations and entitlements may be expressed in monetary terms. This is perhaps the most complete success that the transformative legal process can have: that a general appreciation for the legal process penetrates persons' attitudes even before they engage it in particular cases, so that disputes are rendered tractable in advance of their actually arising.

THE LAWYERLY VIRTUES REVISITED

This chapter has argued, with Parsons, that "the primary function of the legal system is integrative."[122] The law "serves to mitigate potential elements of conflict and to oil the machinery of social intercourse."[123] Moreover, this integrative function is essential to social coordination. "It is, indeed, only by adherence to a system of rules that systems of social interaction can function without breaking down into overt or chronic covert conflict."[124]

The law integrates through the transformative powers of the legal process, which operate through the efforts of the lawyers who administer this process and invite disputants to engage it. To be sure, lawyers, including perhaps particularly adversary ones, may encourage conflict in particular cases. But when viewed from a more fundamental perspective—which asks not how persons decide about incremental assertions of their legal rights but rather how persons who face intractable disagreements at every level of principle can nevertheless sustain peaceful social coordination at all—lawyers are peacemakers. And lawyers can successfully invite litigants to engage the legal process (and open themselves up to the transformations that the process engenders) only if they resist themselves judging their clients—only, that is, if they serve their clients faithfully, exercising the negative capability that I have described.

By embedding lawyerly fidelity (with its attendant negative capability) in a political context, this approach achieves two successes for lawyers' ethics that have remained beyond the grasp of more traditional arguments that sound in morality and develop, in one way or another, the adversary system excuse for partisan lawyering.

First, and most obviously, the political approach justifies a greater degree of lawyerly partisanship, in a wider range of contexts, than does the adversary system excuse. To be sure, there exist significant limitations on the forms of partisan lawyering that best promote retail political legitimation: as I have repeatedly said, unconstrained partisanship, and in particular partisanship in which advocates abandon their negatively capable role in favor of exercising their positive capabilities to speak, on their own behalf, in support of clients with whom they make common cause, is not legitimating. Moreover, these limitations may well depart, substantially, from the current partisan practices of the adversary bar, so that the political reconstruction of lawyers' ethics is anything but a whitewashing of the status quo. (Two respects in which the argument has shown its critical bite especially clearly are: first, that legitimation requires a much more even distribution of legal services than exists virtually anywhere today; and, second, that the political argument offers no defense for partisanship among government lawyers and indeed underwrites a harsh critique of the adversary self-conception that government lawyers, at least in the United States, have in recent years increasingly brought to their practice.) The precise contours of the partisanship that the argument for legitimacy recommends (and hence the precise extent of the revisionary pressure that it exerts on current practice) have yet to be identified, of course. But the crucial point has been made plain, namely that the political defense of partisan lawyering avoids the conclusion that repeatedly embarrasses the traditional adversary system defense, namely that adversary advocacy should be reduced to a residual category, to be indulged only insofar as it has no appreciable effect on outcomes.

Second, and more subtly but no less importantly, the political reconstruction of fidelity and negative capability as lawyerly virtues establishes a role-ethic that lawyers may aspire to in the first-person, so that they may reclaim authorship of their professional lives and sustain their integrity even in the face of the conflicts that necessarily arise between their professional obligations and ordinary first-personal moral ambitions. The adversary system excuse *reduces* the case for adversary advocacy to the proposition (however elaborately developed) that it is impartially best for lawyers to be partisans. And this reduction, under which lawyers' partisanship becomes simply a special case of the general commitment to promoting impartiality, renders the adversary system excuse incapable of sustaining lawyers' integrity. The ideals in which the adversary system traffics are precisely those that the earlier argument revealed are unsuited to adoption as integrating first-personal moral ambitions.

The political defense of partisan lawyering developed here is, by contrast, not reductive at all. Although fidelity and negative capability gain in stature from their connections to political legitimacy, and certainly stake no claim to supplanting impartialist morality, they involve forms of empathy and imagination whose general appeal, as first-personal ambitions, stands apart from whatever contributions to legitimacy they make when practiced specifically by lawyers. Fidelity and negative capability possess a thickness—literally, an additional moral dimension—that the idea of impartial bestness (no matter how subtly spun-out) lacks. And this renders these lawyerly virtues capable—at least in principle—of sustaining the integrity of partisan lawyers where the adversary system excuse could not.

In spite of these successes, the political argument cannot, as I have emphasized from the start, sustain the justice of adversary adjudication (indeed, it will necessarily depart from justice in at least some cases), and the argument about legitimacy therefore cannot defend adversary advocacy to the satisfaction of impartial morality. Moreover, although the principle of legitimacy (as I have repeatedly pointed out) does not just authorize partisan advocacy but also forbids certain forms of adversary excess, the demands of impartial morality may constrain the partisanship that lawyers may display within still narrower limits. And although sustaining the integrity of lawyers requires that legal ethics not simply *capitulate* to every one of impartiality's demands, legal ethics must remain *respectful* of impartiality, so that arguments like the one developed here may not simply *supplant* impartialist morality. The connection between adversary advocacy and legitimacy that I have developed here is therefore not sufficient to fix the metes and bounds of lawyers' professional duties of partisanship, all things considered (again, as I have repeatedly emphasized).

But the argument that lawyerly fidelity and negative capability lie at the very center of the law's claim to legitimacy—as a retail analog to the democratic virtues that are so notoriously celebrated throughout the civilized world—is more than sufficient to demonstrate that, far from being makeshift or even sham ideals, and far from relying on mistaken analogies to other moral realms, these lawyerly virtues appear on their proper ground, where they possess substantial moral importance and even dignity. "Viewed in this light, the role of the lawyer as a partisan advocate appears not as a regrettable necessity, but as an indispensable part of a larger ordering of affairs. The institution of advocacy is not a concession to the frailties of human nature, but an expression of human insight in the design of a social framework within which man's capacity for impartial judgment can attain its fullest realization."[125] And this political account of the lawyerly virtues therefore provides the substantive ideals that the formal moral argument about integrity-preserving role-based redescription needs in order to succeed. It provides lawyers with substantial lawyerly virtues that they may adopt in place of the ordinary first-personal ambitions that conflict with their professional obligations to lie and to cheat. It allows lawyers to fulfill their professional obligations even while living a life that they endorse from the inside, even, that is, while sustaining their integrity. And it therefore complements impartialist defenses of adversary advocacy, including the adversary system excuse, to establish a cohort of arguments that, at least in principle, render the legal profession worthy of commitment.

Chapter 9

TRAGIC VILLAINS

I ARGUED IN Part I that the deep structure of the adversary advocate's professional role, which is reflected and elaborated by the positive law governing lawyers, subjects lawyers to professional obligations to lie and to cheat in ways that they would ordinarily regard as vicious. Moreover, I argued in Part II that even if the adversary advocate's professional conduct can be impartially justified, for example, by the adversary system excuse that dominates traditional legal ethics, his moral position nevertheless remains troubling. The tension between his ordinary conceptions of personal virtue, on the one hand, and his professional obligations, on the other, will cast his professional life as a betrayal of self that places his integrity under threat. Accordingly, the arguments that have dominated legal ethics are structurally incapable of rendering the legal profession worthy of commitment, all things considered. Finally, this third part of the book has asked whether legal ethics may nevertheless be brought to a happy conclusion.

The argument has so far been promising, including from the lawyer's point of view. I have proposed that the ethics of role can in principle preserve the lawyer's integrity against the threats that my earlier arguments identified. Although the ethics of role cannot insulate lawyers from the requirements of impartial morality (and philosophers are properly dismissive of the suggestion that it can), role-based ethical argument that complements rather than replaces impartial morality has the right *form* to allow lawyers whose activities are impartially justified on other grounds to preserve their integrity in the face of the charges that they lie and cheat. Role-based redescription can allow lawyers to recast their professional activities in their own minds, recharacterizing the vices attributed to them by common first-personal morality in terms of role-based, distinctively lawyerly virtues that lawyers can affirmatively endorse. Moreover, the argument has displayed a *substantively* attractive version of a distinctively lawyerly role ethic, involving lawyerly fidelity and negative capability, upon which lawyers might focus their efforts at role-based redescription. This account—and in particular the connection that it draws among adversary advocacy, lawyerly negative capability, and the legitimacy of the legal process—demonstrates that the lawyerly virtues are no mere contrivance but instead bear a natural and close connection to substantial and important political ideals.

The argument up to this point therefore has the structure of a comedy: I have identified and explained a problem, the problem of integrity, that philosophical legal ethics has heretofore neglected; but I have gone on to suggest that role-based ethical arguments of the sort practical lawyers make can in general protect integrity, and that at least one substantively attractive version of such role-based argument exists specifically in the case of lawyers. Although the argument begins by calling lawyers liars and cheats, it ends up, at least in principle, vindicating their ethical position.

But the argument up to this point also remains importantly incomplete, specifically in that it emphasizes what is conceptually possible in legal ethics without seriously investigating whether lawyers can in fact exploit the conceptual possibilities that it identifies. The fact that the lawyer's role might in principle sustain her integrity does not guarantee that the problematics of legal ethics will be satisfactorily resolved from the lawyer's point of view. That turns on whether the conceptual promise of the argument so far can be redeemed in practice—whether the lawyerly role that the argument identifies is under current conditions practically available to modern lawyers. Even if the lawyer's professional life is in principle worthy of commitment, is this a commitment that contemporary lawyers can actually make? Can the lawyers whose integrity needs preserving actually develop and sustain the distinctive, negatively capable first-personal moral ideals that I have described?

There are good reasons for thinking that this question will meet with an unhappy answer, at least from the lawyer's point of view. In particular, the development of the content and structure of the American lawyer's role over the long twentieth century (that is, from the years following the Civil War through the present and near future) suggests that contemporary lawyers do not in practice have access to the role-based redescriptions necessary to preserve their integrity against the ethical assaults of their professional lives. On the one hand, the pressures that the norms and practices of the legal profession exert on the integrity of its members have dramatically increased over this period. And on the other hand, the legal profession has over the same period lost the freestanding authority over its members on which the stability of role-based redescription depends.

I now take up these developments and explain their significance for adversary advocates. In each case, my account will refer to facts that recent work on the history and sociology of the American legal profession has made familiar, although in each case the theoretical structure that I have elaborated will lead me to organize these facts into new patterns. Finally, although I describe these developments for the special case of American lawyers, they are not peculiar to the American legal profession or indeed to American social and political life more broadly. Instead, the developments that cut off contemporary American lawyers from the promise of integrity-preserving role-based redescription, or at least the bulk of these developments, reflect the deepest and most general moral and political structure of modernity. And accordingly, although I once again elaborate my arguments through the special case of American legal practice, my general approach applies much more broadly.

New Pressures on Lawyers' Integrity

I have argued that the adversary advocate's professional vices, and the threat to her integrity that these vices engender, do not depend on any particular conception of adversary advocacy—that they are instead written into the genetic code of the adversary lawyer's role, in particular through the structural separation between advocates and tribunals that all forms of adversary adjudication share. But although the basic threat to integrity that I have identified faces all adversary advocates, the intensity of this threat varies (and can vary substantially) with the peculiar content given to the lawyer's professional duties through one or another local elaboration of adversary adjudication. Moreover, two trends that have played out over the twentieth century have combined dramatically to increase the pressures that adversary legal practice exerts on lawyers' integrity.

First, lawyers today are, and are required by the law governing lawyers to be, more aggressively partisan than they were a century ago.* This development has increased the divergence between lawyers' professional obligations and ordinary first-personal moral ambitions and also the related sense that lawyering involves professional vices which attack lawyers' integrity.

And second, the twentieth century has multiplied the division of labor that characterizes the adversary system, by inwardly replicating this division of labor to create, in addition to the old separation between advocate and tribunal, a new separation in which each lawyer more or less exclusively represents clients on only one side of ongoing social and political disputes. This development has increased—by installing an additional higher-order layer of complexity even within the class of adversary advocates—the distance between lawyers and the impartially justified outcomes of the adversary system that their labors support. Lawyers are

---

* Economic forces related to competition among lawyers (including as these forces are refracted through the institutional structure of law firms) may also subject lawyers to increasing pressures toward partisanship.

less able to take ownership of the adversary process—to conceive of themselves as responsible for the process as a whole rather than their particular places in it—when they are always on the same side. And this has increased, for any (fixed) gap between lawyers' professional obligations and ordinary first-personal morality, the degree of alienation associated with putting professional obligations ahead of first-personal morality and so also the threat to their integrity that lawyers who make this choice face.

The first trend, toward greater partisanship, is more familiar but probably less important than the second, toward an increased division of labor. I take up each in turn.

Greater Partisanship

It is commonly observed, especially among proponents of the idea that the legal profession is in decline, that the twentieth century has witnessed an increase in adversary aggression among lawyers—a deepening of the demands of lawyer loyalty and client control—so that lawyers went from being principally custodians of the law to being principally hired guns.[1] The extent of this change is sometimes exaggerated, most commonly by underestimating the adversary loyalty and client-centeredness that nineteenth-century lawyers (especially elite ones) in practice displayed, at least in litigation.[2] Moreover, it is one thing to observe the historical increase in lawyers' adversary conduct and quite another to characterize this trend as a case of moral and political decline: the ideals of fidelity and negative capability that I have introduced and the connections that I have drawn between these ideals and the legitimacy of adjudication suggest that modern lawyers' adversary aggressiveness may also be cast in terms of distinctively lawyerly moral ambitions, which represent an expression of (rather than a retreat from) civic virtue. But however this may be, the basic observation that the lawyer's role has become more adversary is historically accurate, and this historical trend has increased the tensions between lawyer's professional obligations and ordinary first-personal moral ambitions.

Certainly the leading ethics treatises of the nineteenth century—David Hoffman's *Resolutions in Regard to Professional Deportment* and George Sharswood's *Essay on Professional Ethics*—both reject the broad principles of lawyer loyalty, client control, and professional detachment that I have argued characterize the contemporary law governing lawyers. Thus Hoffman insisted that "My client's conscience, and my own, are distinct entities. . . . I shall ever claim the privilege of solely judging to what extent to go. In civil cases, if I am satisfied from the evidence that the fact is against my client, he must excuse me if I do not see as he does and do not press it: and should the principle, also be wholly at variance with sound law it would be dishonorable folly in me to endeavor to incorporate it into the jurisprudence of the country . . . ."[3] And Sharswood similarly proposed that "[i]t is in some measure the duty of counsel to be the keeper of the conscience of the client,"[4] so that the advocate's duty is only "to USE ALL FAIR ARGUMENTS ARISING ON THE EVIDENCE. Beyond that he is not bound to go in any case; in a case in which he is satisfied in his own mind of the guilt of the accused, he is not justified in going."[5] Indeed Sharswood insisted quite generally that a lawyer "should throw up his brief sooner than do what revolts against his own sense of honor and propriety."[6]

Moreover nineteenth-century legal ethics backed up these broad principles by more specific rules fixing the lawyer's rights and duties to pursue his own assessment of a client's case. Thus neither treatise included the duty to preserve client confidences that so prominently contributes to the partisanship of lawyers today. And Hoffman,[7] for example, insisting that "no man's ignorance or folly shall induce me to take advantage of him,"[8] pledged not to engage in "mystery, silence, obscurity, suspicion, vigilance to the letter."[9] He therefore resolved to be fair to witnesses,[10] and he refused to plead the statute of limitations "when based on the mere efflux of time"[11] or to assert the "bar of Infancy, against an honest demand."[12]

Nor were these the idiosyncratic resolutions of specialists in legal ethics. Instead, they reflected widely held views among nineteenth-century lawyers and courts, which could be heard to insist, for example, that the lawyer's first duty is of fidelity to the law, and that "he violates it when he consciously presses for an unjust judgment."[13] Indeed, the principles Hoffman and Sharswood elaborated reflected, or at least became, banalities of nineteenth-century legal ethics, which, Gordon observes, "advised lawyers to be satisfied of the likely merits of clients' causes before instigating suits, to be scrupulous in arguing law and facts to tribunals, and to reach an independent view, not the client's view, of the demands of the governing law. . . ."[14] Even prominent exceptions to these attitudes were in fact deployed to reinforce the orthodoxy. For example, "[t]he famous admonition of Lord Brougham to the effect that the lawyer must fight for his client, heedless of any other interest in the universe, was often quoted [in the nineteenth century], but invariably with disapproval."[15]

This brief discussion of course cannot hope to establish the precise contours of nineteenth-century lawyers' professional obligations. To do so would require elaborating, much as Part I did for contemporary legal ethics, precisely when and precisely how nineteenth-century lawyers were permitted to act on their personal views of the legal and factual merits of their clients' cases and when they were (in spite of the principles just recited) required to promote clients' interests even against their own judgments. But although these grand principles of nineteenth-century legal ethics could not plausibly have dominated every aspect of actual legal practice—that would have undermined the structural separation between lawyers and judges on which the very idea of adversary advocacy depends—they surely were not irrelevant to the daily conduct of lawyers. Certainly the conflict between nineteenth-century lawyers' professional obligations and ordinary first-personal morality was nothing near so stark as the conflict that confronts lawyers today, and the attendant threat to the lawyer's integrity was similarly less potent.

The current discussion also does not establish the precise historical path along which the nineteenth-century conception of legal ethics developed into the modern one, or even fix exactly when this development began. But although the search for precision in such matters is perhaps anyway a fool's errand, as good a starting point as any is the first appearance of the professional duty of confidentiality in Rule 21 of the Alabama Ethics Code of 1887,[16] which was the first formal ethics code adopted in any American jurisdiction and also the model for the many codes to come. "Since then every revision of the codes has moved them further away from the obligation to balance clients' interests against obligations to the legal system, toward almost exclusive duties of loyalty, confidentiality, and zealous advocacy to clients."[17] Throughout the twists and turns in the historical development of legal ethics, the tension between lawyers' professional obligations and ordinary moral ambitions and the pressure that these obligations exert on lawyers' integrity have steadily increased.

The Internal Division of Labor

A second historical development, proceeding in rough parallel to the increase in partisanship, has further intensified the pressure that modern lawyers' professional obligations place on their integrity. Whereas the first development concerns the nature of the representation that lawyers provide for whatever clients they serve, this second development concerns the types of clients that lawyers acquire and thus the patterns of lawyer-client pairings that arise in society.

Nineteenth-century lawyers (including elite lawyers) typically represented a broad range of clients on all sides of disputes. But although the legal profession as a whole continues to represent all sides of disputes, the division of labor has penetrated the profession itself, to create divisions among lawyers that parallel the divisions among clients. Lawyers have become increasingly specialized over the course of the twentieth century, not just by doctrinal expertise but also, and critically, in virtue of becoming increasingly narrowly tied to certain classes of clients, who press distinctive substantive positions, so that lawyers today typically represent exclusively businesses or individuals, defendants or plaintiffs.*[18] Although this narrowing trend is familiar to sociologists of the legal profession, it figures less prominently than the trend toward greater partisanship in philosophical treatments of legal ethics (and indeed in the ethical self-understandings of the bar). It is, however, no less (and probably more) important to the modern lawyer's ethical quandary. And it is therefore worth devoting some energy to identifying this historical development and elaborating its moral significance.

"Before 1900," Gordon observes, "the same lawyers often represented whoever first sought to hire them, whether plaintiffs or defendants."[19] This was true even with respect to issues that were among the most contentious or divisive of the day—so that, for example, "[u]ntil the 1930s lawyers in general corporate practice might still represent labor organizations."[20] Moreover, this habit of representing a broad range of clients on all sides of disputes extended into the upper echelons of the bar. Thus, "[t]he leaders of the bar in 1900 were still mostly generalists, men who made their mark as trial lawyers trying a medley of civil and criminal cases such as wills, divorces, libels, and murders, as constitutional lawyers arguing before the Supreme Court, and as general business advisers."[21]

Perhaps most notably, the nineteenth-century "lawyers ranked by the public and their peers at the top of their profession were rarely exclusively or full-time 'corporate lawyers.'"[22] Instead, although "[a] successful lawyer had important business clients: railroads, financial institutions, insurance companies, and industrial firms," to be sure, "[h]e was also a courtroom lawyer who tried murders, divorces, and will contests as well as commercial cases; who argued appeals before the highest federal and state courts; and who took time off from practice to serve in high elective or appointive office."[23] For example, Rufus Choate, the leading Boston lawyer of his day, represented an injured railway worker in a tort suit against the Boston & Worcester Railroad Co., in an important effort to subject employers to liability for industrial accidents.[24] Similarly, Clarence Darrow famously sought pardons for the Chicago Haymarket defendants even as he was general counsel for the Chicago & Northwestern Railway. And even after Darrow resigned from his position as general counsel in order to represent Eugene V. Debs in his legal battles with the railroads, he kept doing part-time work for the Chicago & Northwestern.[25]

---

* This development is in some measure peculiar, or at least peculiarly well-developed, in the American context. English barristers, by contrast, have retained the cab-rank rule, which forbids precisely the kind of specialization by client-type and cause that American lawyers have embraced.

This generalism began to come undone when, toward the end of the nineteenth century, "the companies most often sued, like railroads, mining companies, and streetcar companies, began to . . . put [their lawyers] on retainer, and forbade them from representing plaintiffs."[26] Lawrence Friedman reports that whereas in-house counsel was "unheard of in 1800" and "exceedingly rare in 1850," this was "by 1900 . . . a well-worn groove of practice."[27] In insurance practice, for example, the Prudential acquired an in-house law shop in 1885, with New York Life following in 1893, and the Metropolitan in 1897.[28] And insurance practice was not in this respect unusual. Lawyers quite generally were becoming "increasing specialized not only by type of case but also by clientele: in labor disputes, lawyers made careers representing exclusively management or labor; in tort cases, plaintiffs or defendants."[29] Indeed, such specialization was, by the early decades of the twentieth century, a familiar bugbear of old-fashioned lawyers such as Samuel Untermeyer, a successful corporate lawyer in New York who warned in 1933 that large corporations who demanded exclusive engagements from their lawyers acted "to draw away from advocacy the best minds of the bar and by money temptations convert them into highly paid clerks to teach financiers to keep 'prayerfully within the law.'"[30]

Today, such specialization is dramatic and extreme. Perhaps most fundamentally, the bar is split, as a famous empirical study revealed, "between lawyers who represent large organizations (corporations, labor unions, or government) and those who represent individuals," two very different forms of practice that distinguish "the two hemispheres of the profession."[31] This division is persistent: "Most lawyers reside exclusively in one hemisphere or the other and seldom, if ever, cross the equator";[32] and very few—as few as 15 percent—spend substantial portions of their professional time in both hemispheres.[33]

Moreover, the division has broad-ranging consequences, including especially narrowing the range of substantive positions that lawyers advocate over the course of their careers. Many organizational clients generate enough work to command most or even all of their lawyers' professional attention. This is trivially true with respect to in-house lawyers, including those that represent the government, but something similar applies to outside counsel, at least for corporations, so that in one survey, large firm lawyers spent an average of 35 percent of their time, over a year, on a single client, with lawyers in certain specializations in certain firms spending up to 60 percent of their time on one client.[34] And although such an intimate affiliation with a few clients is perhaps most natural for the corporate lawyer, who wants (as one commentator put it) nothing more than "a steady and permanent group of well-paying clients,"[35] this narrowing of lawyers' professional engagements is not limited to lawyers who represent business interests. Perhaps the apotheosis of this narrow form of legal practice, not least because it makes a narrow selection of clients self-consciously into one of its aims, is public-interest practice, or cause-lawyering, in which lawyers engage their professional energies in the service of a particular, sectarian political program.[36] And finally, as this last example suggests, in many areas of law the identity of a lawyer's client effectively determines the substantive positions that she takes. The tort bar, for example, is divided between defense lawyers who represent businesses and plaintiffs' lawyers who represent individuals, and includes professional bodies devoted to either side of the divide.*[37]

The division of labor has thus penetrated the legal profession, which is not just separated from the laity by its commitment to partisanship but also internally divided into many camps, each connected to particular classes of clients and therefore pursuing specific substantive positions. And this second, internal division of labor qualitatively increases the pressure that lawyers' professional obligations in favor of partisanship exert against their integrity.†[38] The problem of lawyers' integrity

---

* The plaintiffs' bar, for example, dominates the Association of Trial Lawyers of America (ATLA). In fact, the predecessor organization to the ATLA was known as the National Association of American Claimants' Attorneys (NAACA).

† One might think that the internal division of labor within the legal profession in another way relieves the pressure on lawyers' integrity, by decreasing the likelihood that lawyers represent clients of whom they disapprove. For one thing, the narrowing of lawyers' professional engagements makes it easier for lawyers to sort themselves into varieties of practice in which their clients match their sympathies; and for another, it allows the natural human tendency, in Karl Llewellyn's words, for a person's "sympathies and ethical judgments [to be] determined essentially by the things and the people he works on and for and with," to operate in a uniform way to bring lawyers' personal attitudes into line with their clients' goals. Thus Llewellyn added that "[h]ence the practice of corporation law not only works for business men towards business ends, but develops within itself a business point of view—toward the work to be done, toward the value of the work to the community, indeed, toward the way in which to do the work."

And indeed, modern business lawyers, for example, do tend roughly to approve of their clients' general aims and to favor legal changes that would benefit their clients. According to one surveyor, "three-quarters of the respondents for whom I have complete data have never been faced with a conflict between their personal values and the request of a client." In the same survey, the legal changes that corporate lawyers favored "came out against the government, for management, for the defense in litigation, for wealthy taxpayers, and for banks and creditors." Moreover, "80.2 percent of the responses suggested that the proposed changes would have salutary effects for clients."

Nevertheless, the survey also revealed that "businessmen are substantially more optimistic about the capacity of the market than are the legal elite who represent them," that "[l]arge-firm lawyers almost certainly have a more favorable view of federal administrative involvement in the day-to-day activities of employers than do the business clients they

arises, recall, because even when their partisanship can be impartially justified, the achievements of the adversary system that justify such partisanship are too remote from the lawyer's point of view, too dependent on other interventions by other agents, for lawyers to take authorship of the adversary system as a whole. Instead, adversary advocates are merely cogs in the causal mechanism of the adversary system, who forsake their integrity as agents when, in the more immediate actions of which they can take authorship, they betray their personal moral ambitions and lie and cheat in the service of the system. The internal division of labor that has grown up within the legal profession deepens the lawyer's alienation by further attenuating the connection between her professional inputs and the adversary system's final outputs—by introducing an additional layer of specialization, an additional epicycle of causal instrumentalism, to separate the lawyer's own actions, in lying and cheating, from the just or legitimate outcomes that give the adversary system its impartial justification.

Although even an old-fashioned lawyer, who represented all kinds of clients and argued all sides of disputes, was in each case that she took merely a cog in the adversary system's causal mechanism, she might at least claim to encompass all parts of the adversary system over the course of her career; a modern lawyer, whose work-life is dominated (sometimes exclusively) by one client on one side, cannot claim even that.

---

represent," and that "a substantial segment of the elite strata of the bar regards the distribution of economic rewards to be unjust," all of which "indicate an awareness of substantive inequality and support for some government efforts to redress the unequal access to the resources necessary to meet some basic human needs."

Moreover, the suggestion that a division of labor might save lawyers' integrity misconstrues the nature of the threat against their integrity that lawyers face, specifically by locating that threat, incorrectly, in lawyers' discomfort with their clients' ultimate purposes rather than, as I have been arguing, in tensions between more general first-personal ethical ideals of truth-telling and fair play and the methods that lawyers must employ in serving their clients' purposes, whatever they are. (This is the mistake, against which I have sought from the very beginnings of my argument to build up resistance, of focusing legal ethics unduly on sensational cases of conflicts between lawyers' and clients' ultimate values rather than on more banal, everyday conflicts between ordinary ideals of upstanding conduct and the professional obligations of adversary advocacy.) Whatever legal standard regulates an activity, the participants in the activity will always focus their legal energies on shifting the boundaries of the standard, which means that even lawyers who have internalized their clients' purposes and values will inevitably be regularly engaged in cases in which they believe that their clients, all things considered (that is, applying the prevailing legal rules to the facts as they see them), have the weaker position. And in such cases, lawyers' come under professional obligations to lie and to cheat, and they therefore face the threats against their integrity that I have been describing.

Insular and Cosmopolitan Roles

Over the course of the twentieth century, the law governing lawyers has developed to exacerbate the substantive tension between lawyers' professional obligations and everyday first-personal moral ideals. Moreover, the bar has, during the same period, internalized the division of labor so as to increase (by a full degree of abstraction) the ethical distance between a lawyer's personal contributions to adversary adjudication and the impartial justification of the adversary process itself. Both of these trends—toward greater partisanship and a greater division of labor— have worked systematically to increase the pressures that the professional obligations associated with adversary advocacy exert on the integrity of twentieth-century lawyers. But although these parallel historical developments present the problem of integrity (a problem that I have argued is inherent in adversary advocacy) to modern lawyers in particularly stark terms, they do not render that problem insoluble. In particular, the solution that I have recommended—involving role-based redescription elaborated in terms of the connection between the lawyerly virtues of fidelity and negative capability and the legitimacy of adjudication—remains conceptually open to modern lawyers. The question now to hand is therefore not whether the problem of integrity is posed to lawyers today, or whether a solution to the problem is conceptually possible, but rather whether this solution to this problem is practically available. And this is the question to which I now turn.

In arguing that lawyers might employ the ethics of role to preserve their integrity against the threats raised by their professional obligations, I have focused on what is conceptually possible—on the fact that role-ethics has the right form for preserving integrity and that there exists, in negative capability and surrounding ideas, a substantively appealing account of the lawyer's role. But the fact that an ideal is recognizably ethical is not by itself sufficient for persons to adopt that ideal as their own or indeed even to pursue it. A person may recognize an ideal's ethical bona fides but may nevertheless think it unsuited, or even inappropriate, to the conditions of her own life, so that it never penetrates her own first-personal ambitions. Many people, including boxing fans, never aspire to the boxer's virtues; and many more will admire Jane's dedication to freedom fighting without pursuing her executory ruthlessness for themselves. And the lawyerly virtues have a similarly distant and abstract appeal for most persons, who can recognize that fidelity and negative capability are essential for the legitimacy of adjudication, and therefore useful and even appealing for others, but nevertheless steadfastly retain their own first-personal commitments to truthfulness and fair play.

Accordingly, it remains to be asked, as I have not yet done, whether integrity-preserving role-based redescription along these lines is in fact practically accessible to modern lawyers. In particular, I have not asked what a role must be like—what features it must have—in order to support its occupants in developing role-based, first-personal moral ideals that depart from commonplace morality and that can resist ordinary first-personal moral criticism, and I have not asked whether the modern adversary lawyer's role is in fact like this. I now take up these questions and conclude that the internal construction of the contemporary lawyer's role renders it unable to underwrite distinctively lawyerly first-personal ethical ideals and so renders integrity-preserving role-based redescription practically unavailable to contemporary lawyers.

When a person presents an impartial moral defense of her activities, she must address this defense, in either the third- or the second-person, to the world at large; but when (after having presented this defense) she engages in integrity-preserving role-based redescription, she may proceed in the first-person, addressing only herself. In order to preserve the integrity of someone whose actions (even though they are impartially justified) violate the first-personal ideals ordinarily adopted by good people, role-based redescription need only persuade that person herself that these ideals do not apply to her peculiar circumstances, circumstances that are more properly approached in terms of distinctive, role-based first-personal ideals. Accordingly, role-based redescription's success depends, in effect, on whether or not it is proposed authentically. This is, of course, a much more relaxed standard than the strict standard of general persuasiveness by which arguments concerning impartial morality are measured. Nevertheless, even this lax standard establishes some limits on what a role must be like in order to underwrite integrity-preserving role-based redescription. The role must, after all, be able to sustain its occupants in resisting outsiders' accounts of their role-based conduct and instead understanding this conduct in the terms established by the role. This makes it worth asking what a role must be like in order for its occupants, acting authentically, to see the world stably through its terms.

The remarks I have made about the contrast between Jim's position and Jane's begin to develop an answer to this question. In particular, I have said that Jim could not simply *decide* to redescribe his act without reference to killing the one. Good faith belief is, in an important sense, not discretionary—one cannot simply *choose* what to believe, including what to believe about the nature of one's own actions; belief is instead in some measure compelled by certain features of the circumstance in which it is formed, including, but not limited to, the truth about the object of belief. A bare act of will therefore cannot create a role capable of underwriting role-based redescription,[39] and Jim's position illustrates this. Moreover, Jane's case—the fact that role-based redescription was available to Jane—illustrates the most natural way for a person to come to a role, namely for the role to have been established by the attitudes, expectations, and activities of many others, often (although not necessarily in Jane's case) combining to create a culture,[40] or a practice.[41]

Of course, the role will involve a practice in which not all people participate. The threat to a person's integrity and the need for role-based *re*description arises, after all, because people do not ordinarily see the person's actions in the terms set out by the role that requires them; because ordinary people resist role-based descriptions and consequently insist on approaching even conduct that occurs within roles in terms of ordinary first-personal moral ideals. In the lawyer's case, ordinary people resist describing lawyers' professional conduct in terms of fidelity and negative capability and instead insist on calling such conduct lying and cheating.[42] Where lawyers give the concepts lying and cheating legalistic developments, according to which their application depends narrowly on the desires and expectations of the people involved in an interaction, their ordinary accusers give lying and cheating much more expansive and informal treatments, according to which their application depends primarily on the presence of manipulation and the imposition of avoidable harm. And where lawyers give the negatively capable virtues that they associate with their profession loose and expansive interpretations, their accusers interpret these virtues narrowly and view them skeptically, insisting that goodness depends not on self-effacing empathy but on purity of heart.

This conflict is, of course, just a reprise of the idea, by now familiar,* that every action may come under a wide range of descriptions depending on the aims and conceptual schemes adopted by the describer, and that each of these many descriptions may be accurate when assessed from the point of view of someone who has adopted the appropriate conceptual scheme. The lawyer who seeks to employ role-based redescription to preserve his integrity stands in a very different position, with respect to this idea, from the lawyer who must answer the charge of partiality. He need not address the world at large, and need not worry that his accusers continue (and for good reason) to reject the values and descriptions in terms of which he conceives of his activities, but must instead persuade only himself and his co-practitioners.

Nevertheless—and this is the crucial point here—the lawyer can successfully employ role-based redescription to defend his integrity only if he continues to find the redescription persuasive even in the face of the

---

* Recall the discussion in Chapter 7.

fact that it is rejected by others, indeed by most or all others who are not themselves lawyers, as it inevitably will be. Lawyers' professional activities, after all, are regarded as vicious by ordinary first-personal morality. And lawyers' efforts to recharacterize these activities in terms of role-based virtues will therefore be viewed by non-lawyers not just as eccentric—on the model of the attitude outsiders might take to attributions of virtue made by members of a strange but harmless subculture (for example, to competitive ballroom dancers' claims that a routine displays emotional courage)—but rather as wrongful. If hostility and indeed outright rejection from nonlawyers undermines the lawyer's own commitment to the concepts and descriptions associated with his role— his own belief in role-based redescription—then such redescription cannot save the lawyer's integrity because it will not present him with an alternative to viewing his professional activities as involving a betrayal of his own ends (even if this betrayal is impartially justified).

Accordingly, a role can underwrite integrity-preserving role-based redescription only insofar as it is *authoritatively insular* in matters of first-personal ethics, that is, only insofar as role-occupants, who take their first-personal ethical ideals and ambitions from the role rather than from ordinary morality, are not shaken by the fact that others reject these ethical concepts, or even reject the role outright, for themselves. Above all, if a role is to be capable of underwriting integrity-preserving role-based redescription, it may not be *cosmopolitan.* Its occupants must not think of themselves, in connection with their first-personal ethical ambitions, as members of a role-independent ethical culture, as coming under a duty to satisfy the ethical opinions of the world at large. Thus, the very element of roles that rendered them structurally unsuited to defending lawyers against the accusation of partiality is absolutely central to their capacity to support lawyers' integrity (in the first person) in the face of the independent charge that they lie and cheat.*[43]

---

*This same point may also be expressed in a slightly different vocabulary by saying that a role loses the power to sustain integrity-preserving role-based redescription as its occupants treat the role as less important to their self-conceptions, that is, as they grow more distant from the role. Meir Dan-Cohen has argued that the relationship between lawyers and their role has become more attenuated over time—that lawyers have experienced increasingly greater *role-distance*—and indeed that lawyers have become so distant from their role that their ties to the role have become "too distended" for lawyers to continue counting their role "as [an] integral part[] of the self." (Dan-Cohen borrows the term *role-distance* from Erving Goffman.)

But although this vocabulary provides a natural alternative to my discussion of cosmopolitan roles and the problem of integrity (right down to the suggestion that "an inappropriate role-distance" can lead to "alienation"), Dan-Cohen does not himself deploy the vocabulary in this direction. Instead, he proposes that role-distance, or "detachment" as he also calls it, "may be the self's preferred strategy for dealing with 'dirty hands' types of

It seems likely that there was a time, in the more distant past, when
many roles—including, clerical, military, and merchant roles—were sufficiently insular for their role-based ethics to serve the integrity-preserving
function that I have described. These roles were structured so that their
occupants neither looked nor felt any need to look beyond the roles in
forming their first-personal ambitions, and even persons outside the roles
recognized and respected the roles' distinctive ethical status and authority. Certainly these historical roles openly resisted ethical incursions by
non-members, from the outside world. They commonly exercised strict
control over who might enter the role and subjected new role-occupants
to long periods of apprenticeship, designed to alter their habits and dispositions to conform to the role's standards. Furthermore, these roles
were self-governing, claiming primary (and sometimes even exclusive) authority to resolve disputes amongst role-members: churches, armies, and
even guilds, for example, all staffed and operated their own court systems,[44] and role-occupants made un-selfconscious claims based on the
norms and ambitions that the roles established.[*45] Taken as a unit, these
roles may have been in one way or another accountable to society in general (although the form of this accountability was as a historical matter,
almost certainly not impartial). But the internal affairs of the roles remained strictly internal, governed by role-bound rather than ordinary
ethical standards.[†46]

---

situations, in which social norms call for the performance of horrifying or otherwise repugnant tasks." Dan-Cohen proposes, in other words, that lawyers' role-distance saves
them from the charges that they lie and cheat, because it detaches evaluations of them as
lawyers from evaluations of them as persons. As I understand this argument, it proposes
that as long as a role's occupants insist on appropriate role-distance, the role can shield
them from the criticisms of third-personal impartial morality. And that, it seems to me,
involves a mistake—indeed, precisely the mistake that philosophical critics have accused
role morality of committing quite generally.

* A striking example of this appears in Arthur Applbaum's ethical portrait of Charles-
Henri Sanson, executioner of Paris . . . throughout the period of the French Revolution.
Sanson lost himself, completely and utterly unselfconsciously, inside his role, accepting no
ethical ideas or authority from outside the role. Furthermore, as the fact of Sanson's lon-
gevity reveals, this view of Sanson's role-insularity and unaccountability to ordinary morality was widely shared. Sanson executed noblemen at the beginning of the revolution,
moderates during the Terror, and, finally, Robespierre himself; but no side ever charged
Sanson with the partisan causes his executions served, or indeed treated him as anything
other than the technical functionary his role declared him to be.

† It is worth noting that this extremely insular account of roles, though it may have
been dominant, was not uniformly accepted even in the more distant past. Montaigne, for
example, quite explicitly proposed a cosmopolitan account of roles, saying "we must play
our part [our role] duly, but as the part of a borrowed character. Of the mask and appearance we must not make a real essence, nor of what is foreign what is our very own."
Furthermore, Montaigne, ever modern, realized that this account of roles has profoundly

Assessing the precise character and extent of the insularity of any particular past role, and especially of roles from the more distant past, will
of course always involve considerable historical complexity and difficulty.* Indeed, such historical uncertainty is illustrated even by the early
history of the American bar.

On the one hand, Tocqueville's observation that American lawyers had
acquired "the tastes and habits of the aristocracy," including a "repugnance to the actions of the multitude" and a "secret contempt of the
government of the people,"[47] famously suggests that, at least in the mid-
nineteenth century, the lawyer's role was indeed significantly insular.
Moreover, the early American bar was in many respects authoritatively
self-regulating in the ways that role-insularity requires: "[d]uring colonial
times and for almost two hundred years after the American revolution,
lawyers practiced relatively free of anything like the intricate constraints
of law that now hold lawyers fast."[48]

On the other hand, the full historical record is much more complicated
than Tocqueville's remark suggests. Indeed, the very period in which Tocqueville wrote had been bad for lawyers' insularity. Jacksonian democracy had subjected the legal profession to previously unknown pressures,[49]
and these pressures dramatically reduced the insularity and cohesion of
the bar. Perhaps most dramatically, most American jurisdictions eliminated the apprenticeship system through which the bar had traditionally
exercised control over its membership and shaped its members, and some
jurisdictions even went so far as to open the practice of law to all free
adult men.[50] These developments call Tocqueville's conclusion into question, at the very least, and it has even been suggested that the Jacksonian
period's "hostility to professional privileges destroyed incipient legal guild
organizations in the early nineteenth century."[51] Indeed, the organized
bar is perhaps best understood as an effort to combat Jacksonian attacks
on the lawyer's role and to make Tocqueville's vision a reality. Certainly
the now-familiar institutions of the bar arose in the years following the

---

disturbing ethical implications for their occupants, much like the implications I have developed here. Thus, Montaigne believed that because "in any government there are necessary offices which are not only abject but also vicious," some citizens must "sacrifice their
honor and their conscience . . . for the good of their country."

* Part of the problem here is that applying the distinction between insular and cosmopolitan roles to the distant past risks a serious anachronism. These concepts are designed,
as will become increasingly clear, to characterize roles against the backdrop of certain
fundamental commitments to the universal application of impartial morality. But the
modern idea of moral impartiality, especially in its position as the dominant ideal of
moral argument, is itself a historical development. And this may make it misleading, and
perhaps even incoherent, to apply an account of roles constructed in the shadow of impartiality to premodern societies.

Jacksonian period, after Tocqueville wrote. New Hampshire, for example, which had at mid-century allowed anyone over twenty-one and of
good character to practice law,[52] restored official recognition to an elite
inner bar in 1859 and restored the State Supreme Court's power to exclude people from the practice of law in 1872.[53] And generalized bar
groups, which were previously unknown, began to flourish only in the
latter part of the nineteenth century.*[54]

   These complexities make it an interesting historical question whether
the organized American bar and its institutions were ever insular in the
way necessary for sustaining a distinctive, integrity-preserving role-ethic
among lawyers or whether, instead, the bar's professionalism project
was in this respect doomed to failure from the beginning—the last, des-
perate gasp of an elite being overcome by the increasingly egalitarian
tides of history. But however that question is resolved, and I shall not
say more about it here, the legal profession has undergone a series of
historical developments, beginning almost as soon as the organized bar
was established and continuing throughout the twentieth century, that
have eliminated all the key elements of insularity from the lawyer's role.
Whatever may have been true historically, the modern lawyer's role has
taken on a decidedly cosmopolitan cast, so that it cannot today sustain
integrity-preserving role-based redescription.

   Three features of the modern bar contribute especially substantially to
its cosmopolitanism. First, the bar has come to draw its members from a
much more heterogeneous group of persons and, at the same time, has
become much less involved in shaping lawyers' professional attitudes.
These developments have dramatically diminished the bar's capacity to
establish and sustain a unified and distinctive set of attitudes toward the
practice of law of the sort required for integrity-preserving role-based redescription. Second (and perhaps as a result of the first trend, although I
shall not try to establish the causal connection), the principles of professional conduct through which the bar regulates its members have changed
from being fraternal admonitions that announce the informal standards of
right-thinking lawyers to being fixed rules backed by formal sanctions in a

---

   * The first was the Association of the Bar of the City of New York (1870). Eight further
city and eight state bar associations (in twelve states) were created between 1870 and 1878,
in which year the American Bar Association was formed. The formation of the ABA is,
unsurprisingly, itself a historically complex matter—part an offshoot of a self-conscious
project of professional role-building among American lawyers and part a partisan political
effort to promote laissez-faire economic and social organization. In this respect, the formation of the ABA was perhaps connected to opposition to the Supreme Court's decision in
Munn v. Illinois, which rejected a takings challenge to an Illinois statue regulating prices
charged by grain elevators, although this connection seems unlikely to have figured prominently in the self-understandings of the ABA's founders.

bureaucratic regulatory scheme. This development has deprived the modern law governing lawyers of its aspirational qualities and so rendered it formally unsuited to being adopted in the modality of first-personal moral ambition, as role-based redescription requires. And finally, and perhaps most importantly, control over modern lawyers is no longer the exclusive province of the bar but has instead become colonized by the state through its standard regulatory organs. The modern bar has lost the free-standing authority to regulate its members, whose professional morality increasingly takes instruction from non-lawyers who do not share the idiosyncratically lawyerly ideals on which role-based redescription depends.

Whether or not the American bar was *ever* insular, it is, for all these reasons, *now* clearly and anxiously cosmopolitan. And a cosmopolitan bar cannot sustain its members' integrity against the pressures that their professional circumstances apply.

The Disintegrated Bar

Whereas the bar in 1800 was almost exclusively drawn from elite families, by 1860 lawyers with middle-class origins were much, much more common.[55] But even so, the legal profession remained strikingly homogeneous throughout the nineteenth century: most lawyers were Protestants, although there were a few Catholics and Jews;[56] and virtually all lawyers were white and male.[57] The twentieth century, however, particularly in its latter years, witnessed a sea-change in the composition of the bar. Minority enrollment in law schools increased steadily—from 4.3 percent in 1969,[58] to 13.1 percent in 1990,[59] to 21.4 percent in 2005.[60] More strikingly still, enrollment of women at ABA approved law schools grew from 4.5 percent to 37.7 percent between 1976 and 1983 and by 2005 was 47.5 percent.[61] As a result of these changes, the modern bar, although far from perfectly integrated or egalitarian, is unquestionably "an amorphous and polyglot group."[62] Certainly modern lawyers do not, antecedent to their legal training and practice, share any traits or attitudes that set them apart from non-lawyers in a way capable of sustaining the distinctive first-personal moral ambitions on which integrity-preserving role-based redescription depends.*[63]

---

*The sheer size of the modern bar, which now comprises roughly a million lawyers, exacerbates the dis-integrative effects of the bar's heterogeneity by diluting the professional ties that might otherwise integrate even a diverse profession. Thus it is among the banalities of the sociology of modern lawyers that "as the numbers [of lawyers] grow, the probability of chance transactions between any given pair or any given sets of lawyers decreases. Since individual lawyers' circles of acquaintance are unlikely to expand at the same rate or to the same extent as the growth of the bar, there will be an increasing number of their fellow lawyers with whom they have no ties."

Moreover, even as the bar has admitted lawyers with more various backgrounds, it has asserted less control and exerted much less influence over the education and training of young lawyers, and it has therefore abandoned any prospect of securing convergence among its originally heterogeneous recruits by instilling distinctive and homogenizing professional ideals. Legal education has moved steadily from the apprenticeship to the university law school, first as a matter of practice, and then by express design. Thus whereas most lawyers in 1870 learned their trade as apprentices, by 1950 most lawyers were law school trained instead.[64] And this trend only accelerated over the twentieth century: the ABA issued its first list of approved law schools in 1923;[65] by 1947, there were fifteen jurisdictions in which it was no longer possible to enter the legal profession by apprenticeship;[66] and today it is virtually unheard of to become a lawyer without attending law school.[67] Indeed, the bar—initially motivated to resist the trend toward diversity just mentioned by raising the costs of entrance so that only members of the establishment could pay them—has over this period moved to require its members to possess not just a university-provided legal education but also a prior generalist university degree. The leading law schools had already made a B.A. a requirement of admission by the end of the 1920s,[68] and beginning in that same decade, the ABA and AALS worked strenuously and steadily to require all law schools to follow this lead,[69] so that by 1970,[70] law had everywhere in the United States become an advanced degree.

Finally, the internal division of labor that I earlier observed has grown up within the bar brings additional schismatic pressures to bear on the legal profession, by undermining the idea, which characterized the legal profession's self-understanding through the late years of the nineteenth century, that the bar was as Gordon has said, "an integrated whole, in the sense that if all its projects could have been carried through, they would all have *fit together*."[71] Instead, even lawyers' professional experiences have come to separate them according to the types of clients and causes that they serve.

All these twentieth-century developments have rendered the bar increasingly unable to sustain a distinctive role-ethic. On the one hand, greater diversity in lawyers' backgrounds (concerning class, religion, race, and gender) has increased the integrative burden that the bar's institutions would have to bear in order to sustain an insular legal profession. As lawyers have less and less antecedently in common, it becomes less and less natural for lawyers, in forming their personal and professional ambitions, to look inward to each other rather than outward to non-lawyers with whom they do share a background.

And on the other hand, even as the outward-looking tendencies that an insular legal profession must overcome have increased, the bar's capacity to draw its members inward has diminished. The old apprenticeship system, which molded men (and they were, remember, overwhelmingly white, protestant men) into lawyers by encouraging them to emulate the habits of established practitioners, was a powerful integrative force. The bar took hold of apprentices when they were still very young and subjected them to a more or less uniform, all-encompassing, inward-looking, and utterly distinctive training regimen. Modern legal education, by contrast, has none of these integrative capacities. Law schools take in exclusively older students, who have completed a prior course of study in which their intellectual and ethical characters were shaped wholly apart from the adversary context and ideals of the law.* And law schools themselves belong to a cosmopolitan academic culture. They teach using generally available texts presented by professors (and not practitioners) whose allegiance is to cosmopolitan standards of truth rather than to specifically lawyerly ethical ideals, so that, as one commentator has observed, "[t]here is now an almost total unwillingness within the legal academy to consider the organized bar as the legitimate voice for all lawyers or to accept traditional lawyer ideology as something like the established religion of law practice."[72] Finally, young lawyers become further isolated from one another as they enter forms of practice that are themselves increasingly mutually antagonistic.

Taken together, these developments mean that the twentieth century has seen a growth in the centrifugal forces to which the bar is subject, and a reduction in the centripetal ties it can assert. And the result, inevitably, is a less insular legal profession.

Regulation by Rule

A second development, which proceeded in parallel to (and was plausibly caused by) the dis-integration of the bar, further undermined the insularity of the modern lawyer's role, raising up another obstacle to her practical access to integrity-preserving role-based redescription. The character of the ethical principles governing lawyers' professional conduct has changed dramatically over the last century (even as their content has changed much less).

At the close of the nineteenth century, the principles of legal ethics functioned, in Hazard's words, as "fraternal admonitions."[73] Today these informal standards have been replaced by a law governing lawyers

---

* Note the irony here. A strategy adopted by a professional elite seeking to maintain the insularity of the bar (by keeping out immigrants) turned the keys to the profession over to institutions that would come to embrace the very cosmopolitanism that the elite was trying to resist.

comprised of specific, legally binding rules, backed by sanctions. Thus while earlier regimes of legal ethics expressed the point of view of "right thinking lawyers,"[74] the contemporary law governing lawyers replaces this broad ambition to elaborate the highest ambitions of the bar with a much more narrowly regulatory emphasis. This development, which has exchanged internal aspiration for external compulsion, has also contributed to the anxious cosmopolitanism of the modern lawyer's role. Certainly, modern legal ethics is stylistically unsuited to expressing an ethical point of view that might be held, in the first person, as an insular role-ethic capable of supporting integrity-preserving role-based redescription. It is simply the wrong kind of regime.

The earliest (pre-Revolutionary) regulation of American lawyers openly relied on a shared "sense of decorum and good character."[75] Indeed, even the era's rare legislative incursions into the regulation of lawyers proceeded in such broad and aspirational registers: thus, a New York statute prohibited lawyers from committing "any deceit, malpractice, crime or misdemeanor";[76] and a Maryland statute forbade "any indecent liberties to the lessening of the grandeur and authority of the (magistrate's) respective courts."[77] Moreover, little changed in the century following the American Revolution, so that in the late nineteenth century, Massachusetts contemplated disciplining its lawyers for "deceit, malpractice, or other gross misconduct,"[78] and Pennsylvania allowed disbarment of any lawyer who "shall misbehave himself in his office of attorney."[79] Indeed, the early ethics codes, including most prominently the Canons of Professional Ethics promulgated by the ABA in 1908, generally proceeded in this fraternal and high-minded mode.*[80] And well into the twentieth century, disbarment cases arose almost exclusively when lawyers either were convicted in the criminal courts of a serious offense or had engaged in "plainly outrageous behavior of a similarly repugnant nature" which had not yet resulted in a criminal conviction (although it still might).[81] Until surprisingly recently, "[j]urisdictions seem to have contented themselves with the position that no more precise specification of prohibited wrongs was necessary because a lawyer of suitable learning and character would be well aware of what was permitted and prohibited."[82]

But although "[t]he early history of American legal ethics gave no indication that lawyers would one day become a highly regulated profession,"[83] this is without doubt what the modern legal profession has become.[84] The sea-change happened in 1969, when the ABA replaced

---

* The ABA itself "until well into the twentieth century functioned mainly as an exclusive social fraternal organization of high-status lawyers rather than as a broadly representative and unofficial regulatory body."

the 1908 Canons with the Model Code of Professional Responsibility. The Model Code was, as one commentator has observed, "explicitly regulatory in purpose and design."[85] Although it retained some of the Canons' aspirational language, the Model Code also included specifically identified narrower and mandatory "Disciplinary Rules," which naturally came to dominate its practical application. Moreover, this development was extended, in 1983, by the ABA's promulgation of the Model Rules of Professional Conduct, which consist more or less exclusively of specific, legally cognizable rules drafted by a quasilegislative process and designed to share in the authority of ordinary public law.[86] Whereas earlier legal ethics proceeded in the modality of stating generally what well-disposed lawyers ought to aspire to be, the modern ethics codes aim to identify precisely what every lawyer may and may not do.

As a result of this development, Hazard says, "[t]he rules of ethics have ceased to be internal to the profession; they have instead become a code of law enforced by formal adjudicated disciplinary processes."[87] And this change—the joint emphasis on narrow rules and formal sanctions—inserts a distance between modern ethics regimes and the lawyers that they govern, and so makes these regimes simply the wrong *kind* of thing for grounding first-personal ethical life, which requires the intimacy associated with a natural drive to live up to broad ideals.[88] Indeed it is one of the banalities of the sociology of the professions that "[f]ormal, codified disciplinary procedures do not therefore fit easily and comfortably into any professional community," and are instead a "second best or a last resort, tantamount to a breakdown of normal, communal life."[89]

One might say, using the language that I have introduced, that the increasingly formal character of the legal ethics codes has made the legal profession's most prominent collective ethical regime more cosmopolitan than insular, and therefore unable to sustain any distinctive first-personal ethical creed that might replace more ordinary ethical ambitions and protect lawyers' integrity against the pressures associated with their professional obligations.

External Controls

Finally, and most importantly, the twentieth century has witnessed a dramatic shift, in the law governing lawyers, away from self-regulation and towards external control over lawyers. To be sure, the bar's official statements continue to insist that lawyers are a self-regulating profession—the Preamble to the Model Rules of Professional Conduct, for example, refers to the "special responsibilities of self-government."[90] And the bar continues both to draw up the regulatory codes that govern lawyers' professional conduct and to adjudicate cases of misconduct that arise under these codes. But the legal profession's assertions of self-regulation are becoming increasingly (and by now perhaps even principally) a myth. The organized bar's direct contributions to regulating its members are increasingly distant from the traditional forms of professional self-regulation. And other institutions, including most strikingly the political branches of government, are increasingly asserting authority over the regulation of lawyers.

These developments have further undermined the insularity of the modern bar, because a legal profession that lacks the collective authority to control the obligations its members come under will hardly be able to sustain a distinctive ethical outlook for individual lawyers. Instead, insofar as the bar's collective regulation involves external control, lawyers' individual ethical aspirations will inevitably be outward-looking also. And such cosmopolitan lawyers will, as I have argued, be unable to sustain their integrity against the threats presented by their professional lives.

The undoing of the bar's prerogative of self-regulation has proceeded on two fronts.*[91] First, although the modern bar retains trappings of self-regulation that traditionally accompanied professional status, including, most notably, as the formal author of the ethics codes that govern admission to the practice of law and professional discipline, even these traditional bar-authored structures of self-governance are no longer purely within the control of a free-standing private bar, so that often only a shadow of self-regulation remains in place. And second, bar-authored legal ethics codes are increasingly no longer the exclusive, or in some circumstances even the dominant, sources of the law governing lawyers.

With respect to the first front, even where the bar continues to draft the rules that govern its members, the processes through which breaches of such bar-codes are adjudicated have been transformed by contact with external authorities. Certainly this is true of disbarment proceedings, which today proceed in the shadow of the fact that the license to

---

* The independence of the bar has come under attack along a third front also, which is more sociological and economic than legal, although it does have significant implications for the law governing lawyers. In particular, the bar has lost its monopoly control over the admissions process, first, as noted earlier, to universities (for many candidates, getting into law school is more burdensome than passing the bar), and then to new competitors in the market for providing legal services.

These competitors range from the purely symbolic (the accused criminal who conducts his own defense rather than hiring a lawyer) to the substantially revolutionary. Thus non-lawyers, and in particular accountants and other allied servants of business, have begun to encroach on the very core of the lawyer's special competence. Such firms (and in particular firms of accountants), are "coming to dominate corporate financial and tax transactional practice in Europe. In the United States they already employ some five thousand professionals, trained as lawyers but not claiming to practice law and unregulated by the bar . . . ."

practice has been characterized by the Supreme Court as a right, so that people may not be deprived of it save by procedures that satisfy the external ideal of due process of law.[92] And this approach has been extended to the disciplinary process quite generally. Thus, it is commonly observed that over the course of the twentieth century, "the dominant bar associations directly involved in bar discipline [were transformed] from private clubs into quasi-governmental organs,"[93] so that discipline is nowadays "administered with vigor and consistency through a professional bureaucracy."[94] And it naturally follows that "[a]s disciplinary staffs have become more professionalized, they tend to identify less with the lawyers who appear before them and more with the system of rules they are charged to uphold,"[95] with the result that the organized bar "exert[s] only mild influence"[96] on processes of professional discipline under ethics codes that are "only under the indirect control of lawyers and their bar associations."[97]

Moreover, the independence and self-governance of the legal profession has been further diminished insofar as ordinary courts, which exist completely outside the traditional disciplinary process, have become directly involved in applying the ethics codes that the bar draws up. The most important judicial mechanism for the external enforcement of lawyers' professional ethics involves tort, and in particular legal malpractice, which after a long and stagnant career has achieved a new prominence in the legal regime regulating lawyers' professional conduct.*[98]

Thus the increase in the frequency and size of malpractice suits has been accompanied by a reconstruction of the doctrinal and conceptual foundations of legal malpractice claims, which has made malpractice law a much more potent cosmopolitan regulatory tool. Whereas the law of legal malpractice was, until the 1970s, dominated by contract notions, it is today dominated by ideas concerning professionalism and reasonable professional care.[99] And in conjunction with this development, malpractice suits have become a means of enforcing ethics codes outside of the bar's disciplinary processes: in some jurisdictions, a breach of professional ethics creates a rebuttable presumption of malpractice;[100] and in others, it can be nearly conclusive evidence.[101] Thus, "it is now

---

* According to one study, malpractice decisions, which accumulated at a slow and steady pace from the 1790s through 1959, display a "spectacular increase" that "began in the 1960s and continued through the 1970s and beyond." Another study reports that "[m]alpractice claims doubled in the seven years between 1979 and 1986, and the average settlement went from $3,000 to $45,000." Yet another study comparing data from 1980 to 1985 with data from 1990 to 1995 found that the number of malpractice claims closed *without* payment to the claimant decreased 16.5 percent, and the number of claims resulting in settlement after the commencement of litigation rose 8.5 percent. The relative frequency of payments over $50,000 was roughly stable, increasing by just over 2 percent.

well established in many American jurisdictions that claimants in any and all [litigation seeking a tort remedy for lawyer misconduct] can invoke a theory of breach of duty that rests at least in some important way on a provision of a lawyer code."[102] These developments have been resisted by the bar, which has "tried to separate 'malpractice' from 'discipline,'" but "these efforts have been largely unsuccessful."[103] Certainly courts have increasingly ignored the statements in both the Model Code and the Model Rules that the provisions they contain do not underwrite civil liability for lawyers who violate them.[104]

The second front along which the bar's self-governing status has been eroded involves not just the external application of ethics standards that the bar has drafted, but instead the external establishment of ethics regimes that stand wholly apart from the organized bar. Courts, legislatures, and the executive (principally through administrative agencies) are all increasingly asserting free-standing authority to regulate the practice of law, not just derivatively by applying the bar's rules, but by creating new rules of their own.

Courts have moved to impose free-standing and previously unknown regulatory regimes on the bar in a number of ways. Perhaps most straightforwardly, they have, in several doctrinal areas, been increasingly willing to apply generally applicable law against lawyers, including in circumstances in which it imposes standards of conduct that are stricter than those imposed by the lawyers' own ethics rules.[105] In the context of public law, courts have insisted that the bar's internal regulations must respect independently established rights associated with antidiscrimination law and personal privacy and autonomy.[106] And in private law, courts hearing malpractice suits have become less willing to defer to the bar in establishing the standard of care that lawyers owe their clients, specifically by expressing doubts about the exemption that lawyers have traditionally enjoyed from the rule that industry custom does not create a safe-haven from tort liability,[107] so that even as violating the ethics codes may trigger tort claims, conforming to the codes no longer guarantees immunity from liability.[108] In addition, this process of tortification has extended the judicial regulation of lawyers beyond merely policing the lawyer-client relation. The common law rule making privity of contract a necessary prerequisite for negligence claims against a lawyer is no longer absolute,[109] and privity is no bar for intentional torts, such as fraud,[110] so that lawyers are increasingly exposed to tort claims when their services are used by clients who make false or deceptive statements. To be sure, the bar's ethics rules also forbid lawyers from counseling client fraud, but that prohibition is narrower, so that the ethics rules "provide greater protection to lawyers in discipline proceedings than other law provides them in other contexts."[111]

Moreover, courts have increasingly come to regulate lawyers under their own rules, including most notably (in the Federal System) Rule 11 of the Federal Rules of Civil Procedure, which has over the last decades been amended in ways that give "federal courts an opportunity to enforce professional responsibility rules that state disciplinary bodies have been unable or unwilling to enforce."[112] Indeed, the ABA, through amendments to the Model Rules, has recognized and capitulated to the power of the courts to regulate lawyers in these ways, specifically in recent amendments to Model Rule 1.6, which governs the duty to preserve client confidences. The original version of the Rule made no exception to the duty of confidentiality for cases in which other law required disclosure[113] and indeed was adopted following an express rejection of an alternative that contemplated the exception.[114] But a recent amendment to Rule 1.6 now expressly allows disclosure of client confidences in order to comply with a court order,[115] and the official comments to the Model Rules adopt an expansive reading of the exception that the Amendment creates, so that "[i]f . . . other law supersedes this Rule and requires disclosure, paragraph (b)(6) permits the lawyer to make such disclosures as are necessary to comply with the law."[116]

Legislatures have similarly displayed an increasing inclination to regulate lawyers directly and outside of the practices of self-governance that the bar has created and manages. As the ABA recognizes, "[e]fforts are made on a recurring basis" further to decrease the bar's influence over its own governance by "remov[ing] authority for the regulation of lawyers from the judicial branch and . . . transfer[ing] it to the legislative or executive branches of government."[117] To be sure, some of these encroachments, especially those that "would significantly prejudice the judicial branch in its essential activity of adjudicating disputes,"[118] have been struck down by courts—although as assertions of judicial prerogatives under provisions of State Constitutions guaranteeing the separation of powers, rather than out of any respect for the independence of the bar. But legislative regulation "that does not substantially differ from similar regulation applicable to members of other professions"[119] typically survives such challenges.

Thus state legislatures have been allowed, for example, to authorize the suspension of attorneys pending appeal from a felony conviction or for failure to pay contributions to a professional liability fund,[120] to permit public inspection of records concerning lawyers' professional conduct,[121] to regulate the choice of lawyers employed to conduct internal investigations of corporate officials,[122] to create a cause of action for malicious prosecution by frivolous ethics complaint,[123] and even to define the practice of law.[124] Certainly, as the Connecticut Supreme Court has explained, "[t]hat . . . a statute of general applicability[] may overlap with disciplinary rules specific to attorney conduct does not render the statute unconstitutional."[125] And instead of responding to these efforts by asserting its traditional prerogatives of independence, the bar, through the ABA, has distanced itself from self-regulation properly so-called and instead embraced regulation by courts, admitting that "[r]egulation of lawyer conduct must be exercised by the judiciary and not by the organized bar,"[126] and that "[r]eform is required to insulate disciplinary counsel from control or influence by the organized bar."[127]

And finally, administrative agencies (housed in the executive branch) have established the most substantial, and certainly the most prominent, external controls over lawyers, as they have "either set up and enforced regulatory regimes to deal specifically with lawyers who practice before the agency or used their regulatory authorization and administrative regulations to enforce remedies against lawyers in courts."[128] These regimes, which are often in direct conflict with the bar's own ethics codes and are often adopted over the bar's express resistance, constitute a frontal assault on the regulatory independence and self-governance of lawyers.

This form of external regulation achieved notoriety following the Savings and Loan crisis of the 1980s, when the Office of Thrift Supervision (OTS) asserted authority to sanction lawyers who committed professional misconduct before it,[129] including in cases in which the bar took the view that the conduct in question was permitted or even required by its ethics code.*[130]

To begin with, the OTS interpreted the ABA's Model Rules to require the lawyers representing thrifts to make disclosures to bank examiners that the ABA, whose Working Group on Lawyers' Representation of Regulated Clients took a more adversary view of practice before the OTS, interpreted the Rules to forbid.[131] Moreover, the OTS also asserted an independent authority to impose standards on lawyers who practice before it that went beyond even the OTS's interpretation of the Model Rules, requiring thrift lawyers who suspected their clients of wrongdoing to report their suspicions to the clients' boards of directors (and not just to lower-level officers) and in some instances even to outside regulators.[132] And although the OTS's position "provoked heated protests that the government was bent on destroying both attorney-client privilege

---

* This administrative assertion of authority to regulate the bar was probably connected to the expansion of judicial authority over lawyers' ethics discussed a moment ago. The OTS was charged to recover the losses that the federal government sustained in connection with the Savings and Loan scandal, and one effective way to do so was to bring tort suits against the responsible parties. The developments in malpractice law that made breaches of legal ethics into the predicates of tort liability therefore made it natural for the OTS to incorporate legal ethics arguments into its litigation strategy.

and the ethical rule of confidentiality, and imposing by fiat a radical new regime of whistle-blowing by counsel for regulated business entities,"[133] law firms against which the OTS applied its new standards, including prominent and reputable firms such as Jones Day and Kaye Scholer, effectively abandoned their protests and agreed to large penal settlements before the OTS enforcement actions against them came to trial.[134] Indeed, the ABA itself appeared, at least at some moments, to concede that the OTS might in principle encroach on the self-regulation of the bar and to argue only that the OTS had, in this instance, failed to follow the regime of notice-and-comment rule-making required under the Administrative Procedures Act.[135] And Congress eventually enacted legislation that effectively codified the OTS's view of lawyers' ethical obligations.[136] This pattern of administrative assertiveness concerning legal ethics followed by resistance and then capitulation from the bar proved immensely damaging to the bar's claims to autonomous self-regulation. The regulation of banking lawyers was, in the words of one prominent commentator, "slipping away from the bar and into the hands of agencies and courts."[137]

Moreover the OTS is not the only agency that asserts the free-standing authority to regulate the lawyers who practice before it. In particular, subsequent corporate scandals have repeated the pattern—lawyer complicity in client misconduct followed by assertions of regulatory authority from a government bureaucracy, followed by opposition and then capitulation from the ABA—that the Savings and Loan crisis introduced. The most prominent and far-reaching such story involves the Securities and Exchange Commission's (SEC) increasingly aggressive assertion of regulatory authority over securities lawyers following the recent wave of corporate scandals (including Enron, WorldCom, and Global Crossing).[138]

The SEC traces its authority to regulate the securities bar to the Securities Exchange Act of 1934, which authorizes the SEC "to determine whether any person has violated, is violating, or is about to violate any provision of this title,"[139] and to the SEC's Rule 2(e), promulgated under the 1934 Act, which allows the commission to "censure" a person and to deny her "the privilege of appearing or practicing before it in any way" if it finds (among other things) that she has "engaged in unethical or improper professional conduct" or "willfully violated, or willfully aided and abetted the violation of any provision of the Federal securities laws or the rules and regulations thereunder."[140] But in spite of this relatively long history, the SEC's assertive use of its authority to regulate *lawyers* is much more recent. Rule 2(e) began to be used to discipline lawyers only in the 1980s, and even then only tentatively.

Thus in the first case applying the rule against lawyers, an administrative law judge's order suspending two lawyers for continuing to assist in

filing documents that they knew misrepresented their client's financial
condition was eventually reversed by the full commission on the ground
that the ethical standard that the administrative law judge had applied
was stricter than the established rules of legal ethics.[141] This was, to be
sure, an attack on the independence of the bar—indeed, the bar resisted
even the milder final ruling, and, "the SEC rejected a proposed compromise with bar officials that would have given state bar disciplinary
committees exclusive jurisdiction to investigate and prosecute similar allegations of lawyer misconduct."[142] But as the full Commission's final
decision makes plain, the SEC's early interventions in legal ethics, even
though they exceeded what the bar desired, fell short of claiming free-
standing authority not just to apply the bar's ethics codes but to create
additional ethical standards in its own name. As one observer summed
up these developments, although the SEC "made some noises" in favor
of aggressive rules requiring lawyers to report securities violations, it
was keenly aware "of the legal profession's bitter opposition to SEC
regulation and discipline of lawyers" and so, at least until the Enron
scandal (discussed below) the SEC showed "little interest" in imposing
such an aggressive position.[143]

Moreover, the modesty of the SEC's initial foray into the regulation
of lawyers displayed itself in other ways also, for example when the full
commission, reversing its own Division of Enforcement, held that the
Securities Exchange Act did not give the SEC authority to sanction lawyer misconduct by issuing orders of general future compliance with the
Act (of the sort extracted by the OTS in the Kaye Scholer settlement)
but only to issue more limited remedies such as orders requiring corrective filings.[144] Similarly, courts were also reluctant to make the regime
regulating securities into a free-standing fount of legal ethics norms,
concluding that "an award of damages under the securities laws is not
the way to blaze the trail toward improved ethical standards in the legal
and accounting professions. Liability depends on an existing duty to
disclose. The securities law therefore must lag behind changes in ethical
and fiduciary standards."[145] Indeed, courts were reluctant even where
the SEC was not. For example, they refused to determine the precise remedial measures that lawyers must take in the face of their clients' securities frauds or to issue injunctions commanding future compliance with
the securities laws even when the SEC asked for them,[146] and they refused to allow private plaintiffs to employ §10(b) of the Securities Exchange Act to bring aiding and abetting suits against lawyers whose
clients violated the Act.[147]

But however callow and however halting the SEC's initial forays into
the law of lawyering, the early modesties have fallen away and the SEC
is now without question a free-standing regulator of the lawyers who

practice before it. Congress (in response to the courts' rejection of aiding and abetting liability under §10(b)[148]) enacted the Private Securities Litigation Reform Act, which expressly gives the SEC authority to prosecute secondary actors, such as attorneys, for aiding and abetting a violation of federal securities law.[149] Moreover, following the Enron and other recent corporate scandals, Congress again sought to increase the SEC's role in regulating the securities bar. Section 307 of the Sarbanes-Oxley Act[150] expressly gives the SEC authority to write rules of professional conduct for lawyers representing public companies before the SEC, and it requires the SEC to issue rules setting forth minimum standards of professional conduct for the lawyers who practice before it, including a rule, to be issued within 180 days of the act's passage, requiring lawyers to engage in up-the-ladder reporting of securities violations committed by their clients including, if they are not rectified, all the way to the clients' highest decision-making officers.[151]

The rules that the SEC promulgated pursuant to Sarbanes-Oxley—which require lawyers for publicly traded corporations to report evidence of material violations of applicable securities law or breaches of fiduciary duties by corporate officers, directors, employees, or agents all the way up to a corporation's board of directors,[152] and which permit lawyers whose corporate boards do not take appropriate rectifying action to report the evidence (including confidential information related to their representations of the corporate client) to the SEC, without the client's consent[153]—are clearly more demanding than the bar-created ethics rules that they replaced.[154] Indeed the ABA's House of Delegates had rejected similar up-the-ladder reporting requirements three times, in 1983, 1991, and 2002. Partly because of these ongoing differences, Sarbanes-Oxley was enacted over the express, although hopelessly ineffectual,*[155] opposition of the ABA.[156] And even after recent, capitulatory moves by the ABA to amend its Model Rules in light of the Enron scandal and its fallout,[157] the SEC continues—with respect to mental state,[158] seriousness of wrongdoing,[159] and discretionary freedom[160]—to impose more demanding reporting requirements on securities lawyers than does the bar.[161] All in all, as one commentator has observed, Sarbanes-Oxley "transfers primary regulatory authority in this area of practice from the state courts that now promulgate the profession's ethics rules to the SEC."[162]

Nor is the SEC unique among contemporary executive agencies in asserting free-standing authority to regulate lawyers who practice before

* Sarbanes-Oxley came about as a result of widespread popular, democratic pressure for reform, which was pushed through because "the weight of corporate scandals . . . [which] were increasingly hurting the stock holdings and pension funds of tens of millions of Americans," so much so that "it became politically risky to oppose reform measures."

it. The IRS regulates tax lawyers: both directly, by claiming authority to "censure, suspend or disbar any practitioner from practice before the Internal Revenue Service if the practitioner is shown to be incompetent or disreputable, fails to comply with any regulation in this part, or, with intent to defraud, willfully and knowingly misleads or threatens a client or prospective client";[163] and also in less direct ways, for example by bringing enforcement proceedings (over the express objections of a defense bar that asserts attorney-client privilege) against criminal defense lawyers who do not identify clients who pay them more than $10,000 in cash.[164] The Department of Justice, expressly overriding a provision of the Model Rules barring lawyers or their agents from contacting represented opposing parties without their lawyer's permission,[165] has asserted that its prosecutors may use wiretaps and informants to investigate represented parties whom they suspect of crimes. (After an initial effort at resistance, the ABA, as it has done in other cases, capitulated and rewrote the official comments to the Model Rules to acknowledge the government's investigative techniques.[166]) Even the U.S. Patent Office regulates lawyers, requiring lawyers filing patent applications to disclose the existence of prior art that is adverse to the patent sought,[167] including in ways that stand in tension with the bar codes' duties to preserve client confidences.[168] And this list is not exhaustive.[169]

Thus, while it was possible to say, as recently as fifteen years ago, that when the bar's rules of legal ethics clashed with the state's conception of how lawyers should behave, the state was only "weakly committed" to its ideals and did not insist on overruling the bar,[170] one cannot say this any longer. Courts, legislatures, and executive agencies today all aggressively assert their prerogatives to regulate lawyers with whom they come into contact, and private bar organizations, after initial periods of resistance, have repeatedly retreated before the state's assertion of its authority. In all these ways, the modern regulatory state, as is often observed, has proved "inexorable in its appetite,"[171] so that "the vastly broadened scope of regulation of almost all other professions and forms of business [has] made it politically and intellectually impossible for lawyers to claim exemption from regulation."[172] Moreover, practical considerations reinforce this principled reason for extending the regulatory state to the governance of lawyers: In many of the practice-areas in which administrative regulation of clients is prominent, the success of legal regimes relies substantially on voluntary compliance, and lawyers (as agencies,[173] courts,[174] and commentators[175] have all noted) are overwhelming best-placed to promote compliance.

As one commentator has remarked, "[i]t stretches the point only slightly to say that the practice of law in America is now, as with many other areas of corporate or personal economic endeavor, a regulated industry,"[176] so that, in the words of another, the modern lawyer's role "belongs ... to the state."[177] And the bar's insularity simply cannot withstand the pressures brought to bear by an increasingly intrusive and increasingly insistent state.

• • •

The legal profession in the late nineteenth century may have been insular. Lawyers controlled membership in their profession and educated and acculturated their own in ways that created a unified, homogeneous bar. They self-consciously pursued fraternal ideals of decency and propriety. And they developed and administered these ideals from within their own ranks.

But over the course of the twentieth century, the bar has lost the essential elements of role insularity. Outsiders can force their way into a legal profession that is educated and develops ethical sensibilities according to universalist academic standards and is too large and too diffuse to be the locus of any unified (or indeed coherent) role morality. The rules of professional conduct are too narrow and too mechanical for any personal moral vision to grow up around them. And the mechanisms of professional control are so compromised by external influences that they undermine any free-standing, idiosyncratically lawyerly ethic that might otherwise arise. Whatever was true in the past, the modern lawyer's role has become thoroughly cosmopolitan.

Tragic Villains

In order for a role to sustain integrity-preserving role-based redescription, it must be authoritatively insular, providing for its members the resources necessary to resist ordinary first-personal moral ideals and to construct, in their place, distinctive role-based alternatives. But even as changes in the nature of legal practice (in particular, greater partisanship and a new division of labor within the bar) have over the course of the twentieth century increased the pressures on modern lawyers' integrity, a second group of changes (in particular, greater heterogeneity, more mechanistic regulation, and increased external control) have denied the bar the insularity needed to sustain lawyers' integrity in the face of these pressures. Even as it has become more urgently necessary, integrity-preserving role-based redescription, built around distinctively lawyerly fidelity and negative capability, is no longer practically available to today's anxiously cosmopolitan lawyers.

These developments are hardly surprising and may even seem, with hindsight, to have been inevitable. Certainly the other professions have, over the same period, shared in the trends toward dis-integration, mechanistic rather than organic solidarity, and external regulation that lawyers have experienced.[178] The egalitarian and democratic ideals that underwrite the modern state and its broad grant of authority do not, nor could they coherently, respect boundaries raised up by a mere clique like the legal profession (this is just to reprise the philosophers' well-justified disdain for any suggestion that role-based ethics might supplant impartial morality).*[179] As Marx understood (even at the start of the period of professional decline that I have documented), "[t]he Bourgeoisie has stripped of its halo every occupation hitherto honored and looked up to with reverent awe. It has converted the physician, the lawyer, the priest, the poet, the man of science, into its paid wage laborers."[180] No role-ethic could have survived these forces, nor could integrity-preserving role-based redescription withstand them, so that today, this time in Weber's words, "[t]he idea of duty in one's calling prowls in our lives like the ghost of dead religious beliefs."[181]

The recent history of the legal profession has much to recommend it, of course, and I do not wish to romanticize the past or to call for a return to lawyers' self-regulation. The bar is a much fairer and more open institution than it was a century ago. Moreover, some of these benefits have accrued to legal ethics: external regulation through mechanistic rules (backed by sanctions) has, perhaps unsurprisingly, had more bite than fraternal admonition, and it has likely increased lawyers' compliance with their ethical obligations.[182] But the developments have also

---

* This development is awash with ironies. To begin with, the very egalitarian sensibilities that have today deprived lawyers of their independence functioned, in more primitive renderings in an earlier age, to propel lawyers to the prominence whose memory makes their independence so cherished. As one historian has noted, "in a society without a landed class, a clearly defined clergy, or others who might impose social control, the need for order ultimately meant that law would become the primary form of social control in the United States," and this need, coupled with the end of colonial administration, "emphasized the importance of the legal profession in the country's government [so that] [l]awyers were catapulted into a political and social prominence which the profession had not enjoyed in England." Thus the same egalitarianism that elevated the legal profession developed into a form that has come, later, to tear it down.

Moreover, lawyers participated actively in the rise of the bureaucratic institutions and sensibilities that have now deprived them of their independence. Certainly one segment of the legal profession was instrumental in crafting the administrative state during the New Deal. Moreover, even the resistance to New Deal administration displayed so prominently by other parts of the bar, including by the fledgling ABA, ultimately backfired, contributing to the profession's loss of independence. Having taken sides in the great political struggle of the age and lost, the bar could no longer plausibly defend its freedom from state control by claiming to stand above politics.

imposed a great cost on lawyers' ethical position, as seen from the lawyers' own points of view. Cosmopolitan lawyers, who can no longer develop their first-personal moral ideals exclusively within their roles or resist the authority of the ordinary first-personal moral concepts employed by the world at large, also cannot sustain their integrity in the face of their professional duties.

Thus, although role-based redescription is formally suited to preserving integrity and although the adversary advocate's role may be given a substantively attractive content based on fidelity and negative capability, modern American lawyers have been denied practical access to this route to preserving their integrity. Some elements of the historical development that has cut lawyers off—for example, the segmentation of the legal profession so that lawyers are engaged systematically on one side of ongoing disputes—are probably historically contingent, at least in the sense that they could have been different in a society that remains otherwise morally and politically like the one that we have become.*[183] But other elements of the recent history of the bar—including its increasing demographic heterogeneity, its increasing reliance on regulation by mechanistic rules, and its increasing subjugation to external control— are not really contingent at all, but are instead the natural and necessary concomitants of the rise of egalitarian democracy in the broader society in which lawyers live and work.

If all this is correct, then the very same pluralism and egalitarianism that cause the legitimacy of adjudication to depend on the ministrations of negatively capable lawyers (and therefore give the lawyerly virtues the ethical weight necessary to sustain integrity-preserving role-based redescription in principle) also undermine the social practices and institutions through which lawyers might gain access to a negatively capable role-ethic (and therefore undermine integrity-preserving role-based redescription in practice). Put a little differently, modernity's insistent cosmopolitanism makes social solidarity depend on a class of persons who can experience their ethical life as satisfactory only if they inhabit an insular role.

Even as modern society depends on its lawyers to display some version of the lawyerly virtues, modern society at the same time denies lawyers the cultural resources that they need to fashion these virtues into their own, distinctive first-personal moral ideals, and instead leaves lawyers in the grip of cosmopolitan first-personal ideals, according to

* English barristers, after all, are not subject to this internal division of labor, and early twentieth-century American lawyers considered a two-tiered bar on the English model. But note that even here economic realities of corporate legal representation make an increasingly segmented legal profession hard to resist (so that even the English bar is under threat).

which they must see their professional activities as vicious and cast themselves as villains. This is not, of course, to reject the good egalitarian reasons for which modernity has undercut the insularity of the bar; nor does it entail that the lawyer's villainous self-understanding involves a mistake. But it does reveal that modern lawyers are villains neither by inclination nor by choice, but rather because they have been cast as villains by historical forces beyond their control. And that is itself just a roundabout, modern way of articulating a thought the ancients would have given a much more elegant expression, namely that my argument has the form of a tragedy, and that lawyers are *tragic* villains.

POSTSCRIPT

ALTHOUGH THIS book has taken narrowly legal ethics—the question whether the legal profession is worthy of commitment—for its real as well as its nominal subject, the argument that it has pursued has implications for modern moral life more broadly.

First, the methodology that the book has employed may be applied elsewhere also, in order better to understand ethical practices besides adversary advocacy.

This is important. The low regard in which most philosophers hold applied ethics quite generally and the disregard for applied ethics usually displayed by persons who actually inhabit the circumstances that applied ethics addresses suggest that there is widespread dissatisfaction with the casuistic approach that applied ethics traditionally adopts, including even in its natural constituencies. This state of affairs encourages making a fresh start, and the method pursued here is presented in this radical spirit: the shift in ethics from casuistry to reconstruction is as dramatic, for example, as a shift in literature from plot-driven to character-driven fiction. It involves reorienting, in a basic way, the point of an enterprise—from story-telling to portraiture in literature, and from advice to understanding in ethics.

Of course, not every new beginning bears fruit, and doubts always arise about whether an ambition is worth pursuing and whether it is being pursued by suitable methods. The analogy to literature is again informative here. The first doubt confronts both character-driven fiction and reconstructive ethics with the question whether contemplative problems are important enough to justify the rigors and demands of the disciplines directed at answering them. It seems to me that there is no reason why not—indeed, no reason why contemplative problems should be thought any less real or important than other sorts of problems. Certainly the prominence of character in "serious" literature suggests that even the most purely contemplative problems merit sustained and energetic attention. And it seems that a philosophical ethics that addresses the reflective demands of practical agents but not necessarily their demands for guidance is similarly worthwhile. The second doubt worries, in the case of character-driven fiction, whether successful literary portraiture is possible and, in the case of reconstructive applied ethics, whether it is possible to say what an ethical condition is like in a philosophically serious way. This doubt can be resolved only by actually succeeding in the tasks at hand. The realist novel provided the resolution for fiction.

The account of lawyers developed here, insofar as it is convincing, represents a first step for reconstructive applied ethics.

Second, the book's argument has broader implications because the ethical difficulties that adversary advocates encounter are not isolated anomalies but instead reflect, and indeed foreshadow, the ethical problems of modern life more generally.

The pattern that the book reveals in lawyers' ethical circumstances—the threat to integrity that arises when persons must betray their ordinary first-personal ideals in the service of an impartially justified moral division of labor, the hope that this threat might be answered by intensifying the division of labor through the ethics of role to give it a stronghold in first-personal morality, and the weakening and ultimately insecure influence of role-based ethical ideals—repeats itself throughout modern moral life. Indeed, this pattern might be thought to reflect *the* problem of modern ethics.

Modernity has, for good egalitarian reasons, dramatically expanded the range of application of impartial morality, and this insistent expansion of impartialist ideals has increased the diversity and flexibility of the burdens that impartiality imposes on persons who are (properly) susceptible to its imperatives. At the same time, again acting in the service of egalitarianism (although now, as I shall argue, perhaps misguidedly), modernity has quite generally dismantled the forms of organization and control, involving insular social roles, that might support persons, who must necessarily mediate their responses to impartiality through idiosyncratic and contingent commitments, in order to sustain their integrity against the burdens that impartiality imposes. Simply put, modernity has increased the demand for and reduced the supply of ethical diversity.*

Lawyers therefore cast a quite general problem into particularly sharp relief, serving as archetypes of the modern moral condition. The explicit specialization of lawyers and the precision of their professional obligations presents a particularly crisp rendition of a much broader tension between impartiality and ordinary first-personal ethical ideals, and the elaborate institutional structure of their role presents a particularly vivid example of the modern attack on cultural support for ethical particularity. Moreover, lawyers—by serving as specialists in political legitimation—make it their particular and contingent ambition to subordinate their own

* Modernity has of course increased certain kinds of diversity—most notably religious diversity and diversity of lifestyle—that might be associated with ethics. But it has done so principally by recasting such diversity as no longer ethical in any deep sense, so that religions (for example) are treated as different expressions of a shared spirituality or, insofar as they are truly at odds, merely as tastes. Once again, real ethical diversity—in the sense of variety concerning the most basic aims and ambitions of life—is smaller in modern egalitarian societies than it was in their caste-based predecessors.

ambitions to the incompatible particular and contingent ambitions of others. And insofar as they do, lawyers live, one might say, on the hinge of modernity's ethical project, and therefore face its most intense and concentrated pressures. But although lawyers serve in all these ways to emphasize and indeed to magnify the difficulties of modern moral life, the root cause of these difficulties precedes their intervention. It is modernity quite generally that opened up the gap between the demands of impartialist and first-personal moral justification: the modern lawyer has merely fallen in.

Third, the book has implications outside of narrowly legal ethics insofar as the ways in which lawyers try to respond to the predicament that I have diagnosed illuminate responses to the broader predicament of modernity that arise outside the narrow confines of the bar.

On the one hand, familiar calls to return the bar to the "professionalism" of past eras—calls, in effect, to recreate the insularity of the lawyer's role—find parallels in familiar calls in politics more broadly to reinstate thick forms of moral community throughout society. These proposals,[1] however, fail to credit the weight of the impartialist objection to the forms of community that they champion. Modernity has for good egalitarian reasons dismantled traditional insular social roles and replaced them with impartial cosmopolitan forms of social organization and governance. This is just the practical development of the philosophical skepticism about role-morality that I described in chapter 7. Thick and insular roles and the communities that sustain them are, as Applbaum says, quite generally "suspect to liberals who have no nostalgia for societies divided into castes, estates, or classes, and who fear any retreat from the idea of universal humanity."[2] Accordingly, any backward-looking attempt to recreate the traditional, insular social role of the lawyer comes (if it comes at all) only at a very great cost. This reveals, finally, that although the ever-increasing cosmopolitanism that fuels the dilemma of modern moral life (both for lawyers and more generally) may be a historical phenomenon, it is not merely of fleeting, local, or in any narrow sense contingent concern. Instead, cosmopolitanism is inextricably intertwined with the conditions of modern moral and political justification and describes (although of course only in rough outline) the way things will be—for lawyers and indeed for persons generally—for as long as the broader conditions of modernity persist.

And on the other hand, calls to embrace this cosmopolitanism—calls, in effect, to abandon any peculiarly lawyerly ethics in favor of a social-scientific, progressive, and realist[*3] conception of the lawyer not as a

---

*The connection to legal realism here is deep and important. The legal realist rejects *tout court* what she sees as the sentimentality of any professional ethics that focuses on

negatively capable servant of his clients but as a positively capable man-
ager of conflict (on the model of Brandeis's "lawyer for the situation")
who produces, through skill and expertise, the best long run results
overall[4]—find parallels in familiar calls in politics more broadly to embrace bureaucratically rational forms of social and moral organization.

These proposals,[5] however, fail to recognize that because persons are
only imperfectly rational, society is inevitably an accommodation among
divergent contingent commitments and that the peculiar professional
commitments of lawyers—the traditional lawyerly virtues—are essential
to sustaining this accommodation. Although some lawyers—I am thinking specifically of public interest lawyers who adopt causes rather than
take cases—may succeed at using the realist gambit to bridge the gap
between first-personal and impartial ethical justification,*[6] the costs of
populating an entire legal system exclusively with legal realists would be
enormous. Even if the lawyer's role-ethic of negative capability cannot
be sustained in the modern world, the difficulty it answered—the difficulty of regulating the "perpetual conflicts between rival impulses and
ideals" that threaten all forms of social order[7]—remains and has perhaps even intensified. The realist lawyer cannot help the law preside
over the conflict because she self-consciously declares herself to be outside of the law and a part of the conflict,† and this is why modern society has never allowed all, or even most, of its lawyers to act like realists

---

the distinctive relation between lawyer and client and instead seeks mercilessly to manipulate laws and legal institutions in pursuit of what she thinks impartially best. (Such a
lawyer recites approvingly Llewellyn's "old anecdote of Marshall"—"Judgment for the
plaintiff. Mr. Justice Story will furnish the authorities.")

A lawyer who thinks in this realist way—displaying a surfeit rather than a deficit of cosmopolitanism, as it were—adopts a tame version of Jane's soldierly first-personal ethic, according to which the executory virtues are king. She prides herself on her tactical skills and
also on her thick-skinnedness, her disciplined willingness to make sacrifices (including sacrifices of virtues) for the greater good and therefore finds no threat to her integrity in the fact
that the professional means by which she pursues the good may involve lying and cheating.

The realist lawyer can sustain her integrity even in the face of her professional activities,
and she can, as Llewellyn himself said, "merge" her "trade, culture and profession all in
one."

*Thus, a lawyer who abandoned a job representing an insurance company in the tradi-
tional way to become a cause lawyer in the realist mode could say: "My work and my
life, they've become one. No longer am I schizophrenic."

†The connection, noted earlier, between the realist lawyer and Jane makes it worthwhile to recall an observation I made earlier regarding Jane's first-personal ethic, namely
that the integrity of a person who adopts this executory ideal is threatened whenever procedural values require her to accept an outcome she disapproves of. Just as the traditional
lawyer, like Jim, finds his integrity threatened when called on to betray his own values in
the name of outcomes, so the realist lawyer, like Jane, finds her integrity threatened when
called on to betray her own values in the name of procedures.

but has instead retained, in the positive law governing lawyers, the substance of the traditionally lawyerly role-ethic, even as it has undermined the institutional and cultural structure—the insular role—that allowed lawyers to take this ethic for their native ambition rather than merely, as today, mimicking a defunct role to meet its demands.

And finally, elaborating the ethics of modern lawyers makes vivid a lesson that applies to morals more generally, but that modern morality has not internalized. This is the idea that the structure of value entails that persons must always choose among incompatible goods— that the pursuit of some virtues forecloses the pursuit of others so that there can never be, as Isaiah Berlin might say, a social world without loss.

Just as social roles give their occupants access to forms of first-personal moral life from which others are excluded, so also do roles exclude their occupants from the more ordinary forms of first-personal moral life that they displace. The earlier examples of role-based redescription illustrate this point as well: Prizefighters, who replace ordinary disgust at violence with an ethic of physical grace and courage are precluded, by this very ethic, from being gentle; executioners cannot be compassionate; and military commanders such as Jane cannot be sentimental. Indeed, loss like this is particularly acute in the context of professional ethics. MacMillan, for example, observed that doctors and clergyman (two of the great professions in MacMillan's England) displayed role-vices alongside their role-virtues: the doctor, MacMillan said, must acquire an eerie and unsettling "calmness in the presence of the emergencies and tragedies of life," a calmness that is hard not to connect to indifference;[8] and the clergyman, who has "[b]y his profession . . . circumscribed his freedom, for he has pledged himself to certain beliefs which he cannot question if he is to remain in his profession," becomes peculiarly susceptible to "dogmatism with its ugly companions, intolerance and persecution, and casuistry, with its accompanying lack of candor."[9]

The point, moreover, is illustrated particularly vividly, and in particularly elaborate detail, by the discussion of adversary advocates presented here. To begin with, lawyers who achieve negative capability abandon ordinary first-personal moral ideals of truthfulness and fair play. And furthermore, negatively capable lawyers also forsake certain impartial values. Keats, discussing himself as a poet, observed that "[i]t is a wretched thing to confess; but it is a very fact that not one word that I ever utter can be taken for granted as an opinion growing out of my identical nature—how can it be when I have no nature?"[10] And the lawyer's self-effacement, his commitment to speaking his client's part rather than his own, has a similar influence on his character. Simply put, "[n]o advocate can be a *sincere* . . . man in the performance of his daily business,"[11] so that the lawyer's character becomes in this respect disfigured.*[12]

Similarly, the lawyer's capacity to argue all sides and his allegiance to procedures rather than outcomes makes him unsuited to moral leadership. The lawyer will, as Bacon says, "desire rather commendation of wit, in being able to hold all arguments, than of judgment in discerning what is true; as if it were a praise to know what might be said and not what should be thought."[13] These two shortcomings, moreover, are related. Because lawyers' experience of life is at once infinitely various and absolutely vicarious—because lawyers' "experience of human affairs is made up of an infinite number of scraps cut out of other people's lives"—lawyers (at least insofar as they pursue their negatively capable professional ethic†) "see too much of life in one way, too little in another, to make them safe guides in practical matters."[14] Even as the lawyer's distinctive virtues make him the guardian of our political life, they render him a suspect leader.

Moreover, if the description of lawyers' professional duties presented here elaborates the idea that there can be no social world without loss, then the normative parts of the overall argument—including both discussion of bounded rationality and integrity and the discussion of the legitimacy of adjudication—emphasize that this thesis invokes an unusual kind of loss. Usually, describing something as a moral "loss" implies that it might be avoided, in the strong sense that an all-things-considered better state of affairs is possible. (This is perhaps an expression of the broad influence on moral thought of the idea that "ought implies can.") But the "losses" associated with the value of integrity are losses only in the weaker sense of selecting among a range of imperfect alternatives to fix the specific form that our imperfections will take.

This recognition—which interprets the idea that every virtue forecloses others (and that many virtues invite vices) as an expression of the inevitable divergence between inertial first-personal ambitions and the ever-changing demands of impartial morality—opens up the possibility of a rapprochement between egalitarian impartial morality and the idea of role. Insofar as *all* first-person ambitions, including the first-personal ambitions of ordinary good people, necessarily depart in some way from impartial morality (which is to say that they involve loss), then role-based

---

* This is chillingly illustrated by an extraordinary story Charles Curtis tells about Arthur Hill, the lawyer who represented Sacco and Vanzetti (taking a case, Curtis says, and not adopting a cause) and who, twenty years later, still refused to express his own opinion about their guilt, telling Curtis, "I have never said, and I cannot say, what I think on the subject because, you see, Charlie, I was their counsel."

† A person who happens also to be a lawyer may of course display all kinds of virtues outside of her professional capacity.

ambitions simply pose a different, rather than a distinctive, problem for impartiality.* And it should be possible, in the light of this realization, to reorient role-insularity so that it does not compete with impartial morality but rather gives one cultural and institutional expression (among many) to the need for boundedly rational beings to engage impartial morality through the mediation of contingent and particular commitments. It should be possible, in other words, for even an egalitarian moral culture to accept roles that are insular in just the way that the demands of integrity require them to be.

The diagnosis of the modern lawyer's ethical condition that the book has made its ambition therefore does, in the end, suggest something like a cure, although it is not a cure on the traditional model of instruction or advice. It is instead a proposal for a reflective reorientation toward modern ethical life, which might assist persons seeking to live well in modernity with the independently ethical task of actually deciding, given the totality of their circumstances, how best to proceed.

---

* Even if the liberal is right that the incidental practices of insular communities cannot, finally, be authoritative even for the communities themselves but must instead answer to some ideal of universal humanity, the communitarian is right that we cannot (because we are only boundedly rational) have direct access to this ideal but must instead get access through the practical example of a contingent community. And, moreover, once we have done so we cannot (again because of our bounded rationality) treat the particular community that we have, contingently, engaged as an example only—that is, as nothing but a freely modifiable rule of thumb for applying the more general principle of universal humanity. It is true that the particular can be valuable only against the backdrop of a valuable general category. But once the general has been given expression in a particular way, the value of *this* particular will, at least for those who live and act within it, never be reducible to the general category. Moreover, because no person can engage universal humanity directly or perfectly, every actual attempt to recast particular practices as special cases of general values eventually runs up against the limits of the generalism of the person who makes it.

NOTES

INTRODUCTION

1. Here I follow PLATO, THE REPUBLIC § 352d (Paul Shorey trans., 1930) *in* THE COLLECTED DIALOGUES OF PLATO (Edith Hamilton & Huntington Cairns eds., 1961). *See also* BERNARD WILLIAMS, ETHICS AND THE LIMITS OF PHILOSOPHY 1–21 (1985).

2. Notwithstanding the absurd suggestions otherwise that are currently popular among political figures.

3. The adversary advocate's duty of loyalty to her client appears on the face of all the major statements of the law governing lawyers in the past century. See CANONS OF PROF'L ETHICS Canon 15 (1908) (requiring a lawyer to represent a client with "warm zeal"); MODEL CODE OF PROF'L RESPONSIBILITY Canon 7 (1969) (requiring a lawyer to "represent a client zealously within the bounds of law"); MODEL RULES OF PROF'L CONDUCT R. 1.3 cmt. 1 (2003) (requiring a lawyer to act "with zeal in advocacy upon the client's behalf"). I address these provisions in greater detail in chapter 1.

4. This observation is one of the banalities of legal ethics. Prominent statements include: DAVID LUBAN, THE ETHICS OF LAWYERS, at xiii (1994) ("The problematic aspect of lawyers' ethics . . . consists in duties (such as demolishing the truthful witness) that contradict . . . everyday morality."); Charles Fried, *The Lawyer as Friend: The Moral Foundations of the Lawyer-Client Relation*, 85 YALE L.J. 1060, 1060 (1976) ("The lawyer is conventionally seen as a professional devoted to his client's interests and as authorized, if not in fact required, to do some things (though not anything) for that client which he would not do for himself."); David Luban, *Introduction* to THE GOOD LAWYER: LAWYERS' ROLES AND LAWYERS' ETHICS 1 (David Luban ed., 1983) ("The authors [in this collection] address the fundamental problems of legal ethics: does the professional role of lawyers impose duties that are different from, or even in conflict with, common morality?"); Gerald Postema, *Moral Responsibility in Professional Ethics*, 55 N.Y.U. L. REV. 63 (1980) ("Yet, lawyers also claim special warrant for engaging in some activities which, were they performed by others, would be likely to draw moral censure.") [hereinafter Postema, *Moral Responsibility in Professional Ethics*]; Gerald Postema, *Self-Image, Integrity, and Professional Responsibility, in* THE GOOD LAWYER: LAWYERS' ROLES AND LAWYERS' ETHICS, *supra*, at 286, 287–88 [hereinafter Postema, *Self-Image, Integrity, and Professional Responsibility*] ("Sometimes with discomfort, sometimes with pride, lawyers acknowledge that the legal profession permits or requires actions that would draw moral censure if performed by others."); Bernard Williams, *Professional Morality and Its Dispositions, in* THE GOOD LAWYER: LAWYERS' ROLES AND LAWYERS' ETHICS, *supra*, at 259, 259 ("[I]t is the possibility of a divergence between professional morality and 'ordinary' or

'everyday' morality that lends particular interest to the notion of a professional morality.").

5. 1 GEOFFREY C. HAZARD, JR. & W. WILLIAM HODES, THE LAW OF LAWYER-ING: A HANDBOOK ON THE MODEL RULES OF PROFESSIONAL CONDUCT § 1.3:106, at 75 n.1 (2d ed. Supp. 1993) [hereinafter HH].

6. See, for example, ARTHUR APPLBAUM, ETHICS FOR ADVERSARIES 175 (1999) ("Part of what adversaries in public and professional life do for a living is violate persons by deceiving and coercing them.") [hereinafter APPLBAUM, ETHICS FOR ADVERSARIES]; 9 JEREMY BENTHAM, Constitutional Code, in WORKS OF JEREMY BENTHAM 77–78 (John Bowring ed., Edinburgh, W. Tait 1843) ("Every criminal uses the weapons he is most practiced in the use of; the bull uses his horns, the tiger his claws, the rattle-snake his fangs, the technical law-yer his lies. Unlicensed thieves use pick-lock keys; licensed thieves use fictions."); Arthur Applbaum, Are Lawyers Liars?, 4 LEGAL THEORY 63, 63 (1998) ("Law-yers might accurately be described as serial liars, because they repeatedly try to induce others to believe in the truth of propositions or in the validity of argu-ments that they believe to be false."); Charles P. Curtis, The Ethics of Advocacy, 4 STAN. L. REV. 3, 9 (1951) ("A lawyer is required to be disingenuous. He is required to make statements as well as argument which he does not believe in."); Marc Galanter, The Faces of Mistrust: The Image of Lawyers in Public Opinion, Jokes, and Political Discourse, 66 U. CIN. L. REV. 805 (1998) (citing as the premises of commonplace lawyer jokes that "'lawyers are hard to under-stand; they charge too much; they are miserable people; they lie all the time; and they should die.'" (quoting David L. Yas, First Thing We Do Is Kill All the Lawyer Jokes, MASS. LAW. WKLY., Oct. 20, 1997, at 11)).

7. Hazard and Hodes, for example, insist that, far from being built into the genetic structure of adversary advocacy, a professional duty to lie arises only on extremist accounts of lawyers' professional obligations, according to which "the law of lawyering is worse than amoral [and] compels persons of normal sensibilities to discard their moral autonomy and to slavishly engage in any immoral action that will benefit a client so long as it is legal." 1 HH § 5.8, at 5–25 (3d ed. 2001, Supp. 2004). And they attack this view of legal ethics as "plainly incorrect," id., and insist that under the law of lawyering as it has ac-tually developed "the formal rules of professional conduct are crowded with provisions permitting or even requiring" lawyers to avoid partisan extremes like lying. Id.

8. The phrase comes from Robert W. Gordon, The Radical Conservatism of the Practice of Justice, 51 STAN. L. REV. 919, 920 (1999).

9. Support for the claims made in this footnote may be found in MARY ANN GLENDON, A NATION UNDER LAWYERS 300 (1994) (claiming lawyers' billable hours have increased dramatically in recent years); Patrick Schiltz, On Being a Happy, Healthy, and Ethical Member of an Unhappy, Unhealthy, and Unethical Profession, 52 VAND. L. REV. 871 (1999) (making the same claim). See also LORRAINE DUSKY, STILL UNEQUAL 171–72 (1996); Carl T. Burges, The Death of an Honorable Profession, 71 IND. L.J. 911 (1996); Nancy D. Holt, Are Lon-ger Hours Here to Stay? A.B.A.J., Feb. 1993, at 62, 64; Benjamin Sells, Stressed-Out Attorneys, S.F. DAILY J., May 25, 1994, at 3A.

10. 1 HENRY BROUGHAM, SPEECHES OF HENRY LORD BROUGHAM 105 (Edinburgh, A. & C. Black, 1838) (quoted in LORD MACMILLAN, LAW AND OTHER THINGS 195 (1937)). MacMillan, it should be noted, did not himself approve of this extreme position.

11. Indeed, it is not clear that even Lord Brougham himself believed what he said. Brougham intended the remark as a threat, made during a dispute, and designed to induce settlement. And he later characterized his statement as "anything rather than a deliberate and well-considered opinion." *See* WILLIAM FORSYTH, HORTENSIUS: AN HISTORICAL ESSAY ON THE OFFICE AND DUTIES OF AN ADVOCATE 389 n.1 (2d. ed. 1875); *see also* DAVID J.A. CAIRNS, ADVOCACY AND THE MAKING OF THE CRIMINAL TRIAL, 1800–1865, at 139 (1998).

Moreover, Brougham's statement probably did not represent the mainstream view among either his English contemporaries or their nineteenth-century American counterparts. Certainly David Hoffman and George Sharswood, the two most prominent American legal ethicists of the nineteenth century, both accepted what today seem surprisingly strong limits on the lawyer's partisan commitment to his clients' interests. I take up these matters in more detail in chapter 9.

12. The need to moderate adversary advocacy in the face of imperfections in the legal system is emphasized by David Luban and by William Simon. *See* DAVID LUBAN, LAWYERS AND JUSTICE 67–103 (1988); WILLIAM SIMON, THE PRACTICE OF JUSTICE 53–76 (1998).

13. The need to moderate adversary advocacy in the face of nonconsequentialist moral ideas is emphasized by David Luban and especially by Arthur Applbaum. *See* LUBAN, *supra* note 12, at 50–103; APPLBAUM, ETHICS FOR ADVERSARIES, *supra* note 6 at 113–35, 175–203. As Applbaum remarks, a successful development of the adversary system defense "will have to do more than simply invoke the balance of consequences," *id.* at 177, but will instead have to be "reasonably acceptable" even to those whom the adversary system harms. *Id.* at 258.

14. *See generally*, MONROE FREEDMAN, LAWYERS' ETHICS IN AN ADVERSARY SYSTEM (1975).

15. ANTHONY KRONMAN, THE LOST LAWYER: FAILING IDEALS OF THE LEGAL PROFESSION 14 (1993).

16. *Id.* at 2. The idea of integrity that I develop in Part II of the book explains why an account of lawyerly virtue is necessary for rendering the lawyer's life worthy of commitment in this way.

17. Support for the claims made in this footnote may be found in *id.* at 380 (invoking the country lawyer as one of the pillars of statesmanship). The quoted text is taken from *id.* at 16.

18. *Id.* at 364.

19. *Luke* 11:46 (King James).

20. *See* MODEL RULES OF PROF'L CONDUCT R. 2.4 (2003).

21. *See id.* R. 2.3.

22. *See* MIRJAN DAMASKA, THE FACES OF JUSTICE AND STATE AUTHORITY (1986).

23. John H. Langbein, *The German Advantage in Civil Procedure*, 52 U. CHI. L. REV. 823, 824 (1985).

24. *Id.*

25. *Id.*

26. *Id.* at 841.

27. *Cf.* Robert H. Mnookin & Lewis Kornhauser, *Bargaining in the Shadow of the Law: The Case of Divorce*, 88 YALE L.J. 950 (1979).

28. The ethics rules governing tax advice do not require lawyers to imagine themselves as impartial judges of their clients' returns but, instead, permit them to advise their clients to take positions on tax returns as long as the positions have "a realistic possibility of success if litigated." ABA Comm. on Ethics and Prof'l Responsibility, Formal Op. 85–352 (1985). This replaces an even more permissive rule (which still applies in some areas of tax practice) allowing lawyers to advise clients to take any positions that have a "reasonable basis." ABA Comm. on Ethics and Prof'l Responsibility, Formal Op. 314 (1965). This standard expressly allows a lawyer to act as a partisan for her client and advise reporting a position "even where the lawyer believes the position probably will not prevail, there is no 'substantial authority' in support of the position, and there will be no disclosure of the position on the return." ABA Comm. on Ethics and Prof'l Responsibility, Formal Op. 85–352. A task force of the ABA Tax Section elaborated that "having a 5 percent or 10 percent likelihood of success, if litigated, should not meet the new standard. A position having a likelihood of success closely approaching one-third should meet the standard." Paul Sax, James P. Holden, Theodore Tannenwald, Jr., David Watts & Bernard Wolfman, *Report of the Special Task Force on Formal Opinion 85–352, reprinted in* 39 TAX LAW 633, 638–39 (1986). Strikingly, the standard was adopted in the context of an express recognition that the realities of the audit lottery (fewer than 1 percent of all tax returns are audited) makes it likely that such contentious positions will never come to the Internal Revenue Service's attention. *See id.*

29. *See* MODEL RULES OF PROF'L CONDUCT R. 1.6 (2003). I take up these rules in greater detail in chapter 2. For now, note merely that although the rules concerning client confidences were relaxed in 2003 to allow for disclosure in certain cases in which clients use a lawyer's services in furtherance of a crime or fraud, *see id.* R. 1.6(b)(2)–(3), they remain strikingly strict.

30. *See id.* R. 3.3 & cmt. 14.

31. This point incidentally, has been thought directly illustrated by lawyers' ethical lives. Thus Anthony Kronman's proposal that lawyers are specialists in practical wisdom is a detailed elaboration of the features of ethical life that casuistry inevitably ignores. *See generally,* ANTHONY KRONMAN, *supra* note 15, at 53–164.

32. This case is emphasized, for example, in Monroe H. Freedman, *Professional Responsibility of the Criminal Defense Lawyer: The Three Hardest Questions*, 64 MICH. L. REV. 1469, 1478 (1966).

33. The classic case is *Spaulding v. Zimmerman*, 116 N.W.2d 704 (Minn. 1962), in which a lawyer defending a tort action learned that the victim had suffered a potentially fatal aortic aneurism and kept this secret in order to secure an advantageous settlement.

34. This case figures in MARTON MINTZ, AT ANY COST: CORPORATE GREED, WOMEN, AND THE DALKON SHIELD (1985).

35. This case, which actually occurred, *see* Annesley v. Anglesea, 17 How. St. Trials 1139 (1743), is discussed in LUBAN, *supra* note 12, at 3–10 (1988).

36. *See* Northern Sec. Co. v. United States, 193 U.S. 197, 400 (1904) (Holmes, J., dissenting) ("Great cases like hard cases make bad law.").

37. JAMES AGEE & WALKER EVANS, LET US NOW PRAISE FAMOUS MEN, at xlvii (3d ed. 1988).

CHAPTER 1
THE WELLSPRINGS OF LEGAL ETHICS

1. William Simon is a prominent example. According to Simon, the view that "the lawyer must—or at least may—pursue any goal of the client through any arguably legal course of action and assert any nonfrivolous legal claim," is "assumed in the most important provisions of each of the two ethical codes promulgated by the American Bar Association—the *Model Code of Professional Conduct* [sic] of 1969 and its successor, the *Model Rules of Professional Conduct* of 1983." WILLIAM SIMON, THE PRACTICE OF JUSTICE 7, 8 (1998).

2. An excellent example of this response appears in Ted Schneyer, *Moral Philosophy's Standard Misconception of Legal Ethics*, 1984 WIS. L. REV. 1529.

3. See CANONS OF PROFESSIONAL ETHICS Canon 15 (1908). The phrase comes from George Sharswood's pioneering essay on legal ethics, which instructed lawyers to display "[e]ntire devotion of the interests of the client [and] warm zeal in the maintenance and defense of his rights . . . ." GEORGE SHARSWOOD, AN ESSAY ON PROFESSIONAL ETHICS, 78–80 (photo. reprint 1993) (5th ed., Philadelphia, T. & J.W. Johnson 1896).

4. MODEL CODE OF PROF'L RESPONSIBILITY Canon 7 (1969).

5. *Id.* DR 7–101(A)(1).

6. MODEL RULES OF PROF'L CONDUCT R. 1.3 (2003) ("A lawyer shall act with reasonable diligence and promptness in representing a client.").

7. *Id.* Preamble ¶ 14.

8. *Id.* R. 1.3 cmt. 1.

9. *See Id.* Preamble ¶¶ 2, 8, 9.

10. RESTATEMENT (THIRD) OF THE LAW GOVERNING LAWYERS § 16(1) (2000).

11. 1 GEOFFREY C. HAZARD, JR. & W. WILLIAM HODES, THE LAW OF LAWYERING: A HANDBOOK ON THE MODEL RULES OF PROFESSIONAL CONDUCT § 1.2:103, at 24 (2d ed. 1990) [hereinafter HH]. Hazard elsewhere says that "the partisanship principle remains at the core of the profession's soul." Geoffrey Hazard, *The Future of Legal Ethics*, 100 YALE L.J. 1239, 1245 (1991).

12. There is another facet to the lawyer's duty of loyalty, which I do not emphasize. The duty protects clients against various forms of lawyer laziness. Indeed, most lack of zeal cases involve lawyers who are excessively lazy rather than excessively scrupulous. A typical example is *Haynes v. Al. St. Bar*, 447 So. 2d 675, 677 (Ala. 1984), in which DR 7–101 of the Model Code was violated when a lawyer agreed to take on a matter but did nothing. *See also In re* Haupt, 444 A.2d 317, 325 n.3 (D.C. 1982) (collecting authorities). But the fact that the

loyalty rules promote quality control does not mean that they cannot be rules of professional morality as well.

13. *See, e.g.*, MODEL RULES OF PROF'L CONDUCT R. 1.7(b)(4).

14. *See, e.g., id.* R. 1.7(b)(1).

15. *Id.* R. 1.7(a)(1).

16. *Id.* R. 1.7(a)(2).

17. *See, e.g., id.* R. 1.8(b). The Rule adds that lawyers may use such information to the disadvantage of their clients "as permitted or required" by other parts of the Model Rules.

This scheme of course implicates the lawyer's duty to preserve client confidences and also the exceptions to this duty. *See id.* R. 1.6, 3.3, 4.1. I take up client confidences in chapter 2.

18. *Id.* R. 1.7(b)(3).

19. *See id.* R. 1.8(c).

20. *See id.* R. 1.8(d).

21. *See id.* R. 1.8(a).

22. *See id.* R. 1.8(f); *see also id.* R. 5.4(c).

23. Specifically, Rule 1.2 says: "Subject to paragraphs (c) and (d) [concerning, respectively, contractual limits on the scope of representation and limits imposed by the criminal law and the law of fraud], a lawyer shall abide by a client's decisions concerning the objectives of representation . . . ." *Id.* R. 1.2(a). A general account of the workings of the Rule appears in Judith L. Maute, *Allocation of Decisionmaking Authority under the Model Rules of Professional Conduct*, 17 U.C. DAVIS. L. REV. 1049 (1984).

24. MODEL CODE OF PROF'L RESPONSIBILITY DR 7–101(A)(1) (1980). The Model Code, like the Model Rules, limits client control by allowing lawyers to refuse to aid unlawful conduct. *See id.* DR 7–101(B)(2).

25. RESTATEMENT (THIRD) OF THE LAW GOVERNING LAWYERS § 21(2)–(3) (2000). The Restatement once again creates exceptions to this rule of client control that allow the lawyer and client to vary the rule by contract (section 21(1)) and that subject client control to limits set by otherwise applicable law, including most notably criminal law and the law of fraud (section 23).

26. The several ethics regimes differ, for example, in how friendly they are to efforts to change the boundaries of client control by contract.

27. Olfe v. Gordon, 286 N.W.2d 573, 577 (Wis. 1980) (quotation marks and citation omitted). Note, moreover, that even the rule that lawyers must pursue clients' instructions and not their interests may be explained in these terms. Thus a lawyer who disobeys her client's instructions cannot defend against malpractice suits (which sound in tort and agency law) by arguing that the instructions did not serve her clients best interests. *See* Note, *Attorney Malpractice*, 63 COLUM. L REV. 1292, 1302 (1963) (citing W.L. Douglas Shoe Co. v. Rollwage, 63 S.W.2d 841 (Ark. 1933); Lally v. Kuster, 177 Cal. 783 (1918)).

28. Thus the Restatement of Agency identifies agency as "the fiduciary relationship that arises when one person (a 'principal') manifests assent to another person (an 'agent') that the agent shall act on the principal's behalf and subject to the principal's control, and the agent manifests assent or otherwise consents so to act." RESTATEMENT (THIRD) OF AGENCY § 1.01 (2006).

29. Specifically, Rule 1.2 says that "as required by Rule 1.4, [the lawyer] shall consult with the client as to the means by which [the client's objectives] are to be pursued." MODEL RULES OF PROF'L CONDUCT R. 1.2(a) (2003). Rule 1.4 addresses consultation and communication between lawyer and client. *See id.* R. 1.4.

30. *Id.* R. 1.2 cmt. 2. See also RESTATEMENT (THIRD) OF LAW GOVERNING LAWYERS § 23 & cmt. c (2000) for more on the client's control of her lawyer's actions with respect to harming third parties.

31. MODEL RULES OF PROF'L CONDUCT R. 1.2 cmt. 2.

32. *Id.* R. 2.1. The official Comment adds that "[p]urely technical legal advice . . . can sometimes be inadequate" so that "[i]t is proper for a lawyer to refer to relevant moral and ethical considerations in giving advice." *Id.* R. 2.1 cmt. 2.

33. DAVID A BINDER, ET AL., LAWYERS AS COUNSELORS: A CLIENT-CENTERED APPROACH 279 (1991).

34. Williams v. Chrans, 742 F. Supp. 472, 478 (N.D. Ill. 1990). The words are the lawyers' as reported in the court's opinion. The lawyers further admitted that this "strategy was developed to accommodate [the lawyers] and not [the] client." *Id.*

35. *Id.* at 480 n.5.

36. *Id.* The court rejected the habeas petition. There appears to be have been no subsequent ethics case.

37. *See* RESTATEMENT (THIRD) OF AGENCY §§ 7.01, 7.03 (2006).

38. This privilege is, fundamentally, a creature of tort law. *See* RESTATEMENT (SECOND) OF TORTS § 586 (1977). The privilege is also recognized by the law of agency, *see* RESTATEMENT (THIRD) OF AGENCY § 7.01 cmt. e (2006), and the law governing lawyers, *see* RESTATEMENT (THIRD) OF LAW GOVERNING LAWYERS § 57(1) (2000); *see also* 1 HH, *supra* note 11, § 1.1:205, at 18.38 (Supp. 1998). Cases applying the privilege are collected in 1 RONALD E. MALLEN & JEFFREY M. SMITH, LEGAL MALPRACTICE § 6.25, at 353–54 (3d ed. 1989). The privilege is critically appraised in Paul Hayden, *Reconsidering the Litigator's Absolute Privilege to Defame*, 54 OHIO ST. L.J. 985 (1993).

39. *See, e.g.*, Salaymeh v. Interqual, Inc., 508 N.E.2d 1155 (Ill. 1987). An exception exists for cases in which the lawyer's advice reflects "actual malice" against the victim of the breach that is "unrelated to [her] desire to protect [her] client." *Id.* at 1160.

40. Reves v. Ernst & Young, 507 U.S. 170 (1993) (interpreting the "conduct or participate" language of the Federal RICO statute). Similarly, a lawyer who files an application on behalf of a client seeking to seize goods on the basis of trademark violations is not an "applicant" under the Lanham Act and so not liable if the seizure turns out to be unwarranted. *See, e.g.*, Electronic Laboratory Supply Co. v. Cullen, 977 F.2d 798 (3d Cir. 1992).

41. *See* RESTATEMENT (SECOND) TORTS § 772 (1979). See also 1 HH, *supra* note 11, § 1.1:205, at 18.37 (Supp. 1998). *See also* 1 MALLEN & SMITH, *supra* note 38,§ 6.23, at 348–52.

42. RESTATEMENT (SECOND) OF TORTS § 10, cmt. d (1965). ("The most frequent instances of such absolute or indefeasible privileges are those given to the

judiciary and to other persons such as witnesses, jurymen, and counsel who aid in the administration of the law.").

43. Support for the claims made in this footnote regarding the differing fee shifting regimes adopted in Great Britain and the United States may be found in the following sources. In Britain, see CIV. PROC. R. 44.3(2)(a) (Eng.); see also Michael Zander, *Will the Revolution in the Funding of Civil Litigation in England Eventually Lead to Contingency Fees?*, 52 DEPAUL L. REV. 259, 292 n.192 (2002) ("The general rule is that the unsuccessful party will be ordered to pay the costs of the successful party."). In the United States, see 42 U.S.C. § 1988 (2006), which entitles certain successful civil rights plaintiffs to recover their fees and costs, and also Rules 11 and 37 of the Federal Rules of Civil Procedure, which (among other things) require payment of costs (in the narrow sense of court costs) associated with suits that are unreasonable or without substantial justification.

44. MODEL RULES OF PROF'L CONDUCT R. 3.1 (2003). Rule 1.2(d) similarly forbids lawyers from counseling clients to do something illegal but allows them to counsel clients to make good faith efforts to determine the "validity, scope, meaning or application of the law." *See id.* R. 1.2(d) (2003).

45. *See* FED. R. CIV. P. 11; *see also id.* 26(g) (extending Rule 11 to the discovery process); 28 U.S.C. § 1927 (2006) (making lawyers personally liable for costs and attorney's fees that result when they "multipl[y] the proceedings in any case unreasonably and vexatiously" in federal court).

46. The traditional common law tort of malicious prosecution applies only to legal proceedings that, in addition to being wrongful, have a "quasi-criminal" character, substantially interfere with a person's liberty or damage her reputation, or interfere with property interests (such as in attachment or involuntary bankruptcy proceedings). *See* WILLIAM L. PROSSER, HANDBOOK OF THE LAW OF TORTS 851–52 (4th ed. 1971). Although a growing majority of jurisdictions, and also the Restatement Second of Torts, recognize malicious prosecution without the requirement of special injury, RESTATEMENT (SECOND) OF TORTS § 674 (1977), a substantial minority of jurisdictions continue to follow the "English rule," which denies actions for malicious-prosecution-based, groundless civil suits in the absence of special harms of the type just described. *See, e.g.*, Bickel v. Mackie, 447 F. Supp. 1376, 1380 (N.D. Iowa 1978); Garcia v. Wall & Ochs, Inc., 389 A.2d 607, 608, 610 (Pa. 1978); PROSSER, *supra*, at 850–53. Most U.S. jurisdictions also recognize the tort of abuse of process. *See* RESTATEMENT (SECOND) OF TORTS, *supra* § 682; PROSSER, *supra* § 121, at 856–58.

Note that no jurisdiction recognizes the tort of malicious defense. See Jonathan K. Van Patten and Robert E. Willar, *The Limits of Advocacy: A Proposal for the Tort of Malicious Defense*, 35 HASTINGS L.J. 891 (1984).

47. 2 JAMES BOSWELL, THE LIFE OF SAMUEL JOHNSON LL.D. 47 (George Birkbeck Hill ed., 1887). For examples of modern commentaries that repeat this remark, see 1 HH, *supra* note 11, Introduction § 403, at Intro-26 to Intro-27 (Supp. 1998); Simon H. Rifkind, *The Lawyer's Role and Responsibility in Modern Society*, 30 THE RECORD 534 (1975).

48. This position, or something very like it, appears in Ted Schneyer, *The Promise and Problematics of Legal Ethics from the Lawyer's Point of View*, 16

Yale J.L. & Hum. 45, 61–62 (2004) and Alec Walen, *Criticizing the Obligatory Acts of Lawyers: A Response to Markovits's Legal Ethics from the Lawyer's Point of View*, 16 Yale J.L. & Hum. 1, 13 (2004).

49. I borrow the term "role distance" from Meir Dan-Cohen. Meir Dan-Cohen, *Mediating Institutions: Beyond the Public/Private Distinction*, 61 U. Chi. L. Rev. 1213, 1222 (1994). *See also id.* at 1220; Meir Dan-Cohen, *Responsibility and the Boundaries of the Self*, 105 Harv. L. Rev. 959, 967 (1992); Meir Dan-Cohen, *Law, Community, and Communication*, 1989 Duke L.J. 1654, 1654 (1990). Dan-Cohen borrows it from Erving Goffman, Encounters 85–152 (1961) and Erving Goffman, *The Underlife of a Public Institution: A Study of Ways of Making Out in a Mental Hospital, in* Asylums: Essays on the Social Situation of Mental Patients and Other Inmates 171, 318–20 (1961). Dan-Cohen believes that lawyers have sufficient role distance to avoid the charge that they lie. Dan-Cohen, *Law, Community, and Communication, supra.* For the reasons given in the main text, I disagree.

50. 1 HH, *supra* note 11 § 3.4:600, at 646.2 (Supp. 1996). Hazard and Hodes add, moreover, that "[i]n practice, this proper "influencing" of the jurors is not far removed from "testifying" about the believability of evidence." *Id.* Indeed, Hazard and Hodes believe that a lawyer may go so far as, for example, to weep as she describes her client's injuries during summation in a tort suit. *See* 1 HH, *supra* note 11 § 3.5:203, at 658 (Supp. 1998). At the same time, there are of course limits on how far a lawyer may go in promoting her client's cause. Below, I take up one important such limit—that the lawyer may not personally vouch for the cause. *See infra* notes 56–57 and accompanying text.

51. Robert Post, *On the Popular Image of the Lawyer: Reflections in a Dark Glass*, 75 Cal. L. Rev. 379, 388 (1987).

52. *Id.*

53. Miller v. State, 623 N.E.2d 403, 408 (Ind. 1993); *accord.* People v. Hawthorne, 841 P.2d 118 (Cal. 1992). In each case, prosecutors sought to tell juries about this difference by reciting Justice White's observation that "[i]f [defense counsel] can confuse a witness, even a truthful one, or make him appear at a disadvantage, unsure, or indecisive, that will be his normal course." United States v. Wade 388 U.S. 218, 256–58 (White, J., dissenting in part and concurring in part).

54. Bardonner v. State, 587 N.E.2d 1353, 1361 (Ind. Ct. App. 1992).

55. Such warnings are nevertheless often proposed, for example by Alec Walen when he suggests that lawyers might preface their professional statements with a warning that listeners should "not . . . conclude that [they] personally accept the argument[s] [they are] about to express." Walen, *supra* note 48, at 14.

56. Model Rules of Prof'l Conduct Rule 3.4(e) (2003). Although sophisticated listeners of course know that lawyers may not vouch for the claims that they make, unsophisticated listeners, probably including most jurors, are less secure in this knowledge. Adversary lawyers naturally seek to take advantage of this lack of sophistication by conveying a sense (often false) of their own convictions in favor of their clients through means that fall just within the limits imposed by rule against vouching. This stratagem, moreover, is probably an inevitable feature of every adversary legal practice.

57. I develop these ideas at greater length in Daniel Markovits, *Contract and Collaboration*, 113 YALE L.J. 1422–28 (2004).

58. Hazard and Hodes appear at one point to suggest that lawyers lie and cheat only when they continue pressing a client's cause even in the face of a "moral certainty that a client is lying or engaged in an ongoing fraud or crime." 1 HH, *supra* note 11, Introduction § 403, at Intro-28 (1998 Supp.). Hazard and Hodes observe that only extreme versions of adversary advocacy—which oblige lawyers to serve their clients at virtually any cost—require or indeed even permit such conduct. And they conclude on this basis that the law governing lawyers as it stands does not require lawyers to lie.

59. *See* Berger v. United States, 295 U.S. 78, 88 (1935).

60. *See In re* Gahan, 279 N.W.2d 826 (Minn. 1979).

61. I would like to thank Michael Graetz and Jerry Mashaw for encouraging me to emphasize that point.

62. MODEL RULES OF PROF'L CONDUCT R. 1.2 cmt. 1 (2003).

63. *Id.* R. 1.3 cmt. 1. An earlier version of the comments to Model Rule 1.2 made the same point, observing that although clients are entitled to fix the ends of a representation, "at the same time, a lawyer is not required to pursue objectives or employ means simply because a client may wish that the lawyer do so." MODEL RULES OF PROF'L CONDUCT R. 1.2 cmt. 1 (1983).

64. This case is emphasized, for example, in Monroe H. Freedman, *Professional Responsibility of the Criminal Defense Lawyer: The Three Hardest Questions*, 64 MICH. L. REV. 1469, 1478 (1966).

65. The classic case is *Spaulding v. Zimmerman*, 116 N.W.2d 704 (Minn. 1962), in which a lawyer defending a tort action learned that the victim had suffered a potentially fatal aortic aneurism and kept this secret in order to secure an advantageous settlement.

66. This case figures in MARTON MINTZ, AT ANY COST: CORPORATE GREED, WOMEN, AND THE DALKON SHIELD (1985).

67. This case, which actually occurred, *see* Annesley v. Anglesea, 17 How. St. Trials 1139 (1743), is discussed in DAVID LUBAN, LAWYERS AND JUSTICE 3–10 (1988).

68. This statement of the extreme adversary position comes from SIMON, *supra* note 1, at 8, who associates it with the ABA's Model Rules. *See supra* note 1. Simon's critics have pointed out that this mischaracterizes the positive law. *See, e.g.*, Schneyer, *supra* note 2.

69. Bruce Green, *The Role of Personal Values in Professional Decisionmaking*, 11 GEO. J. LEGAL ETHICS 19, 22–23 (1997).

CHAPTER 2
THE LAWYERLY VICES

1. Note that the Model Rules expressly establish these prohibitions as limits on the principle of client control. Thus Rule 1.16(a)(1) expressly requires a lawyer to withdraw from any ongoing representation when the representation "will

result in violation of the rules of professional conduct or other law." Model Rules of Prof'l Conduct R. 1.16(a)(1) (2003).

2. *See id.* R. 3.3(a)(1)–(3).

3. *See id.* The application of this rule is illustrated by *United States v. Shaffer Equipment*, 11 F.3d 450 (4th Cir. 1993). In that case, government lawyers were found to have violated Rule 3.3 when they failed to advise a court that a witness whose credibility they had judged material to the dispute (as a matter of law) had falsely claimed to hold academic degrees related to the technical content of his testimony and also failed to inform the court of ongoing civil and criminal investigations into the witness' false claims. The lawyers were also found to have violated rule 26(e)(2) of the Federal Rules of Civil Procedure by obstructing opposing counsel's efforts to discover the falsehood. I would like to thank Brad Wendel for pointing *Shaffer Equipment* out to me.

4. *See* Model Rules of Prof'l Conduct R. 3.3(b). This requirement is an innovation in the Model Rules, and it has narrowed the scope of lawyers' professional obligations to lie. This may be seen, for example, in the contrast between the American Bar Association's Commission on Ethics and Professional Responsibility, Formal Opinions 287 (1953) and 87–353 (1987). The earlier opinion, which preceded the Model Rules, held that a defense lawyer need not correct a sentencing court's misapprehension that his client had no prior criminal record. The later opinion, applying Rule 3.3, concludes that the lawyer must correct the court's mistake insofar as her client has falsely denied having a prior record. *See* 1 Geoffrey C. Hazard, Jr. & W. William Hodes, The Law of Lawyering: A Handbook on The Model Rules of Professional Conduct § 3.3:203, at 584–85 (2d ed. 1990, Supp. 1997) [hereinafter HH]; *id.* § 3.3:204, at 585–88 (Supp. 1998); *id.* § 3.3:205, at 590–91.

5. 475 U.S. 157, 171 (1986).

6. See Model Rules of Prof'l Conduct R. 3.3(c). This can make it important to decide whether or not the addressee of a lie is a tribunal within the meaning of the rule. The issue played a prominent role in the Kaye Scholer affair, in which the law firm Kaye, Scholer, Fierman, Hays, and Handler, which represented Lincoln Savings and Loan before the Office of Thrift Supervision (OTS) failed to correct false submissions Lincoln Savings had made to the OTS—technically to the Federal Home Loan Bank Board (predecessor to OTS)—or to disclose material facts relevant to these submissions. *See* William H. Simon, *The Kaye Scholer Affair: The Lawyer's Duty of Candor and the Bar's Temptations of Evasion and Apology*, 23 Law & Soc. Inquiry 243, 248–51 (1998). Kaye Scholer was accused of misconduct and although it initially fought the accusation ultimately accepted a settlement that subjected it to a $41 million fine and to an ongoing injunction concerning future representations. *See id.* at 244.

Nevertheless the ABA, in a formal ethics opinion, defended Kaye Scholer's conduct, concluding that although a lawyer who represents a client in a bank examination "may not under any circumstances lie to or mislead agency officials . . . she is under no duty to disclose weaknesses in her client's case or otherwise reveal confidential information protected under Rule 1.6" and indeed may not correct her client's false submissions insofar as doing so would require revealing confidences. ABA Comm. on Ethics and Prof'l Responsibility, Formal Op. 93–375 (1993) (concluding that "the duty to disclose takes precedence over the duty to keep client confidences only in the context of an 'adjudicative proceeding' before a 'tribunal' under Rule 3.3 or a 'nonadjudicative proceeding' under Rule 3.9."). The ABA Opinion turned on the view that a bank examiner is not a tribunal within the meaning of Rule 3.3 but only a third party, and accordingly that the lawyer's duties of candor in such a case do not arise under Rule 3.3, which expressly trumps the duty of confidentially, but only under Rule 4.1, which is expressly subordinate to confidentiality.

There is good reason to doubt the Opinion's reasoning on this point and also to suspect that courts would follow the Kaye Scholer precedent over the Opinion and treat bank examiners as tribunals for purposes of Rule 3.3. *See* 1 HH, *supra* note 4, § 3.3:204, at 589 (Supp. 1998). Moreover, recent changes in the Model Rules narrow the duty of confidentially to allow a lawyer to disclose confidences to prevent or correct substantial financial fraud in which she has participated, and these changes would give a lawyer in Kaye Scholer's position an affirmative duty to disclose even to a third-party bank examiner under Rule 4.1. And, finally, the interaction between the law governing lawyers and the underlying law of fraud may have made Kaye Scholer a participant in Lincoln Savings' fraud and therefore given it a duty at least to withdraw (perhaps noisily) even under the Model Rules as they stood at the time (particularly under Rule 1.2). These last two points are elaborated below; *see also* Ted Schneyer, *From Self-Regulation to Bar Corporatism: What the S&L Crisis Means for the Regulation of Lawyers*, 35 S. Tex. L. Rev. 639 (1994).

7. *See* Model Rules of Prof'l Conduct R. 3.3(a)(3).

8. *See id.* R. 3.4(a). Even a criminal defense lawyer may not hold evidence for a client in a way that obstructs police access to it but must instead either turn the evidence over to the police or return it to its original location. But even so, a lawyer who gives the evidence over to the police is prevented, by the attorney-client privilege, from revealing that she has received the evidence from her client. Consequently if the police cannot connect the evidence to the client in some other way, then it will be inadmissible because it is without foundation. *See* 1 HH, *supra* note 4, § 3.4:204, at 631 (Supp. 1998).

9. *See* Model Rules of Prof'l Conduct R. 3.4(b).

10. *See id.* R. 1.2(b). This rule is generally taken to forbid lawyers from telling their clients which lies will be legally effective, as (in a case made prominent by the book and film *Anatomy of a Murder*) by telling a criminal defendant how to construct a false insanity defense. Even adversary advocacy's most insistent proponents have come to accept this principle, including in the context of criminal defense. (A prominent example is Monroe Freedman's change of mind about this question. *Compare* Monroe H. Freedman, *Professional Responsibility of the Criminal Defense Lawyer: The Three Hardest Questions*, 64 Mich. L. Rev. 1469, 1478–82 (1966) *with* Monroe H. Freedman, Lawyers' Ethics in an Adversary System 59–76 (1975).) As Hazard and Hodes say, "[t]he client, having told the truth to the lawyer about his situation, is entitled to have his confidences respected, but he is not entitled to the lawyer's participation in the fabrication of a new story with better facts." 1 HH, *supra* note 4, § 1.2:505, at 53 (Supp. 1994).

11. *See* MODEL RULES OF PROF'L CONDUCT R. 3.1; *see also* FED. R. CIV. P. 11. More specifically, Rule 11(b)(2) requires that the "claims, defenses and other legal contentions therein are warranted by existing law or nonfrivolous argument for the extension, modification, or reversal of existing law . . . ." Rule 11(b)(3) requires that the "allegations and other factual contentions have evidentiary support or . . . are likely to have evidentiary support after a reasonable opportunity for further investigation or discovery . . . ." *Id.* 11(b)(3).

12. *See* MODEL RULES OF PROF'L CONDUCT R. 3.3(a)(1)–(2). The requirement that lawyers reveal controlling directly adverse precedents is often treated as requiring broad disclosures, for example by an ABA Formal Opinion that concludes disclosure is required whenever a judge would feel misled by a failure to disclose. *See* ABA Comm. on Ethics and Prof'l Responsibility, Formal Op. 280 (1949). But the technical limits of the duty should not be ignored. Thus lawyers are under no duty to disclose adverse rulings from other jurisdictions (although they may not, because of Model Rule 3.3(a)(1), falsely deny that such rulings exist). Indeed, a lawyer who discloses an adverse but not controlling precedent almost certainly violates the duty of loyalty (at least insofar as the disclosure is motivated by desire that the tribunal should learn of the precedent rather than being a tactical effort to preempt the other side).

13. *See* MODEL RULES OF PROF'L CONDUCT R. 3.1; FED. R. CIV. P. 11; *see also supra* note 11.

14. *See* MODEL RULES OF PROF'L CONDUCT R. 1.16(b)(4).

15. *See id.* R. 6.2(c).

16. For the rule against assisting client fraud, see, e.g., *id.* R. 1.2 (2003). Some version of this basic principle—that adversary advocacy is not a license to general lawlessness—appears in all ethics codes. *See, e.g.,* MODEL CODE OF PROF'L RESPONSIBILITY DR 7-101(B)(2) (1980) ("A lawyer may refuse to aid or participate in conduct that he believes to be unlawful, even though there is some support for an argument that the conduct is legal.")

For the rule against knowingly making false statements of material fact or law, see MODEL RULES OF PROF'L CONDUCT R. 4.1(a). Straightforward examples of forbidden affirmative representations include falsely telling a debtor that he will lose his driver's license if he defaults on a loan owed to a client, *see In re Eliasen,* 913 P.2d 1163 (Idaho 1996), falsely telling a hospital that treated an injured client that the client's recovery in a tort action based on the injury is insufficient to pay his medical bills, *see* Fla. Bar v. McLawhoun, 505 So. 2d 1338 (Fla. 1987), falsely telling an interlocutor that a telephone conversation is not being taped, *see* Miss. Bar v. Attorney, 621 So. 2d 229 (Miss. 1993), and falsely identifying an employee of the defendant who is engaging in misconduct, *see* Ausherman v. Bank of Am., 212 F. Supp. 2d 435 (D. Md. 2002).

More subtly, even silence may in some cases amount to an affirmative misrepresentation of the kind forbidden by Rule 4.1(a). Thus a lawyer must inform both the court and opposing counsel that her client has died before she may accept a proposed settlement on behalf of the client's estate. ABA Comm. on Ethics and Prof'l Responsibility, Formal Op. 95-397 (1995). Failure to disclose the death to the court is "tantamount to making a 'false statement of material fact . . . to a tribunal' within the meaning of Rule 3.3," and failure to disclose the death of a client to the other side "is tantamount to making a false statement of material fact within the meaning of Rule 4.1(a)." *Id.*; *see also* Neb. State Bar v. Addison, 412 N.W.2d 855 (1987) (employing similar reasoning, but under the Model Code, to suspend a lawyer for negotiating a favorable settlement of his client's hospital bill in which he allowed the hospital to remain unaware of existence of an insurance policy that might have covered the bill).

17. *See* MODEL RULES OF PROF'L CONDUCT R. 4.1(b).

18. *See id.* R. 1.6(b)(1)–(3), 4.1(b).

19. *See id.* R. 1.6(b)(1); *see also* RESTATEMENT (THIRD) OF LAW GOVERNING LAWYERS § 66(1) (2000), which mimics the Model Rule's language about reasonably certain death or serious bodily harm.

This provision expands lawyers' permissions to break confidences—the Model Rules as originally enacted, for example, allowed disclosure only in connection with *criminal* acts that posed an *imminent* threat of death or serious harm. *See* MODEL RULES OF PROF'L CONDUCT R. 1.6(b); *see* 1 HH, *supra* note 4, § 1.6:304, at 173–74 (Supp. 1993). The inadequacies of the narrower permission are famously illustrated by the facts of *Spaulding v. Zimmerman*, 116 N.W.2d 704 (Minn. 1962), in which lawyers representing a defendant in an accident did not disclose that the plaintiff had suffered a life-threatening aortic aneurism. Both the law governing lawyers in effect in 1957, when the events occurred, and the 1983 Model Rules would have forbidden disclosure of these facts. For an excellent discussion of the general issues, including the tangential question whether the concealment justified rescission of a settlement entered while the plaintiff was a minor (the court ruled that it did), see Roger Cramton & Lori Knowles, *Professional Secrecy and Its Exceptions: Spaulding v. Zimmerman Revisited*, 83 MINN. L. REV. 63 (1998). The current version of the Model Rules, by contrast, permits (but does not require) disclosure.

For a case in which even the older version of Rule 1.6 permits disclosure, and in which disclosure was made, see *Purcell v. District Attorney*, 676 N.E.2d 436 (Mass. 1997), in which a lawyer disclosed his client's stated intention to set fire to an apartment building.

20. *See* FED. R. CIV. P. 26(a) (describing the various "required disclosures" necessary even "without awaiting a discovery request").

21. An example concerning fraud is *Cresswell v. Sullivan & Cromwell*, 668 F. Supp. 166 (1987) (holding that plaintiffs were free to sue Sullivan & Cromwell for participating in the fraud of its clients in not producing required documents pursuant to a legitimate discovery request). Model Rule 1.6(b)(6) would allow the lawyer to correct the misstatement in such a case. *See* 1 HH, *supra* note 4, § 1.1:204, at 18.27 (Supp. 1998).

22. Disclosure of threats to children figures in Cleveland Bar Association Prof'l Ethics Comm., Formal Op. 92-2, *reproduced in* 8 LAW. MAN. PROF. CONDUCT 299 (1992). An Ohio lawyer was permitted to disclose that her client's husband had committed child abuse but that she intended to take her child back to live with him anyway. Ohio law requires reporting child abuse and makes it a crime to subject children to certain risks, and Model Rule 1.6(b)(6) allowed the lawyer to report the husband's abuse in order to comply with this law.

23. *See* MODEL RULES OF PROF'L CONDUCT R. 3.4(d).

NOTES TO CHAPTER 2

24. *See id.* R. 1.6(b)(6).

25. *Id.* R. 8.4(c).

26. *See, e.g., In re* Siegel, 627 A.2d 156 (N.J. 1993) (applying Rule 8.4(c) against a lawyer who defrauded his own firm by claiming personal expenses as client costs); *In re* Conduct of Busby, 855 P.2d 156 (Or. 1993) (applying Model Code of Professional Responsibility DR 1-102(A)(4), the counterpart to Model Rule 8.4(c), against a lawyer who engaged in other dishonesty against his own firm).

27. *See* Restatement (Third) of the Law Governing Lawyers § 5 cmt. c (2000).

28. It is important (as part of the general project of avoiding the fetish of extreme adversariness) to note that although lawyers have broad professional duties to promote false beliefs they do not have a duty to employ every available means of doing so.

Certain litigator's tricks—for example, substituting an imposter for the defendant at the defense table in order to induce a misidentification by a witness—may properly be forbidden even in adversary systems. *See, e.g.,* United States v. Thoreen, 653 F.2d 1332, 1338–41 (9th Cir. 1981) (arguing that although "vigorous advocacy by defense counsel may properly entail impeaching or confusing a witness, even if counsel thinks the witness is truthful, and refraining from presenting evidence even if he knows the truth," this technique crosses the line between zealous advocacy to obstruction of justice); *see also* Kiner v. State, 643 N.E.2d 950, 954 (Ind. Ct. App. 1994) (acknowledging defense counsel's obligation to present arguments that she disbelieves on behalf of her client, but nevertheless approving a trial court's jury instruction "to disregard . . . testimony regarding the misidentification of a photograph of [someone else] as a photograph of the defendant, as it was procured as a result of defense counsel's misrepresentation").

Moreover, and perhaps more importantly, lawyers need not argue their clients' cases by prejudicial means. This point is illustrated by a case in which lawyers representing police officers accused of forcibly sodomizing a prisoner with a toilet plunger suggested that the victim's injuries came from consensual gay sex. It has been suggested that even if the lawyers privately doubted this argument, they may have been constitutionally required to make it (at least insofar as they thought it would be effective). *See* Joseph Fried, *An Insinuation Revisited during the Louima Trial,* N.Y. Times, May 31, 1999, at B4; Laura Mansnerus, *When the Job Requires a Walk on the Ethical Lines,* N.Y. Times, May 30, 1999, § 4, at 10. But this suggestion ignores the question whether the argument's success depends upon appealing to antigay prejudice in the jury. Even if defense counsel is required to try to make the weaker argument seem stronger, she need not be required to do so by appealing to bigotry.

29. *See* Model Rules of Prof'l Conduct R. 3.3(a)(3).

30. *Id.* R. 3.3 cmt. 8.

31. A characteristic case is *In re Ryder,* 263 F. Supp. 360 (E.D. Va. 1967), in which a lawyer who was given a key to a safe deposit box containing a gun and cash by his client was held to know that the client committed the robbery he was accused of.

32. Model Rules of Prof'l Conduct R. 3.3 cmt. 8.

33. United States v. Schaffer Equip. Co., 11 F.3d 450, 459 (4th Cir. 1993) (a civil case brought by the EPA under the Comprehensive Environmental Response, Compensation, and Liability Act ("CERCLA"), 42 U.S.C. § 9601 *et seq.* (2000)).

34. *See* MODEL RULES OF PROF'L CONDUCT R. 3.3(a)(3).

35. *See Id.* R. 3.3 cmt. 9.

36. *See Id.* cmt. 14. The Comment goes on to say that "the conflicting position is expected to be presented by the opposing party." *Id.* This principle appears even more prominently and forcefully in less moderate treatments of adversary ethics, for example in the American Lawyer's Code of Conduct (drafted under the auspices of the aggressively adversary Roscoe Pound—American Trial Lawyer's Foundation). This code, which adopts the general view that lawyers should use all legal means to pursue their clients' objectives, contemplates that lawyers must in some cases knowingly make false claims to courts. *See* AMERICAN LAWYER'S CODE OF CONDUCT § 3.1 & illustrative cases 3(e)–(f) (1982) (if a judge asks a lawyer whether her client is guilty and the lawyer believes that any answer other than "no" will signal guilt, then the lawyer must deny that her client is guilty even if she knows otherwise).

37. 1 HH, *supra* note 4, § 3.3:209, at 596.1 (Supp. 1998).

38. 1 HH, *supra* note 4, Introduction § 403, at Intro-27 (Supp. 1998).

39. Support for the claims made in this footnote may be found in MODEL RULES OF PROF'L CONDUCT R. 3.3(a)(3) (including the quoted text regarding the lawyer's lack of discretion to refuse to offer the testimony of a criminal defendant). *See also* MODEL RULES OF PROF'L CONDUCT R. 3.3 cmt. 9 ("Unless the lawyers knows the testimony will be false, the lawyer must honor the client's decision to testify."). For instances where courts have suggested that a lawyer may refuse to offer the defendant's testimony only when there is absolute, incontrovertible proof of the testimony's falsehood, see United States v. Long, 857 F.2d 436 (8th Cir. 1988); State v. McDowell, 669 N.W.2d 204 (Wis. Ct. App. 2003) (holding that a lawyer provided ineffective assistance of counsel when he refused to put a client on the stand after the client said "I'll say what I need to help myself out and if I have something untruthful to say I'll say that."). The example and quotation in the final paragraph of the footnote are taken from People v. Lang, 11 Cal. 3d 134, 139 (1974).

40. JEROME FRANK, COURTS ON TRIAL 82 (1949). Frank was not necessarily a fan of all these techniques.

41. MODEL RULES OF PROF'L CONDUCT R. 4.4(a).

42. Here I am influenced by Hazard and Hodes, who observe that "[i]n litigation, it is often the duty of an advocate to 'burden' or 'embarrass' an adverse witness during cross-examination, if doing so will make the witness less likely to be believed. Such tactics do not violate Rule 4.4, however, for there is obviously a 'substantial' and legitimate purpose to them. Legally, the situation is probably no different where the examining lawyer knows that the witness is telling the truth. Even though cross-examining a truthful witness tends to move the trier of fact away from the truth rather than toward it, the advocate may *still* point to a 'substantial purpose' *other* than harassing the witness, namely winning the case at hand." 1 HH, *supra* note 4, § 4.4:102, at 756 (Supp. 1997).

43. *See* 1 HH, *supra* note 4, § 40.3, at 40–4.1 (3d ed. Supp. 2004–2).

44. Support for the claims made in this footnote may be found in United States. v. Wade, 388 U.S. 218, 256–58 (White, J., dissenting in part and concurring in part) (including Justice White's quoted observation); United States v. Thoreen, 653 F.2d 1332, 1338–39 (9th Cir. 1981) (including the quoted language regarding the propriety of deceptive methods of cross-examination); *accord* Kiner v. State, 643 N.E.2d 950, 954 (Ind. Ct. App. 1994). Further support is found in Nix v. Whiteside, 475 U.S. 157, 171 (1986) (indicating that defense counsel is not required to assist a defendant who wishes to commit perjury); Sallie v. North Carolina, 587 F.2d 636, 640 (4th Cir. 1978) (suggesting that courts are generally reluctant to second-guess lawyers' strategic situation sense). The first quotation from the Supreme Court, regarding Sixth Amendment rights of defendants whose counsel "entirely fail to subject the prosecutions case to meaningful adversarial testing" is taken from United States v. Cronic, 466 U.S. 648, 659 (1984) (citing Davis v. Alaska, 415 U.S. 308 (1974)), as is the subsequent quotation regarding the Sixth Amendment's requirement that counsel "must hold the prosecution to its heavy burden of proof." *Id.* at 656 n.19 (citation omitted). The assertion that ineffective assistance of counsel claims generally require showings of both deficient performance and prejudicial effect is supported by Strickland v. Washington, 466 U.S. 668 (1984).

The quotation from the ABA Standards for Criminal Justice is found at ABA STANDARDS FOR CRIMINAL JUSTICE Standard 4–7.6(b) (3d ed. 1993). The quotations from the Commentary are found at ABA STANDARDS FOR CRIMINAL JUSTICE Standard 4–7.6 cmt., at 4.92.

For examples of critics who do not entirely reject the impeachment of truthful witnesses despite seeking narrower constraints on defense counsel's cross-examinations, see Harry I. Subin, *The Criminal Lawyer's "Different Mission": Reflection on the "Right" to Present a False Case*, 1 GEO. J. LEGAL ETHICS 125 (1987); Harry I. Subin, *Is This Lie Necessary: Further Reflections on the Right to Present a False Defense*, 1 GEO. J. LEGAL ETHICS 689 (1988); John B. Mitchell, *Reasonable Doubts Are Where You Find Them: A Response to Professor Subin's Position on the Criminal Layer's "Different Mission,"* 1 GEO J. LEGAL ETHICS 339 (1987); Murray L. Schwartz, *On Making the True look False and the False Look True*, 41 S.W. L.J. 1135 (1988); Robert Lawry, *Cross-Examining the Truthful Witness: The Ideal Within the Central Moral Tradition of Lawyering*, 100 DICK. L. REV. 563 (1996); JOHN M. BURKOFF, CRIMINAL DEFENSE ETHICS at 5–90 (2001).

45. *See* MODEL RULES OF PROF'L CONDUCT R. 3.4(a).

46. *See* 1 HH, *supra* note 4, § 3.4:202, at 628–29 (2d ed. Supp. 1998).

47. *See* MODEL RULES OF PROF'L CONDUCT R. 2.1.

48. See the discussion below of the limits of client-counseling.

49. *See* MODEL RULES OF PROF'L CONDUCT R. 3.4(f); *see also* 1 HH, *supra* note4, § 3.4:704, at 649 (2d ed. 1990). The Model Rules give lawyers greater leeway, in this connection, than did previous regimes, and in particular do not contain an equivalent to DR 7-109(B) of the Model Code of Professional Responsibility, which forbade lawyers from making someone "unavailable as a witness." But although the precise limits of lawyers' involvement in this area

may vary across ethics regimes, this variation is constrained by the core commitments of adversary advocacy, which insist that a lawyer must be permitted to help a client exercise whatever rights to control information the law gives him.

50. *See* FED. R. CIV. P. 26(a) (stating that parties must provide the other side with the name and, if known, contact information for each individual "likely to have discoverable information that the disclosing party may use to support its claims or defenses . . . identifying the subjects of the information"); MODEL RULES OF PROF'L CONDUCT R. 3.4(d) (prohibiting a lawyer from "fail[ing] to make reasonably diligent effort to comply with a legally proper discovery request by an opposing party").

51. *See* MODEL RULES OF PROF'L CONDUCT R. 3.3 cmt. 14.

52. *See id.* R. 4.1 cmt. 1. As no less than Samuel Williston observed, a lawyer who discovers a damaging fact in the course of litigation has (at least as a general matter) a professional duty to remain silent even when he knows that the judge's decision would be critically influenced by the fact. SAMUEL WILLISTON, LIFE AND LAW 271 (1940).

53. For example, a lawyer's duties to cooperate with discovery would not require disclosure of the identity or existence of the doctor who discovered the aneurism in *Spaulding v. Zimmerman*, discussed *supra* note 19, much less of the aneurism itself, because the defendants did not intend to use him as part of their defense. *See* Roger Cramton & Lori Knowles, *Professional Secrecy and Its Exceptions: Spaulding v. Zimmerman Revisited*, 83 MINN. L. REV. 63, 84 (1998).

Similarly, a lawyer who introduced evidence tending to show that her client was home one night need not, absent an adequate discovery request, inform other side of eyewitnesses who say he was out. A lawyer would have to reveal these eyewitnesses only if they were so credible, and their evidence so powerful, that the lawyer came to *know* that the evidence she had previously introduced was false. *See* Murray L. Schwartz, *On Making the True look False and the False Look True*, 41 Sw. L.J. 1135 (1988). *See generally* Wayne D. Brazil, *The Adversary Character of Civil Discovery: A Critique and Proposal for Change*, 31 VAND. L. REV. 1295 (1978).

54. *See supra* notes 17–24 and accompanying text.

55. *See also* 1 HH, *supra* note 4, § 3.4:501, at 646 (Supp. 1996).

56. *See* Michigan State Bar Comm. on Prof'l and Judicial Ethics, Op. CI-1164, *reproduced in* 3 LAWYERS' MANUAL OF PROF'L CONDUCT 44 (1989), *available at* http://www.michbar.org/opinions/ethics/numbered_opinions/ci-1164.html.

57. *See* MODEL RULES OF PROF'L CONDUCT R. 3.3(a)(3).

58. *See* 1 HH, *supra* note 4, § 3.3:203, at 584–85 (Supp. 1997); *Id.* § 3.3:204, at 585–88 (Supp. 1998); *Id.* § 3.3:205, at 590–91 (Supp. 1998). Model Rule 3.3 requires the lawyer to correct the court only if the court's mistake is caused by evidence that the lawyer has herself presented or by her client's fraud toward the tribunal.

59. *See* Michigan State Bar Comm. on Prof'l and Judicial Ethics, Opinion RI-13, *reproduced in* 5 ABA/BNA LAWYERS' MANUAL OF PROF'L CONDUCT 155 (1989), *available at* http://michbar.org/opinions/ethics/numbered_opinions/ri-013.htm.

60. *See* MODEL RULES OF PROF'L CONDUCT R. 3.3(c).

61. 1 HH, *supra* note 4, § 3.3:208, at 596 n.5 (Supp. 1998).

62. See, respectively, MODEL RULES OF PROF'L CONDUCT R. 3.1; FED. R. CIV. P. 11; and MODEL RULES OF PROF'L CONDUCT R. 3.3(a)(2).

63. MODEL RULES OF PROF'L CONDUCT R. 3.1; *see also* FED. R. CIV. P. 11(b) ("By presenting to the court . . . a pleading, written motion, or other paper, an attorney or unrepresented party is certifying that to the best of the person's knowledge, information, and belief, formed after an inquiry reasonable under the circumstances, . . . the claims, defenses, and other legal contentions therein are warranted by existing law or by a nonfrivolous argument for the extension, modification, or reversal of existing law or the establishment of new law . . . .").

64. MODEL RULES OF PROF'L CONDUCT R. 3.1 cmt. 2.

65. A typical case is *Stern v. Coates*, 517 N.W.2d 658, 666 (Wis. 1994).

66. Support for the claim made in this footnote that defense lawyers' are strongly obligated to make legal arguments they privately disbelieve can be found in, for example, United States v. Chee, No. 200001071, 2002 CCA Lexis 304 (N-M. Ct. Crim. App. Dec. 12, 2002); People v. Cropper, 89 Cal. App. 3d 716, 720–21 (1979). That these obligations are not unbounded is supported by, for example, Jones v. Barnes, 463 U.S. 745 (1983); Anders v. California, 386 U.S. 738 (1967).

67. *See* Precision Specialty Metals v. United States, 315 F.3d 1346, 1356 (Fed. Cir. 2003). The reprimand, originally issued by the Court of International Trade, was imposed pursuant to Rule 11 of the Court's Rules, which is identical to Rule 11 of the Federal Rules of Civil Procedure. I would like to thank Brad Wendel for pointing out this case.

68. Recall, for example, the earlier discussion of lawyers' expanded duties of factual disclosure in *ex parte* proceedings. *See supra* text accompanying note 36.

69. ABA Comm. on Ethics and Prof'l Responsibility, Formal Op. 85–352 (1985).

70. *Id.* This standard does impose some limits on the aggressiveness that lawyers may display. In particular, the inclusion of the phrase "if litigated" indicates that lawyers may not take into account the unlikelihood of IRS scrutiny in calculating the possibility that a position will succeed. Moreover, there is authority suggesting that a 5–10 percent chance of success is too low to be realistic. But a 33 percent chance of success almost certainly is realistic. *See* Theodore Tannenwald, David Watts & Bernard Wolfman, *Report of the Special Task Force on Formal Opinion 85–352*, 39 TAX LAW. 635 (1986).

71. *See* IRC § 6662(d)(2)(B)(i).

72. *See* Tannenwald, Watts & Wolfman, *supra* note 70, at 635. The laxer "reasonable basis" standard had previously governed filing tax returns also, *see* ABA Comm. on Ethics and Prof'l Responsibility, Formal Op. 314 (1965), and Formal Opinion 85–352 represents a modest narrowing of lawyers' room to lie. *See* ABA Comm. on Ethics and Prof'l Responsibility, Formal Op. 85–352, *supra*; *see also* ABA Comm. on Ethics and Prof'l Responsibility, Formal Op. 346 (1982) (stating that "[a] false opinion [regarding a tax shelter] is one which ignores or minimizes the serious legal risks or misstates the facts or the law, knowingly or through gross incompetence. The lawyer who gives a false opinion . . . violates the Disciplinary Rules of the Model Code of Professional Responsibility. Quite

clearly, the lawyer exceeds the duty to represent the client zealously within the bounds of the law").

73. *See* MODEL RULES OF PROF'L CONDUCT R. 4.1(a) (2003).

74. *See id.* R. 4.1 cmt. 1. The Comment excuses this lie by saying that "[u]nder generally accepted conventions in negotiation, certain types of statements ordinarily are not taken as statements of material fact." *Id.* But this is not descriptively accurate. The point of the lawyer's claim about her client's settlement reservation price is for the other side to accept, and act on, its truth, and the Comment therefore cannot wish the lie away by claiming that it is not factual or material.

75. *See, e.g.*, Roberts v. Sears Roebuck & Co., 573 F.2d 976 (7th Cir. 1978).

76. I borrow this example from 2 HH, *supra* note 4, § 4.1:204, at 717 (Supp. 1993). Although the lawyer may draft the term as a matter of legal ethics, her silence may make it less likely that the term will have the effect she wishes—the term may be interpreted against her client under the contract law doctrine *contra proferentum*. But this outcome is far from certain, and the lawyer remains free, when it comes time to interpret the contract, to argue that *contra proferentum* does not apply.

77. The 1981 Draft of Rule 1.2(d) would have prohibited a lawyer from drafting a "written instrument containing terms the lawyer knows or reasonably should know are legally prohibited," but this language was deleted from the final Rule by the ABA House of Delegates. And although including a clearly unenforceable term may (perhaps, but not necessarily) be prohibited by the underlying law of fraud, including a term that is only probably unenforceable clearly is not prohibited. For a discussion of these issues, see Bailey Kuklin, *On the Knowing Inclusion of Unenforceable Contract and Lease Terms*, 56 U. CIN. L. REV. 845 (1988); 1 HH, *supra* note 4, § 1.2:512, at 66 (Supp. 1998).

78. MODEL RULES OF PROF'L CONDUCT R. 3.3(c).

79. *Id.* R. 4.1(b).

80. *Id.* R. 1.6 (1983) (amended 2003). The rule also allowed lawyers to make disclosures when necessary "to establish a claim or defense on behalf of the lawyer in a controversy between the lawyer and the client, to establish a defense to a criminal charge or civil claim against the lawyer based upon conduct in which the client was involved, or to respond to allegations in any proceeding concerning the lawyer's representation of a client." *Id.*

81. Even under this regime, lawyers were required to withdraw from representing clients who had deceived them into participating in fraud, and perhaps even to withdraw noisily, insofar as not doing so after discovering the fraud made the lawyers complicit in the client's fraud as a matter of substantive law. In such cases, lawyers' disclosure duties sound in generally applicable law rather than in legal ethics (Model Rules 1.2(d), which forbids lawyers from assisting clients in conduct that they know is criminal or fraudulent, and 1.6(b)(6), which allows lawyers to reveal client confidences in order to comply with "other law," merely give these duties the imprimatur of the law governing lawyers.)

Both lawyers and courts commonly underestimate the constraints that generally applicable law places on the lies lawyers may tell for the clients. One famous example is *In re O.P.M. Leasing Services, Inc.*, 13 B.R. 54 (Bankr.

S.D.N.Y. 1981). Another example is *Schatz v. Rosenberg*, 943 F.2d 485 (4th Cir. 1991), in which a court declined to hold a law firm that prepared and delivered papers containing false representations on which it knew the plaintiff would rely liable for fraud, on the ground that the firm had merely "papered the deal" and that lawyers "do not vouch for the probity of their clients when they draft documents reflecting their clients' promises, statements, or warranties," *Id.* at 494 n.3, 495. This argument is simply wrong about the law of fraud. As the Restatement of Agency makes plain, "An agent who fraudulently makes representations, uses duress, or knowingly assists in the commission of tortious fraud or duress by others, is subject to liability in tort to the injured person although the fraud or duress occurs in a transaction on behalf of the principal." RESTATEMENT (FIRST) OF AGENCY § 348 (1933).

At the same time, however, fraud is a narrow and technical legal category, which applies to lawyers only interstitially, and no one seriously suggests that the law of fraud, or indeed any other generally applicable law, generally eliminates lawyers' professional duties to lie.

82. *See* MODEL RULES OF PROF'L CONDUCT R. 1.6(b)(2)–(3). Before 1983, the Model Code of Professional Responsibility had also incorporated a narrow duty of confidentiality, which allowed lawyers to reveal client intentions to commit any crime, no matter how trivial, and also the information needed to prevent the crime. *See* MODEL CODE OF PROF'L RESPONSIBILITY, DR 4–101(C)(3) (1969). The expansive version of the duty in place between 1983 and 2003 was something of an aberration.

83. The quotation at the end of this footnote is taken from MODEL RULES OF PROF'L CONDUCT R. 1.2 cmt. 10 (2003) (cross-references omitted). *See also* ABA Comm. on Ethics and Prof'l Responsibility, Formal Op. 92–366 (1992).

84. ABA Comm. on Ethics and Prof'l Responsibility, Formal Op. 94–387 (1994). The Opinion goes on to say that "[b]y the same token, a lawyer may not ethically break off negotiations with an opposing party simply because she has doubts about the viability of her client's case."

85. MODEL RULES OF PROF'L CONDUCT R. 1.6(b)(1). Note that even in this case lawyers are not required to break client confidences. Hazard and Hodes report, moreover, that this feature of the rule was not controversial—that "[t]here was broad agreement that lawyers should not be *required* to make disclosure in a case of threatened future harm." 1 HH, *supra* note 4, § 1.6:302, at 168.49–.50 (Supp. 1998).

86. MODEL RULES OF PROF'L CONDUCT R. 1.6(b)(6).

87. The case discussed in this footnote may be found in *Westinghouse Electric v. Kerr-McGee*, 580 F.2d 1311 (7th Cir. 1978).

88. The example comes from 1 HH, *supra* note 4, § 1.6:307 at 179 (Supp. 1996).

89. *See* People v. Belge, 372 N.Y.S.2d 798 (Onondaga County Ct. 1975), *aff'd*, 376 N.Y.S.2d 771 (App. Div. 1975). Hazard and Hodes observe that the lawyers behaved properly under the ethics codes in force at the time, and indeed that "no exception [to the duty of confidentiality] even arguably applies." 1 HH, *supra* note 4, § 1.6:303, at 169 (Supp. 1993). Probably nothing has changed, with the possible exception that Model Rule 1.6(b)(6) might allow (although it would not

require) the lawyers to reveal the body's location if this were necessary for complying with other law, for example, laws governing the burial of corpses.

Other sensational examples that commonly appear in the legal ethics literature include cases in which a criminal defendant tells his lawyer that another person is about to be executed for a crime he committed, *see* Bruce A. Green, *The Role of Personal Values in Professional Decisionmaking*, 11 Geo. J. Legal Ethics, 19, 29 (1997), a child tells his lawyer that he is being abused by his father, *see* Assoc. of Bar of City of N.Y. Comm. on Prof'l & Judicial Ethics, Formal Op. 1997-2 (1997), *available at* http://www.nycbar.org/ethics/eth1996-2.htm; Green, *supra*, at 30–31, a kidnapper tells his lawyer where his victims are confined, *see* McClure v. Thompson, 323 F.3d 1233 (9th Cir. 2003), or a defendant tells his lawyer that he intends to kill a person who is informing against him in a criminal prosecution, *see* San Diego County Bar Assoc. Legal Ethics and Unlawful Practices Comm., Op. 1990-1 (1990), *available at* http://www.sdcba.org/ethics/ethicsopinion90-1.html; 6 ABA/BNA Lawyers' Manual of Prof'l Conduct 394 (1990); 1 HH, *supra* note 4, § 1.6:303, at 169 (Supp. 1993).

For familiar reasons, these sensational cases are not nearly as interesting or important as the commonplace cases emphasized in the main text. Because such cases are rare, they do not figure prominently in most lawyers' professional lives. Moreover, the legal ethics rules (and in particular the duty to maintain client confidences) could easily be changed to allow or even to require disclosure in all these cases without abandoning any of the core principles of adversary advocacy. Indeed, the law governing lawyers as it stands (supplemented by external laws that already exist) would almost certainly permit (and perhaps even require) disclosure in the last three cases (although the San Diego Bar's ethics committee staggeringly concluded that California lawyers are *forbidden* from disclosing the client's intention to kill the informant). *See* San Diego County Bar Assoc. Legal Ethics and Unlawful Practices Comm., Op. 1990–1; 6 ABA/BNA Lawyers' Manual of Prof'l Conduct 394.

The sensational lies that dominate the legal ethics literature therefore reflect neither the lived experience of adversary advocacy nor its structural commitments. The more banal lies emphasized in the main text reflect both.

90. *See, e.g.*, Green, *supra* note 89, at 30–31.

91. Thus it is possible, for example, for a primer on legal ethics to say that "[n]o one, not even the most pro-disclosure zealot, thinks the lawyer ought to be permitted to disclose purely past crimes or frauds in which the lawyer is in no way implicated," and that "[a]s for information relating to purely past conduct, there is practically universal agreement that the lawyer is required to keep those facts secret." W. Bradley Wendel, Professional Responsibility: Examples and Explanations 164 (2004).

92. Model Rules of Prof'l Conduct R. 1.3 cmt. 1 (1999).

93. Note that the Model Rules expressly establish these prohibitions as limits on the principle of client control. Thus Rule 1.16(a)(1) expressly requires a lawyer to withdraw from any ongoing representation when the representation "will result in violation of the rules of professional conduct or other law." *Id.* R. 1.16(a)(1) (2003).

94. *See id.* R. 3.5(a).

95. *See id.* R. 3.5(d).

96. Specifically, the lawyer may not "make an extrajudicial statement that the lawyer knows or reasonably should know will be disseminated by means of public communication and will have a substantial likelihood of materially prejudicing an adjudicative proceeding in the matter." *Id.* R. 3.6(a). Note that the Rule forbids only conduct that generates a substantial likelihood of material prejudice, so that it is not triggered by anything like ever speech to the press. *See* Gentile v. State Bar of Nev., 501 U.S. 1030 (1991); *In Re* Morrisey, 168 F.3d 134 (4th Cir. 1999); United States v. Cutler, 58 F.3d 825 (2d Cir. 1995).

97. *See* MODEL RULES OF PROF'L CONDUCT R. 3.4(c).

98. *See id.* R. 3.5(b).

99. *See id.* R. 3.3(d), which requires lawyers in *ex parte* proceedings to inform tribunals of all known material facts, including adverse facts, even when nondisclosure would not be any fraud on the tribunal. This duty is perhaps most prominent in proceedings before patent officers. *See, e.g.*, Charles Pfizer & Co., Inc. v. Fed. Trade Comm'n, 401 F.2d 574 (6th Cir. 1968).

100. *See* MODEL RULES OF PROF'L CONDUCT R. 4.3. Note that the analogous rule in the Model Code of Professional Responsibility, DR 7-104(A)(2), focused on the specific act of a lawyer's "giving advice" to unrepresented persons rather than more generally on the third persons' misunderstandings of the lawyer's adversary role. Accordingly Ethics Opinions drafted under the Model Code allowed a lawyer to take advantage of the ignorance of unrepresented persons as long as she did not actually "giv[e] advice," so that a lawyer might, for example, exploit an unrepresented person's confusion about her adversary role in the course of settlement negotiations.

Although I will in a moment elaborate a catalogue of ways in which lawyers must cheat even in modest adversary systems which recognize the constraints I am here describing, I will not include this case of cheating in the list. It arises not out of the genetic structure of adversary advocacy but rather out of a drafting error in the Model Code, and it therefore cannot support the argument about the character of adversary advocacy per se that I wish to make.

I will similarly set aside certain ways in which even the Model Rules allow lawyers to take advantage of unrepresented persons, for example by exploiting their superior negotiating skills and technical expertise after announcing their adversary role. See 2 HH, *supra* note 4, § 4.3:103:–105, at 748–52 (Supp. 1991). These forms of advantage-taking once again reflect the idiosyncrasies of positive law rather than the deep structure of adversary advocacy and might be eliminated by legal changes that respect the basic commitments of the adversary legal process (for example, by the state provision of lawyers even in civil cases).

101. Support for the claims made in this footnote may be found in 2 HH, *supra* note 4, § 8.4:501, at 961 (Supp. 1998) (suggesting that Model Rule 8.4 "appears redundant"); RESTATEMENT (THIRD) OF THE LAW GOVERNING LAWYERS § 5 cmt. c. (2000) (warning of due process concerns); Hirschfeld v. Superior Court, 908 P.2d 22 (Ariz. Ct. App. 1985) (applying Rule 8.4(d) to berating and verbally assaulting an opposing party in the courthouse hallway); *In re* Palmisano, 70 F.3d 483 (7th Cir. 1995) (applying Rule 8.4(d) to a reckless charge that the judge was "crooked").

102. *See*, respectively, MODEL RULES OF PROF'L CONDUCT R. 3.1; FED. R. CIV. P. 11; 28 U.S.C. § 1927 (2006) (a lawyer in Federal court who "multiplies the proceedings in any case unreasonably and vexatiously" may be made personally liable for costs and attorney's fees reasonably incurred as a result); Cambers v. NASCO, Inc., 501 U.S. 32 (1991) (trial courts' inherent powers to regulate their own affairs extend to imposing money sanctions against a party who abused process very badly).

Note that the standard of frivolousness established by these principles is probably objective rather than subjective. In particular, the standard established by FED. R. CIV. P. 11 is clearly objective, *see* Bus. Guides, Inc. v. Chromatic Comm'ns Enters., Inc. 498 U.S. 533 (1991), and Model Rule 3.1, which borrows its language from Rule 11, will likely be interpreted in the shadow of Rule 11 law. *See* 1 HH, *supra* note 4, § 3.1:102, at 547–48 (Supp. 1996); *id.* § 3.1:201, at 549.

103. MODEL RULES OF PROF'L CONDUCT R. 3.2.

104. *Id.* R. 3.2 cmt. 1.

105. *See In re* Levine, 847 P.2d 1093 (Ariz. 1993).

106. *See* NASCO, Inc. v. Calcasieu Television & Radio, Inc., 894 F.2d 696, 708 (5th Cir. 1990), *aff'd sub nom.*, Chambers v. NASCO, Inc., 501 U.S. 32 (1991).

107. 1 HH, *supra* note 4, § 3.2:102, at 570.1 (Supp. 1996).

108. A striking example is *Mungo v. UTA French Airlines*, 212 Cal. Rptr. 369 (Ct. App. 1985), in which the plaintiffs represented that they were ready to go to trial even though they knew that their key witness was abroad and not under subpoena and when they knew that defendants would spend thousands of dollars bringing witnesses to trial from around the world. The plaintiffs were sanctioned for acting in bad faith and for causing frivolous and unnecessary delay, which are among the principles codified by Model Rule 3.2. The sanctioning court did not cite the Model Rules, which have not been adopted in California, but acted under analogous principles established by CAL. CIV. PROC. CODE § 128.5 (Deering 2006).

109. *See* MODEL RULES OF PROF'L CONDUCT R. 3.4(d); *see also* FED. R. CIV. P. 26(g), which requires that discovery requests and responses be certified as made in good faith, after reasonable inquiry, and in accordance with the rules.

Recent changes to FED R. CIV. P. 26(a)(1)(B), which went into effect December 1, 1993, now place an affirmative disclosure duty on the parties. Thus, parties must disclose, "without awaiting a discovery request," "a copy of, or a description by category and location of, all documents, data compilations, and tangible things that are in the possession, custody, or control of the party and that the disclosing party may use for its claims or defenses . . . ." *Id.* While these changes were implemented in an attempt to increase the level of cooperation between the parties, critics have argued that these changes simply add a new layer to the contestation over pretrial discovery by employing vague discovery requirements to be applied to the wide range of cases handled by courts. *See* Ronald J. Gilson & Robert H. Mnookin, *Disputing Through Agents: Cooperation and Conflict Between Lawyers in Litigation*, 94 COLUM. L. REV. 509, 519 n.28 (1994).

110. MODEL RULES OF PROF'L CONDUCT R. 3.4(e).

111. *Id.* R. 4.4(a).

112. *See generally* Harry I. Subin, *The Criminal Lawyer's "Different Mission": Reflection on the "Right" to Present a False Case,* 1 GEO. J. LEGAL ETHICS 125 (1987) (discussing the limits on the methods a lawyer should be willing to use when presenting a case inconsistent with the truth); Harry I. Subin, *Is This Lie Necessary: Further Reflections on the Right to Present a False Defense,* 1 GEO. J. LEGAL ETHICS 689 (1988) (rejoinder to responses); Joseph D. Piorkowski, Note, *Professional Conduct and the Preparation of Witnesses for Trial: Defining the Acceptable Limitations of "Coaching,"* 1 GEO. J. LEGAL ETHICS 389 (1987) (considering the limitations of witness preparation as a tool in the adversarial process). Shield laws, which protect victims of child abuse and rape against certain forms of intimidating or chauvinist cross-examination give an independent statutory expression to one application of this duty. Such laws have, moreover, been held consistent with the constitutional confrontation rights of criminal defendants. *See, e.g.,* Maryland v. Craig, 497 U.S. 836 (1990) (upholding the constitutionality of a Maryland law protecting victims of child abuse from facing cross-examination in the defendant's physical presence).

Model Rule 4.4 also likely condemns intimidating or chauvinistic conduct designed to prevent witnesses or even parties from getting to court in the first place, for example the efforts, by lawyers for the Dalkon Corporation, to suppress tort claims that they believed baseless by investigating the sexual histories of the women who made the claims. *See* MARTON MINTZ, AT ANY COST: CORPORATE GREED, WOMEN, AND THE DALKON SHIELD (1985).

113. *See* ABA Comm. on Ethics and Prof'l Responsibility, Formal Op. 92-363 (1992).

114. *See* MODEL RULES OF PROF'L CONDUCT R. 4.4(b), which establishes that if the lawyer reasonably knows that the document was inadvertently sent, she must notify the sender. The Rule does not address other circumstances, for example in which a document is intentionally sent (perhaps by a friendly third party), and the Official Comments to the Rule expressly decline to flesh out any full regime for the handling of any such documents (and expressly defer to other law in this connection), although they do say that "the decision to voluntarily return such a document is a matter of professional judgment ordinarily reserved to the lawyer." *See id.* cmt. 3.

But although lawyers' precise obligations concerning misdirected confidential documents are uncertain, some generalizations may nevertheless be made. Thus, lawyers clearly may not participate in wrongfully acquiring the documents and generally have a duty not to take advantage of mistakes by an opposing party or counsel. *See* ABA Comm. on Ethics and Prof'l Responsibility, Formal Op. 92-368 (1992). The hard case arises when the lawyers obtain confidential material because some third party (perhaps a whistleblower) has sent it to them. The American Bar Association takes the view that lawyers may not take advantage of the information even in this case, although it makes exceptions when the lawyer should have received the information anyway or the sender is protected by a whistleblower statute. *See* ABA Comm. on Ethics and Prof'l Responsibility, Formal Op. 94-382 (1994). Courts sometimes come down against exploitation, *see, e.g.,* Resolution Trust Corp. v. First of Am. Bank, 868 F. Supp. 217

(W.D. Mich. 1994); Kusch v. Ballard, 645 So. 2d 1035 (Fla. Dist. Ct. App. 1994), and sometimes come down in favor, *see, e.g.*, Aerojet-General Corp. v. Transp. Indem. Ins., 18 Cal. App. 4th 996 (Ct. App. 1993); NLRB v. Monfort, Inc., 29 F.3d 525 (10th Cir. 1994*). See* 1 HH § 3.4:402–1 at 642 (2d ed. Supp. 1998). The last two cases suggest that lawyers may even have a *duty* (of zealous advocacy) to use the information.

115. 1 HH, *supra* note 4, § 3:102, at 537 (Supp. 1997).

116. MODEL RULES OF PROF'L CONDUCT R. 3.1.

117. 1 HH, *supra* note 4, § 3.1:204, at 553 (Supp. 1994). As one well-known judge (Frank Easterbrook) has said, a position is legally frivolous only if "99 out of 100 practicing lawyers would be 99 percent sure that the position is untenable, and the other 1 percent would be 60 percent sure it's untenable." Sanford Levinson, *Frivolous Cases: Do Lawyers Know Anything at All*, 24 OSGOODE HALL L.J. 353, 375 (1987) (quoting Letter from Judge Frank Easterbrook to Sanford Levinson, January 29, 1986).

118. 1 HH, *supra* note 4, § 3.1:205, at 558.8–.9 (Supp. 1996). The lawyer is probably obligated to accept her client's version of the facts as long as "[t]he story is coherent, internally consistent, and gives the lawyer no reason . . . to doubt it." 1 HH, *supra* note 4, § 3.1:302, at 562 (Supp. 1994). Indeed, "even if there was reason for some doubt, the lawyer should give his client the benefit of those doubts." *Id.* This leeway is even greater, moreover, for lawyers who represent defendants, because of "the principle that a defendant is not required to admit factual matters where he lacks knowledge or is in good faith doubt about where the truth lies." 1 HH, *supra* note 4, § 3.1:205, at 558.9 (Supp. 1996).

Of course, none of this is to deny that Model Rule 3.1 and its cognates prevent forms of cheating that amount to outright fraud.

119. *See supra* text accompanying notes 11–13.

120. For an overview of Rule 11 and the other cognates to Model Rule 3.1, including 28 U.S.C. § 1927, *see* SANCTIONS: RULE 11 AND OTHER POWERS (M. Nelken ed., 3d ed. 1992); *see also* 1 HH, *supra* note 4, § 3.1:207, at 558.12–558.13 (Supp. 1996); *id.* § 3.2:103, at 570.1–.2 (Supp. 1996).

121. Sussman v. Bank of Isr., 56 F.3d 450 (2d Cir. 1995); *see also* 1 HH, *supra* note 4, § 3.1:202, at 550 n.1.01 (Supp. 1996). The case arose under Rule 11 of the Federal Rules of Civil Procedure, but the analysis would have been the same under Model Rule 3.1.

The lawyer's zone of discretion under Model Rule 3.1 is not unlimited, of course, and even otherwise nonfrivolous claims may become sanctionable if a lawyer brings them with a sufficiently improper motive or in sufficiently bad faith. *See, e.g., In re* Levine, 847 P.2d 1093, 1100 (Ariz. 1993) ("Therefore, if an improper motive or a bad faith argument exists, respondent will not escape ethical responsibility for bringing a legal claim that may otherwise meet the objective test of a nonfrivolous claim.") But securing an advantageous settlement by exploiting an opposing party's unusual sensitivity to otherwise nonfrivolous counterclaims does not, by itself, involve an improper motive.

122. Sanctions are typically applied against lawyers in such cases only when lawyers bring tort claims that are not just unsuccessful but rather truly outrageous or vexatious. A typical example is *Raine v. Drasin*, 621 S.W.2d 895 (Ky.

1981), in which a lawyer argued that a hospital had broken his client's shoulder when it had in fact attempted to treat a preexisting break.

123. Even those who generally defend lawyers' professional morality acknowledge that lawyers must cheat in this way. For example, Ted Schneyer, writing about the Model Code, admits that "The Code does at least tolerate many litigation techniques that can not only harm witnesses or adverse parties, but make judicial decision-making less reliable to boot. Examples include "using pre-trial motions, refusals to stipulate, and discovery requests to exploit a client's greater staying power." Ted Schneyer, *Moral Philosophy's Standard Misconception of Legal Ethics*, 1984 WIS. L. REV. 1529, 1555.

124. MODEL RULES OF PROF'L CONDUCT R. 3.2 (2003).

125. *Id*. R. 3.2 cmt. 1.

126. *Id*.

127. *Id*. Much has been made of the fact that the Model Rules, by emphasizing the *purpose* of a dilatory tactic, introduce a subjective standard into this area of legal ethics. Some commentators have even gone so far as to worry whether introducing questions of a lawyer's subjective motive renders to Model Rule constitutionally dubious. *See* Carol Rice Andrews, *The First Amendment Problem with the Motive Restrictions in the Rules of Professional Conduct*, 24 J. LEGAL PROF. 13 (2000).

But it is not clear that the Rules in fact do place the lawyer's subjective motive for delay at the center of the ethics of expediting litigation, as the Official Comment's emphasis on the views of "a competent lawyer acting in good faith" reveals. *See generally* Principe v. Assay Partners, 586 N.Y.S.2d 182 (Sup. Ct. 1992) (blending together the Model Code's objective standard, a more subjective court rule permitting sanctions for behavior "undertaken primarily . . . to harass or maliciously injure another," and the Rule 11 ban on pleadings "interposed for any improper purpose," to craft an objective, "reasonable attorney" standard). Moreover, the critical feature of the Rule, from the perspective of the lawyer's professional duty to cheat, is not whether it emphasizes the subjective intent to harm or the objective likelihood of harm, but rather the recognition, common to both the Model Rules (in the reference to a "substantial purpose other than delay") and the Model Code (in the reference to conduct that "serve[s] merely" to harm others), that dilatory tactics do not violate professional ethics if they promote ends besides delay. This underwrites the forms of cheating described in the main text.

128. As another example, consider whether Rule 3.2 forbids attempting to delay answering a complaint on grounds of a technical defect in the service of process, even though the complaint was in fact received in plenty of time to answer on the merits. *See* John C. Martin, *Expedition and Professionalism: Considering the Utility of Model Rule 3.2*, 2 LITIG. ETHICS 1 (2004).

129. *See supra* notes 102–10 and accompanying text. Indeed, one commentator making a similar observation has gone so far as to say that cases applying Rule 3.2 almost always "afford[] it little, if any, independent meaning" but instead view it as merely a corollary of other rules, including most notably Rules 1.3 and 3.1. *See* Martin, *supra* note 122 (collecting cases).

130. Martin, *supra* note 128.

131. MODEL RULES OF PROF'L CONDUCT R. 4.4(a) (emphasis added).

132. *See, e.g.*, Shepherd v. Am. Broad. Corp., 62 F.3d 1469, 1483–84 (D.C. Cir. 1995). The court did acknowledge that a lawyer's conduct may become "so harassing that it merits sanctioning, notwithstanding the existence of a substantial purpose" that the conduct serves, *id.* at 1483, but this acknowledgment was designed to discourage exceptional and outrageous tactics rather than to forbid the broad class of behaviors exploiting third parties that Rule 4.4's reference to a substantial other purpose expressly allows. (Note, also, that the procedural posture of the case prevented the *Shepherd* court from applying Rule 4.4 directly, and that the court instead took Rule 4.4 as a guide in the exercise of its inherent powers to supervise the conduct of litigation before it.)

133. Ellen Yankiver Suni, *Who Stole the Cookie from the Cookie Jar?: The Law and Ethics of Shifting Blame in Criminal Cases*, 68 FORDHAM L. REV. 1643, 1667 (2000).

134. *See, e.g.*, Attorney M. v. Miss. Bar, 621 So. 2d 220 (Miss. 1992). The court held that a lawyer prosecuting a malpractice action did not violate Model Rule 4.4 when he warned a doctor that although the doctor "didn't do anything wrong," he might be "forced" to join the doctor as a codefendant if the doctor refused to testify to certain facts that aided the lawyer's case. This conduct was found ethical because the legal action threatened against the doctor was colorable (and also, of course, because the testimony that the lawyer sought to elicit was truthful).

135. *See* ABA Comm. on Ethics and Prof'l Responsibility, Formal Op. 92-363 (1992); *see also* Michigan State Bar Comm. on Prof'l and Judicial Ethics, Op. RI-78 (1991) (A lawyer may advise a client to either forego or pursue criminal proceedings, if the advice serves to protect the client's rights and does not contravene any specific statutory or other duty). The criminal matter must be related to the client's civil claim, the lawyer must have a well-founded belief that both the civil claim and the criminal charges are warranted by the law and the facts, and the lawyer must not attempt to exert or suggest improper influence over the criminal process. *See* ABA Comm. on Ethics and Prof'l Responsibility, Formal Op. 92–363. Finally, a lawyer may not make strategic use of criminal charges if doing so would itself be criminal, not least because a lawyer may not "commit a criminal act that reflects adversely on the lawyer's honesty, trustworthiness or fitness as a lawyer in other respects." MODEL RULES OF PROF'L CONDUCT R. 8.4(b). The Model Penal Code expressly refuses to criminalize bargains that settle civil claims in exchange for agreements not to press criminal charges. *See* MODEL PENAL CODE § 223.1(3) (1962).

Note that the Model Rules depart from previous practice in this respect, and that the Model Code of Professional Responsibility (which remains in force in some states) forbade lawyers from presenting or threatening to present criminal charges in order to obtain an advantage in a civil case. *See* MODEL CODE OF PROF'L RESPONSIBILITY DR 7-105(A) (1980).

136. *See In re* Wallingford, 799 S.W.2d 76 (Mo. 1990) (en banc).

137. *Id.* at 78.

138. MODEL RULES OF PROF'L CONDUCT R. 3.1 cmt. 1 (emphasis added).

139. *Id.* Preamble ¶ 2.

140. *See* Zabella v. Pakel, 242 F.2d 452, 455 (7th Cir. 1957). The purely technical character of the defense in this case is particularly striking, because the plaintiff's morally valid claim foundered not on the statute of limitations standing alone but on the interplay between this and the law of bankruptcy. This meant that technical answers that might ordinarily overcome the debtor's technical defense were in this case unavailing. As the court noted:

> Plaintiff was in a difficult and somewhat anomalous position in endeavoring to maintain this suit. An oral promise to pay the debt might avoid the effect of a discharge in bankruptcy but would not remove the bar of the statute of limitations. On the other hand, a part payment would not remove the bar of the discharge in bankruptcy but might remove the case from the statute of limitations. The reason why a less or different proof is required in one than the other is due to the wording of the Illinois Statutes. *Id.*

These features of the case removed it from the policy rationales behind the technical defenses that it involved, so that even these probably gave no comfort to the defendant or his lawyer. But none of this had any effect on the debtor's lawyer's unambiguous professional obligation to make the arguments that would win the case for his client.

Rule 11 of the Federal Rules of Civil Procedure was in the past sometimes interpreted to support sanctioning lawyers who filed time-barred claims. *See, e.g.*, Brubaker v. City of Richmond, 943 F.2d 1363, 1384 (4th Cir. 1991). The Brubaker court found "no logical reason" why a permission to file time-barred claims would not extend to a permission to file all frivolous claims, and so "effectively abolish Rule 11," Brubaker, at 1384. But the reason is in fact obvious. A defendant who fails to assert an affirmative defense is not entitled to its protection, so that a verdict against him is (in respect of the defense) correct. This means that bringing a time-barred claim does not threaten to deceive the tribunal hearing it, and that forbidding time-barred claims in effect either changes the substantive rights of the parties or (more radically still) abandons the adversary process and requires plaintiffs to assert defendants' rights. An ordinary frivolous claim, by contrast, should be rejected regardless of whether or not its flaw is exposed. And this means that the claim's success constitutes a legal mistake, and deceives the tribunal hearing the claim, regardless of how the other side has responded. Prohibiting ordinary frivolous claims therefore neither changes the substantive law nor abandons the adversary system but instead merely protects tribunals against fraud.

The current version of Rule 11, moreover, unambiguously rejects sanctions against lawyers for bringing time-barred claims. Rule 11 now requires opposing counsel to give a lawyer a warning and 21 days to withdraw papers before seeking Rule 11 sanctions. Fed. R. Civ. P. 11(c)(1)(A). This means that lawyers may test whether opposing counsel knows that a claim is time-barred and withdraw the claim without sanction if opposing counsel does know. A creditor's lawyer must therefore exploit an uninformed debtor's ignorance if her client wishes. To fail to pursue the debt, or to inform the debtor that the statute of limitations has run, would violate Rules 1.3 and 1.6. *See* ABA Comm. on Ethics and Prof'l Responsibility, Formal Op. 94-387 (1994) ("A lawyer has no ethical duty to inform an opposing party in negotiations that the statue of limitations has run on her client's claim; to the contrary, it would violate Rules 1.3 and 1.6 to reveal such information without the client's consent. It follows that where the opposing party and his counsel appear to be unaware that the limitations period has expired, the lawyer may not discontinue negations simply on this ground, in the absence of agreement by her client that she should do so.").

141. *See* Walkovszky v. Carlton, 18 N.Y.2d 414 (1966).

142. *See* Ball v. Gambro, Inc., 584 N.E.2d 104 (Ill. 1991). The lawyer may not, of course, seek delay through frivolous or vexatious means.

143. *See supra* text accompanying notes 69–72.

144. Familiar such examples include helping an agri-business obtain water subsidies intended for individual farmers by holding its land through individual trustees, all under its control, *see* SIMON, supra note 1, at 4–5, delaying regulation to allow a client to distribute wine containing a chemical soon to be banned as a carcinogen, *see* ARTHUR H. GOLDMAN, THE MORAL FOUNDATIONS OF PROFESSIONAL ETHICS 102 (1980), and informing a client that the Environmental Protection Agency does not enforce antipollution laws until pollution exceeds twice the limit that the laws establish, *see* Stephen L. Pepper, *Counseling at the Limits of the Law: An Exercise in the Jurisprudence and Ethics of Lawyering*, 104 YALE L.J. 1545 (1995); Stephen L. Pepper, *The Lawyer's Amoral Ethical Role: A Defense, a Problem, and Some Possibilities*, 1986 AM. BAR FOUND. RES. J. 613.

145. State v. Leon, 621 P.2d 1016 (Kan. 1981).

146. MODEL CODE OF PROF'L RESPONSIBILITY DR 7-101(A)(1) (1980).

147. *In re* Harshey, 740 N.E.2d 851 (Ind. 2001).

148. *Id.* at 854.

149. There are, to be sure, also cases that criticize lawyers who cheat on behalf of their clients and that acquit lawyers who refuse to cheat of professional misconduct. This is not surprising, given (as I have earlier elaborated) that the law governing lawyers limits the lawyer's professional obligations to cheat by secondary rules that forbid certain narrowly defined forms of cheating. And although some cases may gesture toward generic ideals of fair play, they all recur, eventually, to one or another of these narrowly defined rules.

A typical example is *Virzi v. Grand Trunk Warehouse & Cold Storage Co.*, 571 F. Supp. 507 (E.D. Mich. 1983), in which a court held that a lawyer must inform the opposing party when his client dies during settlement negotiations. The opinion speaks in general terms about the importance of the client's testimony to the outcome of the case and the consequent unfairness of proceeding as if the client were alive when he was in fact dead. But the resolution of the case turned on a much narrower argument about the court's role in supervising the settlement, and the case was in fact decided on technical grounds under Model Rule 3.3 (concerning candor to tribunals) rather than on the basis of general principles of fairness. (In this respect the case resembles *Spaulding v. Zimmerman*, discussed earlier at notes 19 & 53.)

A second, similar example is *Transcraft, Inc. v. Galvin, Stalmack, Kirschner & Clark*, 39 F.3d 812 (7th Cir. 1994), in which the court found that it was not malpractice for a tort lawyer to refuse to engage in trial tactics whose expected costs exceeded their expected benefits or to refuse to introduce questionable expert testimony when no respectable experts were willing to testify for his clients. Once again, although the opinion employed broad language about fairness, saying, for example, that "[a] refusal to violate professional ethics—or even to approach as near to the line as humanly possible—is not professional misconduct," *id.* at 817, the actual grounds of decision were much narrower and more technical. They had little to do with fundamental fairness or the lawyer's right to impose her ethical sense on her client and everything to do with the other half of the division of control under Model Rule 1.2, namely the lawyer's authority over tactical and technical questions concerning her craft.

Both cases illustrate the same theme, namely that language that seems to give lawyers rights and even duties to abide by broad principles of fair play in fact sounds in the much narrower technical rules against cheating discussed earlier in this chapter, whose inability to relieve lawyers of the generic duty to cheat is developed in the main text.

150. MODEL RULES OF PROF'L CONDUCT R. 6.2 (2003).

151. *Id.* R. 6.2(c). The same language appears in the Official Comment. *See id.* cmt. 2.

152. *See id.* R. 6.2(a). The Official Comment elaborates this theme in greater detail, identifying as cases of "good cause" that "the lawyer could not handle the matter competently," and that "the representation would result in an improper conflict of interest." *Id.* cmt. 2.

153. 2 HH, *supra* note 4, § 6.2:401, at 840 (Supp. 1991).

154. MODEL CODE OF PROF'L RESPONSIBILITY EC 2–29 (2003).

155. *Id.* EC 2–30.

156. *Id.* EC 2–29 .

157. An example is *Jones v. State*, 738 P.2d 525 (Okla. Crim. App. 1987), which quotes the Model Code's statement that "the belief of a defense lawyer that his client is guilty is insufficient to excuse him from a court appointment in a criminal proceeding." *Id.* at 530.

158. Bd. of Prof'l Responsibility of the Supreme Court of Tennessee, Formal Op. 96-F-140 (1996), *available at* http://www.tbpr.org/Attorneys/EthicsOpinions/Pdfs/96-F-140.pdf.

159. The suggestion appears, for example, in Ted Schneyer, *The Promise and Problematics of Legal Ethics from the Lawyer's Point of View*, 16 YALE J. L. & HUM. 45, 65 (2004).

160. Support for the claims made in this footnote can be found in MODEL RULES OF PROF'L CONDUCT R. 1.16(a)(2) (2003) (allowing lawyers to withdraw representation for health reasons); *id.* R. 1.16(b)(5) (allowing withdrawal due to breakdown in the lawyer-client relationship); McGuive v. Wilson, 735 F. Supp. 83 (S.D.N.Y. 1990) (same); Kannewurf v. Johns, 32 N.E.2d 711 (Ill. App. Ct. 1994) (providing an example of when an ordinary commercial dispute between client and lawyer becomes so serious as to make competent representation impossible); Ambrose v. Detroit Edison, 237 N.W.2d 520 (Mich. Ct. App. 1975) (same).

161. *See* MODEL RULES OF PROF'L CONDUCT R. 1.16(b)(1) (2003).

162. *Id.* R. 1.16(a)(1).

163. Although the argument that the Rules require withdrawal in such cases is straightforward, it is not always recognized by a legal culture that takes client loyalty and zealous advocacy very much to heart.

This blindness to the clear requirements of the Model Rules is illustrated by *Norris v. Lee*, No. 93-0441, 1994 WL 143119 (E.D. Pa. Apr. 15, 1994), in which a court denied a motion to withdraw made by a lawyer who concluded that the plaintiffs he represented (in a civil rights case) were offering perjured testimony. (The court acted under Model Rule 1.16(c), which commands lawyers to comply with court rules that require them to obtain court permission before withdrawing, and instructs lawyers who have been denied permission to continue on a case notwithstanding good cause for terminating the representation.) MODEL RULES OF PROF'L CONDUCT R. 1.16(c). The court did not doubt that the clients' testimony was in fact perjured but instead observed that bearing the burdens of being a hired gun belongs to the lawyer's job.

Although other cases reaching similar results exist, it would be a mistake to draft these cases into the service of my claim that the possibility of withdrawal does not relieve adversary advocates of their professional duties to lie. As others have remarked, the cases are wrongly decided under the Model Rules. *See* 1 HH, *supra* note 4, § 1.16:401, at 486.5 (Supp. 1998). Moreover, and much more importantly, even if the positive law were different and the cases were correct, this would be merely an idiosyncratic feature of the positive law and not an essential element of adversary advocacy. An adversary system can forbid lawyers from assisting perjury, including by requiring them to withdraw from representations that would involve perjury, without abandoning its core commitments (and the Model Rules illustrate this). And accordingly, an argument claiming that adversary advocates must inevitably lie and cheat, and that withdrawal cannot possibly relieve them of this duty, may not rely on cases that forbid withdrawal even in the face of perjury, no matter how common they are as a matter of positive legal practice.

164. *See, e.g.*, Whitig v. Lacarn, 187 F.3d 317 (2d Cir. 1999), which observed that even if a lawyer refused to proceed with the frivolous claims that the client insisted upon she could not ethically continue in the representation, because the breakdown of the lawyer-client relation that would follow the lawyer's flat refusal to press the claims would render competent representation impossible and result in a violation of Model Rule 1.1.

Similar results have been reached under predecessors to the Model Rules, including under the Model Code. *See, e.g.*, Kirsch v. Duryea, 146 Cal. Rptr. 218 (1978), which held (in dismissing a legal malpractice claim filed against a withdrawing lawyer) that under California State Bar Rules of Professional Conduct, 2-111(A)(2) (an analog of DR 2-110 of the Model Code), a lawyer may withdraw if she thinks her client's claim cannot be made in good faith.

165. Support for the claims made in this footnote can be found at United States v. Long, 857 F.2d 436, 445 (8th Cir. 1988) (providing the "firm factual basis" standard, quoted in the footnote, for when a lawyer can withdraw in the face of client perjury). *See also* Lowery v. Cardwell, 575 F.2d 727 (9th Cir. 1978) (holding that even though a criminal defense lawyer's withdrawal conformed to

the ethics rules requiring withdrawal when a client insists on giving perjured testimony, it nevertheless constituted unconstitutionally ineffective assistance of counsel). *Cf.* Nix v. Whiteside, 475 U.S. 157, 171 (1986) (regarding a lawyer's obligation to withdraw when her client's perjury is certain).

The quotation from *Anders v. California* can be found at 386 U.S. 738, 744 (1967). *See also* Penson v. Ohio, 488 U.S. 75 (1988) (indicating that failure to file an *Anders* brief requires reversal).

166. MODEL RULES OF PROF'L CONDUCT R. 1.16(b)(2).

167. *Id.* R. 1.16(b)(3).

168. A lawyer may also sometimes be *required* to withdraw when her clients involve her services in crime or fraud: Rule 1.2 forbids lawyers from assisting client crime or fraud, and Rule 1.16(a)(1) therefore requires withdrawal when continuing in a representation amounts to assisting in crime or fraud. The withdrawal rules therefore engage the complex of arguments which turn to both the ethics rules and other substantive law to regulate cases in which a lawyer becomes an accessory to her client's crimes and frauds.

One important question that arises in this connection asks whether withdrawal is mandatory only from representations that directly concern a client's crimes or frauds or also from representations that assist the client on other matters, for example, on the theory that even unrelated representations, by comforting and supporting the client, assist in the client's crimes or frauds. (This issue is addressed, for example, in ABA Comm. on Ethics and Prof'l Responsibility, Formal Op. 92–366 (1992), which tangentially refers to the alternative, permissive withdrawal regime of Rule 1.16(b)(2)–(3).) Another important question asks how certain of the client's crime or fraud a lawyer must be before withdrawal becomes mandatory. Rule 1.16(a)(1) refers to cases in which continuing a representation *will* result in a violation of the Model Rules or other law, but that language is imprecise, and there is some reason to read the Rule as requiring withdrawal only when the lawyer is *certain. See* 1 HH, *supra* note 4, 1.16:203, at 472.2–.3 (Supp. 1998).

169. MODEL RULES OF PROF'L CONDUCT R. 1.16(b)(4).

Earlier versions of the Model Rules adopted slightly different language, allowing lawyers to withdraw when a client insisted upon "pursuing an objective that the lawyer considers repugnant or imprudent." *Id.* R 1.16(b)(3) (1995). Alternative statements of the law governing lawyers contain similar provisions. The Model Code, for example, allows withdrawal when a client "insists, in a matter not pending before a tribunal, that the lawyer engage in conduct that is contrary to the judgment and advice of the lawyer but not prohibited under the Disciplinary Rules." ABA Model Code of Professional Responsibility DR 2-110(C)(1)(e) (1980). And the Restatement allows withdrawal when "the client insists on taking an action that the lawyer considers repugnant or imprudent." RESTATEMENT (THIRD) OF THE LAW GOVERNING LAWYERS § 32(3)(f) (2000).

The present version of the Model Rules therefore somewhat narrows the grounds for withdrawal, compared to earlier regimes. In particular, it no longer allows a lawyer to withdraw merely because she regards her client's conduct as "imprudent." I shall comment on this change in a moment and defend the present version by reference to the deep structure of adversary advocacy.

170. Support for the claims made in this footnote may be found in 1 HH, *supra* note 4, § 1.3:101, at 71 (Supp. 1991) (emphasis added) (including the observation of Hazard and Hodes quoted in the footnote); MODEL RULES OF PROF'L CONDUCT R. 1.16 cmt. 2 (2003) (reminding lawyers that they should comply with their obligations of confidentiality when explaining their withdrawal); *id.* R. 1.16(d) (including the quoted language requiring that a lawyer who may prejudicially withdraw shall take steps to protect a client's interests); RESTATEMENT (THIRD) OF THE LAW GOVERNING LAWYERS § 33(1) (2000) (including nearly identical language, also quoted in the footnote); *id.* § 32(4) (indicating that withdrawal is not permitted when the harms thereby imposed significantly exceed the harms of continuing in representation); 1 HH, *supra* note 4, § 1.16:303, at 486 (Supp. 1998) (requiring that a lawyer who withdraws rather than press a repugnant claim must take steps to ensure that substitute counsel is secured quickly and that the change harm the client's prospects as little as possible).

171. But note that lawyers are not always granted leave to withdraw even in such sensational cases. For example, a court has expressly insisted (even in the face of the contrary view taken by the Model Rules) that lawyers who oppose the death penalty may withdraw from representing a client who directs them to seek it only if this withdrawal can be accomplished without prejudice. *See* Red Dog v. State, 625 A.2d 245, 247 (Del. 1993). (And, although the opinion never takes up the issue, this must, given Rule 1.2, mean prejudice to the *client's* ends, that is, to the end of securing the death penalty that the lawyers oppose. As the Red Dog court said, "A defendant's wish to forego further appeals and accept the death penalty, like other decisions relating to the objectives of litigation, is essentially that of the client, whose decision the attorney must respect." *Id.* at 247.)

172. This case comes from Hazard and Hodes, *see* 1 HH, *supra* note 4, § 1.2:303, at 38 (Supp. 1996), who addressed the pre-2002 version of the repugnant-client withdrawal rule. *See* MODEL RULES OF PROF'L CONDUCT R. 1.16(b)(3) (1995). The 2002 amendments have not changed the analysis.

173. E. Wayne Thode, *The Ethical Standard for the Advocate*, 39 TEX. L. REV. 575 (1961).

174. Some commentators have proposed an interpretation of the repugnant-client withdrawal rule that is narrower still, according to which the rule adds virtually nothing to the other withdrawal regimes discussed above. *See, e.g.,* Monroe H. Freedman, *Legal Ethics and the Suffering Client*, 36 CATH. U. L. REV. 331, 332–33 (1987); Harold S. Lewis, *Shaffer's Suffering Client, Freedman's Suffering Lawyer* 38 CATH. U. L. REV. 129, 132 (1988). For an argument against this narrow view, see Thomas L. Shaffer, *Less Suffering When You're Warned: A Response to Professor Lewis*, 38 CATH. U. L. REV. 871, 877 (1989).

175. *See* MODEL RULES OF PROF'L CONDUCT R. 1.16(b)(4). This precise language comes from 2002 amendments to the Rule, which replaced language that allowed withdrawal when a lawyer found the client's conduct "repugnant or imprudent." The current version of the rule is therefore in this respect stricter than its predecessor. The 2002 amendments did in one way broaden the right of withdrawal—by replacing the rule's reference to "pursuing an objective" with "taking an action" and thereby extending the permission to withdraw to cases in which clients employ repugnant means in addition to cases in which they

pursue repugnant ends. All in all, the narrowing effect of the amendments outweighs their broadening effect.

176. Versions of the rule that allow withdrawal in cases of repugnant or *imprudent* client conduct, *see id*. R. 1.16(b)(3) (1995); RESTATEMENT (THIRD) OF THE LAW GOVERNING LAWYERS § 32(3)(f) (2000), should be read (especially when imprudent is set against the backdrop of repugnant) to require conduct that is irresponsible, foolhardy, or even reckless, and certainly more than just conduct that is somehow suboptimal or that lawyer would prefer to avoid. Indeed, allowing withdrawal in the face of more broadly imprudent actions would, as one commentator has pointed out, unacceptably compromise client autonomy. Stephen Gillers, *What We Talked About When We Talked About Legal Ethics*, 46 OHIO ST. L.J. 243, 260 (1985). And although the Model Code version of the rule, allows withdrawal in the face of "conduct that is contrary to the judgment and advice of the lawyer" and therefore might seem to countenance withdrawal whenever a client presses a claim that the lawyer would prefer to concede, this regime expressly limits the rule's application to "matter[s] not pending before a tribunal," MODEL CODE OF PROF'L RESPONSI-BILITY DR 2–110(C)(1)(e) (1980), and makes no allowance for repugnant client withdrawal, even in sensational cases, once a dispute enters adjudication. The strictness of this regime—the total ban on repugnant-client withdrawal once a dispute has entered adjudication—has not been lost on courts. *See, e.g.*, United States v. Lopez, 98 F.2d 1032, 1043 (9th Cir. 1993) (Fletcher, J., concurring) (observing that in California repugnance is not grounds for withdrawal in cases before tribunals).

177. *See, e.g.*, State v. Jones, 923 P.2d 560, 566 (Mont. 1996), which applied the pre-2002 version of the Model Rules' repugnant-client withdrawal rule, MODEL RULES OF PROF'L CONDUCT R. 1.16(b)(3) (1995).

178. Van Gieson v. Magoon, 20 Haw. 146, 154 (1910).

179. *See, e.g.*, Ray Vann v. Shilleh, 126 Cal. Rptr. 401 (Cal. App. 1975); Borup v. Nat'l Airlines, Inc., 159 F. Supp. 808 (S.D.N.Y. 1958).

180. *Cf.* 1 HH, *supra* note 4, § 1.16:306, at 486.3–4 (Supp. 1998), who adopt a similar interpretation of the Model Rules.

181. *See, e.g.*, Jones v. Feiger, Collison & Killmer, 903 P.2d 27 (Colo. Ct. App. 1994).

182. This approach tracks the treatment that requests to avoid court-appointed representations of repugnant clients receive under Model Rule 6.2(c). *See supra* notes 150–53 and accompanying text. Note that a lawyer whose distaste for her client rendered her ineffective could not continue in the representation without violating Model Rule 1.1 on competence and would therefore anyway be required to withdraw under Model Rule 1.16(a)(1). Under the Model Code, the lawyer could not continue without violating DR 6-101 on competence and would therefore be required to withdraw under DR 2-110(B)(2). The lawyer might also be permitted to withdraw under DR 2-110(C)(1)(d), on the grounds that the client's repugnant conduct "renders it unreasonably difficult for the lawyer to carry out his employment effectively."

183. *In re* Crystal G. v. George G., No. A100905, 2003 WL 22520417 (Sonoma County Sup. Ct. Nov. 6, 2003) (quoting People v. Brown, 203 Cal.

App. 3d 1335, 1341 (Ct. App. 1988)). The decision applied CALIFORNIA RULES OF PROF'L CONDUCT R. 3-700(C)(1)(d), the California version of MODEL CODE OF PROF'L RESPONSIBILITY, DR 2-110(C)(1)(d) (1980).

184. *Id.* Note that the court added that CALIFORNIA RULES OF PROF'L CONDUCT R. 3-700(B)(1)—which requires withdrawal where a client insists upon unfounded harassing litigation techniques—did not apply because the client's requests to file complaints against the human services commissioner fell outside the scope of representation. For analog of the California rule, see MODEL CODE OF PROF'L RESPONSIBILITY DR 2-110(B)(1) (1980).

185. *See, e.g.,* State v. Lynch, 796 P.2d 1150 (Okla. 1990).

186. Even those who defend adversary advocacy finally recognize this. As one commentator recognized, in writing about the Model Code, "the Code does at least tolerate many litigation techniques that . . . make judicial decision-making less reliable . . . . Examples include discrediting a truthful witness on cross-examination; counseling a client not to retain certain records because they could be damaging in future litigation; cultivating an expert witness by feeding her only favorable information until she is locked into supporting the client's position; and using pre-trial motions, refusals to stipulate, and discovery requests to exploit a client's greater staying power." Schneyer, *supra* note 123, at 1555.

CHAPTER 3

THE SEEDS OF A LAWYERLY VIRTUE

1. MODEL RULES OF PROF'L CONDUCT R. 1.2(b) (2003).

2. *See* ABA Comm. on Ethics and Prof'l Responsibility, Formal Op. 324 (1970).

3. *See, e.g.,* CAL. BUS. & PROF. CODE §§ 6067, 6068(h) (Deering 2006); RULES REGULATING THE FLORIDA BAR R. 1-3.1(a) (quoted at *In Re* Amendments to the Rules Regulating the Fla. Bar, 573 So. 2d 800, 803 n. 8 (Fla. 1991)); MICH. BAR R. 15 § 3.

4. A famous bar report, for example, insists that "[n]o member of the bar should indulge in public criticism of another lawyer because he has undertaken the representation of causes in general disfavor. Every member of the profession should, to the contrary, do what he can to promote public understanding of the service rendered by the advocate in such situations." Lon L. Fuller & John D. Randall, *Professional Responsibility: Report to the Judicial Conference,* 44 A.B.A.J. 1159, 1217 (1958).

5. *See* RESTATEMENT (SECOND) OF TORTS § 586 (1977); *see also* 1 GEOFFREY C. HAZARD, JR. & W. WILLIAM HODES, THE LAW OF LAWYERING: A HANDBOOK ON THE MODEL RULES OF PROFESSIONAL CONDUCT § 1.1:205, at 18.38 (2d ed. 1990, Supp. 1998) [hereinafter HH]. Note that because the immunity is absolute, it applies even to statements made in bad faith, as long only as they display the required connection to litigation. For a collection of cases, see 1 RONALD E. MALLEN & JEFFREY M. SMITH, LEGAL MALPRACTICE § 6.25, at 353–54 (3d ed. 1989). For a critical discussion see Paul Hayden, *Reconsidering the Litigator's Absolute Privilege to Defame,* 54 OHIO ST. L.J. 985 (1993).

6. *See, e.g.*, Salaymeh v. Interqual, Inc., 508 N.E.2d 1155 (Ill. 1987); *see also* 1 MALLEN & SMITH, *supra* note 5, § 6.25, at 353–54 (citing RESTATEMENT (SECOND) OF TORTS § 772 (1979)).

7. *See* 1 HH, *supra* note 5, § 1.1:205, at 18.37. Note that this immunity depends on the lawyer's good faith. Lawyers who proceed in bad faith may be liable as accessories to their clients' torts.

8. In trademark, see, e.g., *Electronic Laboratory Supply Co. v. Cullen*, 977 F.2d 798 (3d Cir. 1992), which held that lawyers who filed an application on behalf of a client who sought to seize goods on the basis of trademark violations were not "applicants" under the Lanham Act and so not liable when the seizure turned out to be unwarranted. In conspiracy, see, e.g., *Azrielli v. Cohen Law Offices*, 21 F.3d 512, 521–22 (2d Cir. 1994), which held that a law firm that advises a business but does not participate in its management does not "conduct or participate" in the enterprise and so is not guilty of racketeering under the Federal RICO statute. *See also* Bailey v. Trenam, Simmons, Kemker, Scharf, Barkin, Frye & O'Neill, P.A., 938 F. Supp. 825, 827 (S.D. Fla. 1996).

9. *See supra* ch. 2, note 10 and accompanying text. This form of liability has been expanding in recent years. *See infra* ch. 9, note 110 and accompanying text.

10. A classic case, concerning a mob lawyer, is *In re Disbarment Proceedings*, 184 A. 59 (Pa. 1936). A more recent case is *Ryan v. United States*, 74 F.3d 1161 (11th Cir. 1996), in which a lawyer who charged drug smugglers a $10,000 retainer in exchange for promising to defending them if they were caught was convicted of conspiracy to import illegal drugs.

11. Fuller & Randall, *supra* note 4, at 1217.

12. David Luban, *Selling Indulgences: The Unmistakable Parallel Between Lynne Stewart and the President's Torture Lawyers*, SLATE, Feb. 14, 2005, http://www.slate.com/id/2113447/. Luban is of course a critic of lawyers' nonaccountability.

13. Support for the claims made in this footnote may be found in CANONS OF PROFESSIONAL ETHICS, Canon 5 (1965) (including the quotations regarding the express rights and duties of defense counsel); MODEL RULES OF PROF'L CONDUCT R. 3.4(e) (2003) (including the quotations regarding the prohibition of asserting personal knowledge of facts in issue and personal opinions); MODEL CODE OF PROF'L RESPONSIBILITY DR 7-106(C)(4) (1980) (issuing a virtually identical command); RESTATEMENT (THIRD) OF THE LAW GOVERNING LAWYERS § 107(1) (2000) (same); LORD MACMILLAN, LAW AND OTHER THINGS 181 (1937) (including the quotation from MacMillan).

14. Johns v. Smyth, 176 F. Supp. 949 (E.D. Va. 1959).

15. The lawyer "stated that the evidence against [his client] was overwhelming and that he was not going to insult the jury's intelligence" and added "that if they found [the client] guilty they should 'not ever look back' and agonize regarding whether they had done the right thing." People v. Swanson, 943 F.2d 1070 (9th Cir. 1991), (citing Osborn v. Shillinger, 861 F.2d 612, 629 (10th Cir. 1988)).

16. People v. Lang, 11 Cal. 3d 134, 138 (1974).

17. The lawyer, acting in a capital sentencing hearing, "made public statements to the effect that [his client] was not amenable to rehabilitation," compared the

client "to sharks feeding in the ocean in a frenzy; something that's just animal in all respects," and told the court that "in essence his client deserved the death sentence." Osborn v. Shillinger, 861 F.2d 612, 628–29 (10th Cir. 1988).

18. See the discussion of lying in chapter 2.

19. See the discussion of cheating in chapter 2.

20. Recall that although the ethical rule against proffering perjured testimony may constitutionally be applied even to the testimony of a criminal defendant, *see* Nix v. Whiteside, 475 U.S. 157, 171 (1986), the degree of certainty that is required before the rule is triggered is higher in the criminal than in the civil context. When Model Rule 3.3(a)(3) permits lawyers to refuse to offer evidence that they reasonably believe is false it excludes the testimony of a criminal defendant. *See* MODEL RULES OF PROF'L CONDUCT R. 3.3(a)(3) (2003). And the cases following *Nix v. Whiteside* insist that criminal defense lawyers must have a firm factual basis for treating their client's testimony as perjured and observe that this standard will rarely be satisfied. *See, e.g.,* United States v. Long, 857 F.2d 436, 445 (8th Cir. 1988). These matters are discussed in chapter 2.

21. Recall that criminal defense lawyers whose clients wish to appeal convictions may not ignore frivolous grounds for appeal altogether but must, if their clients insist, identify everything in the record that arguably supports their client's appeals. *See* Anders v. California, 386 U.S. 738 (1967).

22. Von Molke v. Gillies, 332 U.S. 708, 725 (1948). The point is also made elsewhere. *See, e.g.,* Wood v. Georgia, 450 U.S. 261, 271–72 (1981) (holding that the Sixth Amendment right to counsel contains a "correlative right to representation that is free from conflicts of interest"); State v. Christenson, 820 P.2d 1303, 1306 (Mont. 1991) (holding that the Sixth Amendment right to effective assistance of counsel includes a right to counsel's "undivided loyalty").

23. People v. Lang, 11 Cal. 3d 134, 139 (1974).

24. *Id.*

25. United States *ex rel* Wilcox v. Johnson, 555 F.2d 115, 122 (3d Cir. 1977); *see also* State v. Jones, 923 P.2d 560, 566 (Mont. 1996).

26. Frazer v. United States, 18 F.3d 778, 782 (9th Cir. 1994) (quoting United States v. Swanson, 943 F.2d 1070, 1074 (9th Cir. 1991)).

27. *Jones,* 923 P.2d at 566.

28. *Frazer,* 18 F.3d at 782. The idea that a lawyer who abandons professional detachment and acts on her private doubts about her client's cause suffers a conflict of interest is not special to Frazer. For other cases that advance this idea *see, e.g., Osborn v. Shillinger,* 861 F.2d 612, 629 (10th Cir. 1988) ("A defense attorney who abandons his duty of loyalty to his client and effectively joins the state in an effort to attain a conviction or death sentence suffers from an obvious conflict of interest."); *Swanson,* 943 F.2d at 1075 ("[A]n attorney who is burdened by a conflict between his client's interests and his own sympathies to the prosecution's position is considerably worse than an attorney with loyalty to other defendants, because the interests of the state and the defendant are necessarily in opposition."); *Jones,* 923 P.2d at 566 ("An attorney who abandons his or her duty of loyalty may create a conflict of interest.").

29. Johns v. Smyth, 176 F. Supp. 949, 953 (E.D. Va. 1959). The court in question was hearing a federal habeas petition brought by a prisoner whose

trial counsel had refused to contest the charges, asserting that given his private beliefs about the case, "you can talk about legal duty to client all you want, but I consider it dishonest to get up before a jury and try to argue [for acquittal]." *Id.* The court recognized that "[n]o attorney should 'frame' a factual defense in any case," *id.*, and, moreover, that under the standards that applied at the time, "error[s] of judgment, such as an election with respect to trial tactics . . . [were] not properly reviewable in habeas corpus unless the trial [was] a farce." *Id.* at 952. But the court concluded that "the defendant was entitled to the faithful and devoted service of his attorney uninhibited by the dictating conscience," *id.* at 953, so that "when defense counsel, in a truly adverse proceeding, admits that his conscience would not permit him to adopt certain customary trial procedures, this extends beyond the realm of judgment." *Id.* at 952. The court therefore crafted an exception to the general rule and granted habeas, reflecting that "indeed it would be a dark day in the history of our judicial system if a conviction is permitted to stand where an attorney . . . candidly admits that his conscience prevented him from representing his client according to the customary standards prescribed by attorneys and the courts." *Id.* at 954.

30. *Frazer*, 18 F.3d at 782 (quoting *Swanson*, 943 F.2d at 1074 (quoting *Osborn*, 86 F.2d at 625 (quoting United States v. Cronic, 466 U.S. 648, 666 (1984)).

31. Sanctions have been recommended against lawyers who breach their duties of professional detachment. *See, e.g., Swanson*, 943 F2d at 1076.

32. *See* Strickland v. Washington, 466 U.S. 668 (1984).

33. United States v. Cronic, 466 U.S. 648, 659 (1984); *see also* Cuyler v. Sullivan, 446 U.S. 335, 349–50 (1980) ("a defendant who shows that a conflict of interest actually affected the adequacy of his representation need not demonstrate prejudice in order to obtain relief."); Wood v. Georgia, 450 U.S. 261, 272 (1981); Burger v. Kemp, 483 U.S. 776, 783 (1986); Mickens v. Taylor, 535 U.S. 162 (2002).

34. State v. Jones, 923 P.2d 560, 566 (Mont. 1996) (quoting *Frazer*, 18 F.3d at 784). A loyal and professionally detached counsel is in this respect like an impartial and engaged factfinder (that is, a fact-finder that seeks without bias to impose its view of the truth), which is also essential to the authority of the judicial process. *See, e.g.*, United States v. Nelson, 277 F.3d 164 (2d Cir. 2002). The different requirements that apply in the two cases—the lawyer's loyalty and detachment and the factfinder's impartiality and engagement—are explained by the different contributions that lawyers and factfinders make to the overall authority of adjudication. I take up the lawyer's contribution in detail in Part III.

35. *See, e.g., In re* Harshey, 740 N.E.2d 851 (Ind. 2001). I discuss the case in greater detail in chapter 2.

Moreover, the rule that a lawyer may not impose her private judgment of a client's claim on settlements applies even outside the immediate shadow of a tribunal. For example, "a lawyer may not ethically break off negotiations with an opposing party simply because she has doubts about the viability of her client's case." *See* A.B.A. Comm. on Ethics and Prof'l Responsibility, Formal Op. 94–387 (1994).

36. *See, e.g.*, Singleton v. Foreman, 435 F.2d 962, 970 (5th Cir. 1970). The Singleton court expressly added that the conflict can arise even when the adversity between lawyer and client is not "of an economic character." *Id.*

37. 1 HH, *supra* note 5, § 3.3:201, at 581–82 (Supp. 1994).

38. This language, quoted in Ted Schneyer, *Professionalism as Politics: The Making of a Modern Legal Ethics Code*, in LAWYERS' IDEALS/LAWYERS' PRACTICE: TRANSFORMATIONS IN THE AMERICAN LEGAL PROFESSION 95, 122 (Robert L. Nelson et al. eds., 1992), was used by the American Trial Lawyer's Association to support the expansion of the duty to keep client confidences enacted by the 1983 version of the Model Rules. That version of the confidentiality principle was probably too broad, and the principle has since been narrowed. *See* MODEL RULES OF PROF'L CONDUCT R. 1.6(b)(2)–(3) (2003). But although the trial lawyers employed the idea that lawyers must serve rather than judge their clients to support an extreme and unjustified conclusion, this conception of the adversary advocate clearly does support some duty of confidentiality, which requires lawyers to lie in some measure.

39. Charles P. Curtis, *The Ethics of Advocacy*, 4 STAN. L. REV. 3, 9 (1951).

40. MODEL RULES OF PROF'L CONDUCT R. 3.1 cmt. 1. This idea also appears in the Model Code, which says that "[a] lawyer shall not intentionally fail to seek the lawful objectives of his client through reasonably available means . . . ." MODEL CODE OF PROF'L RESPONSIBILITY DR 7-101(A)(1) (1980).

41. The word "intolerable" is Charles Fried's, who applied it to refusals to plead technical defenses such as the statute of limitations and the statute of frauds. *See* Charles Fried, *The Lawyer as Friend: The Moral Foundations of the Lawyer-Client Relation*, 85 YALE L.J. 1060, 1085 (1976).

42. Moreover, even civil advocates acquire greater affirmative duties to promote the truth before tribunals at which no adversary is present. Model Rule 3.3(d) states, in general terms, that "[i]n an ex parte proceeding, a lawyer shall inform the tribunal of all material facts known to the lawyer that will enable the tribunal to make an informed decision, whether or not the facts are adverse." MODEL RULES OF PROF'L CONDUCT R. 3.3(d) (2003). The contrast to this broad, affirmative, and nontechnical commitment to truth emphasizes the many ways in which adversary advocates' professional duties to lie survive the more modest duties of candor that apply in ordinary circumstances. And the fact that the broader duties to truth arise when no adversary is present underlines the connection between the lawyers' duties to lie and her adversary role.

Finally, although only as a curiosity, note that applicants for bar admission and lawyers in connection with bar admissions or disciplinary matters also face broader affirmative duties to disclose. In particular, they may not "fail to disclose a fact necessary to correct a misapprehension known by the person to have arisen in [a] matter . . . except that this rule does not require disclosure of information otherwise protected by Rule 1.6." MODEL RULES OF PROF'L CONDUCT R. 8.1.

43. ABA STANDARDS FOR CRIMINAL JUSTICE Standard 3-3.9(a) (3d ed. 1993). This standard also forbids prosecutors from bringing charges that are not supported by probable cause, *see id.*, as do the Model Rules. *See* MODEL RULES OF PROF'L CONDUCT R. 3.8(a).

44. *Id.* Standard 3–3.9(f).

45. *Id.* Standard 3–3.9(b).

46. *Id.* Standard 3–3.9(b)(1). Indeed, "[a] prosecutor should not be compelled by his or her supervisor to prosecute a case in which he or she has a reasonable doubt about the guilt of the accused." *Id.* Standard 3–3.9(c).

47. *See id.* Standard 3–5.7(b).

48. "[T]he advocate has a duty to use legal procedure for the fullest benefit of the client's cause." MODEL RULES OF PROF'L CONDUCT R. 3.1 cmt. 1 (2003). This idea also appears in the Model Code, which says that "[a] lawyer shall not intentionally fail to seek the lawful objectives of his client through reasonably available means . . . ." MODEL CODE OF PROF'L RESPONSIBILITY DR 7–101(A)(1) (1980).

49. ABA STANDARDS FOR CRIMINAL JUSTICE Standard 3–3.11(a). Note also Standard 3–3.11(c), which forbids prosecutors from intentionally avoiding pursuit of evidence because it damages the prosecution's case. See also MODEL RULES OF PROF'L CONDUCT R. 3.8(d). The prosecutor's ethical duties are broader than the constitutional requirement to reveal evidence to the defense established by *Brady v. Maryland*, 373 U.S. 83 (1963). In particular, they are not limited by considerations involving the significance of the evidence or the propriety of the defense's request.

50. *See* ABA STANDARDS FOR CRIMINAL JUSTICE Standard 3–1.2(c); *see also* Berger v. United States, 295 U.S. 78 (1935).

51. In practice, of course, states may seek injustice (including through their prosecutors). But states may not legitimately seek injustice, whereas private parties may.

52. Support for the claims made in this footnote may be found in Marvin E. Frankel, *The Search for Truth: An Umpireal View*, 123 U. PENN. L. REV. 1031 (1975) (setting forth Frankel's proposal that advocates ought to pursue truth above their clients' interests); *id.* at 1052 (claming to wish merely to "modify (not abandon) the adversary ideal"); *id.* at 1056 (including the quoted language acknowledging his proposal's inconsistency with more fundamental ideals and that his proposal stretches our conception of the partisan advocate); *id.* at 1059 (concluding that he would sacrifice truth if forced to choose).

Support for the footnote's discussion of the New Jersey rule can be found at N.J. RULES OF PROF'L CONDUCT R. 3.3(a)(5) (1984); 2 HH, *supra* note 5, §AP4:104, at 1264 (2d ed. 1990) (containing the quoted language calling the rule a "'radical proposition'"); Michael P. Ambrosio, *The "New" New Jersey Rules of Professional Conduct: Reordered Priorities for Public Accountability*, 11 SETON HALL LEGIS. J. 121, 138 (1987) (including the quotation observing that the rule "'seems to conflict with the basic premise that an advocate must present a client's cause in its best light.'"); Raymond R. Trombadore, *The New Jersey Rules of Professional Conduct: A Recipe for Good Lawyering*, 18 SETON HALL L. REV. 606, 610 (1988) (including the quotation from the chair of the New Jersey Supreme Court Disciplinary Review Board); Supreme Court of New Jersey, *Administrative Determination in Response to the Report and Recommendation of the Supreme Court Commission on the Rules of Professional Conduct*, N.J. L.J., Sept. 22, 2003, at 59, 65, 173 N.J.L.J. 1131, 1137 (retreating from the rule and including the quotation observing that "the very nature of the rule makes compliance difficult"); N.J. RULES OF PROF'L CONDUCT R. 3.3(a)(5) (2004) (continuing to cabin lawyers' obligations to lie more narrowly than do the Model Rules); *In re* Seelig, 180 N.J. 234, 850 A.2d 477 (2004) (showing some inclination to enforce New Jersey's higher standards).

The discussion in this footnote benefited enormously, especially in its account of the particulars of New Jersey's experience, from Daniel Walfish, *Making Lawyers Responsible for the Truth: The Influence of Marvin Franklin's Proposal for Reforming the Adversary System*, 35 SETON HALL L. REV. 613 (2005).

53. 1 HH, *supra* note 5, § 5.8, at 5–25 (3d ed. Supp. 2004). Hazard and Hodes associate such slavish devotion with the view that the law of lawyering "*compels* persons of normal sensibilities to discard their moral autonomy," *id.*, and call this complex of views "plainly incorrect." *Id.* But although they are right to attack any suggestion that lawyers must unconstrainedly serve their clients, Hazard and Hodes are wrong to conclude that lawyers retain their moral autonomy. Even constrained loyalty involves a significant sacrifice of autonomy, as Hazard has elsewhere acknowledged. *See* Geoffrey C. Hazard, Jr., *Equal Opportunity in the Practice of Law*, 27 SAN DIEGO L. REV. 127, 136 (1990).

54. *Id.* at 135–38.

55. As Heidegger, quoting Hölderlin, was fond of saying, "But where the danger is, grows / The saving power also." MARTIN HEIDEGGER, *The Question Concerning Technology, in* THE QUESTION CONCERNING TECHNOLOGY AND OTHER ESSAYS 3, 28 (William Lovitt trans., 1977).

56. Something like an ideal of lawyerly fraternity is developed in ANTHONY T. KRONMAN, THE LOST LAWYER: FAILING IDEALS OF THE LEGAL PROFESSION (1993).

57. The canonical account of lawyerly friendship appears in Charles Fried, *The Lawyer as Friend: The Moral Foundations of the Lawyer-Client Relation*, 85 YALE L.J. 1060 (1976).

58. *Id.* at 1071 (acknowledging that "the ordinary concept of friendship provides only an analogy").

59. *See, e.g.*, William H. Simon, *The Ideology of Advocacy: Procedural Justice and Professional Ethics*, 1978 WIS. L. REV. 29, 108 ("Fried has described the classical notion, not of friendship, but of prostitution.").

60. ARISTOTLE, THE NICOMACHEAN ETHICS bk. VIII, at 1156b (David Ross trans., J.L. Ackrill & J.O. Urmson eds., Oxford University Press 1998) ("Perfect friendship is the friendship of men who are good, and alike in virtue.").

61. Recall Model Rule 1.2 and the discussion of the rule in chapter 1.

62. Thus lawyers may take measures that damage their clients' interests when this is necessary to collect their fees. MODEL CODE OF PROF'L CONDUCT DR 4-101(C)(4) (1980). And even the lawyer's duty of confidentiality includes an exception that allows lawyers sometimes to divulge client confidences in self-defense. *See* MODEL RULES OF PROF'L CONDUCT R. 1.6(b)(5) (2003).

63. The analogy between lawyers and poets is not, as it happens, without precedent. Charles Curtis observed the analogy half a century ago, when he proposed to "[c]ompare the lawyer with the poet whose speech goes to the heart of things," and added, quoting Thoreau, that the lawyer "is that one especially

who speaks civilly to Nature as a second person and in some sense is the patron of the world. Though more than any he stands in the midst of Nature, yet more than any he can stand aloof from her." Charles P. Curtis, *The Ethics of Advocacy*, 4 STAN. L. REV. 3, 23 (1951) (quoting 7 THE WRITINGS OF HENRY DAVID THOREAU 289 (1906)).

64. Note, however, that where Plato's analogy is between two harmonies—between a state governed by the wise and a soul governed by reason—the analogy that I shall develop is between two disharmonies. The lawyer and the poet both preside, as we shall see, over perpetual conflict. (Plato, of course, had his own views about poets, *See* PLATO, THE REPUBLIC § 603a (Paul Shorey trans., 1930) *in* THE COLLECTED DIALOGUES OF PLATO (Edith Hamilton & Huntington Cairns eds., 1961), and I shall not even try to address the complicated question of the relation between Plato's account of poets and Keats's, *see infra*.)

65. Keats introduced the term "negative capability" in JOHN KEATS, *Letter to George and Tom Keats, 21, 27 (?) Dec. 1817, in* LETTERS OF JOHN KEATS 43 (Robert Gittings ed., 1970).

66. JOHN KEATS, *Letter to Richard Woodhouse, 27 Oct. 1818, in* LETTERS OF JOHN KEATS, *supra* note 65, at 157.

67. KEATS, *supra* note 65.

68. 1 HH, *supra* note 5, Introduction § 403, at Intro-26 (2d ed. Supp. 1998).

69. KEATS, *supra* note 65.

70. Fuller & Randall, supra note 4, at 1160 (excerpted in Lon L. Fuller, *The Forms and Limits of Adjudication*, 92 HARV. L. REV. 353, 383 (1978)).

71. In this feature, my account of negative capability displays some similarity to certain ideas Roberto Unger has developed under the same heading. *See, e.g.,* Roberto Mangabeira Unger, *The Critical Legal Studies Movement*, 96 HARV. L. REV. 561, 650–53 (1983).

72. KRONMAN, *supra* note 56, at 66–74.

73. Support for the claims made in this footnote can be found at MODEL RULES OF PROF'L CONDUCT R. 3.3(a)(3) (2003) (indicating that lawyers must reveal adverse legal authority); 1 HH, *supra* note 5, § 3.3:206, at 591 (Supp. 1998) (giving the traditional explanation, quoted in the footnote, for the asymmetry between revealing adverse precedent and adverse facts).

74. Support for the claims made in this footnote can be found in 24 CHARLES ALAN WRIGHT & KENNETH W. GRAHAM, JR., FEDERAL PRACTICE AND PROCEDURE § 5484, at 318, 328 (1986) (indicating that attorney-client privilege can be exercised to block attorney testimony with respect to communications whose content the client himself may be forced to reveal). *See also* Upjohn Co. v. United States, 449 U.S. 383, 395–96 (1981) ("The privilege only protects communications, it does not protect disclosure of the underlying facts by those who communicated with the attorney . . . . The client cannot be compelled to answer the question, 'What did you say or write to the attorney?' but may not refuse to disclose any relevant fact within his knowledge merely because he incorporated a statement of such fact into his communication to his attorney."); Fisher v. United States, 425 U.S. 391, 404 (1976) (indicating that the attorney-client privilege extends to prevent the lawyer from revealing facts that she knows apart from privileged communications in criminal contexts when the client

could refuse to reveal these facts by citing his Fifth Amendment privilege against self-incrimination.)

75. See MODEL RULES OF PROF'L CONDUCT R. 1.6, 4.1, and the discussion of these rules *supra* chapter 2.

76. Support for the claims made in this footnote can be found at D.C. RULES OF PROF'L CONDUCT R. 3.3(b) (2007) (allowing witnesses whose testimony their lawyer knows is false to proceed in narrative form); Conn. Bar Formal Op. 42 (1992) (same); People v. Johnson, 77 Cal. Rptr. 2d 805 (Cal. App. 1998) (same); State v. Long, 714 P.2d 465 (Ariz. Ct. App. 1986) (same); Sanborn v. State, 474 So. 2d 309 (Fla. Ct. App. 1985) (same); Model Rule 3.3(a)(3) & cmts. 6–7 (setting forth the majority view that the narrative approach does not satisfy the duty of candor); *see also* Nix v. Whiteside, 475 U.S. 157, 170 n.6 (1986) (same); State v. McDowell, 669 N.W.2d 204 (Wis. Ct. App. 2003) (forbidding the narrative approach on the grounds that it impermissibly discloses client perjury).

77. See 1 HH, *supra* note 5, §1.6:102, at 132–134.2 (Supp. 1998) for cites.

78. *See* MODEL RULES OF PROF'L CONDUCT R. 1.7(b)(3); RESTATEMENT (THIRD) OF THE LAW GOVERNING LAWYERS § 122(2)(b) (2000); United Sewage Agency v. Jelco, 646 F.2d 1339 (9th Cir. 1981); Baldasarre v. Butler, 625 A.2d 458, 467 (N.J. 1993). Note that earlier ethics regimes were even stricter in this connection and made conflicts involving adverse positions even in unrelated matters nonwaivable. *See, e.g.*, Cinema 5 v. Cinerama, 528 F.2d 1384 (2d Cir. 1976).

79. Fuller & Randall, *supra* note 4, at 1160 (excerpted in Lon L. Fuller, *The Forms and Limits of Adjudication*, 92 HARV. L. REV. 353, 382 (1978)).

80. As Fuller says, "If it is true that a man in his time must play many parts, it is scarcely given to him to play them all at once." *Id.*

81. *See* MODEL RULES OF PROF'L CONDUCT R. 3.7; MODEL CODE OF PROF'L RESPONSIBILITY DR 5–101(B) & 5–102 (1981).

82. 1 HH, *supra* note 5, § 2.7:102, at 679 (Supp. 1996). Sometimes commentators go on to say that for a lawyer to testify would create a conflict of interest with the client, *see, e.g., id.* § 3.7:103, at 680, but this does not add much, as it does not explain what the conflict consists in. Finally, the rule is sometimes explained in historical terms as a descendant of the common law rule that parties and their agents (including their lawyers) were generally barred from testifying in their own causes. *See id.* § 3.7:102, at 678. The explanation of course justifies nothing.

83. Support for the claims made in this footnote may be found in MODEL RULES OF PROFESSIONAL CONDUCT R. 3.4(e) (2003) (indicating that a lawyer may not express her personal opinions about a client's cause or vouch for her client); 1 HH, *supra* note 5, § 3.4:101, at 624 (2d ed. 1990) (including the quotation in the footnote opining that this rule "is troublesome precisely because it protects less substantial interests and is not vital to the protection of the system itself").

84. *See, e.g.*, Willy v. Coastal Corp., 647 F. Supp. 116 (E.D. Tex. 1986), *rev'd on jurisdictional grounds*, 855 F.2d 1160 (5th Cir. 1988); Balla v. Gambro, Inc., 584 N.E.2d 104 (Ill. 1991); Herbster v. N. Am. Co. for Life & Health Ins., 501

N.E.2d 343 (Ill. App. Ct. 1986); 1 HH, *supra* note 5, § 1.16:206, at 477 (Supp. 1998); Grace M. Giesel, *The Ethics or Employment Dilemma of In-House Counsel*, 5 GEO. J. LEGAL ETHICS 535, 557–62 (1992); Sara A. Corello, Note, *In-House Counsel's Right to Sue for Retaliatory Discharge*, 92 COLUM. L. REV. 389, 399–415 (1992). Sometimes lawyers do succeed at bringing such claims. *See, e.g.*, Wieder v. Skala, 609 N.E.2d 105 (N.Y. 1992) (breach of contract); Mourad v. Auto. Club Ins. Ass'n, 465 N.W.2d 395 (Mich. Ct. App. 1991).

85. MODEL RULES OF PROF'L CONDUCT Preamble ¶ 8 (1983).

86. *Id.* Preamble ¶ 8.

87. *Id.* Preamble ¶ 8.

88. *See supra* ch. 1, note 2 and accompanying text.

CHAPTER 4
INTRODUCING INTEGRITY

1. MODEL RULES OF PROF'L CONDUCT Preamble ¶ 8 (1983).

2. 1 GEOFFREY C. HAZARD, JR. & W. WILLIAM HODES, THE LAW OF LAWYERING: A HANDBOOK ON THE MODEL RULES OF PROFESSIONAL CONDUCT §1.2:301, at 36 (2d ed. Supp. 1996) [hereinafter HH]. Such remarks lead William Simon to call the idea that "the lawyer must—or at least may—pursue any goal of the client through any arguably legal course of action and assert any nonfrivolous claim" the "Dominant View" of legal ethics. WILLIAM SIMON, THE PRACTICE OF JUSTICE: A THEORY OF LAWYERS' ETHICS 7 (1998).

3. This point is powerfully developed in SIMON, *supra* note 2.

4. MODEL RULES OF PROF'L CONDUCT Preamble ¶ 8 (1983).

5. The need to moderate adversary advocacy in the face of imperfections in the legal system is emphasized by David Luban and by William Simon. *See* DAVID LUBAN, LAWYERS AND JUSTICE 67–103 (1988); SIMON, *supra* note 2, at 53–76.

6. The need to moderate adversary advocacy in the face of nonconsequentialist moral ideas is emphasized by David Luban and especially by Arthur Applbaum. *See* LUBAN, *supra* note 5, at 50–103; ARTHUR APPLBAUM, ETHICS FOR ADVERSARIES 113–35, 175–203 (1999). As Applbaum remarks, a successful development of the adversary system defense "will have to do more than simply invoke the balance of consequences," *id.* at 177, but will instead have to be "reasonably acceptable" even to those whom the adversary system harms. *Id.* at 258.

7. This example is discussed in detail in chapter 2.

8. *See, e.g.*, FED. R. EVID. 412; N.Y. CRIM. PROC. LAW § 60.42 (McKinney 2006); CAL. PENAL CODE § 1347(b) (Deering 2006); Maryland v. Craig, 497 U.S. 836 (1990). *But see* Crawford v. Washington, 541 U.S. 36 (2004). Note, however, that not all developments in this connection have been salutary. In particular, recent decades have seen a systematic undermining of the legal services corporations through which the legal system had sought to bring the distribution of access to lawyers more nearly into line with what the adversary system excuse requires. *See, e.g.*, Legal Aid Soc'y v. Legal Servs. Corp., 145

F.3d 1017 (9th Cir. 1998); Reg'l Mgmt. Corp. v. Legal Servs. Corp., 186 F.3d
457 (4th Cir. 1999); W. Ctr. On Law & Poverty v. Legal Servs. Corp., 592 F.
Supp. 338 (D.D.C. 1984).

9. William Simon perhaps comes closest to recommending that the legal profession abandon adversary advocacy outright, when he argues for a "Contextual View" of legal ethics, whose "basic maxim is that the lawyer should take
such actions as, considering the relevant circumstances of the particular case,
seem likely to promote justice." SIMON, *supra* note 2, at 9. For Simon, moreover, "justice" means resolution of the case on the "legal merits," with law
being understood in a broad sense, so that a lawyer should "decide questions of
justice . . . [by] think[ing] about them as she would if she were a judge." *Id.* at
138–39. This standard—which seems to eliminate the gap between lawyer and
judge that, I have said, constitutes adversary advocacy's core—suggests that
Simon is contemplating a complete departure from adversary ethics.

But Simon seems finally reluctant to go quite so far, and elsewhere insists that
"[t]he Contextual View incorporates much of the traditional lawyer role, including the notion that lawyers can serve justice through zealous pursuit of clients' goals," *id.* at 11, and adds that "thinking like a judge does not necessarily
mean reaching the same decisions that one would make as a judge," *id.* at 139.
Moreover, Simon certainly accepts that differences in institutional competence
may sometimes lead the conclusions of judges and lawyers properly to diverge.

This leaves it unclear how completely Simon distances himself from adversary
advocacy, and in particular whether Simon acknowledges a distinctive, and distinctively adversary, social function for lawyers or instead treats adversary lawyering as a shallow and contingent feature of our legal practice, that reflects
differences only in technical capacity and not in basic ideals or social purposes.

10. Geoffrey C. Hazard, Jr., *The Future of Legal Ethics*, 100 YALE L.J. 1239,
1245 (1991).

11. Geoffrey Hazard is a case in point. Hazard is persuaded that the adversary system excuse straightforwardly justifies lawyers' partisanship. *See* Hazard,
supra note 10. But rather than simply redirecting this same argument to answer
my charges that lawyers lie and cheat, Hazard feels the need to refute these
charges directly, denying that lawyers are professionally vicious at all. *See* Geoffrey Hazard, *Humanity and the Law*, 16 YALE J.L. & HUMAN. 79 (2004).

12. Bernard Williams, *History, Morality, and the Test of Reflection*, *in* CHRIS-
TINE M. KORSGAARD, THE SOURCES OF NORMATIVITY 210, 210–11 (1996).

13. *See* ARISTOTLE, THE NICHOMACHEAN ETHICS, bk. I, chs. 4–12 (David
Ross trans., J.L. Ackrill & J.O. Urmson eds., Oxford University Press 1998).

Plato, incidentally, also believed the just man to be happier than the unjust
one. Specifically, Plato argued that "[t]he just soul and the just man then will
live well and the unjust ill" and that "he who lives well is blessed and happy,
and he who does not the contrary." PLATO, THE REPUBLIC § 353e–354a (Paul
Shorey trans., 1930) *in* THE COLLECTED DIALOGUES OF PLATO (Edith Hamilton &
Huntington Cairns eds., 1961). Plato's position, however, is in fact the polar opposite of Aristotle's. Thus, Aristotle took well-being to be the fundamental idea
and derived an ethical theory from the conditions for promoting well-being.
Plato, by contrast, took ethical obligation to be the fundamental idea and sought

to explain why a person who violates the principles of ethics will always and inevitably suffer diminished well-being. (This is the source of Plato's well-known concern to show that even a person possessing the power to violate ethical principles with impunity even—to use Plato's own example, the wearer of the Ring of Gyges—will be happiest if he nevertheless resists temptation and acts justly. *See id.* at § 359c).

14. This view of Christianity owes much to Isaiah Berlin. *See* ISAIAH BERLIN, *Two Concepts of Liberty*, § III (The Retreat to the Inner Citadel), *in* FOUR ESSAYS ON LIBERTY (1969). Of course, as Pascal's wager makes plain, it is a dubious proposition whether asceticism adopted with this motive involves any genuine self-sacrifice at all. Indeed, even an ascetic who did not take heaven seriously might (as Berlin observed) adopt asceticism as simply a self-interested effort to limit her desires in the face of the prospect that whatever desires she has will be frustrated.

The reference to Christianity in this context proceeds only by way of presenting a historically familiar example. There is no reason to think that the form of perverse asceticism that I am discussing is peculiarly Christian, and certainly none to think that Christianity possesses a monopoly on this form of self-abnegation.

15. It is an open question whether the advances can be sustained without suffering the pathologies. In particular, it is plausible that the institutions and practices that in fact sustain and express the ideal of human equality throughout the modern world are hostile to the institutions and practices through which persons most naturally seek to take authorship of their lives. I elaborate this connection in Part III.

16. This paragraph borrows loosely from Thomas Hill's similar expressions of related ideas, *see* THOMAS HILL, AUTONOMY AND SELF-RESPECT 176–77 (1991), although my development of these ideas will ultimately depart from Hill's. In particular, Hill approaches authorship and related considerations in the shadow of his commitment to Kant's ethics, whereas I believe (as I argue in chapters 6 and 7) that Kant's moral thought, like all impartialist theories, is fundamentally hostile to this more intimate tradition in ethics. Indeed, Hill's Kantianism limits his interest in authorship from the outset, by way of his express intention to apply such ideas only in connection with ambitions and actions that "do not have to do with the welfare, rights, or interests of others." *Id.* at 174. By contrast, I shall extend ethical considerations concerning authorship to cases in which other persons' moral claims are at stake and expressly argue that these considerations can sometimes outweigh such claims.

17. This suggestion is expressed in the liberating elements of Nietzsche's thought. *See, e.g.*, FRIEDRICH NIETZSCHE, ON THE GENEALOGY OF MORALS 1–56 (Walter Kaufman ed. & trans., 1969).

18. *See* Bernard Williams, *A Critique of Utilitarianism, in* J.J.C. SMART & BERNARD WILLIAMS, UTILITARIANISM: FOR AND AGAINST 76, 98 (1973) [hereinafter Williams, *A Critique of Utilitarianism*].

19. *Id.* at 108.

20. *Id.* at 109.

21. THOMAS NAGEL, THE VIEW FROM NOWHERE 182 (1986). Nagel adds that this will produce "an acute sense of moral dislocation." *Id.*

22. Williams, *A Critique of Utilitarianism, supra* note 18, at 116 n.18.

23. *Id.* at 117.

24. *Id.* at 98.

25. I am skeptical about whether such considerations can finally do much to salvage Jim's integrity, for reasons that I address in greater detail below.

CHAPTER 5
AN IMPARTIALIST REJOINDER?

1. The statement of third-personal impartiality that I present in the main text borrows heavily from T.M. SCANLON, WHAT WE OWE TO EACH OTHER 79–81 (1998).

2. The dictum is attributed to Bentham by Mill. *See* JOHN STUART MILL, UTILITARIANISM 60 (George Sher ed., Hackett 1979) (1863). Although it is commonly thought that Bentham never used this form of words himself—and Mill certainly provides no citation—Bentham in fact did utter almost the exact phrase that Mill reports, saying that "every individual in the country tells for one; no individual for more than one." See JEREMY BENTHAM, *Rationale of Judicial Evidence, in* 7 THE WORKS OF JEREMY BENTHAM 334 (John Bowring ed., Edinburgh, W. Tait 1843).

3. This is of course a highly schematic account, which abstracts from a host of familiar questions about the more detailed structure of third-personal impartiality. Such questions have been most systematically addressed in connection with the utilitarian version of third-personal impartiality, specifically in the debate over what David Lyons has called the forms and limits of utilitarianism. *See generally* DAVID LYONS, THE FORMS AND LIMITS OF UTILITARIANISM (1978). The questions include: whether value should be understood purely quantitatively, for example as the difference of pleasure over pain, or whether value is a qualitatively varied phenomenon, as in John Stuart Mill's famous discussion of higher and lower pleasures, *see* MILL, *supra* note 2, at 10; whether the value contained in a state of affairs is the sum or the average of the values that inhere in the individuals who make up the state of affairs, *see generally* JOHN RAWLS, A THEORY OF JUSTICE 161–92 (1971) [hereinafter RAWLS, A THEORY OF JUSTICE]; Gregory S. Kavka, *Rawls on Average and Total Utility*, 27 PHIL. STUD. 237 (1975); and whether third-personal impartiality calls on persons, in discharging their duty to maximize value, to choose optimal individual actions or optimal general rules for action, *see generally* J.J.C. SMART & BERNARD WILLIAMS, UTILITARIANISM: FOR AND AGAINST 76, 98 (1973); Robert Adams, *Motive Utilitarianism*, 73 J. PHIL. 467 (1976).

4. CHRISTINE KORSGAARD, "The Reasons We Can Share: An Attack on the Distinction between Agent-Relative and Agent-Neutral Values," in CREATING THE KINGDOM OF ENDS 275, 292 (1996).

5. BARBARA HERMAN, THE PRACTICE OF MORAL JUDGMENT 39 (1993).

6. RAWLS, A THEORY OF JUSTICE, *supra* note 3, at 27. As Rawls says, on the utilitarian view "separate individuals are thought of as so many different lines along which rights and duties are to be assigned and scarce means of

satisfaction allocated in accordance with rules so as to give the greatest fulfillment of wants." *Id.*

7. This way of putting the point paraphrases remarks of T. M. Scanlon and Thomas Nagel. *See* T.M. SCANLON, WHAT WE OWE TO EACH OTHER 82 (1998) [hereinafter SCANLON, WHAT WE OWE TO EACH OTHER]; THOMAS NAGEL, THE VIEW FROM NOWHERE 178 (1986).

8. KORSGAARD, *supra* note 4, at 275.

9. Here Korsgaard cites, unsurprisingly, to Kant's *Groundwork. Id.* at 295 (citing IMMANUEL KANT, FOUNDATIONS OF THE METAPHYSICS OF MORALS 430 (Lewis White Beck trans., 1969)).

10. More precisely, Scanlon's contractualism "holds that an act is wrong if its performance under the circumstances would be disallowed by any set of principles for the general regulation of behavior that no one could reasonably reject as a basis for informed, unforced general agreement." SCANLON, WHAT WE OWE TO EACH OTHER, *supra* note 7, at 153; T.M. Scanlon, *Contractualism and Utilitarianism, in* UTILITARIANISM AND BEYOND (Amartya Sen & Bernard Williams eds., 1982) [hereinafter Scanlon, *Contractualism and Utilitarianism*].

11. The emphasis on impartiality in the Kantian tradition begins in Kant's own work, especially in the formulation of the Categorical Imperative that commands one always to treat all others as ends in themselves and never merely as means. IMMANUEL KANT, GROUNDWORK OF THE METAPHYSICS OF MORALS 95–96 (H.J. Paton trans. 1958) (1785). It may be seen equally clearly in the efforts of modern Kantians, beginning with John Rawls, to develop Kantian moral ideas through the mechanisms of social contract theory—mechanisms expressly designed to construct moral principles that would be generally acceptable to equally situated people. *See, e.g.,* BRUCE ACKERMAN, SOCIAL JUSTICE AND THE LIBERAL STATE (1980); JOHN RAWLS, POLITICAL LIBERALISM (1993); RAWLS, A THEORY OF JUSTICE, *supra* note 3; SCANLON, WHAT WE OWE TO EACH OTHER, *supra* note 7; Scanlon, *Contractualism and Utilitarianism, supra* note 10.

12. This purpose is declared in the title Korsgaard gives to her argument: "The Reasons We Can Share: An Attack on the Distinction between Agent-Relative and Agent-Neutral Values." *See* KORSGAARD, *supra* note 4, at 275. The most immediate subject of Korsgaard's attention is an earlier attempt by Nagel to come to grips with the ethical ideas involved in Jim's problem, *see* NAGEL, *supra* note 7, at 175ff., and Korsgaard devotes substantial textual attention to Nagel's arguments. But in spite of styling her argument "an attack," Korsgaard's stance toward Nagel's presentation of the problem is substantially friendly. In particular, both Nagel and Korsgaard find the core of Jim's dilemma in the requirement that Jim must justify any killing he commits to his victim in a way in which he need not justify the dictator's killings to anyone. Korsgaard's disagreement with Nagel is not about this characterization of the problem but rather about the problem's solution, when it is characterized in this way. Nagel doubted whether Jim could provide the required justification; Korsgaard, as will become clear in a moment, believes that he can.

The argument in the main text will demonstrate that Korsgaard's approach to Jim's dilemma does not dissolve the problem of integrity. This argument applies to Nagel's approach to the dilemma also, and I mention Nagel here only to emphasize this fact, especially in light of Nagel's remarks, reported earlier, concerning the problem of Jim's potential moral dislocation. *See supra* ch. 4 text accompanying note 21. In spite of making these remarks, the bulk of Nagel's analysis of the ethical problem raised by circumstances like Jim's does not in the end focus on the problem of integrity at all.

13. KORSGAARD, *supra* note 4, at 292.

14. *Id.* at 296 (emphasis in original).

15. The consent of the victim was, as Korsgaard acknowledges, present in Williams's statement of the original example. *See id.* at 292; Bernard Williams, *A Critique of Utilitarianism, in* SMART & WILLIAMS, *supra* note 3, at 76 [hereinafter Williams, *A Critique of Utilitarianism*]. It did not, however, figure prominently in Williams' discussion.

16. KORSGAARD, *supra* note 4, at 296.

17. *Id.*

18. *Id.* at 309 n.42 (emphasis in original).

19. *Id.*

20. This argument is developed in detail in ARTHUR APPLBAUM, ETHICS FOR ADVERSARIES 136–74 (1999). Applbaum worries that although it is reasonable for each innocent to consent to the lottery in such cases, it may not, to borrow Scanlon's language and form of thought, be *unreasonable* for any of the innocents to reject such an arrangement. And accordingly, Applbaum is unsure whether this form of argument may be *forced* on the innocents and, relatedly, whether, "[i]f the loser [of a fair lottery] sees a way to escape both Jim and the [dictator], . . . he is obligated to stick around." *Id.* at 164. These concerns are especially important to the second-personal reconstruction of the adversary system excuse, which must (because of the large numbers of persons involved) make do with the hypothetical rather than the actual consent of the persons whose disputes will be resolved by adversary procedure and which defends a process that (like the lottery) is Pareto superior only *ex ante* and therefore invites resistance by those who discover themselves to be ill-served *ex post.*

21. APPLBAUM, ETHICS FOR ADVERSARIES, *supra* note 20, at 136–74.

22. It is possible that the Kantian reconstruction of the adversary system excuse is slightly more forgiving, so that it does not require adversary advocacy to be most just for every person but only most just for the person for whom it is least just (so that the greatest individual rights violation that adversary advocacy imposes is smaller than the greatest individual rights violation imposed by any alternative). This complication does not change the basic argument, however (or if it does, it only strengthens the argument by increasing the extent of lawyers' lying and cheating that the Kantian approach condones). Accordingly, I shall not take it up here.

23. APPLBAUM, ETHICS FOR ADVERSARIES, *supra* note 20, at 166–74.

24. KORSGAARD, *supra* note 4, at 296.

25. Williams, *A Critique of Utilitarianism, supra* note 15, at 116.

26. Support for the claims made in this footnote may be found in KORSGAARD, *supra* note 4, at 296 (proposing the smaller world in which Jim and the adversary must think of themselves as acting); IMMANUEL KANT, *On a Supposed Right to Lie from Altruistic Motives, reprinted in* IMMANUEL KANT: CRITIQUE

of Practical Reason and Other Writings in Moral Philosophy (Lewis White Beck trans. 1949) (suggesting that it is always wrong to use deception or coercion); *See* Christine Korsgaard, *The Right to Lie: Kant on Dealing With Evil, in* Creating the Kingdom of Ends, *supra* note 4, at 133 (trying, within the Kantian frame, to open up a space for abandoning moral scruples in order to combat evil).

27. *Id.* at 117.

28. The answer to this question may depend on whether the source of the dilemma an agent faces is another agent's wrongful conduct, as in the examples in the main text, or instead a genuinely natural phenomenon. Thus it is interesting to compare Jim's case with one in which a hospital administrator facing a power shortage must disconnect one life support machine in order to prevent twenty such machines (including that one) from failing for want of adequate power. This new case may (perhaps) be easier, because although it involves the same balance of lives, and once again challenges ordinary ideals and ambitions, the act that it requires can never be characterized as unnecessary, not even in a larger world. This difference may affect the degree of tension between an agent's personal ideals and ambitions and the acts that impartial morality requires of him.

Chapter 6
Integrity and the First Person

1. The reference to moral purity borrows from Thomas Hill. *See* Thomas E. Hill Jr., Autonomy and Self-Respect 68 (1991). In spite of worrying about excessive moral purity, Hill eventually accepts that a concern for integrity can be ethically justified, although he does not put the point in quite this way. Moreover, Hill's defense of integrity proceeds by an argument that is very different from the argument I develop here.

2. The arguments and quotation presented in the footnote may be found in David Hare, The Absence of War 84 (1993).

3. Barbara Herman, The Practice of Moral Judgment 39 (1993).

4. *Id.*

5. John Rawls, A Theory of Justice 27 (1971).

6. Arthur Koestler, Darkness at Noon (1941). Similarly, some lawyers resist the charge that adversary advocates lie by arguing that truthfulness just *consists in* a person's causal contribution to true belief and that the adversary system defense therefore casts even lawyers who utter falsehoods as truthful. This position removes every element of truth-*telling* from truthfulness and so, like Rubashov's view, deprives the virtue it extols of any subjects who might possibly display it.

7. Herman, *supra* note 3, at 39.

8. *Id.* at 40 (emphasis in original).

9. *Id.*

10. I borrow the idea of impartiality as a limiting condition from Barbara Herman. *See id.* at 31, 39.

11. I borrow the metaphor of appellate review from Thomas Nagel, who proposes to "take the conflict between [first-personal] and [third-personal] back to

the [third-personal] standpoint on appeal." THOMAS NAGEL, THE VIEW FROM NOWHERE 202 (1986).

12. HERMAN, *supra* note 3, at 39.

Herman adds that morality's refusal to honor unconditional attachments is not necessarily unique—that "[u]nconditional attachments can be as much at odds with one's loves, one's other interests, even with the physical limitations on action, as they may be in conflict with the limits imposed by morality." *Id.* Herman regards this observation as providing further support for her claim that morality's authority to review first-personal ambitions does not undermine integrity, but I am not so sure. It seems more natural to me to reverse the inference and say that when a person abandons her attachments in the face of these other phenomena her integrity suffers, and that this illustrates the threat to integrity that morality also poses. Certainly this interpretation more naturally accords with the experience of abandoning an attachment in response to one of the forces Herman mentions—for example, abandoning a love in the face of an infatuation—an experience in which a person generally feels her integrity to have suffered a blow.

13. *Id.* at 38.

14. *Id.* at 40.

15. *Id.*

16. Support for the claims made in this footnote can be found at IMMANUEL KANT, GROUNDWORK OF THE METAPHYSIC OF MORALS (H.J. Paton trans., 1958) (1785) (especially ch. 3, *Passage from a Metaphysic of Morals to a Critique of Pure Practical Reason*) (arguing that making second-personal impartiality into a first-personal project is *required* for integrity); *id.* at 88 (including the quoted Formula of the Universal Law); *id.* at 35 (including the quoted Formula of the Kingdom of Ends); CHRISTINE M. KORSGAARD, THE SOURCES OF NORMATIVITY 131–66 (1996) (connecting autonomy to impartiality only by reference to additional ideas about the nature of Enlightenment practical identity and the public character of reflection and deliberation).

17. BERNARD WILLIAMS, *Persons, Character and Morality*, *in* MORAL LUCK 1, 13 (1981).

18. *Id.* at 12. This does not in any straightforward way entail that the frustration of a person's ground project requires him to see no reasonable alternative to suicide or even to contemplate suicide at all. For one thing, the decision to commit suicide, as much as any other decision, needs reasons to back it up. For another, as Williams says, "[o]ther things, or the mere hope of other things, may keep him going." *Id.* at 13.

19. For a point related to the one made in this footnote, see Thomas Nagel, *Universality and the Reflective Self*, *in* KORSGAARD, *supra* note 16, at 200, 206.

20. *See* CHRISTINE KORSGAARD, *The Reasons We Can Share: An Attack on the Distinction between Agent-Relative and Agent-Neutral Values*, *in* CREATING THE KINGDOM OF ENDS 275, 296 (1996) (giving no consideration to the question of Jim's possible pacifism).

21. *Id.* at 14.

22. *See* Bernard Williams, *Professional Morality and Its Dispositions*, *in* THE GOOD LAWYER: LAWYERS' ROLES AND LAWYERS' ETHICS 259, 267 (David Luban

ed., 1983). Here I should make clear that the argument in the main text does *not* stand for the proposition that impartial morality has no role to play in constructing a person's character. That quite absurd claim is obviously belied by ordinary moral experience, as for example by the experience of the person whose character is to be fair (or in some other way to conform, in certain circumstances, to the principles of impartial morality). The argument presents only the much less sweeping claim that impartial morality cannot be the exclusive or hegemonic source of a person's character.

23. *Id.*

24. *Id.*

25. The argument is also open to narrower objections, involving the details of its construction. For one thing, persons' ambitions are not generally arranged in such a way as to produce a neatly, or even only roughly, distinguishable ground project, but instead overlap so that no subset is necessary, and many subsets are sufficient, for producing meaning in their lives. And persons' engagements with morality are accordingly much more resilient in the face of impartialist interventions than Williams supposes. For another, the scope of our intuitive concern for integrity is not limited to cases that involve the psychological intensity conjured up by Jim's example and rendered concrete by the idea of betraying a ground project. Instead—as the case of the adversary advocate perhaps illustrates—integrity seems equally clearly at issue even in less dramatic and instantaneously intense conflicts between impartiality and first-personal ambitions. And the resistance against impartial morality that the argument must sustain is accordingly much broader than Williams's argument can deliver.

26. Samuel Scheffler has also sought to develop Williams's initial insight about integrity into a sustained practical argument against the hegemony of impartial morality, at least in its consequentialist, third-personal form, and in favor of what he calls an "agent-centered prerogative" which permits persons sometimes to act in ways that do not produce the third-person impartially best overall state of affairs. *See* SAMUEL SCHEFFLER, THE REJECTION OF CONSEQUENTIALISM 5 (rev. ed. 1994).

Scheffler's argument is more limited than mine in one obvious way: it takes aim only at third-personal impartiality rather than at hegemonic impartiality *tout court*, and indeed suggests that the second-personal approach to impartiality might solve the problem of integrity. *See id.* at 4–5.

Scheffler's approach differs from mine in another important way also. Although Scheffler seeks to connect his argument to "the way in which concerns and commitments are *naturally* generated from a person's point of view quite independently of the weight of those concerns in an impersonal [impartial] ranking of overall states of affairs," *id.* at 9 (emphasis in original), and although he seeks to develop a moral theory that takes adequate account of the "independence of the personal point of view," *id.* at 62, "as a fact about human agency," *id.* at 64, Scheffler makes no sustained effort to elaborate on this idea. Although Scheffler recognizes that moral theory must be sensitive to what it is "reasonable" to demand of human agents given how their concerns and commitments arise," *id.* at 125, and although he recognizes that the idea of reasonableness must in this connection refer to "the structure of a unified personality," *id.* at 18, he presents no substantive standard of what is, in this sense, reasonable.

Scheffler presents no articulate account of what I call the "architecture of the first person." Moreover, the intuitive view of the first person that lies behind Scheffler's arguments is inconsistent with the view that I elaborate. In particular, Scheffler claims that "[t]he promotion of the general good . . . can be undertaken from *within* one's personal standpoint," *id.* at 97 (emphasis in original), so that "if someone *wants* to bring about the best state of affairs, either out of a supererogatory willingness to sacrifice his own projects or because bringing about the best *is* his project, there is no reason from the standpoint of integrity to forbid that." *Id.* at 22 (emphasis in original). Scheffler takes the only alternative to this approach to be the view that "to have a [first-]personal point of view is to have a source for the generation and pursuit of personal commitments and concerns that is independent of the impersonal [impartial] perspective," *id.* at 57, a view that he expressly rejects. My argument concerning bounded practical rationality seeks to develop a third way, which insists that first-personal ambitions must be distinct form impartial morality but not that their source must be independent.

27. MICHAEL BRATMAN, INTENTION, PLANS, AND PRACTICAL REASON 28 (1987).

28. *Id.* at 10.

29. *Id.* at 16.

30. *Id.*

31. *Id.* at 70. Bratman distinguishes among several forms of inertia, which he calls nonreflective, deliberative, and policy-based nonreconsideration. *See id.* at 60–61. He argues for the rationality of nonreconsideration at id, 64ff.

32. *Id.* at 30.

33. *Id.* at 32.

34. This possibility is associated with the categories of nonreconsideration that Bratman calls nonreflective and policy-based. *See id.* at 60–61.

35. *Id.* at 65–66.

36. This distinction is not always appreciated in the philosophical literature, which has a tendency to lump together all cases in which a person fails to do what she judges best. A notable exception is Richard Holton, who distinguishes between *akrasia*, which he uses (unconventionally) to refer to the state of intending to do other than what one judges best and weakness of will, by which he means (again unconventionally) the state of too readily reconsidering (and abandoning) one's intentions in the face of inclinations that the intentions were designed to defeat. *See* Richard Holton, *How is Strength of Will Possible, in* WEAKNESS OF WILL AND PRACTICAL IRRATIONALITY 39 (S. Stroud and C. Tappolet eds., 2003).

37. *See id.* at 40–41. This account of will-power is not quite true to Holton's own views, because it treats will-power as both enabling intentions to track decisions about what is best and enabling endeavors to track intentions. Holton, by contrast, (following the distinction between *akrasia* and weakness of will reported *supra* note 36) limits will-power to the second function.

38. *See* Ray Fisman, Shachar Kariv, and Daniel Markovits, *Individual Preferences for Giving*, 97 AM. ECON. REV. 1858 (2007).

39. *See* Holton, *supra* note 36, at 56.

40. *See id.* at 56–57.

41. *See* Holton, *supra* note 36, at 49.

42. Support for the claims made in this footnote can be found in *id.* (claiming that will-power, like a muscle, can be trained to become stronger).

43. This possibility finds a natural point of attachment to Bratman's views in his discussion of short-circuiting the full costs of deliberation by blocking the application of a policy to a special case even without reconsidering the policy. Bratman observes that such blocking must overcome the deliberative costs that even it involves. *See* BRATMAN, *supra* note 27, at 89–91. One might add that it must also overcome the motivational costs associated with the redirection of inclination that blocking requires.

44. JED RUBENFELD, FREEDOM AND TIME 95–97 (2001).

45. *Id.* at 97. I am not quite using *commitment* as Rubenfeld does, because I am proposing that all intentions and endeavors possess motivational inertia and that commitments (or ambitions) merely possess greater inertia than usual. Rubenfeld, by contrast, treats commitments as qualitatively (and not just quantitatively) different from ordinary intentions, which, by implication, possess no motivational inertia (or at least nothing like the inertia possessed by commitments). This difference frees me from worrying, as Rubenfeld must, about what commitments add to mere intentions (Rubenfeld thinks that they add something like, but only like, a promise to oneself, *id.* at 101, 125) and whether commitments are in fact possible at all (as a person might always release himself from promises he has made to himself). On my approach, commitments (including in their inertial properties) are no more mysterious than ordinary intentions.

46. A similar point is made by Rubenfeld, when he suggests that our ambitions can be "normative for us only if they are and remain ours. We must have given them to ourselves, and they must remain recognizable as self-given, if they are to be normatively forceful at all." RUBENFELD, *supra* note 44, at 96–97.

47. Critics of approaches to integrity like mine tend to be particularly insensitive to the boundedness of our motivational capacities. Korsgaard, for example, suggests that once a person understands the similarities between herself and others, which she cannot help but do when others address moral claims to her, then she must take impartiality as her overriding reason. (Thus she suggests that simply "*[b]y making you think these thoughts [about our shared humanity]*, I force you to acknowledge the value of *my* humanity, and I obligate you to act in a way that respects it." KORSGAARD, *supra* note 16, at 143.

48. Alec Walen, building on some ideas from Korsgaard, has worried that my account of integrity cannot be right because first-personal ambitions are private in a way that renders them a philosophical nonsense. *See* Alec Walen, *Criticizing the Obligatory Acts of Lawyers: A Response to Markovits's Legal Ethics from the Lawyer's Point of View*, 16 YALE J.L. & HUMAN. 1 (2004).

Thus, Korsgaard insists that just as "the idea of a private language is inconsistent with the normativity of meaning," KORSGAARD, *supra* note 16, at 137, so also the idea of private (or agent-relative) reasons is inconsistent with the normativity of reasons, which are "public in their very essence," *id.* at 134–35, or, put a little differently, "inherently shareable." *Id.* at 135. Moreover, Korsgaard believes that this inherent shareability determines the *content* of reasons and in particular underwrites the hegemony of impartial morality in its second-personal reconstruction. She proposes that in order to value anything at all, that is to "acknowledge the existence of any practical reasons," a person "must value [her] humanity as an end in itself." *Id.* at 125. And she adds that "valuing humanity in your own person somehow implies, entails, or involves valuing it in that of others." *Id.* at 132. Walen approves of this reasoning and argues that it threatens, in one stroke, to cast the first-personal ambitions my argument elaborates as incoherent and to cast the public reasons presented by impartiality (on a second-personal account) as unconditional.

Korsgaard's argument may of course be resisted at many points. The incoherence of private meanings may be questioned, and Korsgaard acknowledges that the incoherence of private practical reasons is still less immediate or obvious than the incoherence of private language. *See id.* at 141–42. Moreover, even if private practical reason is incoherent, the connection that Korsgaard draws between the formal claim that reasons are inherently public and the substantive hegemony of impartial morality depends on a connection between valuing one's own humanity and being open to the humanity of others that is famously difficult to forge. Although it may be that when I take my humanity to give me reasons this commits me to recognizing that your humanity gives you reasons (roughly, because we each stand in analogous relations to our own humanity), it is hard to see how this commits *me* to taking *your* humanity as a reason (or *you* to taking *mine*). (This doubt is shared by Williams, who also worries how an analogy between two persons' relations to their own humanity can ever underwrite a relation between each and the other's humanity. *See* BERNARD WILLIAMS, ETHICS AND THE LIMITS OF PHILOSOPHY 54–64 (1985).) Indeed it seems, at some points, that Korsgaard is reduced to *insisting* that persons are a law to each other, and it is not clear how the publicity of reasons is meant to help here (after all, even the weaker analogy just drawn makes reasons public in some sense).

It is not necessary for me to take up these questions here, however. As the main text argues, my account of integrity resists the hegemony of impartialist morality without proposing any fundamentally private realm of reasons or indeed denying that all persons must value humanity in general in the sense that Korsgaard insists on.

49. Nagel addresses something very much like the possibility that a person's ambitions may generate reasons when he discusses what he calls "reasons of autonomy." *See* NAGEL, *supra* note 11, at 166ff. Here Nagel is contemplating the possibility that a person's adopting certain ambitions might give him reasons to succeed at these ambitions—Nagel imagines that a person's ambition to climb Mount Kilimanjaro might give him a reason to get to the top. *See id.* at 167. Furthermore, Nagel asks a question about such reasons that is very much like the question I am asking, namely "how far the authority of each individual runs in determining the objective value of the satisfaction of his own desires and preferences." *Id.* at 168.

Nagel's inquiry, however, is importantly different from mine. Nagel is concerned with the question whether a person's ambitions might create reasons for others—impartial reasons—to promote the success of these ambitions. (Nagel rejects this possibility, at least for ambitions other than those involved in seeking out or avoiding basic sensations such as pleasure or pain. "It seems," he says, "too much to allow an individual's desires to confer impersonal value on something outside himself . . . ." *Id.* at 169.) But I am concerned not with whether a person's ambitions might create impartial reasons but rather with whether they might create first-personal reasons (which are capable of resisting impartial morality). Furthermore, I am concerned with the way in which a person's ambitions may create first-personal reasons for her that are connected to her integrity as an agent, and not just to her own welfare as a patient. For this reason, my argument is different also from the suggestion, to which Nagel is sympathetic, *see id.* at 173, that a person might properly display a limited preference for her own interests over the interests of others, and that insofar as satisfying her ambitions promoted her interests, she might therefore display a special first-personal concern for her ambitions.

The reason for the difference between my approach and Nagel's harkens back, I believe, to my somewhat unusual construction of the idea of first-personal *morality*. The examples Nagel thinks of when he thinks of ambitions—including quintessentially the desire to climb Mount Kilimanjaro—are self-regarding in their substance as well as first-personal in their form. This leads Nagel, when he asks about the relationship between the first-personal reasons that ambitions give rise to and impartial morality, to treat these first-personal reasons as involving something like the pursuit of pleasure and hence to analogize to the question of a person's preference his own well-being over the well-being of others instead of to the question of a person's more intimate concern with his own actions (the actions whose author he is) than with the actions of others. My unusual construction of the idea of first-personal morality as involving reasons having to do with the treatment of others helps me to see the second possibility as well as the first.

CHAPTER 7

INTEGRATION THROUGH ROLE

1. Annesley v. Anglesea, 17 How. St. Trials 1139, 1248 (1743) (cited in DAVID LUBAN, LAWYERS AND JUSTICE 5 (1988)).

2. The idea that roles may be logically prior to the actions done within them comes from John Rawls's idea of practice rules, *see* John Rawls, *Two Concepts of Rules*, 64 PHIL. REV. 3 (1955), and John Searle's idea of constitutive rules, *see* JOHN R. SEARLE, SPEECH ACTS: AN ESSAY IN THE PHILOSOPHY OF LANGUAGE 33–42, 50–53 (1969); *see also* JOHN R. SEARLE, THE CONSTRUCTION OF SOCIAL REALITY (1995). For a subtle development of these ideas in the context of legal ethics (to which the account I present in the main text owes a substantial debt), see ARTHUR APPLBAUM, ETHICS FOR ADVERSARIES 76ff. (1999).

3. In fact, this argument depends on one further idea, namely that the lawyer's role does not internalize moral content that makes ordinary morality a part of the lawyer's role morality. I suspect that the lawyer's role has in fact incorporated some ordinary moral ideas into its role-morality, but that the two moral views nevertheless remain sufficiently distinct so that this does not undercut the role-based argument. For more on this question, see APPLBAUM, *supra* note 2, at 98–109.

Here it is worth pointing out that even though the *substance* of the lawyer's role-morality converges on the *substance* of ordinary morality, the lawyer's morality may remain distinctively a *role*-morality, because the *authority* of the lawyer's morality may continue to depend not on ordinary morality, but on the lawyer's role. Of course, instead of being merely recast (as this note imagines), the lawyer's role might be eliminated entirely, so that the lawyer's morality loses both its distinctive substance and its distinctive authority. I take up one important form of this last suggestion later on in the argument.

4. Arthur Applbaum states this attitude clearly when he says that "the redescriptive strategy seeks to pre-empt [moral] evaluation and bypass the hard work of moral argument." APPLBAUM, *supra* note 2, at 77–98.

5. F.H. BRADLEY, ETHICAL STUDIES 160–213 (2d ed. 1927). David Luban reports that Bradley borrowed the phrase from the Anglican catechism in DAVID LUBAN, LAWYERS AND JUSTICE 106 (1988).

6. *See, e.g.,* LUBAN, *supra* note 5, at 128.

7. Later on, it will be important that in some circumstances those who are interested in one description may care about how people with other descriptive interests respond to it. The sociologist, for example, cares whether the young lovers view the ring exclusively as a symbol of pure love or also as an indication of future earnings potential.

8. *See* BERNARD WILLIAMS, MORALITY: AN INTRODUCTION TO ETHICS 55 (1972).

9. *See, e.g.,* APPLBAUM, *supra* note 2, at 91–98.

10. Applbaum applies the argument specifically to the case of executioners in Arthur Applbaum, *Professional Detachment: The Executioner of Paris*, 109 HARV. L. REV. 458 (1995).

11. Support for the claims that made in this footnote may be found in ROBERT L. NELSON, PARTNERS WITH POWER: THE SOCIAL TRANSFORMATION OF THE LARGE LAW FIRM 256 (1988) (reporting that 75 percent of corporate lawyers surveyed claimed to have experienced no ethical dilemmas at work).

12. The fact that the actions in question are impartially best means that role-occupants can provide an impartial defense for their own allegiance to their roles, even if they cannot convince others to accept these roles for themselves.

13. Bernard Williams, *History, Morality, and the Test of Reflection, in* CHRISTINE M. KORSGAARD, THE SOURCES OF NORMATIVITY 210, 210–11 (1996).

14. STUART HAMPSHIRE, INNOCENCE AND EXPERIENCE 189 (1989).

15. Hampshire, with a nod to Heraclitus, proposes that "justice" is this steward, *id.*, a suggestion that (uncharacteristically for Hampshire) turns to a concept when what is plainly needed is a way of proceeding and a form of personality.

16. *See generally* RICHARD L. ABEL, AMERICAN LAWYERS 142–57 (1989).

CHAPTER 8
LAWYERLY FIDELITY AND POLITICAL LEGITIMACY

1. Support for the claims made in this footnote may be found in ABA STANDARDS FOR CRIMINAL JUSTICE Standard 3–5.7(b), 3–3.9, 3–3.11(a) & (c) (3d ed.

1993) (recognizing restrictions on partisanship in the narrow context of criminal prosecutions).

2. As Thomas Nagel has observed, persons may all be "motivated by an impartial regard for one another" but be "lead into conflict by that very motive if they disagree about what the good life consists in, hence what they should want impartially for everyone." THOMAS NAGEL, EQUALITY AND PARTIALITY 154 (1991).

3. And therefore about whether collective arrangements should serve the needs of this world or of the next.

4. Where faith is available to all.

5. John Rawls has famously called this the "fact of pluralism." See JOHN RAWLS, POLITICAL LIBERALISM 36, 64, 144 (1993).

6. The clearest contemporary statement of this position appears in ROBERT PAUL WOLFF, IN DEFENSE OF ANARCHISM (1970).

7. See RAWLS, POLITICAL LIBERALISM, supra note 5; see also RAWLS, A THEORY OF JUSTICE (1971).

8. RAWLS, POLITICAL LIBERALISM, supra note 5, at 217 (and on the back of the dust jacket).

9. Id. at 218.

10. Id. at 217 (and on the back of the dust jacket).

11. Support for the claims made in this footnote may be found in JOHN RAWLS, A THEORY OF JUSTICE, supra note 7, at 86, 120 (1971) (including the text quoted in the footnote).

12. My emphasis on the need for political philosophy to take into account disagreement not just about the first-order uses of political power that a theory of legitimacy seeks to justify but also about legitimacy itself (disagreement, in other words, at ever level of the theory) resembles Jeremy Waldron's emphasis on the importance of taking into account disagreement about justice. See JEREMY WALDRON, LAW AND DISAGREEMENT (1999).

13. This is a familiar and, I take it, uncontroversial point. See, e.g., Thomas Nagel, Moral Conflict and Political Legitimacy, 16 PHIL. & PUB. AFFAIRS 215, 218 (1987); Joseph Raz, Facing Diversity: The Case for Epistemic Abstinence, 19 PHIL. & PUB. AFFAIRS 3, 32 (1990). In order for political philosophy even to get off the ground as a rational and critical enterprise, it must answer to standards apart from persons' actual, brute beliefs.

14. This formulation of course tracks Rawls's account of reasonable moral pluralism. Rawls characterizes reasonable moral pluralism as "the inevitable long-run result of the powers of human reason at work within the background of enduring free institutions," RAWLS, POLITICAL LIBERALISM, supra note 5, at 4, and he therefore insists that it is "not an unfortunate condition of human life." Id. at 144.

By applying the same logic to reasonable pluralism about political legitimacy, I am turning the method of pluralist political philosophy in on itself. (The relation to Waldron's work, see supra note 12, is particularly close here.)

15. This characterization of the practical approach to political legitimacy may make it seem unfair of me to place Rawls—at least in his later work and in particular in Political Liberalism—in the theoretical camp. The idea that citizens who disagree about which policies are good or just may nevertheless unite around a set

of institutions and practices that command allegiance based on free-standing political considerations may seem to bear a close resemblance to Rawls's idea of an
overlapping political consensus among reasonable moral views. *See* RAWLS, PO-
LITICAL LIBERALISM, *supra* note 5, at 10 ("[P]olitical liberalism looks for a political conception of justice that can gain the support of an overlapping consensus of
reasonable religious, philosophical, and moral doctrines in a society regulated by
it."); *see also id.* at 15, 133–72. And Rawls, in essays leading up to *Political Liberalism*, does say that his conception of political legitimacy "is practical" and
"presents itself not as a conception of justice that is true, but one that can serve as
a basis for informed and willing political agreement." John Rawls, *Justice as Fairness: Political Not Metaphysical*, 14 PHIL. & PUB. AFFAIRS 223, 230 (1985).
  But in spite of these superficial similarities, the practical approach to legitimacy as I understand it departs dramatically from even the later Rawls's views.
First, it understands political disagreement to be both broader and deeper than
Rawls supposes, so that the overlapping consensus among reasonable moral
conceptions simply cannot be had. (This point is powerfully developed in Raz,
supra note 13, at 32.) And second, it proposes, against the backdrop of this
broad and deep disagreement, that politics must be practical in a much more
intensive sense than Rawls supposes. Even in his later work, Rawls retains his
conviction that legitimacy can be achieved by finding abstract principles upon
which all citizens can agree apart from any actual political engagements with
one another. Rawls's views remain theoretical in this sense—that they take philosophical theorizing about politics to be fundamental to political legitimacy.
The view that I am proposing is practical in the strong sense that it rejects the
centrality of philosophy. Political legitimacy depends, instead, on actual and affective participation in political life.
  16. Support for the claims made in this footnote may be found in RAYMOND
GEUSS, THE IDEA OF A CRITICAL THEORY: HABERMAS AND THE FRANKFURT
SCHOOL (1981) (regarding the practical approach to legitimacy that imposes
only the test of critical theory).
  17. As the declaration states:

  1. Everyone has the right to take part in the government of his
      country, directly or through freely chosen representatives.
  2. Everyone has the right of equal access to public service in
      his country.
  3. The will of the people shall be the basis of the authority
      of government; this will be expressed in periodic and gen-
      uine elections which shall be by universal and equal suf-
      frage and shall be held by secret vote or by equivalent
      free voting procedures.

Universal Declaration of Human Rights art. 21, G.A. Res. 217A, at 71, U.N.
GAOR, 3d Sess., 1st plen. mtg., U.N. Doc. A/810 (Dec. 12, 1948).
  18. This discussion reprises a longer argument that appears in Daniel Markovits, *Democratic Disobedience*, 114 YALE L.J. 1897, 1905–21 (2005).
  19. RAWLS, A THEORY OF JUSTICE, *supra* note 7, at 231. Rawls's views were
of course more subtle than this simple remark reveals. He acknowledged, for

example, that the difference principle applies in this area to justify inequalities that benefit the worst off, so that political inequality is justified as long as it is "to the benefit of those with the lesser liberty." *Id*. at 232

20. RONALD DWORKIN, SOVEREIGN VIRTUE: THE THEORY AND PRACTICE OF EQUALITY 184 (2000).

21. These procedural accounts of democracy face conceptual difficulties concerning both the idea that democracy is about the distribution of political *power* and the idea that democracy renders this distribution *equal*. With respect to power, Dworkin distinguishes between impact and influence—roughly, between the difference a person can make "just on his own, by voting for or choosing one decision rather than another," and the difference he can make "not just on his own but also by leading or inducing others to believe or vote or choose as he does." *Id*. at 191. With respect to equality, he distinguishes between horizontal and vertical dimensions—which compare "the power of different private citizens or groups of citizens" and "the power of private citizens with individual officials." *Id*.

Dworkin observes that a democratic theory of equal power must insist on a vertical as well as a horizontal component, because authoritarian states that completely disempower ordinary citizens satisfy horizontal equality of power but clearly are not democratic. *See id*. Next, he observes that vertical equality of power must be understood in terms of influence rather than impact, because vertical equality of impact cannot possibly obtain in states that distinguish between public officials and private citizens, even though many such states obviously are democratic. *Id*. at 192. And finally, he observes that equality of influence is itself a dubious ideal, because it can be achieved only by suppressing forms of political engagement—for example, persuasive speech on matters of political principle—that are manifestly valuable, and indeed essential, to both liberal equality and democratic politics. *Id*. at 194–98. Together, these observations deny that democracy can combine conceptions of equality and power in an appealing way, and they therefore undermine the suggestion that democracy involves equal political power.

22. *Id*. at 186. Dworkin calls the formal conception of democracy "detached" and the substantive conception that he adopts "dependent." *Id*.

23. *Id*. at 204.

24. *Id*. Dworkin reveals how narrow this class is when he observes that "[t]hough it might seem odd," he believes that it is "sensible" even "to speak of a decision . . . to give aid to the [Nicaraguan] Contras as either accurate or inaccurate," so that his liberal conception of democracy requires that this decision be made accurately, regardless of citizens' actual preferences or the outcomes of a majoritarian process. *Id*. at 204. As an example of a choice-sensitive issue, Dworkin imagines the decision "whether to use available public funds to build a new sports center or a new road system," although even here he suggests that choice-insensitive issues like distributive justice may "merge in that decision." *Id* at 204.

25. Support for the claims made in this footnote may be found in RAWLS, A THEORY OF JUSTICE, *supra* note 7, at 62 (discussing substantive requirements restricting the democratic process).

26. *Id.* at 355. Here it is worth noting that the later Rawls may well have been more of a democrat, insofar as he came to emphasize the need for free-standing political ideals and institutions capable of adjudicating reasonable disagreement among competing comprehensive moral doctrines. *See generally* RAWLS, POLITICAL LIBERALISM, *supra* note 5.

27. ALEXANDER BICKEL, THE MORALITY OF CONSENT 15 (1975). Bickel was commenting approvingly on Edmund Burke, who famously championed the right of elected representatives to vote their consciences and connected this practice to the authority of representative government. *See* EDMUND BURKE, *Speech on Fox's India Bill* (Dec. 1, 1783), *in* 5 THE WRITINGS AND SPEECHES OF EDMUND BURKE: INDIA: MADRAS AND BENGAL, 1774–85, at 378 (Paul Langford et al. eds., 1981).

28. *See e.g.*, Robert Post, *Equality and Autonomy in First Amendment Jurisprudence*, 95 MICH. L. REV. 1517, 1538 (1997) (book review) ("Approaches that attempt to maximize other kinds of equality of ideas or of persons are either implausible or inconsistent with the principle of collective self-governance [that is, democracy].").

29. I borrow use of *authorship* in this connection from Robert Post. *See* Robert Post, *Democracy and Equality*, 1 LAW CULTURE & HUMAN. 142, 144 (2005) ("Self-government is about the authorship of decisions, not about the making of decisions."); *see also* Robert C. Post, *Between Democracy and Community: The Legal Constitution of Social Form*, *in* NOMOS XXXV: DEMOCRATIC COMMUNITY 163, 170 (John W. Chapman & Ian Shapiro eds., 1993) (arguing that democracy makes collective self-government possible by "social processes anterior to majoritarian decision making that somehow connect the democratic system as a whole to the autonomous will of the entire citizenry"). In both essays, Post is following Hans Kelsen, who observed that "[a] subject is politically free insofar as his individual will is in harmony with the 'collective' (or 'general') will expressed in the social order. Such harmony of the 'collective' and the individual will is guaranteed only if the social order is created by the individuals whose behavior it regulates." HANS KELSEN, GENERAL THEORY OF LAW AND STATE 285 (Anders Wedberg trans., 1945). The idea of authorship also appears in Habermas, who observes that "legal person can be autonomous only insofar as they can understand themselves, in the exercise of their civic rights, as authors of just those rights which they are supposed to obey as addressees." Jürgen Habermas, *On the Internal Relation Between the Rule of Law and Democracy*, 3 EUR. J. PHIL. 12, 15 (1995).

30. JEAN-JACQUES ROUSSEAU, ON THE SOCIAL CONTRACT 53 (Roger D. Masters ed. & Judith R. Masters trans., St. Martin's Press 1978) (1762).

31. *Id.* at 110.

32. *Id.* at 111.

33. Friendships and family relations constitute the most familiar forms of nonpolitical communal engagement. And other forms also exist, including forms that do not require the intimacy that friendships and families necessary involve. I cast promise and contract as examples of communal engagement even among strangers in Daniel Markovits, *Contract and Collaboration*, 113 YALE L.J. 1417 (2004).

34. I owe this way of putting the point to Bernard Williams.

35. WALDRON, *supra* note 12, at 102.

36. This is the theme that unifies the several approaches to deliberative democracy. *See, e.g.*, BENJAMIN BARBER, STRONG DEMOCRACY: PARTICIPATORY POLITICS FOR A NEW AGE (1984); 1–2 JÜRGEN HABERMAS, THE THEORY OF COMMUNICATIVE ACTION (Thomas McCarthy trans., 1984).

37. The best historical account of the role of political parties in sustaining democratic legitimacy appears in RICHARD HOFSTADTER, THE IDEA OF A PARTY SYSTEM: THE RISE OF LEGITIMATE OPPOSITION IN THE UNITED STATES, 1780–1840 (1969). An underappreciated early account is MARTIN VAN BUREN, INQUIRY INTO THE ORIGIN AND COURSE OF POLITICAL PARTIES IN THE UNITED STATES (Smith T. Van Buren et al. eds., 1867).

38. These suggestions appear in ROUSSEAU, *supra* note 30.

39. K.N. LLEWELLYN & E. ADAMSON HOEBEL, THE CHEYENNE WAY: CONFLICT AND CASE LAW IN PRIMITIVE JURISPRUDENCE 293 (1941).

40. Support for the claims made in this footnote may be found in W. Bradley Wendel, *Professionalism as Interpretation*, 99 Nw. U. L. REV. 1167, 1168–69 (2005) (including the quoted text). *See also* W. Bradley Wendel, *Civil Obedience*, 104 COLUM. L. REV. 363, 385 (2004). The quotation from Robert Gordon is found in Robert W. Gordon, *Why Lawyers Can't Just Be Hired Guns*, *in* ETHICS IN PRACTICE: LAWYERS' ROLES, RESPONSIBILITIES, AND REGULATION 42, 48 (Deborah L. Rhode ed., 2000). For one study of mechanisms for settling disputes in close-knit communities, see ROBERT C. ELLICKSON, ORDER WITHOUT LAW: HOW NEIGHBORS SETTLE DISPUTES (1991). Especially important is the discussion in *id*. at 64 (including the quoted language regarding "bad apples" and "odd ducks").

41. WILLIAM H. SIMON, THE PRACTICE OF JUSTICE: A THEORY OF LAWYERS' ETHICS 138 (1998).

42. Robert W. Gordon, *The Radical Conservatism of the Practice of Justice*, 51 STAN. L. REV. 919, 922 (1999) (reviewing SIMON, *supra* note 41).

43. *Id.*

44. Support for the claims made in this footnote may be found in Drew A. Swank, *The National Child Non-Support Epidemic*, 2003 MICH. ST. L. REV. 357, 358–59 (2003) (discussing the collection of child support from absentee fathers); Ronald K. Henry, *Child Support at a Crossroads: When the Real World Intrudes Upon Academics and Advocates*, 33 FAM. L.Q. 235, 237 (1999) (suggesting that there is reason to believe that delinquency is caused by inability rather than unwillingness to make payments).

45. David Trubek, *The Handmaiden's Revenge: On Reading and Using the Newer Sociology of Civil Procedure*, 51 LAW & CONTEMP. PROBS. 111, 115 (1988). "Transparent procedure," as Trubek says, takes the litigants as they come to the court." *Id*. at 115. It "does not add or subject anything" to their dispute, so that it "should not make a difference to the [right] outcome of a dispute." *Id*. at 114.

46. *See* William L.F. Felstiner, Richard L. Abel & Austin Sarat, *The Emergence and Transformation of Disputes: Naming, Blaming, and Claiming*, 15 LAW & SOC'Y REV. 631, 640 (1980–81).

47. Lynn Mather & Marbara Yngvesson, *Language, Audience, and the Transformation of Disputes*, 15 LAW & SOC'Y REV. 775, 791 (1980–81).

48. RONEN SHAMIR, MANAGING LEGAL UNCERTAINTY: ELITE LAWYERS IN THE NEW DEAL 38 (1995).

49. Maureen Cain, *The General Practice Lawyer and the Client: Towards a Radical Conception*, 7 INT'L J. SOC. LAW 331, 343 (1979).

50. Mather & Yngvesson, *supra* note 47, at 792.

51. Stewart Macaulay, *Lawyers and Consumer Protection Laws*, 14 LAW & SOC'Y REV. 115, 125 (1979).

52. Felstiner, Abel & Sarat, *supra* note 46, at 646.

53. Jeffrey Fitzgerald & Richard Dickins, *Disputing in Legal and Nonlegal Contexts: Some Questions for Sociologists of Law*, 15 LAW & SOC'Y REV. 681, 698 (1980–81).

54. This effect emphasizes "the impact on the client of the lawyer's *attitude*, his expression or implied approval of this as so legitimate that a lawyer is willing to help him get it, whereas other elements of the client's goals are disapproved and help in getting them is refused." Talcott Parsons, *The Law and Social Control, in* LAW AND SOCIOLOGY: EXPLORATORY ESSAYS 56, 70 (William M. Evan ed., 1962).

55. Support for the claims made in this footnote may be found in Felstiner, Abel & Sarat, *supra* note 46, at 641 (including the quotation regarding the narrowing of disputes); Terence Halliday, *Politics and Civic Professionalism: Legal Elites and Cause Lawyers*, 24 LAW & SOC. INQUIRY 1014, 1034–35 (1999) (reviewing SHAMIR, *supra* note 48 and CAUSE LAWYERING: POLITICAL COMMITMENTS AND PROFESSIONAL RESPONSIBILITIES (Austin Sarat & Stuart Scheingold eds., 1998)) (including the quotation regarding the transformation of a putatively moral issue into a technical-legal issue); Lynn Mather, *Ethnography and the Study of Trial Courts, in* PUBLIC LAW AND PUBLIC POLICY 52, 182–83 (J.A. Gardiner ed., 1977) (including the quotation regarding highly personal and idiosyncratic perceptions).

56. *See* Lon L. Fuller, *The Forms and Limits of Adjudication*, 92 HARV. L. REV. 353, 368 (1978). Fuller imagines a baseball player who transforms his brute claim to play catcher into a claim of right based on his being the best catcher available and therefore implicitly acknowledges that he must abandon his claim in case a more skilled catcher appears.

57. Macaulay, *supra* note 51, at 128.

58. Lon L. Fuller, *Mediation: Its Forms and Functions*, 44 S. CAL. L. REV. 305, 325 (1971). Fuller wrote these words as part of a discussion of mediation, which he sought in certain respects to contrast with adjudication, *see id.* at 328, so that my appropriation of Fuller's characterization stands in some tension with his official position on adjudication. I quote Fuller nevertheless because I believe that my account is generally in sympathy with Fuller's broader emphasis on the legitimating character of adjudication. *See, e.g.*, Fuller, *supra* note 56.

59. Felstiner, Abel & Sarat, *supra* note 46, at 650 (emphasis added).

60. Support for the claims made in this footnote may be found in Tom R. Tyler, *The Psychology of Disputant Concerns in Mediation*, 3 NEGOTIATION J., Oct. 1987; TOM R. TYLER, WHY PEOPLE OBEY THE LAW 105 (1990) (suggesting

that the importance of process for legitimacy increases when the stakes are high).

61. TYLER, *supra* note 60, at 103.

62. *Id.* at 102.

63. *Id.* at 126.

64. *Id.* at 149.

65. *Id.* at 149.

66. ALEXIS DE TOCQUEVILLE, DEMOCRACY IN AMERICA 357 (F. Bowen ed., 1876)

67. Abraham Blumberg, *The Practice of Law as a Confidence Game: Organizational Cooptation of a Profession*, 1 LAW & SOC'Y REV. 15, 28 (1967).

68. Macaulay, *supra* note 51, at 159.

69. *Id.* at 124.

70. *See* Felstiner, Abel & Sarat, *supra* note 46, at 644, *citing* James Weinstein, *Big Business and the Origin of Workman's Compensation*, 8 LAB. HIST. 1560 (1967).

71. Trubek, *supra* note 45, at 122.

72. Felstiner, Abel & Sarat, *supra* note 46, at 650.

73. Trubek, *supra* note 45, at 125.

74. An excellent and fair-minded study is R. Moorhead, A. Sherr, and A. Paterson, *What Clients Know: Client Perspectives on Legal Competence*, INTERNATIONAL JOURNAL OF THE LEGAL PROFESSION, vol. 10, no. 1, pp. 5–35 (2003).

75. Support for the claims made in this footnote may be found in ROBERT BOLT, A MAN FOR ALL SEASONS 39 (1961) (including the first quotation); *id.* at 74 (including the second quotation).

76. See TYLER, *supra* note 60, at 155.

77. RICHARD L. ABEL, AMERICAN LAWYERS 34–35 (1989).

78. *Id.*

79. Robert Gordon, *"The Ideal and the Actual in the Law": Fantasies and Practices of New York City Lawyers, 1870–1910, in* THE NEW HIGH PRIESTS: LAWYERS IN POST–CIVIL WAR AMERICA 51, 53–54 (Gerald W. Gewalt ed., 1984).

80. Support for the claims made in this footnote can be found in MIRJAN DAMASKA, THE FACES OF JUSTICE AND STATE AUTHORITY: A COMPARATIVE APPROACH TO THE LEGAL PROCESS 143 (1986) ("The invocation of counsel as officer of the court is designed to constrain the excessive amalgamation of the lawyer's interest with that of his client and to forestall the transformation of privately managed litigation into a melee of self-seeking."); MODEL RULES OF PROF'L CONDUCT R. 1.7 cmts. 29–31, R. 2.4 (2003) (governing lawyers who function as intermediaries or third party neutrals); ABA ETHICS 2000 COMMISSION, RULE 2.2 REPORTER'S EXPLANATION MEMO (2002) (including the quoted language explaining the deletion of Model Rule 2.2).

81. Parsons, *supra* note 54, at 63.

82. Tyler, *supra* note 60. See also J. Casper, *The Criminal Courts: The Defendant's Perceptive*, NATIONAL INSTITUTE OF LAW ENFORCEMENT AND CRIMINAL JUSTICE (Washington, D.C.: 1970); Casper, J., Tyler, T., and Fisher, B., Procedural Justice in Felony Cases, Working Paper 87–03, American Bar Foundation, Chicago, Ill. (1987).

83. *Id.*

84. Gordon, *supra* note 79, at 53–54.

85. *Id.*

86. Support for the claims made in this footnote may be found in Ronald Gilson & Robert Mnookin, *Disputing Through Agents: Cooperation and Conflict Between Lawyers in Litigation*, 94 Colum. L. Rev. 509 (1994) (claiming that lawyers, as repeat participants in the legal process, can establish reputations for cooperation that improve the efficiency of outcomes); *id.* at 551 (including the quotation observing that "client-centered advocacy presents a serious problem for the lawyer seeking to establish or to maintain a reputation for cooperation").

87. Richard Abel, *A Comparative Theory of Dispute Institutions in Society*, 8 Law & Soc'y Rev. 217, 265 (1973).

88. *Id.*

89. *Id.*

90. Parsons, *supra* note 54, at 67. These ideas are also emphasized in the client-counseling literature. *See, e.g.*, David A. Binder et al., Lawyers as Counselors (1991); Anthony G. Amsterdam, 1 Trial Manual 5 for the Defense of Criminal Cases 106–10 (1988).

91. The capacity to understand and abide by fair terms of social cooperation is, as Rawls says, one of the basic powers of human moral personality. *See, e.g.*, Rawls, Political Liberalism, *supra* note 5, at 19.

92. *See* Dan M. Kahan, *The Logic of Reciprocity: Trust, Collective Action, and Law*, 102 Mich. L. Rev. 71 (2003); *see also* Ernst Fehr & Simon Gächter, *Fairness and Retaliation: The Economics of Reciprocity*, 14 J. Econ. Persp. 159 (2000).

93. This is perhaps most evident in the criminal context, where "[i]n the eyes of many defendants, their attorney is the most despicable member of the cast of characters who have conspired to deprive them of their liberty; of all the figures in the courtroom, only defense counsel *pretends* to be on their side." Charles Silver, *Truth, Justice, and the American Way*, 47 Vand. L. Rev. 339, 364 (1994).

94. Jeffrey Fitzgerald & Richard Dickins, *Disputing in Legal and Nonlegal Contexts: Some Questions for Sociologists of Law*, 15 Law & Soc'y Rev. 681, 698 (1980–81).

95. The quotation in this footnote is taken from Monroe H. Freedman, Lawyers' Ethics in an Adversary System 2 (1975).

96. For an illustration of this development using the example of the American tort system, see, Samuel Issacharoff and John Fabian Witt, *The Inevitability of Aggregate Settlement: An Institutional Account of American Tort Law*, 57 Vanderbilt L.J. 1571 (2004).

97. For a recent survey of some of the issues, see the essays collected in *Symposium: The Civil Trial and its Alternatives*, 57 Stanford L. Rev. 1255–676 (2005).

98. Felstiner, Abel, and Sarat, *supra* note 46, at 651.

99. *See* Macaulay, *supra* note 51, at 153.

100. Fuller, *supra* note 56, at 364 (emphasis added).

101. *Id.*

102. Stuart Scheingold, *Taking Weber Seriously: Lawyers, Politics, and the Liberal State*, 24 LAW & SOC. INQUIRY 1061, 1063 (1999).

103. Support for the claims in this footnote may be found in Susan Sturm, *Second Generation Employment Discrimination: A Structural Approach*, 101 COLUM. L. REV. 458 (2001) (regarding the claim that the law of sexual harassment actively encourages employers to internalize its substantive norms).

104. Specifically, the law approaches sexual harassment through a framework established by Title VII of the Civil Rights Act of 1964, 42 U.S.C. § 2000e-2(a) (2000), which says "It shall be an unlawful employment practice for an employer to . . . fail or refuse to hire or to discharge any individual, or otherwise to discriminate against any individual with respect to his compensation, terms, conditions, or privileges of employment, because of such individual's race, color, religion, sex, or national origin; or . . . to limit, segregate, or classify his employees or applicants for employment in any way which would deprive or tend to deprive any individual employee of employment opportunities or otherwise adversely affect his status as an employee because of such individual's race, color, religion, sex, or national origin."

105. *See* Burlington Indus., Inc. v. Ellerth, 524 U.S. 742, 752 (1998); Meritor Sav. Bank v. Vinson, 477 U.S. 57, 65 (1986).

106. Vicki Schultz, *Reconceptualizing Sexual Harassment*, 107 YALE L.J. 1683, 1686 (1988); *see also* Kathryn Abrams, *The New Jurisprudence of Sexual Harassment*, 83 CORNELL L. REV. 1169 (1998).

107. Schultz, *supra* note 106, at 1712.

108. The Supreme Court first acknowledged this branch of sexual harassment in *Meritor Savings Bank v. Vinson*, 477 U.S. at 65.

109. Some early cases took this view. *See, e.g.*, Tomkins v. Public Serv. Elec. & Gas Co., 422 F. Supp. 553 (D.N.J. 1976). The cases are discussed in Schultz, *supra* note 107, at 1701–5.

110. *See* Title VII of the Civil Rights Act of 1964, 42 U.S.C. § 2000e (2000) (discussed in Schultz, *supra* note 106)

111. For an early example of this form of argument, which emphasizes that quid pro quo sexual harassment is just a special case of an already familiar antidiscrimination claim, see *Barnes v. Costle*, 561 F.2d 983, 987 (D.C. Cir. 1977). For a statement of this principle by the Supreme Court, see *Oncale v. Sundowner Offshore Servs.*, Inc. 523 U.S. 75 (1998).

112. Abrams, *supra* note 106, at 1219.

113. Schultz, *supra* note 106, at 1687.

114. *See, e.g.*, Price Waterhouse v. Hopkins, 490 U.S. 228, 250–51 (1989).

115. *See, e.g.*, Oncale v. Sundowner Offshore Servs., Inc. 523 U.S. 75 (1998); *see also* Doe v. City of Belleville, 119 F.3d 563 (7th Cir. 1997), *vacated*, 523 U.S. 1001 (1998) (mem.) (remanded for reconsideration in light of *Oncale*).

116. Here I follow Noah Zatz, who proposes that "[i]f employers insist that employees conform to [sex-based] stereotypes regarding interactions with other [sex] groups, employment practices enforcing those stereotypes constitute actionable discrimination because of race or sex." Noah D. Zatz, *Beyond the Zero-Sum Game: Toward Title VII Protection for Intergroup Solidarity*, 77 IND. L.J. 63, 108 (2002). Reprisals against employees who support harassed coworkers

are unlawful, under this approach, "as simply a special case of the prohibition on . . . gender stereotyping." *Id.* at 69.

117. The final expansion of sexual harassment law just mentioned—the aim to treat reprisals against those who stand up for the victims of harassment as harassment in their own right—may be approaching the limits of the doctrine. Certainly courts have not yet embraced this expansion of sexual harassment law. In a typical case, a court granted a motion to dismiss the Title VII claims of white male police officers who suffered reprisals after complaining about the harassment of their black and female colleagues on the ground that the practices these officers complained of were "biased in their favor." Childress v. City of Richmond, 907 F. Supp. 934, 939 (E.D. Va. 1995), *summary judgment granted*, 919 F. Supp. 216 (E.D. Va. 1996), *vacated*, 120 F.3d 476 (4th Cir. 1997), *aff'd en banc*, 134 F.3d 1205 (4th Cir. 1998) (per curiam), *cert. denied*, 524 U.S. 927. The black female officers were permitted to proceed with their own claims of harassment.

118. The case discussed in this footnote is reported in Cole v. Lehman, No. 85CV2187 (Adams County Colo. Dist. Ct. filed 1985), *dismissed per stipulation*, No. 87-CA0943 (Colo. Ct. App. Dec. 15, 1988). For a more complete account of the dispute, which emphasizes the failure of the legal process's transformative ambitions, see Penelope Canan, Gloria Satterfield, Laurie Larson & Martin Kretzmann, *Political Claims, Legal Derailment, and the Context of Disputes*, 24 LAW & SOC'Y REV. 923, 936–39 (1990).

119. Mather & Yngvesson, *supra* note 47, at 784.

120. *Id.* at 783.

121. The final quotations come from Felstiner, Abel & Sarat, *supra* note 46, at 648. Felstiner, Abel, and Sarat take a much less salutary view of this development than I do, observing that it does less to serve collective safety than to serve the lawyers who might get paid out of damage awards. *Id.* My present argument, however, does not require me to take any view of the effectiveness of tort damages as deterrents against dangerous conduct. True to my announced ambitions, I am considering not the justice or efficiency of tort law but, what is very different, its practical legitimacy.

122. Parsons, *supra* note 54, at 58.

123. *Id.*

124. *Id.*

125. Lon L. Fuller & John D. Randall, *Professional Responsibility: Report of the Joint Conference*, 44 A.B.A.J. 1159, 1161 (1958) (excerpted in Fuller, *supra* note 56, at 384).

CHAPTER 9
TRAGIC VILLAINS

1. The most sophisticated and authoritative statement of this position is ANTHONY T. KRONMAN, THE LOST LAWYER: FAILING IDEALS OF THE LEGAL PROFESSION (1993). A more typical statement, in the form of a professional lament by an old lion of the bar, is SOL M. LINOWITZ, THE BETRAYED PROFESSION (1994).

The hinge of this swing toward adversariness is sometimes said to have been the Civil War. Thus one commentator suggests that before the Civil War, lawyers' "professional loyalties were more to [political] parties and their principles than to clients and their interests," but that after, the bar was "left tethered to nothing more substantial than the fluctuating desires of its clientele." Mark DeWolfe Howe, Book Review, 60 HARV. L. REV. 838, 839, 840 (1947) (reviewing 1 ROBERT T. SWAINE, THE CRAVATH FIRM AND ITS PREDECESSORS, 1819–1947 (1946)).

2. For example, while it is often reported that Abraham Lincoln flatly refused to defend clients he believed were guilty, *see, e.g.*, Andrew L. Reisman, *An Essay on the Dilemma of "Honest Abe": The Modern Day Professional Responsibility of Abraham Lincoln's Representations of Clients He Believed to Be Culpable*, 72 NEB. L. REV. 1205 (1993), the more aggressively adversary actions of famous nineteenth-century lawyers, such as David Dudley Field's representation of his railroad clients, are less noticed today. Field's case is especially noteworthy because he publicly rejected the adversarial ethic yet proceeded to betray his public position in railroad litigation. *See* James M. Altman, *Modern Litigators and Lawyer-Statesmen*, 103 YALE L.J. 1031, 1055 (1994) (reviewing ANTHONY T. KRONMAN, THE LOST LAWYER (1993)) ("Field's own scurrilous conduct as an attorney in the 1868 Erie Railroad dispute underscores the hazard of relying on the words of ethical commentators to determine how litigators actually practiced."). A general historical argument that nineteenth-century litigators especially displayed substantial partisanship appears in Norman Spaulding, *The Myth of Civic Republicanism: Interrogating the Ideology of Antebellum Legal Ethics*, 71 FORDHAM L. REV. 1397 (2003).

3. DAVID HOFFMAN, *Resolutions in Regard to Professional Deportment, in* 2 A COURSE OF LEGAL STUDY 752, Resolution XIV, at 755 (photo. reprint 1972) (2d ed., Baltimore, Joseph Neal 1836).

4. GEORGE SHARSWOOD, AN ESSAY ON PROFESSIONAL ETHICS 110 (photo. reprint 1993) (5th ed., Philadelphia, T. & J.W. Johnson 1896).

5. *Id.* at 107.

6. *Id.* at 74–75.

7. Sharswood's treatise, which came a little later than Hoffman's, was already less committed to the specifics of a justice-centered approach to lawyering. Sharswood concluded, for example, that a lawyer is not responsible for acts of his client "in maintaining an unjust cause," *id.* at 83, and insisted that a lawyer may neither reveal to the court facts damning to his client's case, nor withdraw if the case is in adjudication, *id.* at 84–85. Indeed, Sharswood originated the language of "[e]ntire devotion of the interests of the client [and] warm zeal in the maintenance and defense of his rights" that survives in the codes of ethics even today. *Id.* at 78–79.

8. HOFFMAN, *supra* note 3, Resolution V, at 752.

9. *Id.* Resolution XXXII, at 764.

10. *Id.* Resolution XLII, at 770.

11. *Id.* Resolution XII, at 754. Hoffman added that "I shall claim to be the sole judge (the pleas not being compulsory) of the occasions for their proper use." *Id.* Resolution XIII, at 755.

12. *Id.* Resolution XIII, at 754.

13. Rush v. Cavenaugh, 2 Pa. 187, 189 (1895). It has recently been argued that Chief Justice Gibson's opinion in *Rush* departed from views of Hoffman and Sharswood in that *Rush* insisted that lawyers display fidelity to the court, as a matter of professional conscience, whereas Hoffman and Sharswood emphasized personal conscience instead. *See* Fred Zacharias and Bruce Green, *Reconceptualizing Advocacy Ethics*, 74 GEO. WASH. L. REV. 1 (2005).

I accept this distinction and its historical attribution to Gibson's opinion in *Rush* but doubt that it makes a difference to the larger argument that I am developing here. First, the historical reception of *Rush* (including by both Hoffman and Sharswood) seems not to have adopted its distinction between professional and personal conscience, so that nineteenth-century legal ethics more generally retained a commitment to the separate restrictions on partisanship associated with deference to personal conscience. And second, although, as Zacharias and Green point out, the idea of professional conscience has established a footprint in contemporary legal ethics, the trend over much of the long twentieth century was toward an increasingly partisan conception of advocacy even in this respect (with only a very recent and modest reversal).

Finally note that although the idea of professional conscience has some purchase on legal ethics, for example with respect to the lawyer's duties of candor toward tribunals before which she appears, it cannot, as a matter of philosophical principle, generally resolve the ethical complexity of the lawyer's professional circumstances. In particular, it glosses over the disagreements about the proper *application* of law that give rise to the problem of the legitimacy of adjudication. I take up this point in somewhat greater detail, although still only briefly, in chapter 8, in the discussion of W. Bradley Wendel's philosophical reconstruction of professional conscience.

14. Robert W. Gordon, *The Legal Profession*, *in* LOOKING BACK AT LAW'S CENTURY 287, 301 (Austin Sarat et al. eds., 2002) [hereinafter Robert Gordon, *The Legal Profession*.]

15. Robert Gordon, *Law as a Vocation*, *in* THE PATH OF THE LAW AND ITS INFLUENCE: THE LEGACY OF OLIVER WENDELL HOLMES, JR., 7–32, 9 (Steven J. Burton ed., 2000).

16. *See* Allison Marston, *Guiding the Profession: The 1887 Code of Ethics of the Alabama State Bar Association*, 49 ALA. L. REV. 471, 471 (1998) (identifying the 1887 Alabama code as the "first code of ethics for lawyers officially adopted in the United States").

17. Gordon, *The Legal Profession*, *supra* note 14, at 301.

18. Support for the claims made in this footnote may be found in CHARLES W. WOLFRAM, MODERN LEGAL ETHICS § 10.2.2, at 571–72 (student ed. 1986) (regarding English retention of the cab-rank rule).

19. *Id.* at 315.

20. *Id.* at 294.

21. *Id.*

22. *Id.* at 303–4.

23. *Id.*

24. This example is reported in Robert Gordon in *Is Law Still a Profession? Was it Ever One? And Does it Matter?* (inaugural lecture as Chancellor Kent

Professor of Law and Legal History). For a more complete discussion, see
CHRISTOPHER L. TOMLINS, LAW, LABOR AND IDEOLOGY IN THE EARLY AMERI-
CAN REPUBLIC (1993).

25. This case is reported in Robert Gordon in *Is Law Still a Profession? Was
it Ever One? And Does it Matter?* (inaugural lecture as Chancellor Kent Professor of Law and Legal History). For more complete discussions, see J. ANTHONY
LUKAS, BIG TROUBLE 311 (1997); and CLARENCE DARROW, THE STORY OF MY
LIFE 62 (1932).

26. Gordon, *The Legal Profession, supra* note 14, at 315.

27. LAWRENCE M. FRIEDMAN, A HISTORY OF AMERICAN LAW 641 (2d ed.
1985).

28. *Id.* at 641.

29. Gordon, *The Legal Profession, supra* note 14, at 312. Unsurprisingly, the
new divisions did not split the bar into even parts. Rather, "the most successful
lawyers were drawn into the orbit of powerful corporate clients like railroads
and financial institutions." *Id.* at 311.

30. Samuel Untermeyer, *What Every Present-Day Lawyer Should Know*, 167
ANNALS AM. ACAD. POL. & SOC. SCI. 173, 173 (1933) (quoted in Wayne K.
Hobson, *Symbol of the New Profession: Emergence of the Large Law Firm,
1870–1915, in* THE NEW HIGH PRIESTS: LAWYERS IN POST–CIVIL WAR AMERICA
3, 21 (Gerald W. Gawalt ed., 1984)).

31. John P. Heinz & Edward O. Laumann, *Chicago Lawyers: The Social
Structure of the Bar, in* LAWYERS: A CRITICAL READER 27, 31 (Richard L. Abel
ed., 1997).

32. *Id.*

33. According to a 1975 survey of the Chicago bar, only one in seven lawyers
spent 25 percent of their time in both hemispheres. Heinz & Laumann, *supra*
note 31, at 31. And an update of this research using a 1995 survey confirms the
basic story. For example, of lawyers in litigation, real estate, and tax, "about
three-quarters of them . . . do not cross the client-type line for even 5% of their
time, and only about a seventh devote substantial [over 25 percent] amounts of
time to both types of work." John P. Heinz, Robert L. Nelson, Edward O. Laumann & Ethan Michelson, *The Changing Character of Lawyers' Work: Chicago
in 1975 and 1995*, 32 LAW AND SOC'Y REV. 751, 756 (1998).

34. Robert L. Nelson, PARTNERS WITH POWER: THE SOCIAL TRANSFORMATION
OF THE LARGE LAW FIRM 250–51 (1988).

35. FRIEDMAN, *supra* note 27, at 636.

36. Cause-lawyering (somewhat ironically) has its historical roots in certain
forms of probusiness practice. It was "pioneered by elite lawyers and judges to
establish judicial interpretations of private and constitutional law that would
fortify rights to ownership and control of business property against (what these
elites perceived to be) impulsive populist redistributive or regulatory legislation
and trade-union actions such as strikes and boycotts." Gordon, *The Legal Profession, supra* note 14, at 319. Indeed, by the time of the New Deal, the elite
lawyers who argued for the *Lochner* era constitutional order had become so
entangled with their business clients (whom they had been representing more or
less exclusively since the early years of the century) that they were treated, in

politics, as mere propagandists. *See, e.g.*, RONEN SHAMIR, MANAGING LEGAL UNCERTAINTY: ELITE LAWYERS AND THE NEW DEAL 46 (1995).

In spite of these roots, the business bar turned dramatically against cause-lawyering when, in the 1950s, it began to take up the cause not of property rights but of the poor. Throughout that decade, the ABA waged a systematic campaign to prevent the creation of political institutions that would provide comprehensive legal services for poor people including by creating a "Special Committee to Study Communist Tactics, Strategy, and Objectives" whose aim was to "drive such [communist] lawyers from the profession." MARTHA F. DAVIS, BRUTAL NEED: LAWYERS AND THE WELFARE RIGHTS MOVEMENT 1960–1973, at 19 (1993). The ABA eventually reversed its decades long opposition to federally funded legal services, recognizing that federally supported poverty law programs, subjected to the Bar's general ethics rules, would in fact be in the interest of lawyers. *Id.* at 33.

37. Support for the claims made in this footnote may be found in Judith Kilpatrick, *Speciality Lawyer Associations: Their Role in the Socialization Process*, 33 GONZ. L. REV. 501, 511 (1997/98) (regarding the plaintiff's bar's domination of the Association of Trial Lawyers of America); Sara Parikh & Bryant Garth, *Philip Corby and the Construction of the Plaintiffs' Personal Injury Bar*, 30 LAW & SOC. INQUIRY 269, 278 (2005) (regarding the predecessor organization to the ATLA).

38. Support for the claims made in this footnote may be found in K.N. Llewellyn, *The Bar Specializes—With What Results?*, 167 ANNALS 177, 177 (1933) (quoted in NELSON, *supra* note 34, at 249 (including both quotations of Karl Llewellyn); NELSON, *supra* note 34, at 233 (including the quotation regarding the prevalence of conflicts among lawyers between personal values and requests of clients); *id.* at 247 (including the quotation regarding the legal changes that corporate lawyers favor and the quotation regarding responses suggesting that the proposed changes would have salutary effects for clients); *id.* at 239 (including the quotation regarding businessmen's relative optimism about the capacity of the market and the quotation regarding large-firm lawyers' more favorable views of government regulation); *id.* at 240 (including the quotation regarding the elite strata of the bar's view of the distribution of economic rewards and the quotation regarding an awareness of substantive inequality); *see* George L. Priest & Benjamin Klein, *The Selection of Disputes for Litigation*, 13 J. LEGAL STUD. 1 (1984) (regarding the focus of legal energies on shifting the boundaries of legal standards).

39. I do not mean to suggest that the will is never involved in generating good faith beliefs but only that good faith beliefs cannot themselves be the product of a single discrete act of will, a single discrete choice. People constantly choose which questions to pursue and which to avoid and which evidence to emphasize and which to ignore, and these choices affect what they come to believe. People choose, that is, how to go about forming beliefs. But although these choices influence which beliefs people do in the end form, this is very different from the case the main text contemplates, in which people choose, directly, what to believe. This kind of case almost certainly involves pathologies of belief, as in Aquinas's idea that to learn to believe in God one must first pray to

him or, more familiarly, in the common case of the person who refuses to accept a lover's infidelity.

40. In emphasizing the importance of the lawyer's role to sustaining role-based redescriptions that proceed in terms of negative capability, I am departing significantly from Keats's view of the poet's negative capability. Poetic negative capability, for Keats, had to be achieved out of the poet's inner resources rather than on the back of an external institution such as a social role. This feature of Keats's views no doubt contributed to his belief that, as Kenji Yoshino has pointed out to me, poetic negative capability was a sign of greatness, which most poets fail to achieve. (Lionel Trilling observes that for Keats, negative capability depends, "upon the strength of one's sense of personal identity. Only the self that is certain of its integrity and validity can do without the armor of systematic certainties." Lionel Trilling, *Introduction to* THE SELECTED LETTERS OF JOHN KEATS 29 (2002).) Because I am holding out the possibility that even ordinary lawyers might achieve lawyerly negative capability, the suggestion that they might receive external support in this endeavor becomes particularly important to my view.

41. Thus it is one of the banalities of social psychology that "the agreement of others is necessary in sustaining a particular perception of phenomena in the face of other competing conceptions." Jeffrey Fitzgerald & Richard Dickens, 15 LAW & SOC'Y REV. 681, 699 (1980–81), citing MUZAFER SHERIF & CAROLYN W. SHERIF, AN OUTLINE OF SOCIAL PSYCHOLOGY 245–67 (1948). Nevertheless, I say only that role-based redescription is most *naturally* supported by a broad-based practice, and leave open just how much external support is strictly necessary for adopting a conceptual scheme. Perhaps a clique or a family or even an individual person could create a set of attitudes capable of sustaining the functional equivalent of role-based redescription, as long as these attitudes were more than just a tool employed to disguise purely willful redescription, although very few people, to be sure, possess the imagination and force of personality to sustain such redescription all on their own. To do so would involve a kind of genius such as appears, for example, in Robert Frost's successful effort to construct and assume the originally foreign and fanciful persona of a stylized New England farmer. These remarks naturally return to Keats's views about the elusiveness of poetic negative capability and its connection to poetic greatness. *See supra* note 40.

42. Ordinary people may continue to employ these descriptions even as they recognize that the role is impartially justified. They may conclude that "on the question of *moral* deformation, it may be that some socially useful roles require the development of vices and the suppression of virtues, so that good professionals become bad people." ARTHUR APPLBAUM, ETHICS FOR ADVERSARIES 66 (1999).

43. Support for the claims made in this footnote may be found in Meir Dan-Cohen, *Mediating Institutions: Beyond the Public/Private Distinction*, 61 U. Chi. L. Rev. 1213, 1222 (1994) (including the quoted text); ERVING GOFFMAN, ENCOUNTERS 85–152 (1961) (introducing the term "role-distance"); ERVING GOFFMAN, *The Underlife of a Public Institution: A Study of Ways of Making Out in a Mental Hospital, in* ASYLUMS: ESSAYS ON THE SOCIAL SITUATION OF

MENTAL PATIENTS AND OTHER INMATES 171, 318–20 (1961) (same); Meir Dan-Cohen, *Law, Community, and Communication*, 1989 DUKE L.J. 1654, 1659 (1990) (making the suggesting that an inappropriate role-distance can lead to alienation); Meir Dan-Cohen, *Responsibility and the Boundaries of the Self*, 105 HARV. L. REV. 959, 1001 (1992) (proposing that role-distance may be the self's preferred strategy for dealing with "dirty hands" types of situation).

44. *See, e.g.*, WILLIAM MITCHELL, ESSAY ON THE EARLY HISTORY OF THE LAW MERCHANT (1904) (describing the work of merchant courts); BRIAN L. WOODCOCK, MEDIEVAL ECCLESIASTICAL COURTS IN THE DIOCESE OF CANTERBURY (1952) (describing the work of church courts).

45. Support for the claims made in this footnote may be found in Arthur Applbaum, *Professional Detachment: The Executioner of Paris*, 109 HARV. L. REV. 458 (1995) (giving an ethical portrait of Charles-Henri Sanson).

46. Support for the claims made in this footnote may be found in MICHEL DE MONTAIGNE, *Of Husbanding Your Will*, *in* THE COMPLETE ESSAYS OF MONTAIGNE 3 (Donald Frame ed., 1958) (including the quotation proposing a cosmopolitan account of roles); *id.* at 600 (including the quotation claiming that some citizens must sacrifice their honor and their conscience for the good of their country).

47. 2 ALEXIS DE TOCQUEVILLE, DEMOCRACY IN AMERICA 284 (H. Reeve trans. P. Bradley ed., 1945).

48. Charles W. Wolfram, *Toward a History of the Legalization of American Legal Ethics—I. Origins*, 8 U. CHI. L. SCH. ROUNDTABLE 469, 470 (2001). The bar was never entirely free of outside supervision, but such supervision was limited, so that "colonial lawyers in their roles as such were not the object of significant regulation outside of the process of admission to practice and the occasional regulation of their fees." *Id.* at 472–73. Even the disbarment proceedings (which changed very little from colonial times until the 1960s) were "generally conducted as an equity suit or more specifically as a contempt proceeding. Most importantly, that meant that the court invariably tried charges without a jury." *Id.* at 474–75.

49. Robert Stevens, *Two Cheers for 1870: The American Law School*, *in* LAW IN AMERICAN HISTORY 405, 417 (Donald Fleming & Bernard Bailyn eds., 1971) ("The guild feeling within the legal profession and the somewhat mystical view with which the common law was regarded were put under pressures they had never had to face in England.").

50. Thus "[i]n 1800, fourteen out of nineteen jurisdictions required a definite period of apprenticeship. By 1840 it was required by not more than eleven out of thirty jurisdictions. By 1860 it was required in only nine out of thirty-nine jurisdictions." *Id.* Indeed, "in the 1840's and 1850's New Hampshire, Maine, Wisconsin, and Indiana provided that anyone twenty-one and over and of 'good moral character' could practice as a lawyer. In the Utah territory there was apparently an attempt to prevent the existence of any professional bar whatsoever." *Id.* at 418.

51. Gordon, *The Legal Profession*, *supra* note 14, at 290. Nevertheless, it is worth noting that "for all the talk of Jacksonian democracy and for all the changes in formal rules, there seems little doubt that in major cities like Boston

the leading members of the bar played a role, led a life, and enjoyed a status little different from that of their counterparts in 1800 or 1900." Stevens, *supra* note 49, at 421.

52. *See* Stevens, *supra* note 49, at 418.

53. *Id.* at 425.

54. Support for the claims made in this footnote may be found in FRIEDMAN, *supra* note 27, at 648–50 (regarding the creation of city and state bar associations); Munn v. Illinois, 94 U.S. 113 (1877). For a discussion of the formation of the ABA, see John A. Matzko, *The Best Men of the Bar: The Founding of the American Bar Association, in* THE NEW HIGH PRIESTS: LAWYERS IN POST–CIVIL WAR AMERICA 75 (Gerard W. Gawalt ed., 1984).

55. FRIEDMAN, *supra* note 27, at 634.

56. *Id.* at 638.

57. *Id.* at 639. Census data lists only three black lawyers in Massachusetts (in 1870), fourteen in North Carolina (in 1890), and roughly twenty-five in Texas (in 1900). *Id.* Similarly, as late as 1900, only about fifty women practiced law in Massachusetts. *Id.*

58. Robert L. Nelson, *The Future of American Lawyers: A Demographic Profile of a Changing Profession in a Changing Society, in* LAWYERS: A CRITICAL READER 20, 25 (Richard L. Abel ed. 1997).

59. *Id.*

60. American Bar Ass'n, Fall 2005 Enrollment Statistics 2 (Jan. 11, 2006), http://www.abanet.org/legaled/statistics/fall2005enrollment.pdf.

61. Gordon, *The Legal Profession, supra* note 14, at 293. In 1993 and 1994, female enrollment was 43 percent. American Bar Ass'n, First Year Enrollment in ABA Approved Law Schools 1947–2004 (Percentage of Women), http://www. abanet.org/legaled/statistics/femstats.html (last visited Oct. 20, 2007). In 2005 female enrollment was 47.5 percent. American Bar Ass'n, Fall 2005 Enrollment Statistics, *supra* note 60, at 2.

62. Charles W. Wolfram, *Toward a History of the Legalization of American Legal Ethics—II The Modern Era*, 15 GEO. J. LEGAL ETHICS 205, 222 (2002).

63. Support for the claims made in this footnote may be found in American Bar Ass'n, Lawyer Demographics, http://www.abanet.org/marketresearch/law-yerdem2004.pdf (2005) (claiming that there are 1.1 million lawyers in America); U.S. DEP'T OF LABOR, BUREAU OF LABOR STATISTICS, OCCUPATIONAL OUTLOOK HANDBOOK (2006), *available at* http://www.bls.gov/oco/ocos053.htm. (claiming that there are 735,000 practicing lawyers in America); Heinz, Nelson, Laumann & Michelson, *supra* note 33, at 770 (including the quotation regarding the effects of the growth of the bar).

64. *See* Stevens, *supra* note 49, at 505–6.

65. *Id.* at 494.

66. *Id.* at 505.

67. *Id.* at 509.

68. *Id.* at 498.

69. In taking this position, the A.B.A. departed from the common practice of the time. "[I]n 1927, of the forty-nine jurisdictions (the forty-eight states and the District of Columbia), thirty-two had no formal requirements for prelegal

studies, eleven required high school graduation or its equivalent, and six required two years of college or its equivalent." *Id.* at 496.

70. *Id.* at 509.

71. Robert Gordon, *The Ideal and the Actual in the Law: Fantasies and Practices of New York City Lawyers, 1870–1910, in* THE NEW HIGH PRIESTS: LAWYERS IN POST–CIVIL WAR AMERICA 51, 57–58 (Gerald W. Gawalt ed., 1994).

72. Wolfram, *supra* note 62, at 227.

73. Geoffrey C. Hazard, Jr., *The Future of Legal Ethics*, 100 YALE L.J. 1239, 1249–50 (1991).

74. *Id.*

75. Wolfram, *supra* note 48, at 479.

76. *In re* Percy, 36 N.Y. 651, 653 (1867) (describing the statute). This and the following sources are collected in Wolfram, *supra* note 48, at 479.

77. *See* Laws of the Colony of Maryland, ch. 48, § 12 (1715) (cited and quoted in *Ex parte* Burr, 4 F. Cas. 791, 793 (C.C.D.C. 1823)).

78. Bar Ass'n of Boston v. Greenhood, 46 N.E. 568, 574 (Mass. 1897).

79. Act of Apr. 14, 1834, Pa. Pamph. L. 354 (cited and quoted in *Ex parte* Steinman, 95 Pa. 220, 237 (1880)).

80. The quotation in this footnote is taken from Wolfram, *supra* note 48, at 485.

81. *Id.* at 480–81.

82. *Id.* at 480. Wolfram adds that "Proper professional deportment was something that was thought to accompany virtue, or at least something to be learned during apprenticeship to a reputable lawyer." *Id.*

83. Wolfram, *supra* note 62, at 206.

84. An extended discussion of the development summarized here appears in Fred C. Zacharias, *Specificity in Professional Responsibility Codes: Theory, Practice, and the Paradigm of Prosecutorial Ethics*, 69 NOTRE DAME L. REV. 223 (1993).

85. Wolfram, *supra* note 62, at 217–18.

86. This similarity should not be exaggerated, of course. Thus even the most modern legal ethics codes fall well short of the specificity associated with penal codes, for example in that, as Richard Abel observes, the ethics codes do not specify penalties or rank infractions in order of seriousness. *See* Richard L. Abel, *Why Does the ABA Promulgate Ethics Rules?*, 59 TEX. L. REV. 639, 649 (1981).

87. Hazard, *supra* note 73.

88. As Dan-Cohen observes, it is natural to "associate the presence of [external] inducements [to comply with a role's rules] with role distance and their absence [and the presence instead of fraternal admonitions] with proximity." Meir Dan-Cohen, *Mediating Institutions: Beyond the Public/Private Distinction*, *supra* note 43, at 1232.

89. Michael Burrage, *Escaping the Dead Hand of Rational Choice: Karpic's Historical Sociology of French Advocates*, 24 LAW & SOC. INQUIRY 1083, 1106 (1999) (reviewing LUCIEN KARPIK, LES AVOCATS: ENTRE L'ÉTAT, LE PUBLIC, ET LE MARCHÉ XIIIe–Xxe (1995)).

90. MODEL RULES OF PROF'L CONDUCT Preamble ¶ 12 (2003).

91. Support for the claims in this footnote may be found in Faretta v. California, 422 U.S. 806 (1975) (regarding the accused criminal who conducts his own defense); Robert W. Gordon, *The Legal Profession, supra* note 14, at 296 (including the quotation regarding accountants and others coming to encroach on the lawyer's special competence).

92. *See* Spevak v. Klein, 385 U.S. 511 (1967) (holding that lawyers may not be disbarred for exercising their privilege against self-incrimination); *In re* Ruffalo, 390 U.S. 544 (1968) (treating disciplinary proceedings as "quasicriminal" and holding that lawyers may not be disbarred without procedural due process).

93. Wolfram, *supra* note 62, at 217.

94. *Id.* at 206.

95. David Wilkins, *Who Should Regulate Lawyers?*, 105 HARV. L. REV. 801, 845 (1992).

96. Wolfram, *supra* note 62, at 207. Wolfram adds that the bar "exert[s] very little influence at all with respect to the prosecutorial agenda of the bar-discipline agencies." *Id.*

97. Wolfram, *supra* note 48, at 470.

98. Support for the claims made in this footnote may be found in Wolfram, *supra* note 62, at 214 (2002), (citing 1 RONALD E. MALLEN & JEFFREY M. SMITH, LEGAL MALPRACTICE § 1.6, at 19 (4th ed. 1996)) (including the quotations regarding the spectacular increase in malpractice decisions); Robert W. Gordon, *The Legal Profession, supra* note 14, at 297 (including the quotation regarding the doubling of the number of malpractice claims between 1979 and 1986); 1 RONALD E. MALLEN & JEFFREY M. SMITH, LEGAL MALPRACTICE § 1.7, at 42 (2005 ed.) (reporting the results of a study comparing data from 1980 to 1985 with data from 1990 to 1995).

99. *Id.* at 483.

100. *See, e.g.*, Lipton v. Boesky, 313 N.W.2d 163, 167 (Mich. Ct. App. 1981). In other jurisdictions, ethics violations are admissible evidence in support of a malpractice claim. *See, e.g.*, Woodruff v. Tomlin 616 F.2d 924, 936 (6th Cir. 1980); Lazy Seven Coal Sales, Inc. v. Stone & Hinds, P.C., 813 S.W.2d 400 (Tenn. 1991); Allen v. Lefkoff, Duncan, Grimes & Dermer, P.C., 453 S.E.2d 719, 720–21 (Ga. 1995).

101. *Day v. Rosenthal*, 170 Cal. App. 3d 1125, 1147 (Ct. App. 1985) (stating that the ethics rules, and not the testimony of an expert witness, establish the standard of care for legal malpractice).

102. Wolfram, *supra* note 48, at 469 (citing RESTATEMENT (THIRD) OF THE LAW GOVERNING LAWYERS § 52(2) cmt. f (2000)). For a more detailed account, see Michael J. Hoover, *The Model Code of Professional Conduct and Lawyer Malpractice Actions: The Gap Between Code and Common Law Narrows*, 22 NEW ENGL. L. REV. 595 (1988).

103. Wilkins, *supra* note 95, at 806.

104. *See* MODEL CODE OF PROF'L RESPONSIBILITY Preliminary Statement (1983); MODEL RULES OF PROF'L CONDUCT Preamble (2003) ("Violation of a Rule should not give rise to a cause of action nor should it create any presumption that a legal duty has been breached . . . . [The Rules] are not designed to be a basis for civil liability. Accordingly, nothing in the rules should be deemed to augment any

substantive legal duty of lawyers or the extra-disciplinary consequences of violating such a duty." Not every jurisdiction has abandoned this approach—Indiana, for example, continues to reject the Code of Professional Responsibility as a basis of civil liability. *See* Sanders v. Townsend, 582 N.E.2d 355, 359 (Ind. 1991) (citing the preambles to the Model Code and Model Rules).

105. The brief catalog of examples that follows is far from exhaustive. Another important case is antitrust law, which courts have applied against the bar to outlaw minimum fee schedules. *See* Goldfarb v. Va. State Bar, 421 U.S. 773 (1975). Similarly, a Justice Department threat to prosecute the A.B.A. for violations of antitrust law and certain constitutional principles caused the bar to amend ethics rules that had been adopted to raise up roadblocks against group legal services plans. *See* Richard L. Abel, *Why Does the ABA Promulgate Ethics Rules?*, 59 Tex. L. Rev. 639, 650 (1981).

106. With respect to antidiscrimination law, bar admissions processes may not discriminate on the basis of race, gender, or religion. *See* Schware v. Bd. of Bar Examiners, 353 U.S. 232, 238 (1957). Indeed, the Americans with Disabilities Act also limits the grounds on which lawyers may be denied admission to the bar and the circumstances in which they may be disciplined. *See, e.g.*, Clark v. Va. Bd. of Bar Examiners, 880 F. Supp. 430 (E.D. Va. 1995); People v. Reynolds, 933 P.2d 1295, 1304–05 (Colo. 1997). With respect to privacy and autonomy, a state bar may not, for example, reject a female applicant on the ground that she lives with a man with whom she is not married, Cord v. Gibb, 254 S.E.2d 71 (Va. 1979), nor may the bar reject an applicant on the grounds of his political affiliations. *See* Baird v. State Bar of Ariz., 401 U.S. 1 (1971).

107. The rule is most famously articulated in *The T.J. Hooper*, 60 F.2d 737, 740 (2d Cir. 1932).

108. Some states expressly "reject the notion that the practice of the majority of attorneys conclusively establishes the standard of care. While the standard of care is based on the degree of care, skill, diligence and knowledge commonly possessed by a reasonable, careful and prudent Vermont lawyer, the conduct of the majority of Vermont lawyers does not define 'reasonableness' per se. It is ultimately the role of the courts to define this standard." Estate of Flemming v. Nicholson, 724 A.2d 1026, 1029 (Vt. 1998). Others imply that legal malpractice should follow the general law of torts. *See, e.g.*, Frullo v. Landenberger, 814 N.E.2d 1105, 1109 (Mass. App. 2004) ("Negligence claims against attorneys do not differ from negligence claims generally in that plaintiffs must demonstrate both that the defendant failed to adhere to an applicable standard of care, and that the failure proximately caused the plaintiffs' losses.").

Moreover, even states that retain the traditional exemption to the *T.J. Hooper* rule, *see, e.g.*, Dawson v. Toledano, 109 Cal. App. 4th 387, 396 (2003) ("The attorney's duty is to use such skill, prudence, and diligence as other members of his profession commonly possess and exercise"), have generally weakened the exemption by expanding the scale of the professional unit whose common practices establish the standard of care so that jurisdiction-wide, rather than just local, practices determine this standard. *See* David A. Barry, *Legal Malpractice in Massachusetts: Recent Developments*, 78 Mass. L. Rev. 74, 77–78 (1993) ("Although some states still adhere to a 'locality rule' by which the lawyer's conduct is measured against the standards prevalent in the particular legal community in which his practices, the majority of states have adopted a 'jurisdiction wide' standard of care."); *see also* RESTATEMENT (THIRD) OF THE LAW GOVERNING LAWYERS § 52 cmt. b (2000).

109. *See, e.g.*, McCamish, Martin, Brown & Loeffler v. F.E. Appling Interests, 991 S.W.2d 787 (Tex. 1999) (following RESTATEMENT (SECOND) OF TORTS § 552 (1977) to allow a claim for negligent misrepresentation against a lawyer when false information generated by the lawyer was supplied to a "limited group of persons" to whom the lawyer knew or should have known the client would give the information). A lawyer's liability under RESTATEMENT (SECOND) OF TORTS § 552(a) (1977) is limited to the "loss suffered by the person or one of a limited group of persons for whose benefit and guidance he intends to supply the information or knows that the recipient intends to supply it." This limitation stems from the fact that § 552 imposes liability on those who have "no intent to deceive, but only good faith coupled with negligence . . . ." RESTATEMENT (SECOND) OF TORTS § 552, cmt. a (1977).

110. Lawyers may be liable in fraud under RESTATEMENT (SECOND) OF TORTS § 531 (1977) to injured parties who reasonably rely on fraudulent misrepresentations and belong to a "class of persons" whom the lawyer "has reason to expect" will so rely. For a comparison with § 552, *see supra* note 109.

111. Roger C. Cramton, *Enron and the Corporate Lawyer: A Primer on Legal and Ethical Issues, in* ENRON: CORPORATE FIASCOS AND THEIR IMPLICATIONS 571, 577 (Nancy B. Rapoport and Bala G. Dharan eds., 2004)

The Model Rules prohibit only cases in which lawyers have "actual knowledge" of the fraudulent nature of the client's conduct, *see* MODEL RULES OF PROF'L CONDUCT R. 1.2(d) (2003), although knowledge may be "inferred from circumstances." *See id.* R. 1.0(a), (f). By contrast, "[f]ederal and state laws dealing with fraud and various deceptive practices generally adopt or are interpreted as embodying a less demanding standard of knowledge of culpable conduct than that of the ABA Model Rules: a lawyer cannot turn a blind eye to facts and circumstances that indicate fraud or illegality—conduct that falls within the 'willful blindness' rubric." Cramton, *supra*, at 578.

For example, the scienter requirement for fraud under the federal securities acts may be met, in the criminal context, by proof that "a defendant deliberately closed his eyes to facts he had a duty to see or recklessly stated as facts things of which he was ignorant." United States v. Benjamin, 328 F.2d 854, 862 (2d Cir. 1964) (citations omitted) (summarizing holdings of prior decisions). And "[t]he federal courts of appeals . . . have almost uniformly concluded that the recklessness and 'willful blindness' sufficient for criminal liability also suffice for civil liability" under § 10(b) of the 1934 Act. Cramton, *supra*, at 579. Cramton reports that "recklessness" is most commonly taken to identify conduct that is "highly unreasonable and that represents an extreme departure from standards of ordinary care . . . [to the extent that the] danger . . . [was] either known to the defendant or [was] so obvious that the [defendant] must have been aware of it." *Id.* The cited language comes from *Hollinger v. Titan Capital Corp.*, 914 F.2d 1564, 1569 (9th Cir. 1990) (en banc). Some courts have adopted an even lower bar to civil liability, requiring just "negligence-plus." *See, e.g.*, Lanza v. Drexel & Co.,

479 F.2d 1277, 1306 n.98 (2d Cir. 1973) (en banc) (recklessness requires only that a defendant who knew of material omissions or misstatements of fact failed to obtain and disclose the facts when this could be done without extraordinary effort).

112. Victor H. Kramer, *Viewing Rule 11 as a Tool to Improve Professional Responsibility*, 75 MINN. L. REV. 793, 798 (1991). Although Rule 11 has since its inception allowed judges to impose sanctions for its violation, these were initially available only for a narrow class of abuses involving signing of the pleadings. *See* FED. R. CIV. P. 11, advisory committee's note on 1983 Amendments. In 1983 the rule was amended because "in practice Rule 11 [in its original version] has not been effective in deterring abuses." *Id.* The amendments authorized judges to impose sanctions more broadly for litigation related misconduct. Note that this seems to have had a practical effect. "In the seven years since Rule 11 was amended, it has generated well over a thousand judicial opinions." Kramer, *supra*, at 793. Moreover, these opinions dramatically underestimate the effect of the rule. A Third Circuit study, for example, discovered that less than 10 percent of the dispositions of requests for Rule 11 sanctions were published. STEPHEN B. BURBANK, RULE 11 IN TRANSITION: THE REPORT OF THE THIRD CIRCUIT TASK FORCE ON FEDERAL RULE OF CIVIL PROCEDURE 11, at 59 (1989). Further Amendments in 1993 have slightly narrowed courts authority to impose sanctions, but that authority remains much broader than it had been before 1983.

In some areas of practice, Rule 11 has even more bite, and clearly imposes duties that exceed those that the Model Rules impose against frivolous claims. *See* MODEL RULES OF PROF'L CONDUCT R. 3.1 (2003). Thus, the Private Securities Litigation Reform Act of 1995, Pub. L. 104–67, 109 Stat. 737 (codified at scattered sections of 15 U.S.C.), amends and partially repeals Rule 11 exclusively for securities cases: "The Act changes the procedure for imposing Rule 11 sanctions and it makes sanctions mandatory, removing any discretion from the district courts. In addition, the Act presumes that the opposing party's attorneys' fees will be the sanction, rejecting the focus on deterrence reflected in Rule 11. These changes apply in all private securities actions, not just class action lawsuits." Jerold S. Solovy, *Sanctions Under Rule 11*, 200 PLI/CRIM 385, 396 (2005). The act also provides more stringent sanctions for complaints than for other pleadings. *Id.* at 401.

113. *See* MODEL CODE OF PROF'L RESPONSIBILITY R. 1.6 (1983).

114. The Kutak Commission, which was charged with drafting the Model Rules, had included an exception to the duty to preserve confidences for cases in which disclosure "is appropriate in the service of a client or is required or permitted by law or these Rules of Professional Conduct." Kutak Commission, Discussion Draft of January 30, 1980, at ¶ 8, *available at* http://www.abanet .org/cpr/ethics/kutak_1-80.pdf. But this exception was rejected by the ABA's House of Delegates.

115. The Amendment was adopted in conjunction with the Ethics 2000 changes to the Model Rules, as MODEL RULES OF PROF'L CONDUCT R. 1.6(b)(4) (2002). Following another round of changes adopted in 2003, the provision was renumbered as R. 1.6(b)(6) (2003).

116. *Id.* R. 1.6 cmt. 12 (2003).

117. *See* COMM'N ON EVALUATION OF DISCIPLINARY ENFORCEMENT, AMERICAN BAR ASS'N, REPORT TO THE HOUSE OF DELEGATES iii (1991). These legislative efforts are becoming increasingly aggressive. *See* Benjamin H. Barton, *An Institutional Analysis of Lawyer Regulation*, 37 GA. L. REV. 1167, 1244–45 (2003).

118. RESTATEMENT (THIRD) OF THE LAW GOVERNING LAWYERS § 1 cmt. c (2000).

119. *Id.* § 1 reporters' note c.

120. *See*, respectively, Bryant v. State, 457 S.W.2d 72 (Tex. App. 1970), and State *ex rel.* Robeson v. Oregon State Bar, 632 P.2d 1255 (Or. 1981). Oregon's is, incidentally, the only such mandatory professional liability fund in the nation.

121. *See* Sadler v. Or. State Bar, 550 P.2d 1218 (Or. 1976).

122. "Corporate law requires, in some circumstances, that internal investigations [of corporate officials] be conducted by 'independent counsel.'" Cramton, *supra* note 111, at 595. *See, e.g.*, MODEL BUS. CORP. ACT § 8.55(b)(2) (Supp. 1998–99) ("Special legal counsel" must be used in making decisions whether or not to indemnify officers and directors."); *see also* OHIO REV. CODE ANN. § 1701.13(E)(4) (Anderson 2001) ("independent counsel" that is, a firm that has not represented the corporation or an indemnified person in last five years, must be used).

123. Friedland v. Podhoretz, 415 A.2d 381 (N.J. Super. Ct. Law Div. 1980).

124. *See* Ga. Bar Ass'n v. Lawyers Title Ins. Corp., 151 S.E.2d 718 (Ga. 1966).

125. Heslin v. Conn. Law Clinic, 461 A.2d 938, 945 (Conn. 1983).

126. *See* COMM'N ON EVALUATION OF DISCIPLINARY ENFORCEMENT, *supra* note 117, at iv.

127. *See* COMM'N ON EVALUATION OF DISCIPLINARY ENFORCEMENT, *supra* note 117, at iii. The A.B.A. Report adds that many of the reforms in question have already been initiated—for example, that disciplinary systems are "[a]lmost without exception . . . staffed by full-time professional disciplinary counsel having statewide jurisdiction . . . ." *See id.* Some states have gone further still, for example adopting legislation requiring lay participation in the management of the disciplinary process, *see* Richard L. Abel, *Why Does the ABA Promulgate Ethics Rules?*, 59 TEX. L. REV. 639, 651 (1981), or even, in the case of California, creating a free-standing, full-time "Bar Court" staffed by "independent professional judges dedicated to ruling on attorney discipline cases." The State Bar Court of California, *available at*, http://calbar.ca.gov/state/calbar/sbc_generic.jsp?cid=13469 (last visited Oct. 20, 2007).

128. Wolfram, *supra* note 62, at 219.

129. Ted Schneyer has taken issue with the suggestion that the interventions by the Office of Thrift Supervision involved a fundamental shift in nature of the regulation of lawyers, towards external controls. *See* Ted Schneyer, *From Self-Regulation to Bar Corporativism: What the S&L Crisis Means for the Regulation of Lawyers*, 35 S. TEX. L. REV. 639 (1994). Schneyer emphasizes the fact that even in the new regulatory schema, outside agencies remain reluctant to interfere in areas in which they perceive lawyers to have a near monopoly on

expertise. But even if Schneyer is right here (and he may well be), his argument misses the point of the account in the main text, namely that the source of *authority* for regulating lawyers has shifted from the bar to the external institutions. That these institutions turn to lawyers to elaborate how their authority should be exercised (as they do more or less whenever they must make legal determinations) does not change this fact.

130. Support for the claims made in this footnote may be found in Dennis E. Curtis, *Old Knights and New Champions: Kaye, Scholer, the Office of Thrift Supervision, and the Pursuit of the Dollar*, 66 S. Cal. L. Rev. 985, 986–87 (1993) (regarding the incorporation of legal ethics arguments into the OTS's litigation strategy).

131. *See* ABA Working Group on Lawyers' Representation of Regulated Clients, Laborers in Different Vineyards? The Banking Regulators and the Legal Profession: Report to House of Delegates at 2 (June 11, 1993).

132. OTS Counsel Harris Weinstein warned thrift attorneys that "the OTS will hold attorneys representing depository institutions to the highest standards of the profession, a standard beyond the 'minimally accepted conduct that avoids disbarment or other form of bar discipline.' Anything less may result in enforcement action." Quoted in *Advice on How to Exploit Loopholes May be Unethical, OTS' Weinstein Says*, 56 BNA Banking Rep. 616, 616 (Apr. 1, 1991).

133. 1 Geoffrey c. hazard, jr. & W. William Hodes, The Law of Lawyering: A Handbook on The Model Rules of Professional Conduct § 1.6:201–1, at 168.39 (2d ed. Supp. 1998) [hereinafter HH]. Arnold & Porter partner Scott Schreiber, for example, said that the OTS position went "beyond what the law requires and what the profession requires," and in this respect took "400 years of jurisprudence and put[] it on its head." Quoted in *Bank, Thrift Attorneys React to Duties Outlined by OTS Chief Counsel Weinstein*, 55 BNA Banking Rep. 547, 547 (Oct. 1, 1990).

134. The Jones Day settlement imposed $51 million in damages, including $19.5 million of the firm's own money, and a three year cease-and-desist order. *See* J. Randolph Evans & Ida Patterson Dorvee, *Attorney Liability for Assisting Clients with Wrongful Conduct: Established and Emerging Bases of Liability*, 45 S.C. L. Rev. 803, 831 (1994); *see also* FDIC v. Shrader & York, 991 F.2d 216, 218 (5th Cir. 1993); *In re* Fishbein, OTS AP-92-19, at 25 (Dep't of the Treas. 1992) (notice of charges and of hearing), 1992 WL 560939.

The Kaye Scholer settlement also involved a large fine and included an agreement that Kaye Scholer, in its future representations of banking clients, would accept the up-the-ladder reporting regime that the OTS preferred, even in spite of the ABA's position that such reporting violated the Model Rules. *See* Edward A. Adams, *Kaye Scholer Agrees to Settle with RTC for Up to $22 Million*, N.Y. L.J., Aug. 6, 1991, at 1, 2.

Nor were these isolated cases. After the savings and loan debacle, federal banking regulators secured more that $400 million in settlements of professional liability related suits from large law firms that did not get disciplined under the Model Rules. *See* Schneyer, *supra* note 129.

135. *See* ABA Working Group on Lawyers' Representation of Regulated Clients, *supra* note 131, at 213–23 (discussion draft, Jan. 1993). The

notice and comment process is mandated by § 553 of the Administrative Procedures Act. 5 U.S.C. § 553.

136. *See* 15 U.S.C. § 7245 (2006). This development is reported in Curtis, *supra* note 130, at 1004–5.

137. Curtis, *supra* note 130, at 1017.

138. For a brief recount of these scandals, see Andre Douglas Pond Cummings, *"Ain't No Glory in Pain": How the 1994 Republican Revolution and the Private Securities Litigation Reform Act Contributed to the Collapse of the United States Capital Markets*, 83 Neb. L. Rev. 979, 1044–58 (2005).

139. Securities Exchange Act of 1934, 15 U.S.C. § 78u(a) (2006).

140. *See* 17 C.F.R. § 201.102(e) (2006).

141. *See In re* Carter & Johnson, Exchange Act Release No. 34–17597, [1981 transfer binder] Fed. Sec. L. Rep. (CCH) ¶ 82,847, at 84,173 (Feb. 28, 1981).

142. Wilkins, *supra* note 95, at 837 n.159 (citing Louis Loss, Fundamentals of Securities Regulation 1064 n.28 (2d ed. 1988)).

143. Cramton, *supra* note 111, at 586–87.

144. The Division of Enforcement had concluded that the broader authority existed under Section 15(c)(4) of the 1934 Act. The Commission rejected this interpretation in *In re* George C. Kern, Jr., Exchange Act Release No. 29356, [1991 Transfer Binder] Fed. Sec. L. Rep. (CCH) ¶ 84,815 (June 21, 1991).

145. Barker v. Henderson, Franklin, Starnes & Holt, 797 F.2d 490, 497 (7th Cir. 1986).

146. *See* SEC v. Nat'l Student Mktg., 457 F. Supp. 682 (D.D.C. 1978). For a helpful discussion of the courts' general reluctance in this period to resolve disputes between the SEC and the bar, see Susan P. Koniak, *When Courts Refuse to Frame the Law and Others Frame it to Their Will*, 66 S. Cal. L. Rev. 1075, 1091–104 (1993).

147. *See* Cent. Bank of Denver, N.A. v. First Interstate Bank of Denver, N.A., 511 U.S. 164, 191 (1994). This was, in the words of one commentator, a "big win" for the bar. Susan P. Koniak, *When the Hurlyburly's Done: The Bar's Struggle with the SEC*, 103 Colum. L. Rev. 1236, 1268 (2003).

148. *See* David J. Beck, *The Legal Profession at the Crossroads: Who Will Write the Future Rules Governing the Conduct of Lawyers Representing Public Corporations?*, 34 St. Mary's L.J. 873, 901–2 (2003).

149. 15 U.S.C. § 78t(e) (2006).

150. *See* Sarbanes-Oxley Act, Pub. L. No. 107–204, § 307, 116 Stat. 745, 784 (2002) (codified at 15 U.S.C. 7245).

151. Section § 307, codified at 15 U.S.C. § 7245 (2006), is entitled "Rules of Professional Responsibility for Attorneys." The regulations that the SEC promulgated in response to the statutory command appear at 17 C.F.R. § 205.3(a), (b)(1) (2006).

152. *See* 17 C.F.R. § 205.3(b)(3)–(4).

153. *See* 17 C.F.R. § 205.3(d)(2).

154. *See* Model Rules of Prof'l Conduct R. 1.6(b), 1.13 (2002).

155. The quotations in this footnote are taken from Brian Kim, *Recent Developments, Sarbanes-Oxley Act*, 40 Harv. J. Legis. 235, 238, 241 (2003).

156. *See* Cramton, *supra* note 111, at 612–13. The ABA did succeed in preventing the SEC from adopting a rule making it mandatory for lawyers to report securities violations out to the SEC, through noisy withdrawal, when reporting up failed to induce the corporate client to cure them.

157. In March 2002, the ABA charged a "Task Force on Corporate Responsibility" with "examin[ing] the systematic issues related to corporate responsibilities arising from the unexpected and traumatic bankruptcy of Enron and other Enron-like situations," with a special focus on "examin[ing] the framework of laws and regulations and ethical principles governing the role of lawyers, executive officers, directors and other key participants." *See* REPORT OF THE ABA TASK FORCE ON CORPORATE RESPONSIBILITY (2003), *available at* http://www.abanet .org/leadership/2003/journal/119a.pdf. The Task Force recommended revising Model Rule 1.6(b) to expand the permission for lawyers to reveal client confidences in the context of substantial financial fraud and (more dramatically) revising Model Rule 1.13 to approach the SEC's rules concerning reporting-up and reporting-out. *See* MODEL RULES OF PROF'L CONDUCT R. 1.6(b)(2)–(3), 1.13(b), (c)(1)–(2) (2003).

158. While the Model Rules use a subjective standard for triggering a lawyer's duty to report (based on actual knowledge, *see* MODEL RULES OF PROF'L CONDUCT R. 1.13(b)), the SEC regulations use a more objective standard (based on reasonable prudence and competence, *see* 17 C.F.R. §205.2(e)).

159. While the Model Rules require reporting only of "a violation . . . [that] is likely to result in substantial injury to the organization," MODEL RULES OF PROF'L CONDUCT R. 1.13(b), the SEC regulations require reporting whenever any "material violation has occurred, is ongoing, or is about to occur." 17 C.F.R. §205.2(e).

160. While the Model Rules say that a lawyer "shall proceed as is necessary in the best interest of the organization," MODEL RULES OF PROF'L CONDUCT R. 1.13(b), the SEC regulations require reporting of all material violations, regardless of what would best serve the firm. *See* 17 C.F.R. § 205.3(b)(1).

161. This has been widely acknowledged among commentators. *See, e.g.,* Drew Kershen, *Sarbanes-Oxley and the Oklahoma Rules of Professional Conduct*, 28 OKLA. CITY U. L. REV. 413, 420–21 (1993); Chi Soo Kim & Elizabeth Laffitte, *The Potential Effects of SEC Regulation of Attorney Conduct Under the Sarbanes-Oxley Act*, 16 GEO. J. LEGAL ETHICS 707, 717 (2003); Larry Cata Backer, *Surveillance and Control: Privatizing and Nationalizing Corporate Monitoring After Sarbanes-Oxley*, 2004 MICH. ST. L. REV. 327, 374–76; Susan Saab Fortney, *Chicken Little Lives: Anticipated and Actual Effect of Sarbanes-Oxley on Corporate Lawyers' Conduct*, 33 CAP. U. L. REV. 61, 67 (2004).

162. Cramton, *supra* note 111, at 609.

163. *See* 31 C.F.R. § 10.50(a) (2007) (providing authority to censure, suspend, or disbar).

164. *See* Breckinridge L. Wilcox, *Martin Marietta and the Erosion of the Attorney-Client Privilege and Work-Product Protection*, 49 MD. L. REV. 917, 940–42 (1990).

165. *See* MODEL RULES OF PROF'L CONDUCT R. 4.2 (2003).

166. *See* 1 HH § 4.2:109–1, at 744.8–.10 (2d ed. Supp. 1998); *see also* Roger Crampton & Lisa Udell, *State Ethics Rules and Federal Prosecutors: The*

Controversies over the Anti-Contact and Subpoena Rules, 53 U. PITT. L. REV. 291 (1992).

167. *See* Duty to Disclose Information Material to Patentability, 37 C.F.R. § 1.56 (1993).

168. *See generally* Alan H. MacPherson et al., *Ethics in Patent Practice (A Brief Visit to Several Areas of Concern)*, 574 PLI/PAT 657 (1999).

169. Further examples are collected at Wolfram, *supra* note 62, at 212 n.27.

170. Susan Koniak, *The Law Between the Bar and the State*, 70 N.C. L. REV. 1389 (1992).

171. Wolfram, *supra* note 62, at 218.

172. *Id.* at 210.

173. *See, e.g., In re* Fields, 45 S.E.C. 262, 266 n. 20 (1973) ("[t]he task of enforcing the securities laws rests in overwhelming measure on the bar's shoulders").

174. *See, e.g.,* Touche Ross & Co. v. SEC, 609 F.2d 570, 580–81 (2d Cir. 1979) ("The role of the accounting and legal professions in implementing the objectives of the disclosure policy has increased in importance as the number and complexity of securities transactions has increased . . . . Recognizing this, the Commission necessarily must rely heavily on both the accounting and legal professions to perform their tasks diligently and responsibly.").

175. *See, e.g.,* Wilkins, *supra* note 95, at 836 n.153 (citing L. Ray Patterson, *The Limits of the Lawyer's Discretion and the Law of Legal Ethics: National Student Marketing Revisited*, 1979 DUKE L.J. 1251, 1253–54, as "predicting that once regulators and the public recognize the power that lawyers exercise in the course of advising clients, they will increasingly demand that lawyers be held accountable for how that power is used.").

176. Wilkins, *supra* note 95, at 207.

177. Meir Dan-Cohen, *Law, Community, and Communication, supra* note 43, at 1669.

178. *See* Gordon, *The Legal Profession, supra* note 14, at 298 ("[T]he story of lawyers' loss of collective control over discipline is part of a more general story of decline in their independence and ability to control the conditions of their work, a trend common to all the professions in the late twentieth century").

179. Support for the claims made in this footnote may be found in Stevens, *supra* note 49, at 423 (including the quotation explaining why law would become the primary form of social control in the United States); *id.* at 409–10 (including the quotation regarding the importance of the legal profession in the country's government); Wolfram, *supra* note 62, at 218 (regarding the centrality of one segment of the legal profession in crafting the administrative state during the New Deal); Robert W. Gordon, *The Legal Profession, supra* note 14, at 298 (making an observation related to the claim that after taking sides with respect to New Deal administration, the bar could no longer plausibly defend its freedom from state control by claiming to stand above politics).

180. KARL MARX & FRIEDRICH ENGELS, *Manifesto of the Communist Party*, *in* THE MARX-ENGELS READER 476 (Robert C. Tucker ed., 1972).

181. MAX WEBER, THE PROTESTANT ETHIC AND THE SPIRIT OF CAPITALISM 182 (Talcott Parsons trans., 1930). Geoffrey Hazard has summed up this Weberian

idea in the context of legal ethics by saying that the legal profession has been transformed from a "traditional" institution in which authority rests on "the sanctity of age-old rules" into a "bureaucratic" institution in which the authority of rules depends on their "expediency" or "value-rationality." Hazard, *supra* note 73, at 1255 (citing MAX WEBER, ECONOMY AND SOCIETY 217, 226 (G. Roth & C. Wittich eds., 1968)).

182. Gordon, *The Legal Profession, supra* note 14, at 297 ("[L]awyers, especially those in the upper tier, are probably much more compliant with ethical obligations than in the old days").

183. Support for the claims made in this footnote may be found in Stevens, *supra* note 49, at 461–62 (regarding early twentieth-century American lawyers' consideration of a two-tiered bar on the English model).

POSTSCRIPT

1. For a typical example of the legal version of the genre, see SOL M. LINOWITZ, THE BETRAYED PROFESSION (1994).

2. ARTHUR APPLBAUM, ETHICS FOR ADVERSARIES 47 (1999).

3. Support for the claims made in this footnote may be found in KARL LLEWELLYN, THE BRAMBLE BUSH 33 (1960) (including the "old anecdote of Marshall"); *id.* at 153 (including the quotations regarding the realist lawyer's ability to merge her trade, culture and profession all in one).

4. This formulation borrows from Robert Gordon, *"The Ideal and the Actual in the Law": Fantasies and Practices of New York City Lawyers, 1870–1910, in* THE NEW HIGH PRIESTS: LAWYERS IN POST–CIVIL WAR AMERICA 51, 62–63 (Gerald W. Gawalt ed., 1994).

5. For a typical example of the legal version of the genre see WILLIAM SIMON, THE PRACTICE OF JUSTICE: A THEORY OF LAWYERS' ETHICS (1998).

6. The quotation in this footnote is taken from STUDS TERKEL, WORKING 539 (1972) (reporting statement of Philip da Vinci).

7. STUART HAMPSHIRE, INNOCENCE AND EXPERIENCE 189 (1989).

8. LORD MACMILLAN, LAW AND OTHER THINGS 259 (1937).

9. *Id.* at 260.

10. JOHN KEATS, *Letter to Richard Woodhouse, 27 Oct. 1818, in* LETTERS OF JOHN KEATS 157, 158 (Robert Gittings ed., 1970).

11. MACMILLAN, *supra* note 8, at 1 (emphasis added).

12. Support for the claims made in this footnote may be found in Charles P. Curtis, *The Ethics of Advocacy,* 4 STAN. L. REV. 3, 17 (1951) (including the quotation of Arthur Hill).

13. FRANCES BACON, *Essay 32: Of Discourse, in* FRANCIS BACON, THE ESSAYS 160 (John Pitcher ed., 1985).

14. FREDERICK SCOTT OLIVER, ORDEAL BY BATTLE 201 (1915).

INDEX OF CASES CITED

INDEX OF MODEL RULES AND OTHER AUTHORITIES

INDEX OF SUBJECTS

221n, 276n89, 288n171; ordinary, 20, 26, 42–43. See also *separate Index of Cases Cited*

casuistry, 17–19, 17n, 18n, 20, 20n

Categorical Imperative (Kant), 139n, 303n11

cause-lawyering, 220, 325n36

character, lawyer's, 142, 142n, 307n22

cheating/exploitation, 9, 34–41, 86; and exploiting the adversary process, 60–64; and exploiting the substantive law, 64–66; limits on, 57–60; as professional obligation, 3–4; and prosecutorial ethics, 86–88; and role-based redescription, 157–58; and substantive law, 64–66. *See also* lying/deception

Choate, Rufus, 218

choice, implications of, 251–53

Christianity, 110, 301n14

civil law, and professional detachment, 84, 84n

Civil Rights Act of 1964: Title VII, 321n104

Civil War, 323n1

Cleveland Bar Association Professional Ethics Commission. See *separate Index of Model Rules and Other Authorities*

client, lawyer's freedom to choose. *See* appointment; withdrawal

client confidences, lawyer's duty to preserve. *See* confidentiality, duty of

client confidences, rules surrounding, 16, 258n29

client control, 3–4, 8, 11, 27–31, 92–93, 264n1; abandonment of, 82–85; and cheating, 66, 78; and legal assertiveness, 31–32, 34; and repugnant-client withdrawal, 76–77

client counseling, 30–31

client fraud, 236; and duty of candor, 46, 46n; and duty of confidentiality, 55–57, 56n

client fraud, assisting, 266n10, 267n16

client instructions, obligation to pursue, 260n27

commitment, use of term, 309n45

commitments, 148, 309n45. *See also* first-personal ambitions

communal engagement, 316n33

community, need for, 181

competition, for provision of legal services, 234n

Comprehensive Environmental Response, Compensation, and Liability Act (CERCLA), 270n33

confidentiality, duty of, 16, 57n, 95, 237, 258n29, 266n6, 294n38; and deceiving third parties, 55–57; and discovery, 52; and duty of candor, 45–47; and negative capability, 96–97; and professional detachment, 85–86

conflict of interest rules, 28, 97

Connecticut Bar Association Commission on Professional Ethics. See *separate Index of Model Rules and Other Authorities*

Connecticut Supreme Court, 237–38

consent, role of, 28, 124–26, 128–29, 304n15, 304n20

consequentialism, 119n. *See also* third-personal impartiality; utilitarianism

consistency, problem of, 140n

conspiracy law, 291n8

Constitution, U.S.: Sixth Amendment, 50n

constitutional law, and professional detachment, 83–84

context, of role, 166–69

"Contextual View," of legal ethics, 300n9

contractualism, 303n10

contra proferentum, 274n76

cooperative lawyering, 196n

corporate law, 220n

corporate scandals, 238–43

cosmopolitanism, of lawyer's role, 13, 222–29, 231n, 232, 243, 245–46, 249–51

country lawyer, and statesmanship, 11n

courts: and appointment of lawyer, 67–69; and client control, 30–31; and enforcement of legal ethics codes, 235–36; and exploitation of adversary process, 61; and principle of professional detachment, 82–85; and regulation of legal profession, 236–37, 240; and repugnant-client withdrawal, 76–77; and role-distance, 38–39. See also *separate Index of Cases Cited*

Cramton, Roger C., 333n111

criminal defense lawyers, 320n93; and capital defense, 30–31; and duty of candor, 45, 266n8; and duty to make legal

first-personal ambitions, 148–50, 307n25, 309n46; context of, 166–69; substance of, 164–66. *See also* first-personal ideals

first-personal ethics, 9, 109–11; and hegemony of impartiality, 144–50; lawyers and, 115–16; and life worthy of commitment, 150–51. *See also* "Jim and Jane"; "Jim and the Innocents"

first-personal ideals, 134, 134n; and lawyer's role, 222–29. *See also* integrity

Florida Supreme Court Rules Regulating the Florida Bar. See *separate Index of Model Rules and Other Authorities*

Formula of the Kingdom of Ends (Kant), 139n

Formula of the Universal Law (Kant), 139n

Frank, Jerome, 50, 270n40

Frankel, Marvin, 88n

fraternity, 90–92

fraud, 47, 275n81. *See also* client fraud

Freedman, Monroe H., 258n32, 266n10

friction: and reconsideration, 143–45; and remotivation, 148. *See also* inertia

frictionless deliberator, 143–44

Fried, Charles, 255n4

Friedman, Lawrence, 219

friendship, 90–92

frivolous claims, 60–61

Fuller, Lon, 97, 189, 203, 298n80, 318n56, 318n58

Galanter, Marc, 256n6

generalism, of legal practice, 217–19

Giffard, James, 157

Gilson, Ronald, 196n

giving voice to the voiceless, 5, 11, 37–38, 37n

Glendon, Mary Ann, 256n9

Goffman, Erving, 263n49

good faith beliefs, 223–24, 326n39

Gordon, Robert W., 185n, 195–96, 216, 218, 230, 256n8

government, and regulation of legal profession, 235–43

government lawyers, and partisanship, 14, 173, 173n, 209. *See also* prosecutors

Graetz, Michael, 264n61

ground projects, 141–42, 148–49, 306n18, 307n25. *See also* first-personal ambitions

Habermas, Jürgen, 316n29

Hampshire, Stuart, 165, 312n15

Hare, David, 136n

harm to others, 30–34. *See also* deception, of third parties

Hayden, Paul, 261n38

Hazard, Geoffrey C., Jr., 3, 27, 49, 52, 60, 73n, 89, 89n, 94, 97n, 104, 231, 233, 256n7, 259n11, 263n50, 264n58, 266n10, 270n42, 275n85, 275n89, 296n53, 300n11, 339n181

Heidegger, Martin, 296n55

Herman, Barbara, 121, 137–38, 305n10, 306n12

Hill, Arthur, 252n

Hill, Thomas, 301n16, 305n1

Hodes, W. William, 3, 27, 49, 52, 60, 73n, 89, 89n, 94, 98n, 104, 256n7, 263n50, 264n58, 266n10, 270n42, 275n85, 275n89, 296n53

Hoffman, David, 215–16, 257n11

Holton, Richard, 146–47, 308n36, 308n37

hostile work environment sexual harassment, 205–6

ideals. *See* first-personal ideals

impartiality, 7, 9, 108, 140, 160, 227n, 248; hegemony of, 135–36, 140–50; and lawyerly vices, 110–11, 115–16; and role, 252–53; and role-based redescription, 158–63; as threat to integrity, 119–21. *See also* "Jim and the Innocents"; second-personal impartiality; third-personal impartiality

impartiality, second-personal. *See* second-personal impartiality

impartiality, third-personal. *See* third-personal impartiality

impeachment of truthful witness, 50, 50n

individual, as example and not representative of morality, 150

inertia, 150, 169, 308n31; of intentions, 143–45, 147; motivational, 309n45

informed consent, and lawyer loyalty, 28

in-house counsel, 219

inquisitorial procedure, 15, 125n, 177n

insularity, of lawyer's role, 12, 222–29, 231n, 234, 243, 249–51, 253. *See also* cosmopolitanism, of lawyer's role

integrating professional commitments into life well-lived, 1–2, 41

professional vices. *See* vices, lawyerly

projects, first-personal. *See* first-personal ambitions

prosecutorial ethics, and lawyerly vices, 86–88

prosecutors, 41, 86–88

psychologism, 141–42

public interest lawyers, 250

quid pro quo sexual harassment, 204, 206n

racketeering, 32

Rawls, John, 121–22, 121n, 175, 179–80, 302n6, 303n11, 311n2, 313n5, 313n15, 314n19, 316n26, 320n91

reasonableness, in legal ethics and in tort law, 32–34

reconsideration: and friction, 143–44; and inertia, 147, 147n

reconstructive ethics, 19; analogy to character-driven fiction, 247–48

redescription. *See* role-based redescription

regulation, of legal profession, 231–43

remotivation, 148

repeat disputants, 200

representation, court-appointed, 67–69

repugnant-client withdrawal rule, 73–77

res judicata, 37

respect for persons, in second-personal impartiality, 123–29

Restatement (First) of Agency. See *separate Index of Model Rules and Other Authorities*

Restatement (Third) of Agency, 260n28. See also *separate Index of Model Rules and Other Authorities*

Restatement (Third) of Law Governing Lawyers, 27, 29, 260n25. See also *separate Index of Model Rules and Other Authorities*

Restatement (Second) of Torts, 262n46. See also *separate Index of Model Rules and Other Authorities*

rights, as constraint on adversary system excuse, 105

role, of lawyer, 10. *See also* cosmopolitanism; insularity; role-based redescription; statesmanship

role-based redescription, 156–58, 212, 251–53, 327n40, 327n41; as complement to impartiality, 161–63; as

substitute for impartiality, 158–61; unavailability of, 12–13, 213, 222–29, 243–46. *See also* cosmopolitanism, of lawyer's role; insularity, of lawyer's role

role distance, 38–39, 225n, 263n49

role ethic, lawyerly, 171–73, 209, 212, 230

role morality, 10, 155–58, 311n3; and preservation of integrity, 169–70

roles, historical, 226–28

Roscoe Pound—American Trial Lawyer's Foundation, 270n36

Rousseau, Jean-Jacques, 181

Rubenfeld, Jed, 148, 309n46

rule of law, 184. *See also* adjudication, legitimacy of

rules of procedure, and duty of candor, 47

rules of thumb, 148n

San Diego County Bar Association Legal Ethics and Unlawful Practices Commission. See *separate Index of Model Rules and Other Authorities*

Sanson, Charles-Henri, 226n

Sarbanes-Oxley Act, 241, 241n

Savings and Loan crisis, 238–39

Scanlon, T. M., 123, 303n7, 303n10

Scheffler, Samuel, 307n26

Schiltz, Patrick, 256n9

Schneyer, Ted, 281n123, 335n129

second-personal impartiality, 121–27, 310n48; and first-personal ideals, 138–40; and "friction" of reconsideration, 144–45; and integrity, 130–33, 138–40; and "Jim and the Innocents," 121–27. *See also* deontological ethics

Securities and Exchange Commission (SEC), 239–41; Rule 2(e), 239

Securities Exchange Act, 239–40

self-government, by legal profession, 226, 229, 231–43

self-reflective morality, 14

self-sacrifice, 109–10

separation: between advocate and tribunal, 4, 8, 14–15, 34, 300n9; between party and judge, 34

serve rather than judge, duty to, 83–86, 85n, 294n38

settlement, 75–76

sexual harassment, 203–8, 321n104, 322n117